D1570347

HUSSERL AND TRANSCENDENTAL INTERSUBJECTIVITY

Series in Continental Thought

HUSSERL
and
Transcendental
Intersubjectivity

A Response to the Linguistic-Pragmatic Critique

DAN ZAHAVI

Translated by Elizabeth A. Behnke

Ohio University Press
ATHENS

Ohio University Press, Athens, Ohio 45701

English translation © 2001 by Dan Zahavi
Copyright © Kluwer Academic Publishers 1996
Originally published in German as
Husserl und die transzendentale Intersubjektivität:
Eine Antwort auf die sprachpragmatische Kritik
in 1996 by Kluwer Academic Publishers,
Dordrecht, The Netherlands

First published in English translation by
Ohio University Press 2001
Printed in the United States of America

09 08 07 06 05 04 03 02 01   5 4 3 2 1

Library of Congress Cataloging-in-Publication Data
Zahavi, Dan.
  [Husserl und die transzendentale Intersubjektivität. English]
  Husserl and transcendental intersubjectivity : a response to the
linguistic-pragmatic critique / Dan Zahavi ; translated by Elizabeth
A. Behnke.
    p. cm. — (Series in Continental thought ; 29)
  Includes bibliographical references (p.) and indexes.
  ISBN 0-8214-1392-9 (alk. paper)
    1. Husserl, Edmund, 1859–1938—Contributions in intersubjectivity.
  2. Intersubjectivity.
  I. Title. II. Series.

B3279.H94 Z34 2001
193—dc21
                              00-140097

CONTENTS

TRANSLATOR'S PREFACE

I AM HAPPY TO SAY that the author very kindly agreed in advance to read this translation in draft form and suggest whatever changes he thought appropriate. He has indeed read the work with great care and has made numerous suggestions designed to help capture his meaning more precisely. Copyeditor Natalie Wrubel also shaped the flow and phrasing of the text. As a result, there are passages where the English version diverges slightly from the German original; to borrow a phrase used by two of Habermas's translators, William Mark Hohengarten and Thomas McCarthy, at such points "the correspondence between the German and the English versions is not exactly that of translation." There are also cases where in order to bring out his point more clearly, the author has re-quested changes in quotations from existing English translations. Such instances are signaled by the words "trans. altered" following the citation. Our overall aim, however, has been to make the work as readable as possible while remaining true to the author's philosophical intentions. (For the further development of some of the themes of this book, readers may also want to turn to the author's *Self-Awareness and Alterity: A Phenomenological Investigation,* published in 1999 by Northwestern University Press.)

The present work is richly supplied with supporting references, and every effort has been made to help readers locate passages of interest. The conventions used for various types of citations are reviewed below; see also the Abbreviations, preceding the Notes, as well as References at the end of the volume. Note that where several works by the same author appear in part 2 of the reference list, they are given in chronological rather than alphabetic order; and in most cases, they are arranged according to the date of the edition cited. However, primary sources by Gurwitsch, Heidegger, Levinas, Merleau-Ponty, Sartre, Scheler, and Schutz are arranged in order of their original date of composition (indicated, where needed, in square brackets after the title).

Husserl. Where possible, references are to the *Husserliana* edition, cited by volume number, with the page number(s) following a slash—e.g., 8/188; see part 1.B of References for full information, arranged in order of volume number. Where an English translation exists, several different conventions are used. In cases where the English edition includes the *Husserliana* page numbers in the margin, only the German page numbers are provided. But where the marginal page numbers in the English refer to a different edition (as is the case with *Ideas I* and *Formal and Transcendental Logic*), and where no marginal page numbers are provided (as in *Logical Investigations* and the *Crisis*), the corresponding English page number is added in square brackets immediately following the *Husserliana* citation—e.g., 17/248[241], 6/371[360]. However, since not all the supplementary texts in volume 6 of the *Husserliana* are included in the English translation of the *Crisis*, references without the added page numbers— e.g., 6/469—also appear. Furthermore, not all of volume 9 of the *Husserliana* edition has been translated, although material from this volume appears both in *Phenomenological Psychology* and in *Psychological and Transcendental Phenomenology and the Confrontation with Heidegger (1927–1931)*. The former work does include the *Husserliana* pagination in the margins. But since the latter work includes this information in most but not all cases, occasionally the corresponding page number for the English edition has been supplied within square brackets as well. Thus a reader who wants to pursue a specific citation from *Husserliana* volume 9 should consult the inclusive page numbers provided in the entry in the reference list to determine whether the passage in question has been translated and, if so, which English work should be consulted. (See also the entries for *Husserliana* volumes 1, 5, and 17.) Finally, most of the references to *Erfahrung und Urteil* (abbreviated EU) are given by section number to facilitate consulting the work in any of its German editions or in its English translation.

For the most part, I have used standard English translations of Husserl's works. In quotations where I have departed from the wording of the *Logical Investigations,* the English page number has still been included for the convenience of the reader; in such cases, the citation takes the following form: 19/677[cf. 789]. Where no English translation was available, I have provided one; and in all cases where Husserl's unpublished manuscripts are quoted, the original German text can be found in the Notes. In both my own translations from Husserl's work and in the body of the text, I have attempted to follow the author's own terminological preferences so that the English translation conveys his train of thought as accurately as possible.

Heidegger. The author draws on three works: *Being and Time, History of the Concept of Time,* and *The Basic Problems of Phenomenology.* Since each of these English translations includes the corresponding German page numbers, all references to these works are to this German pagination (and the German abbreviations—SuZ, PZ, and GP, respectively—are employed as well). Thus although I have relied on Stambaugh's translation of *Being and Time,* those who wish to consult the Macquarrie and Robinson translation instead can easily find passages of interest, since the German pagination is available in their edition of the work too. It should be pointed out that Stambaugh, Kisiel, and Hofstadter do not always render the same German expressions in exactly the same way. All actual quotations follow the choices of the translator concerned; for Zahavi's own text, however, my main aim has been to keep the flow of his argument clear, using terminology drawn from all three of these translators as appropriate. Finally, although Zahavi's original text simply refers to *"Dasein,"* I have followed Heidegger's "express wish," as reported by Stambaugh in her Translator's Preface to *Being and Time,* that the term Da-sein be given in its hyphenated form.

Sartre and Merleau-Ponty. I have used standard English translations for the quotations; the first page number refers to the original, with the page number for the English edition following the slash. (See the list of abbreviations, which for the most part follow the French titles—e.g., EN, rather than BN, for *L'être et le néant/Being and Nothingness*). Note that Zahavi's original text cites the 1976 Tel Gallimard edition of *L'être et le néant* rather than the pagination of the hardbound French edition first published in 1943, and I have followed him in this regard. Similarly, the English page numbers for this work refer to the paperback edition, originally published in 1966 and still readily available, rather than to the pagination of the hardbound Philosophical Library edition published in 1956. (Full information for all editions used will, of course, be found in the reference list.)

Scheler. I have referred to standard English translations throughout (see the list of abbreviations), and all page references are to these English editions. For the most part, the German editions cited in the reference list are the editions that I myself was able to consult, rather than the editions available to the author.

Apel and Habermas. Existing English translations of works by Apel and Habermas have been used wherever they have been available to me, with only the page number for the edition used given in the citation. However, in some cases the contents of the English version of a given work differ from the contents of the German version. For example, the English translation of Apel's *Towards a Transformation of Philosophy* is a one-volume selection of essays drawn from the two volumes of his *Transformation der Philosophie,* and there are differences between the German and the English editions of several of Habermas's works as well. Thus, for instance, the reader may encounter references both to Habermas's *Zur Logik der Sozialwissenschaften,* abbreviated LSW, and to the corresponding English title, *On the Logic of the Social Sciences,* abbreviated LSS; in all such cases, some indication of the relation between the German and the English versions will be found in the entries in the reference list. The abbreviations used for frequently cited works will be found in the list preceding the Notes, and other works are cited by author and date.

All other secondary sources. Where an English translation has been available to me, I have used it (both for actual quotations and for embedded references), and only the date and the page number(s) of the English edition have been included in the citation; for the convenience of scholars, however, original sources are given along with their English translations in the reference list. Where no English edition was available, references to original page numbers have, of course, been retained, and I have provided translations as needed.

A note on inclusive language. All quotations from existing English translations reproduce the pronouns used by the translators concerned. At the request of the author, I have used the generic "he" in my own translations of quotations from other works and have employed alternating gender pronouns rather than double pronouns ("he or she," etc.) in the body and notes of his own text.

I am grateful to everyone who helped bring this project to completion, from the members of the ISMAM cooperative (Indigenas de la Sierra Madre de Motozintla) in Chiapas, Mexico, who grew the coffee that fueled it, to computer wizard Ken Benthien, who saved my sanity as well as my data on more than one occasion. But others deserve special mention as well.

First of all, I would like to thank Dan Zahavi, not only for cheerfully and patiently answering my numerous questions, but also for reading the manuscript with exceptional care and thoroughness and offering suggestions that have improved it in many ways. Needless to say, I am responsible for any errors or infelicities that may remain. But in many regards, this has been a truly intersubjective effort.

I would also like to acknowledge the help of the Interlibrary Loan staff at the main branch of the Santa Cruz Public Library in Santa Cruz, California. In addition, Prof. Eduardo Mendieta, of the University of San Francisco, very graciously assisted me in obtaining materials by Apel in timely fashion, as well as in solving several problems concerning the references.

Finally, I would like to express my heartfelt appreciation to the series editor, Steve Crowell, for his unfailing support in all phases of the project.

ACKNOWLEDGMENTS

My thanks go first and foremost to Elizabeth Behnke for her painstaking work. She not only translated the entire text in a meticulous fashion but also took on the time-consuming but invaluable editorial task of checking the many references (correcting some imprecisions of my own in the process) and adding references to existing English translations wherever possible. I am proud of having benefited from her dedication. I am also much indebted to Steven Crowell, the Editor-in-Chief of the Ohio University Press Series in Continental Thought. He initiated the project, and without his continuous and generous support the book would never have seen the light of day.

Dan Zahavi
Copenhagen, September 2000

PREFACE TO THE GERMAN EDITION

THE PRESENT WORK WAS WRITTEN in Leuven, Boston, and Copenhagen in 1992–94, and was accepted as a dissertation at the Catholic University of Leuven in August 1994; it is offered here in substantially the same form.

I would like to express my most sincere thanks, first and foremost to Prof. Dr. Rudolf Bernet, who was always ready to assist with advice and criticism. I am also grateful to Prof. Dr. Klaus Held for his constant support and for numerous fruitful suggestions, as well as to Prof. Dr. Richard Cobb-Stevens for many encouraging conversations.

I am indebted to Prof. Dr. Samuel IJsseling (Director of the Husserl Archives in Leuven at the time when the research was carried out), as well as to his co-workers, for access to Husserl's unpublished manuscripts. Prof. Dr. Ullrich Melle, Dr. Dieter Lohmar, and Steven Spileers were especially helpful, both in my work with the manuscripts and in providing stimulating discussions. In addition, I would like to thank Dr. Søren Harnow Klausen (Odense) and Mikael Carleheden (Lund) for their critical remarks on various parts of this work. Finally, many thanks are due to those who helped improve the linguistic expression of the original German version: first of all Karin Hildenbrand, but also Berndt Goossens, Stefan Keymer, Dieter Lohmar, and Heiko Schulz. I also wish to thank Thomas Pepper for his assistance in preparing the English Summary that appeared in the German edition.

Copenhagen, October 1994

INTRODUCTION

THE CRITIQUE MOUNTED BY linguistic philosophy against a philosophy of the subject—a critique that has been so predominant in 20th-century thought—is often interpreted as the manifestation of a far-reaching philosophical paradigm shift: namely, as a shift from a philosophy of *subjectivity* to a philosophy of *intersubjectivity*.

Although the critics of a philosophy of the subject have readily been able to agree that it has to be replaced by an intersubjective alternative, the very concept of "intersubjectivity" has remained conspicuously unthematized. It has often simply sufficed to assert that *language* was intersubjective for it to be taken as the point of departure for philosophical analyses.

However, there are exceptions to the latter procedure as well, i.e., there are philosophers who have also subjected intersubjectivity itself to a thematic treatment. Apel and Habermas belong among these exceptions, and where German is spoken, the view that an intersubjective transformation of philosophy is a real necessity has been principally spread through their works. Both of them have criticized the classical monological or methodologically solipsistic mode of thought in detail from a *linguistic-pragmatic* perspective, and indeed have done so with exceptional thoroughness and singleness of purpose.

Their critique presents a decisive challenge for phenomenology, for both Apel and Habermas understand their position as explicitly overthrowing the phenomenological account, which in their opinion is encumbered with a number of grave aporias. Thus both have reproached the phenomenological theory of intentionality (and the Husserlian version in particular) for having ignored the intersubjective, linguistic, sociocultural, and historical conditions of constitution, as well as for implying a misleading understanding of truth and meaning.

Moreover, both Apel and Habermas deny the possibility of anyone privately following a rule; they accordingly claim that meaning is linked with communication, not with intentional experiences. Hence speakers cannot have any pre-linguistic intentions, for intentionality is conditioned and made possible a priori by the deep grammatical structure and the formal pragmatics of language itself: psychic states are only transformed into intentional contents when these psychic states are inserted into the structures of linguistic intersubjectivity. Thus both thinkers want to replace the primacy of intentionality with the priority of linguistic communication.

Against this background, both Habermas and Apel also find it necessary to emphasize the sharp distinction between a subjective "experience of certainty," on the one hand, and intersubjective, linguistically expressed "validity claims" on the other. In other words, truth is not to be sought in the *private* evidence available to consciousness, but rather in the *linguistic* and *argumentative* grounding of a criticizable validity claim. The truth of an assertion lies in the fact that *everyone* can justifiably be prevailed upon to recognize the validity claim of the assertion as legitimate. Hence truth can only be demonstrated in the successful argumentation through which the validity claim is cashed in.

Insofar as the meaning of truth is measured by the requirement of achieving a consensus, and insofar as the condition of the truth of assertions is the potential agreement of all others, the character of the philosophical paradigm shift we have alluded to is already clear. That is to say, the transformation in question is the one that Apel proposes in his *Towards a Transformation of Philosophy,* where he defends the thesis that a critical reconstruction of the idea of transcendental philosophy from the vantage point of linguistic theory is necessary. It is by no means a matter of abandoning the transcendental mode of inquiry, but of renewing it—indeed, by taking the contemporary insight into the transcendental status of language and of the linguistic community as the starting point. If language is to be taken as the condition of possibility for truth and validity, the earlier paradigm of an epistemology based on the analysis of consciousness will have to be replaced by an epistemology based on the analysis of language. It is no longer possible to proceed on the basis of the transcendental I or ego as the guarantee of the validity of knowledge; rather, as intersubjectively valid, knowledge, experience, and constitution themselves are always already linguistic, and to this extent they are mediated by the synthesis of public communication. Thus instead of speaking any longer of the conditions of the possibility and validity of representations, instead of attempting to ground knowledge in a pre-linguistic and pre-communicative synthetic accomplishment of the individual, what is at stake is reviving the Kantian question as a question regarding the possibility of argumentation, and of intersubjective understanding concerning the meaning and truth of propositions and systems of propositions. Accordingly, the "highest point" of transcendental reflection would no longer be the "unity of the consciousness of the object and of self-consciousness," but the intersubjective unity of interpretation—a unity that has to be attained. The transcendental synthesis of apperception is thus replaced by an intersubjective process of forming a consensus, and the transcendental subject is transformed into a linguistic community.

In the following work, we shall take up the question of the transcendental relevance of intersubjectivity. Hence we wish to analyze *transcendental intersubjectivity*. However, our point of departure will not lie in linguistic pragmatics; on the contrary, we will be arguing for an alternative approach: even within phenomenology—and within Husserlian phenomenology in particular—it is possible to find an intersubjective transformation of classic transcendental philosophy (and this in spite of all the current accusations leveled against phenomenology's "solipsism").

Although the chief task of the present work will consist of providing a systematic presentation of *Husserl's phenomenology of intersubjectivity* (which at the same time will cast new light on a number of his basic phenomenological concepts), at bottom our interest lies in investigating what a phenomenological treatment of intersubjectivity as such is capable of accomplishing. Ultimately, we wish to establish to what extent phenomenology is affected by the linguistic-pragmatic critique; to what extent it can reply to this critique; and to what extent it can contribute to the present discussion of intersubjectivity on the whole. And for this very reason, we shall not limit ourselves to Husserl's work (although we definitely do consider his analyses to be of fundamental significance), but shall also incorporate reflections on intersubjectivity by Heidegger, Sartre, and Merleau-Ponty. And this will allow us to conclude by explicitly confronting the phenomenological account with the linguistic pragmatics developed by Apel and Habermas under the influence of Peirce and Wittgenstein.

However, the fact that our critical confrontation with linguistic pragmatics comes only at the end of the volume does not at all mean that it is only introduced in passing, for as we shall see, the linguistic-pragmatic account, and the critique stemming from it, was decisive for the structure of our interpretation of Husserl. It is not that we simply accept the linguistic-pragmatic critique without further ado—quite the reverse. But in order to make the confrontation and comparison possible at all it was necessary to allow our presentation and analysis to be structured by the questions raised by linguistic pragmatics.

At this point, some remarks on the literature are necessary. In addition to taking into account *Cartesian Meditations, Ideas II, Erste Philosophie II, Phenomenological Psychology, Formal and Transcendental Logic,* and the *Crisis,* our interpretation of Husserl relies chiefly on the three volumes entitled *Zur Phänomenologie der Intersubjektivität* and on a number of as yet unpublished manuscripts. It is thus based in part on Husserl's research manuscripts (both unpublished manuscripts and posthumously published ones). These are research manuscripts that Husserl wrote not for a public audience but for himself—and indeed, often because, as Kern puts it, Husserl was attempting to come up with his insights by working them out in writing (13/xviii-xix).[1] At first it may seem a doubtful procedure to base an interpretation on texts that Husserl had not planned for publication, since perhaps the very reason he never published them was that he was dissatisfied with their content. However, there is actually a more complex connection between the manuscripts and the publications, as we can see from the accounts of Husserl's working procedures and publication plans provided in Kern's introductions to the three volumes on intersubjectivity (cf. 14/xx). And there are in fact a number of reasons for considering our recourse to Husserl's research manuscripts to be legitimate.

First of all, Husserl did write many of his late research manuscripts with an ultimate systematic presentation of his philosophy continually in mind, even though no such all-encompassing presentation ever took satisfactory shape because again and again, he lost himself in detailed analyses of specific themes (15/xvi, lxi). But in addition, and of even greater significance, is the fact that on account of his difficulty in bringing his thoughts to a final systematic expression, Husserl would at times work explicitly for his *Nachlass* (cf. 14/ xix, 15/lxii, 15/lxvii-lxviii). And on more than one occasion, he indicated in writing that the most important part of his work was to be found in his manuscripts—as in, for example, the following letter to Grimme dated March 5, 1931: "Indeed, the largest and, as I actually believe, the most important part of my life's work still lies in my manuscripts, scarcely manageable because of their volume" (15/lxvi; cf. 14/xix).

Finally, however, it must also be pointed out that the following interpretation of Husserl is systematically oriented. If there is any mention of the course of development of Husserl's thinking on intersubjectivity, it is only by way of exception,[2] and our interpretation will attempt on the contrary to present the philosophical culmination of his reflections. The use of research manuscripts is therefore also justified for precisely this reason, provided that such use brings analyses to light that surpass the observations on intersubjectivity that were actually published by Husserl himself.

HUSSERL AND TRANSCENDENTAL INTERSUBJECTIVITY

CHAPTER I

Fundamental Phenomenological Considerations

I.1. PRELIMINARY REMARKS

It is well known that intersubjectivity gradually played an ever greater role in Husserl's transcendental phenomenology. But this does not tell us why Husserl found it necessary to treat intersubjectivity in an explicitly transcendental phenomenological manner. Nor is it yet clear why he considered intersubjectivity to be a *transcendental* problem, and saw its appropriate treatment as a *conditio sine qua non* for a phenomenological philosophy. In order to answer these questions, we would like to begin by presenting the main features characterizing the claims and aims of Husserl's transcendental phenomenology. Although this means that we shall be moving over familiar ground, such a presentation is necessary not only to understand the genuine scope of Husserl's theoretical point of departure but also to ensure that the question-horizon within which the problem of transcendental intersubjectivity emerges— and turns out to be urgent—is not missed from the beginning.

This initial presentation will retain a provisional character. That is to say, it will establish that it is precisely Husserl's reflections on transcendental intersubjectivity that can place a number of fundamental phenomenological concepts in the right light, thereby making a new fundamental understanding of his phenomenology possible.[1] However, we will not be able to treat these themes in depth until Chapters IV and V.

I.2. EPOCHĒ AND REDUCTION

The fundamental phenomenological analysis is motivated by, among
other things, an experience of the inadequacy of the positive (objective) sciences.[2] More specifically, such sciences lack that complete rationality which—according to Husserl's conception—is constitutive for
the idea of science (8/251). Hence the objective sciences, which oper-
ate within the natural attitude—the mundane sciences—are characterized by their being incomplete in principle. Such incompleteness
(which does indeed make the constant progress of these sciences possible and thus, pragmatically speaking, necessarily accompanies them)
is, however, simultaneously incompatible with the true radicality of scientific self-responsibility, and thereby seriously places the rigorously scientific character of such mundane sciences in question (3/137[148-49]).

There are two main question-horizons that remain hidden and unthematized for the sciences operating within the natural attitude, although both indeed are linked with the genuine sense and goal of these
sciences' own undertaking. First, the positive sciences have never advanced to an understanding and thematic treatment of their own intentional accomplishments. Secondly, it is precisely this neglect that has
resulted in these sciences never having advanced to an actual understanding of the genuine ontological sense of their domain of research
and, ultimately, to the genuine ontological sense of the world (17/17-
18[13], 5/160). Hence the positive sciences are lacking in scientific radicality, insofar as they leave their own foundations unthematized and
simply presuppose these foundations dogmatically:

> [I]t would certainly be understandable that all objective sciences
> would lack precisely the knowledge of what is most fundamental,
> namely, the knowledge of what could procure meaning and va-
> lidity for the theoretical constructs of objective knowledge and
> [which] thus first gives them the dignity of a knowledge which is
> ultimately grounded. (6/121[119])

Husserl often speaks in this connection of the *cognitive-ethical con-
science* that is part of the epistemological enterprise, inducing us to de-
scend into the depths of cognizing and theoretical accomplishing in
order to make authentic science understandable and possible (17/20
[15-16]). That is to say, Husserl's reproach to the objective sciences is
also guided by ethical considerations and is closely linked with his idea

of an absolute *self-responsibility* (8/197, 29/115). Here, however, it must be emphasized that according to Husserl, this responsibility also turns out to have intersubjective dimensions, for the self-responsibility of the individual includes a responsibility to and on behalf of the community as well (8/197–98, 15/422, Ms. E III 4 18a). Thus it turns out that there is a similarity between Husserl's conception and the Socratic-Platonic idea of philosophy:

> Socrates' ethical reform of life is characterized by its interpreting the truly satisfying life as a life of pure reason. This means: a life in which the human being exercises, in unremitting self-reflection and radical accountability, a critique — an ultimately evaluating critique — of his life-aims and then naturally, and mediated through them, of his life-paths, of his current means. Such accountability and critique is performed as a process of cognition, and indeed, according to Socrates, as a methodical return *[Rückgang]* to the original source of all legitimacy and of its cognition — expressed in our terminology, by going back to complete clarity, "insight," "evidence." (7/9)

Thus Husserl speaks of an ultimately true, self-responsible life in full clarity and transparency, a life that is made possible precisely through a radical ultimate grounding, a radical self-reflection (8/167). And he emphasizes that with this, the phenomenological attitude is called upon to effect a "complete personal transformation" that is of the highest existential significance (6/140[137]). To put it another way, if for Husserl the theoretical impetus is closely linked with an ethical reflection, its importance becomes particularly obvious at the moment when philosophy, as absolute science, turns out to be an infinite idea. For it is precisely the ideal of absolute self-responsibility that is able to propel us further, through constantly more radical self-critique, toward the infinite search for definitive evidence (cf. 8/196, 8/244, 5/139, 1/53).

The realization of the ideal of science thus implies a radical critique. But it belongs to the sense of this critique that we are to put the being of the world into question instead of simply presupposing it (8/262). Thus Husserl writes that phenomenology is characterized precisely by its "transforming the universal obviousness of the being of the world" — which for it is "the greatest of all enigmas" — into something intelligible, thereby transforming this *"Selbstverständlichkeit"* into a *"Verständlichkeit"*

(6/184[180]; cf. 6/208[204]). And indeed, phenomenology can do this because it investigates the intentional accomplishments of the experiencing, constituting transcendental subject. Husserl's methods for this fundamental questioning of the world and the subject are the (transcendental phenomenological) *epochæ* and *reduction.*

Insofar as Husserl's investigations, and all transcendental phenomenological research, take place within the epochē, it is crucial from the very beginning not to misunderstand its genuine achievement and its goal. At bottom, most of the controversies concerning the claim, scope, and validity of phenomenological analyses (including the clarification of the concept of the noema) rest on different conceptions of the epochē, and a defensible decision in this regard can only be arrived at by way of a precise analysis of this concept.[3]

Our conceptual clarification can immediately take up this issue in terms of the way the tasks of phenomenology are described in the *Crisis:* it is the task of phenomenology to understand the *world*[4] (which is at first simply understood as the totality of objective reality—later, we will have occasion to distinguish between objects in the world and the world itself). In order to be able to begin this infinite research task at all, however, a suspension of our naive and dogmatic pre-understanding of the ontological status of the world is necessary. In order to avoid unjustified ontological pre-judgments, we must let ourselves be led by the principle of all principles, and thus to see every *"originary presentive intuition"* as the *"legitimizing source of cognition"* (3/51[44]; cf. 3/43[36]). The performance of the epochē—which is, according to Husserl, a necessary measure of any fundamentally scientific endeavor—consequently implies, when looked at in the right way, not an exclusion or elimination *(Ausschaltung)* of the world, but rather a suspension of the natural attitude's assumptions regarding the mode and manner of the world's existence (a suspension that makes this attitude itself visible *as* an attitude). In other words, we must give up our natural positing of the world, as well as our blind (ontic) occupation with—and judgments about—its objects, in order to pay attention to the *how of its mode of givenness* (8/502).

The putting-into-question that is accomplished through the epochē therefore means that from now on, the world and its objects may only be considered as acceptance- or validity-correlates *(Geltungskorrelate).* This means that they may only be investigated as recollected, perceived, imagined, judged, valued, etc., and thus in their correlation to a recollecting, perceiving, imagining, judging, and valuing, etc. Consequently, the subjectivity that experiences them becomes a theme *indirectly,* since the phenomenological access to the world necessarily proceeds by way of the world's appearance for subjectivity (8/263)[5]—an observation that already indicates the close connection between world and subjectivity.

This emphasis on the indispensability of an analysis of the experiencing subjectivity can be made plain by briefly recalling Husserl's theory of *intentionality* in the *Logical Investigations,* where the angle of approach is an epistemological one.

Since epistemology is not to be understood as a discipline that follows or coincides with metaphysics, but rather as a discipline that precedes metaphysics, just as it precedes psychology and all other disciplines (19/27[265], 3/8[xxii]), the analysis of intentionality (i.e., the phenomenological analysis of the structure of experience, which Husserl often characterized as the general theme of phenomenology —see, e.g., 3/187[199]) is already guaranteed a fundamental status. And this is because a theory that is occupied with the question of the possibility of cognition cannot allow itself to be led either by dogmatic assumptions about the ontological nature of consciousness or of mundane being, or by dogmatic assumptions about the way in which these are related. Consequently, a radical tracing back *(Rückführung)* to what is phenomenologically given is necessary in order to be able to carry out the analysis of intentionality in a way that is uncontaminated by ontological and metaphysical presuppositions.

An analysis of the structure of experience carried out on the basis of what is purely given quickly shows that it is very questionable, and often even misleading, to speak as though the intended objects "'enter consciousness,'" or conversely, that "'consciousness' . . . enters into this or that sort of relation with them," that they "'are taken up into consciousness' in this or that way," and so on. Likewise, it is misleading to say that the intentional lived experiences or mental processes "'contain something as their object in themselves'" and the like (19/385 [557]). The intentional relation between act and object is precisely intentional and not real, and examined more closely, the being-directed-toward belongs, as Husserl emphasized over and over again, to the act itself. That the intentional lived experience is related to the objectivated object, i.e., intends it and means it, does not imply the presence of two different things—the object and, in addition, the intentional act that is directed to it:

> [O]nly one thing is present, the intentional experience, whose essential descriptive character is the intention in question. According to its particular specification, it constitutes the full and sole presentation, judgement etc. etc., of this object. (19/386 [558])

> That a presentation refers to a certain object in a certain manner, is not due to its acting on some external, independent object, 'directing' itself to it in some literal sense, or doing something to it or with it, as a hand writes with a pen. It is due to nothing that stays outside of the presentation, but to its own inner peculiarity alone. (19/451[603])

Consequently, Husserl's analysis of intentionality implies not only that our acts of consciousness are essentially determined by possessing a directedness-toward but also that all distinctions in the mode of objective reference—thus not only concerning the *that,* but also concerning the *how* and the *what*—are descriptive distinctions pertaining to the intentional lived experiences in question (19/427[587], 3/74 [74]). According to the phenomenological attitude, all objects are what they are only through the acts in which they become objectively present for us. There is nothing but an interwoven web of such intentional acts (19/48[283])—which testifies in all clarity that Husserl's position in the *Logical Investigations* is not one of realism, if by realism one means a theory that explicitly defends the existence of objects independent from consciousness.[6] And it is these considerations that allow Husserl to claim in the *Logical Investigations* that the question of the existence of objects is completely insignificant within a phenomenological perspective (19/59[293], 19/358[537], 19/387[559]).[7] Moreover, the being-directed-toward remains whether the object exists or not. The act, in other words, does not become intentional by virtue of an external influence, nor does it lose its intentionality if the currently intended object ceases to exist. The intentional "relation" between act and object is precisely intentional—not real.[8]

    This in no way implies, however, that the intentional object is immanently contained in consciousness, as Brentano originally claimed

(Brentano 1971, 125). The act does *not* really intrinsically contain the object in itself (19/385[557-58]), for a proper description of intentionality shows that it is not a matter of one psychic content being contained within another psychic content. As Husserl has often demonstrated, there is a decisive difference between the mode of givenness of the intentional lived experience as a really intrinsic content, and the mode of givenness of the intentional object. That which is intended is not immanent to the act (even when it is a matter of something phantasied), but is transcendent to the act.[9]

And with this, the close connection between intentionality and constitution becomes clear. For as Husserl says, the analysis of intentionality leads to the insight that

> the objects of which we are 'conscious', are not simply *in* consciousness as in a box, so that they can merely be found in it and snatched at in it; [rather,] they are first *constituted* as being what they are for us, and as what they count as for us, in varying forms of objective intention. (19/169[385]; see also 2/71-75)

Thus if we see a bottle of ink (i.e., if an object appears, in the mode of perception, as a bottle of ink), then what this means phenomenologically is nothing other than that a certain *objectivating* and *unifying* act-character of apprehension animates a complex of sensations. The intentional object appears thanks to sensations and apperception working together: it is constituted. To put it another way, what is provided by the sensations is a kind of building material that goes to make up the intentional object when this material is submitted to an objectivating interpretation.[10] Thus it becomes clear that our being-directed-toward an object is of a *constitutive* nature. In its objectivating and identifying accomplishment, our intentionality implies the "building up" of objective identity.

How, exactly, constitution is to be understood—as a restitution, as a production, or perhaps as something completely different—cannot yet be answered. We shall, however, take this question up again in Chapter V.

This brief mention of the concept of intentionality has nevertheless shown that even the intentional-constitutive understanding of consciousness does not imply any abstraction from the world, since the intentional acts retain their relation to the worldly even after the epoché. The perception of the table is, precisely, perception of it, both before and after the epochē (no matter how it may stand with the legitimate acceptance of this objective something as a reality). Each *ego cogito* thus intends something and bears what is meant within itself as its currently intended *cogitatum,* although this "bearing" the meant "within" itself does not mean including it as a really intrinsic content. And each *ego cogito* does this in its own way (1/71). Consequently, the analysis of the process of experience ultimately reveals three themes that offer three different directions of regard for an intentional analysis. We must distinguish between the ego's directedness-toward something; the appearance of something in a given act; and this something itself as the objective unity given in and through the various appearances. Although these three themes are inseparable in idea (4/107), one must still tease them apart in systematic analysis—an analysis in which the phenomenologically adequate path does *not* take its point of departure in the *ego:*

> First comes the straightforwardly given life-world, taken initially as it is given perceptually: as "normal," simply there, unbroken, existing in pure ontic certainty (undoubted). When the new direction of interest is established, and thus also its strict epochē, the life-world becomes a first intentional heading, an *index* or *guideline* for inquiring back into the multiplicity of manners of appearing and their intentional structures. A further shift of direction, at the second level of reflection, leads to the ego-pole and what is peculiar to its identity. (6/175 [172]; cf. 9/207)

It must therefore be stressed once again that the explication of the constitutive subjectivity proceeds in inseparable connection with a phenomenological exploration of the world that stands before it.[11] This interdependence is explicitly emphasized by Husserl in his so-called *ontological* way to the reduction, where he describes the way in which constitutive phenomenological research advances in constantly two-sided (and thereby mutually determining) steps. The elucidation of a particular ontological region, which is then designated as a *transcendental leading clue,* systematically leads back to the consciousness phenomenologically constituting it, so that the objectivities in question are made understandable, in their sense and being, as the essentially prescribed products of the correlative structures of cognitive life (17/270[263]; cf. 6/175[172]).[12]

While the ontic sciences only investigate the constituted object-pole (without, of course, ever thematizing it as constituted), transcendental phenomenology analyzes the correlation between the constituted object and the constitutive subjectivity, so that the complete and true ontic sense of objective being—and thus of all objective truth—is established (6/179[176]; cf. 8/457, 9/336, 9/191, 29/135). Consequently, the "ontic" mention of what "objectively exists" actually expresses a *covering over* of transcendental constitution—a covering over that is imperceptible in the natural attitude. For what is precisely not apparent at all within this attitude is that whatever is objective is an intentional unity of validity, and that such objectivity has its true being-in-and-for-itself only by virtue of a transcendental sense-bestowal (9/344). But when the reduction comes into play, the anonymous achievement of acceptance and validity hitherto concealed in a functioning naiveté is revealed.

We can thus state that the epochē is not a method for abandoning the world or robbing it of its genuine sense, but a method of approaching the world in such a way that the sense of this very world of natural life, and of the positive sciences established within it, is first of all revealed (8/457). The epochē is performed in order to make the sense of the world understandable.[13] Thus it is first of all necessary to avoid misunderstanding the transcendental epochē by seeing it as though it were an operation that excluded the being and being-thus of the world from the domain of phenomenological research. Properly speaking, it is better—as Husserl himself also realized in the course of time—to avoid speaking of the "exclusion of the world" entirely, precisely insofar as it can readily mislead us into thinking that the world now drops out of the phenomenological theme (8/432). Rather, the exclusion or "bracketing" of the world is an exclusion or "bracketing" of the naive prejudice that simply *presupposes* the world (8/465): "The real actuality is not 'reinterpreted,' to say nothing of its being denied; it is rather that a countersensical interpretation of the real actuality, i.e., an interpretation which contradicts the latter's *own* sense as clarified by insight, is removed" (3/120[129]).[14]

We can now summarize our interpretation in the following manner. According to Husserl, it is through the epochē that we first *attain* the world as a *phenomenon* (1/60). To be sure, this does not mean that on account of the epochē (and the transcendental phenomenological reduction it makes possible), the world is made into, or reduced into, a *mere* phenomenon behind which the true reality would then have to be sought (15/554). I do not convert the actual world, or the actual object, into a merely immanent appearance through the epochē; rather, it is thanks to the phenomenological analysis that every transcendence is revealed as a phenomenon, i.e., as a *correlate of consciousness,* and I recognize that it would be senseless to suppose something above and beyond this.[15]

When the actual ontic sense of the world is disclosed, what is thereby demonstrated is its relation of dependency upon constituting consciousness. For that reason, Husserl's enterprise can be characterized as a *transcendental philosophical* one. And on the basis of the descriptive analysis, it follows that a meaningful concept of transcendence must necessarily include the experienceability of this transcendence, upon which it turns out to be a constituted validity-correlate of transcendental consciousness (1/117). Thus Husserl writes that the fundamental phenomenological method is called *reduction* because it leads the natural realm of being, with its derivative existential status, back to the primal transcendental realm or basis (1/61; cf. 3/ 159[171]). This simultaneously reveals why Husserl's enterprise must in addition be taken as a *transcendental phenomenological* one. For in distinction to Kant's questions—how are synthetic judgments possible a priori, and what are the conditions of possibility for the experience of an object—Husserl's questions are guided by the phenomenological principle. The transcendental results (the discovery of constituting subjectivity) arise from an explication of the sense of the *world* (1/177).[16]

Thus the epochē and the reduction in no way imply a loss; quite on the contrary, what the shift in attitude makes possible is a fundamental discovery, and thereby a broadening of our sphere of experience:

> "The" world has not been lost through the epochē—*it is not at all an abstaining with respect to the being of the world and with respect to any judgment about it,* but rather it is the way of uncovering judgments about correlation, of uncovering the reduction of all unities of sense to me myself and my sense-having and sense-bestowing subjectivity with all its capabilities. (15/366; emphasis added)

In other words, what is laid open is the transcendental domain of investigation into the "absolute correlation between beings of every sort and every meaning on the one hand, and absolute subjectivity, as constituting meaning and ontic validity in this broadest manner, on the other hand" (6/154[151–52]; cf. 1/66). Hence Husserl also speaks in § 32 of the *Crisis* of the *broadening of dimensions* brought about through the epochē and reduction—an expansion that can be compared with the transition from a two-dimensional to a three-dimensional life (6/121–22 [119]).[17] Suddenly, transcendental subjectivity—whose continual achievements have hitherto remained hidden—is revealed as the indispensable sense-bestowing (sense-revealing) dimension.

Although epochē and reduction are closely linked and stand in functional interconnection, Husserl nevertheless occasionally speaks of the epochē as making the reduction possible (6/154[151]), and we can now differentiate between them. Whereas the epochē entails a suspension of ontic commitment, and is thus characterized as the *gate of entry* (6/260[257]), the reduction is the shift in attitude that is thereby made possible, the shift that thematizes the correlation between consciousness and world in order ultimately to lead back to the primal transcendental realm or basis (1/61).

Against the background of this brief summary, it is now possible to reject certain interpretations of both the aim and the domain of objects of transcendental phenomenology, focusing here on erroneous interpretations that have prevented understanding the problem of intersubjectivity in the proper way. First, it has already become clear that Husserl is by no means inquiring into the structures of a worldless subjectivity. Second, however, it is also inadmissible to see the claims of Husserl's phenomenology as pertaining exclusively to the theory of signification or to epistemology in a strict sense.[18] The phenomenological reduction does not require neutrality with regard to questions of being, nor can Husserl's phenomenology be simply understood as a kind of conceptual analysis (Hutcheson 1981, 168). When the phenomenological analyses deal with the "sense" of the world or describe its constitution, it is not a matter of the explication of a *mere* sphere of sense that is distinguished from the actually existing world, as though besides this phenomenological analysis of *sense*, there would be a separate ontological analysis of *being*. For Husserl, the phenomenological analyses are by no means a mere semantic inquiry, without possessing any metaphysical or ontological implications. And indeed, to describe his analyses in this way means both to misunderstand intentional analysis and to overlook its distinctly transcendental philosophical character, which has rejected the very distinction between "being" and "sense" from the beginning.[19] It is for exactly this reason that it is also useless to support the "semantic" interpretation by pointing to passages where Husserl speaks of the constitution of *sense,* since it is precisely the objectivistic understanding of sense (as something distinct from being) that he has overcome through the performance of the reduction in the first place.[20]

Thus Husserl also writes that the completely developed transcendental phenomenology is *eo ipso* the true and genuine ontology (1/138, 8/215), an ontology whose concepts are all drawn from a transcendental originality that allows no questions of sense and legitimacy to remain in obscurity (9/251).

Radically carrying through the phenomenological analysis of intentionality has accordingly led Husserl to the insight that genuine epistemology is meaningful and possible only as a transcendental phenomenological theory of constitution. Instead of being concerned with countersensical arguments that seek to infer supposed transcendence from supposed immanence, genuine epistemology is exclusively concerned with the systematic elucidation of the accomplishment of cognition—an elucidation in which transcendence is made understandable through and through as an intentional accomplishment. It is precisely thereby that every type of existent, real and ideal, itself becomes understandable precisely as a constituted *formation (Gebilde)* of transcendental subjectivity. And it is making the existent understandable in this way that Husserl then designates as the highest conceivable form of rationality (1/118):

> To go back to the intentional origins and unities of the formation of meaning is to proceed toward a comprehension which, once achieved (which is of course an ideal case), would leave no meaningful question unanswered. (6/171[168])

Above and beyond this, however, Husserl also explicitly turns against the anti-metaphysical misinterpretation mentioned above:

> Finally, lest any misunderstanding arise, I would point out that, as already stated, phenomenology indeed *excludes every naïve metaphysics* that operates with absurd things in themselves, but *does not exclude metaphysics as such.* . . . The intrinsically first being, the being that precedes and bears every worldly Objectivity, is transcendental intersubjectivity: the uni-

verse of monads, which effects its communion in various forms. (1/182; 4. 1/38-39)

Phenomenology is anti-metaphysical insofar as it rejects every metaphysics concerned with the construction of purely formal hypotheses. But, like all genuine philosophical problems, all metaphysical problems return to a phenomenological base, where they find their genuine transcendental form and method, fashioned from intuition. (9/253)

As Landgrebe puts it, the reduction is precisely Husserl's way of approaching the fundamental questions of metaphysics (Landgrebe 1963, 26).[21]

Since the transcendental phenomenological, intentional-constitutive attempt at clarification does not merely pretend to elucidate subjective phenomenon, but is directed toward the world as such, it is obvious that it is precisely this realm of *objectivity, reality,* and *transcendence* that presents a particularly important challenge for phenomenology. For if it were not possible to give a phenomenological elucidation of these matters, phenomenology would be of no use as a fundamental philosophy

I.3. PHENOMENOLOGY AND IDEALISM

The performance of the epochē and of the transcendental reduction leads step by step to an understanding of the constitutive accomplishments of subjectivity. But if dogmatic assumptions are to be avoided, transcendent being must necessarily be related to the experiencing subjectivity and may only be investigated in this correlation; in other words, if every ontological dogmatism is to be overcome, one must turn back to the field of (possible) givenness. Being must accordingly be elucidated as sense for a consciousness that produces validities (see, e.g., 1/171, 8/215). From this it follows that a radical "outside" to concrete transcendental subjectivity is an absurdity (1/32, 3/96[100], 11/19). We must thus come to terms with the question of the idealistic implications of Husserl's phenomenology.

In the introduction to the Second Logical Investigation, Husserl explains that the sole consistent theory of knowledge is an idealistic one (19/112[338]). But at that time, what this referred to was merely a theory that claimed the non-reducibility of ideal objects. Later, in the *Cartesian Meditations,* we come across the thesis of an idealistic theory of knowledge once again (1/118). However, it is clear that something fundamentally different is now meant by this—namely, a claim concerning the ontological dignity of subjectivity (8/215), an ontological dignity that Husserl seemingly sees as a core thesis of phenomenology: "Only someone who misunderstands either the deepest sense of intentional method, or that of transcendental reduction, or perhaps both, can attempt to separate phenomenology from transcendental idealism" (1/119). But although Husserl characterizes phenomenology as the first rigorously scientific form of transcendental idealism (8/181), there is nevertheless still the problem of discovering the particular character of this idealism. For as Husserl never tired of emphasizing, transcendental phenomenological idealism differs radically from traditional idealism (5/149-53, 17/178[170], 1/33-34, 1/118), which—precisely in its traditional opposition to a nonsensical realism—betrays its entanglement within an inadequate, *natural* question-horizon (5/151). Remaining true to his phenomenological point of departure, Husserl does not deny the actual existence of the real world. The kind of idealistic thesis he wants to uphold does not consist in the claim that the transcendence of the world is *dissolved* in *psychic* immanence (3/355[366]), nor does he deny that the world exists independently from human cognition. On the contrary, the task of transcendental idealism (or phenomenology) consists in *elucidating* mundane transcendence through a systematic disclosure of constituting intentionality (1/34).[22] In reality, then, idealism is an explication of the sense that the world has for all of us "prior to any philosophizing" (1/36). And Husserl therefore emphatically stresses (recalling, in so doing, Kant's comments on the relationship between transcendental idealism and empirical realism—*Critique of Pure Reason,* A 370) that this idealism completely contains natural realism within itself (9/254):

> There can be no stronger realism than this, if by this word nothing more is meant than: "I am certain of being a human being who lives in this world, etc., and I doubt it not in the least." But the great problem is precisely to understand what is here so "obvious." (6/190-91[187])[23]

> That the world exists, that it is given as existing universe in uninterrupted experience which is constantly fusing into universal concordance, is entirely beyond doubt. But it is quite another matter

to understand this indubitability which sustains life and positive science and to clarify the ground of its legitimacy. (5/152-53)

Although to all appearances, Husserl advocated the thesis of the dependence of the world upon constituting subjectivity, and thus gave the latter ontological priority (3/104-106[110-12], 3/159[171], 5/153), it is of central importance to take note of the change that the epochē and the reduction bring about in the concept of the "subject." Thus Husserl often emphasizes that it is a fundamental misunderstanding if one misinterprets his reflections on the theory of correlation as though they were to be understood within the traditional subject-object dichotomy (6/265[262]). Being and consciousness belong essentially together, and as belonging together, are also concretely one—one in the absolute concretion: transcendental subjectivity (1/117). In this way, his concept of subjectivity is gradually broadened, so that Husserl not only transcends (or perhaps better, undermines) the traditional subject-object dichotomy, but also takes leave of the notion that the relationship between consciousness and world is to be understood as a strict (and static) subject-object correlation.

These remarks, which touch upon themes that we will go into in detail later (see, e.g., Chap. V.7), can provisionally serve to indicate the complex character of Husserlian idealism. Indeed, Gadamer has praised Husserl's transcendental phenomenology for going beyond the old opposition between realism and idealism (Gadamer 1977, 147).[24] In any case, it is of decisive importance not to confuse Husserl's conception with traditional varieties of idealism.[25]

Now it has often been emphasized that it is precisely intersubjectivity that is a litmus test for Husserl's transcendental-idealistic theory of constitution.[26] We fully agree with this view. As will become clear below, however, instead of following the customary procedure of assuming a particular understanding of the concept of constitution in order to test the tenability of Husserl's theory of intersubjectivity, we will do exactly the opposite. Thus we are claiming that the actual sense of Husserl's idealism—and likewise of his concept of constitution—can only be disclosed when his theory of intersubjectivity is taken into account. This thesis is even expressly confirmed by Husserl himself when he writes in the *Cartesian Meditations* that his reflections on intersubjectivity have made the *"full and proper sense"* of transcendental phenomenological idealism understandable for the first time (1/176).

I.4. THE PROBLEM OF INTERSUBJECTIVITY

An assessment of Husserl's phenomenology of intersubjectivity requires
an understanding of its exact intention. It is decisive to clear away at the
very beginning certain misunderstandings that have primarily been
caused by fixing upon Husserl's presentation in the *Cartesian Meditations.*[27] The goal of Husserl's analyses of transcendental intersubjectivity
is often identified either with a clarification of the constitution of the
sense, "other," in one's own consciousness, or with an exact analysis of
the experience of others.[28] Although Husserl does in fact carry out both
sorts of analyses, in our opinion it would be a mistake to characterize
them as the goal of his phenomenology of intersubjectivity. On the
contrary, we will advocate the view that Husserl's incorporation and
analysis of intersubjectivity is occasioned by the desire for a radical realization of his transcendental philosophical project. Husserl came up
against intersubjectivity in the course of analyzing the constitution of
objectivity, reality, and transcendence, since these categories simply
could not be constituted on a solitary egological basis. And this shows
that his phenomenological treatment of intersubjectivity had the goal
of bringing his constitutive analyses to completion—a completion that
culminates precisely in the insight that transcendental intersubjective
sociality is the basis in which all truth and all true being have their intentional source (cf. 1/35, 1/182, 8/449, 9/295[173-74], 9/344, 9/474).
That the specifically *transcendental problem of intersubjectivity* consists
precisely in clarifying the contribution of intersubjectivity to the constitution of objectivity comes to further expression in the *"Nachwort"* to
the *Ideas,* where Husserl explicitly links the problem of transcendental
intersubjectivity with "the essential relatedness of the world that is valid
for me as the Objective world to the other subjects who have validity
for me" (5/150), as well as in the following passage from *Formal and
Transcendental Logic:* "Let us now attempt to develop the involved set of
transcendental problems concerning intersubjectivity, and therefore
concerning the constitution of the categorial form, 'Objectivity', belonging to the world (which, after all, is our world)" (17/245[238]).

   Against this background, it becomes clear why not only the completion but also the *realization* of transcendental phenomenology—which
Husserl characterizes in this context as a *sociological* transcendental
phenomenology (9/539, 11/220; Ms. C 8 11a)[29]—requires an investigation of intersubjectivity (1/69; cf. 9/345, 8/464). Phenomenology

is transcendental philosophical precisely because it deals with the fundamental transcendental problem of how the transcendence of objectivity is to be understood intentionally-constitutively. And this is only possible by way of an analysis of intersubjectivity (8/465, 17/259 [252], 3/198[209], 1/10). Yet at the same time, it is not only a matter of supplying a phenomenological analysis of transcendental intersubjectivity, but also of demonstrating the possibility of an intersubjective phenomenology. Phenomenology naturally claims to supply analyses that are intersubjectively valid. What "valid for everyone" means, however, is not immediately comprehensible, but itself presupposes an analysis of intersubjectivity. It must therefore be emphasized how important the following project truly is. If Husserl's turn to transcendental intersubjectivity were to miscarry, this would simultaneously imply the failure of transcendental phenomenology itself as a fundamental philosophy.

Although it can be shown that Husserl is striving above all for analysis of *constituting* intersubjectivity, one must nevertheless also add that as a matter of fact, a large part of his investigations seems to be devoted to a different problem. It is not constitutive intersubjectivity, but the constitution *of* intersubjectivity that seems to stand in the center, and it is the latter that has been most frequently treated (and criticized) in the literature. But it is not difficult to see why Husserl was also occupied with this question. If, as we shall indeed establish, objectivity is somehow related back to the concordant agreement of a plurality of subjects, an understanding of such agreement naturally also requires an analysis of my experience of other subjects, for to presuppose intersubjectivity dogmatically—as, for instance, Kant did, in Husserl's opinion, although Kant never granted it a transcendental status (cf. 29/118)—is phenomenologically unacceptable (7/366, 7/370). Hence the legitimacy of this very assumption of plural subjects must itself be investigated and made transcendentally understandable:

> We must, after all, obtain for ourselves insight into the explicit and implicit intentionality wherein the alter ego becomes evinced and verified in the realm of our transcendental ego; we must discover in what intentionalities, syntheses, motivations, the sense "other ego" becomes fashioned in me and, under the title, harmonious experience of someone else, becomes verified as existing and even as itself there in its own manner. (1/122)

Thus when Husserl speaks of the constitution of intersubjectivity, his deliberations have to do with how the *experience of others* comes about, since transcendental intersubjectivity (i.e., the relation of a plurality of transcendental subjects to one another) and its constitutive performance are not at all to be phenomenologically analyzed on some meta-level above and beyond the experience of individual I's, but must be exhibited in each individual life of consciousness. In short, intersubjectivity cannot be treated as a transcendental problem from an external, third-person perspective, but only through an "interrogation of myself" (6/206[202]).

This statement is of fundamental importance, for it signals the decisive difference between Husserl's work and alternative, non-phenomenological treatments of intersubjectivity, while at the same time making the exact character of the phenomenological analysis of intersubjectivity even more precise. For when we are talking about the constitutive performance of transcendental intersubjectivity, what we are referring to is a constitutive performance that is in no way carried out by a *collective* consciousness, but is executed by the *individual subject*— yet has the peculiarity of necessarily presupposing an experience of others, a relation to the other.

As we have indicated above, Husserl's observations on the constitution of intersubjectivity have nevertheless often been criticized, and indeed, in various ways. On the one hand, Husserl is reproached for never having succeeded in describing a genuine concrete sociality, as found, for example, in the I-Thou relationship.[30] This reproach, however, misses his point, for Husserl is interested above all in a transcendental elucidation of transcendence and objectivity, and not in a detailed presentation and analysis of *personal experience*. Thus he does characterize the task of analyzing the multiplicity of forms of social relations as an important one, but emphasizes that it can only be carried out on the basis of his transcendental deliberations (1/157, 1/159, 8/137, 15/19). We shall follow him with regard to these points. Hence although we shall appeal to a number of various types of *relation to others* in connection with our detailed analysis of constitutive intersubjectivity, we shall cover Husserl's reflections on the I-Thou relationship, or on the specific types of communicative acts that constitute sociality, only incidentally, for here it is a matter of higher-order spheres of problems.[31] That an exhaustive treatment and analysis of his phenomenology of intersubjectivity must also include these issues is incontestable; our task here, however, is a more restricted one.

On the other hand, the reproach just mentioned is sometimes broadened to a considerably more serious one, for it is claimed not only that Husserl did not, in fact, address the I-Thou relationship, but also that he was unable, for reasons of principle, to tackle this issue at all. That is to say, the reproach is leveled against Husserl that by carrying out the transcendental reduction, phenomenology must thereby necessarily be restricted to exploring an individual I and *its* phenomena. And if phenomenological intentional-constitutive analysis does indeed have the task of exploring the givenness of the world for *me,* how would it then be simultaneously possible to treat its givenness for another subject—let alone the being of this other subject for itself— in an appropriate way? The question is thus to what extent intersubjectivity can be thought at all within a transcendental idealism, and whether the egological starting point of transcendental phenomenology has not condemned the entire enterprise to solipsism from the very beginning (cf. 1/69).

When in his analyses of the experience of others, Husserl speaks of the constitution of the *alter ego* (1/118, 1/126, 17/246[239], 17/ 275[269]), one must therefore always bear in mind that the other I is naturally to be distinguished from all other intentional objects in that it itself is a constituting subject. The *alter ego* is no mere *cogitatum,* but precisely a *cogitatum cogitans* (13/463–64); in other words, it is a matter of a subjectivity whose own being is not at all to be reduced to its being for me. Husserl thus seems to be confronted with the problem of constituting the *alter ego,* as other, within one's own *ego.* And although he was not particularly interested in investigating the other for its own sake (investigating it instead only when it is relevant for making objectivity, transcendence, and reality transcendentally understandable), it should not be denied either that the topic *"consciousness of others"* presents a particular challenge for transcendental phenomenology, or that Husserl himself had enormous difficulties in dealing with it.[32]

In summary, we can now speak of two fundamental problems. First, it should be possible for me to have a constitutive experience of transcendental *others.* But how is this possible if, according to the idealistic point of departure, all that I can currently experience is merely an intentional acceptance-correlate of my own transcendental consciousness? Second, it should be possible for me to have a constitutive *experience* of transcendental others. But can the other be phenomenologically analyzed and experienced at all? The other's foreign character—its transcendence and alterity—does indeed consist, at least in part, precisely in that the other's originary being for itself is absolutely inaccessible and unexperienceable for me. For "if what belongs to the other's own essence were directly accessible, it would be merely a moment of my own essence, and ultimately he himself and I myself would be the same" (1/139).

It is already clear from this passage that Husserl in no way denies the transcendence of the other; it will even turn out that such transcendence is of absolute importance for understanding the constitutive performance of intersubjectivity. For as Husserl also emphasizes, "it is precisely because the foreign subjectivity does not belong to the sphere of my original perceptual possibilities" that it also cannot be "exhausted in being an intentional correlate of my own life" (8/189).

Nevertheless, Husserl does often say that the beginning philosopher's reflections must be carried out within a solipsistic attitude. For like all other experiences, our experiences of others must be considered critically; its veracity, and therefore the existence of others, must not be presupposed without further ado (1/59, 8/59, 8/65-66). It is for just this reason that it is first necessary, on important methodological grounds, to draw up a systematic egology, i.e., a solipsistic phenomenology (8/176, 17/276[270]).

As we shall see later, these observations will be modified by Husserl himself in very decisive ways. However, that the consequences of this standpoint—and the fact that they put the possibility of a phenomenology of intersubjectivity (and an intersubjective phenomenology) in jeopardy—were very much on Husserl's mind can be seen when we note that Husserl was never tired of emphasizing, over and over again, that although the transcendental reduction does involve going back to transcendental subjectivity, it must not be misunderstood as a restriction to the private life of consciousness (8/436)—a misunderstanding that might especially be occasioned by the Cartesian way to transcendental subjectivity (8/313). Hence it is of fundamental importance to recognize that the scope of transcendental phenomenological experience encompasses not merely the phenomenologist's own transcendentally purified *ego* but also the transcendental community of I's disclosed in this *ego* through its experience of others. And it is precisely thereby that a transcendental philosophy based on the "absolute ontological foundation" of transcendental intersubjectivity is possible (9/345). Husserl's thesis is thus that the reduction to the transcendental ego only *seems* to entail a *permanently* solipsistic science; whereas the consequential elaboration of this science, in accordance with its own sense, leads over a phenomenology of transcendental intersubjectivity and, by means of this, to a universal transcendental philosophy. As a matter of fact, we shall see that, in a certain manner, a transcendental solipsism is only a subordinate stage philosophically; though, as such, it must first be delimited for purposes of method, in order that the problems of transcendental intersubjectivity, as problems belonging to a higher level, may be correctly stated and attacked. (1/69; cf. 9/245-46, 8/129)

Or, more precisely, reduction to transcendental subjectivity simultaneously means reduction to the transcendental intersubjectivity made accessible within it (15/73-75, 15/403). For the introduction of the intersubjective dimension does not mean some kind of external expansion of transcendental subjectivity, but expresses a better understanding of it (15/17)![33]

In Chapter II 5 and Chapter III, we take up the question of the relation between an intersubjective and an egological phenomenology once again, in order to contribute to the discussion of the relation between Husserl's initial point of departure (be it characterized as "solipsistic" or as "primordial") and his reflections on the phenomenology of transcendental intersubjectivity. First, however, we must offer a presentation of the constitutive performance of transcendental intersubjectivity. We have chosen this "reverse" sequence for the following reasons. In the first place, we are of the opinion that Husserl's analyses on the theme of *constituting* intersubjectivity are of philosophical value in their own right, and should therefore not always be placed in the shadow of his analyses of *constituted* intersubjectivity. We even believe that Husserl's true contribution to a phenomenology of intersubjectivity—especially in comparison with later phenomenologists—is precisely to be found in the former domain (cf. 1/173). To put it another way, proceeding in this manner will allow us to keep the genuine goal of Husserl's theory of intersubjectivity in view, since it will allow us to evaluate his observations on this theme instead of letting our gaze be diverted to considerations of the (misguided) problem of whether Husserl's concept of empathy implies a direct or a mediated access to others—as has often happened in the Husserl literature to date.[34]

And in the second place, it is our claim that a presentation whose theme is constituting intersubjectivity can in fact illuminate the question of constituted intersubjectivity. Whenever there is talk of constituted intersubjectivity, this naturally presupposes that there is a constituting level prior to intersubjectivity. Now it was obviously also Husserl's own view on occasion that intersubjectivity is first at work only at a higher level in the hierarchy of constitution (cf. 1/169). However, an investigation of constituting intersubjectivity has the precise task of establishing to what extent constitution is indeed dependent upon intersubjectivity, and must determine, on this basis, the legitimacy and possibility of the constitutive performance of a solipsistic subject (or perhaps also reject the value of such performance). To anticipate the results of our analysis, it will turn out that on the basis of Husserl's later research manuscripts on the problem of intersubjectivity, it is possible to defend the view that at the end of his deliberations, Husserl revised the hierarchy of founding. That is to say, it will turn out to be necessary to distinguish between various types of intersubjectivity. Moreover, one of these types is already in place prior to any concrete experience of the other, and must be seen as its condition of possibility. In other words, it will be demonstrated that Husserl's analyses of the concrete experience of others—analyses that always take the route of spatial experience of foreign lived bodies considered as physical bodies—already move within an intersubjective dimension, so that the scope of the primordial reduction must be reconsidered. However, we will show in Chapter III.3 that this insight in no way leads to giving up the principle of the primordial I, but on the contrary, assumes it and ultimately must be thought in conjunction with it.

I.5. SCHUTZ AND MUNDANE INTERSUBJECTIVITY

It should now have been unequivocally shown that Husserl treats intersubjectivity as a *transcendental problem*. However, it is precisely this approach to the problem that is challenged by Alfred Schutz, most extensively in his influential essay "The Problem of Transcendental Intersubjectivity in Husserl" (which was restricted to material published only up to 1957—see Schutz 1966, 78). In fact, the easiest way to demonstrate the actual radicality of Husserl's undertaking is by contrasting it with Schutz's alternative approach to a phenomenology of intersubjectivity.

In Schutz's view, Husserl's attempt to construct a transcendental theory of the objective world on the basis of a transcendental theory of the experience of others is a failure, and Schutz even denies that such an attempt could ever succeed at all (Schutz 1966, 55). That is to say, intersubjectivity is not some problem of constitution that could be solved within the transcendental sphere, but is a datum of the life-world, and for precisely this reason must be made the theme of an ontology of the lifeworld (Schutz 1966, 82; 1962, 133, 168, 312). According to Schutz, the task of a phenomenology of intersubjectivity consists in undertaking a clarification of the sense-structures of the mundane intersubjectivity that is always already accepted as valid— i.e., in descriptively pursuing this mundane manifestation of intersubjectivity itself.[35] Hence Schutz explicitly refers to a phenomenology of the natural attitude, a phenomenology that can manage without the reduction and that accepts intersubjectivity as a lifeworldly "given" (Schutz 1962, 136-37; 1967, 97-98).[36]

Now it is not at all to be contested that there is much to be accomplished by a description of mundane intersubjectivity that is true to the phenomena, or that this undertaking belongs among the legitimate tasks of a descriptive phenomenology of the lifeworld. However, if, following Schutz, one simply accepts the factual pregivenness of intersubjectivity, then one is simultaneously abandoning the fundamental philosophical claim that characterizes Husserl's phenomenology throughout. That is to say, no genuine elucidation and comprehension of intersubjectivity is attained if it is simply presupposed, and the profound deliberations we shall find in Husserl concerning the relationship between subjectivity, intersubjectivity, and objectivity cannot be attained within Schutz's way of posing the question. In short, to presuppose intersubjectivity (and objectivity) as ontologically pregiven basically means parting with philosophical inquiry.[37]

To what extent Husserl's own attempt at a transcendental theory of intersubjectivity actually succeeds, rather than getting stuck in a transcendental solipsism, as Schutz thinks it does, must still remain open. As we have emphasized, however, it is ultimately the transcendental mode of inquiry as such that Schutz is rejecting. In other words, what is being denied is the possibility of a transcendental phenomenological treatment of intersubjectivity at all. But it should be made clear that this cannot be made evident simply on the basis of a critique of the results of Husserl's analysis. Obviously, we must distinguish between what Husserl himself did in fact accomplish, and what it is possible for transcendental phenomenology to accomplish. And Schutz's critique could only be accepted if it actually furnished objections in principle against the very possibility of this transcendental phenomenological undertaking. It is exactly this, however, that is lacking in his reflections. Nevertheless, in one place we do find the following observation:

> But it must be earnestly asked whether the transcendental Ego in Husserl's concept is not essentially what Latin grammarians call a "singular tantum," that is, a term incapable of being put into the plural. Even more, it is in no way established whether the existence of Others is a problem of the transcendental sphere at all, i.e., whether the problem of intersubjectivity does exist between transcendental egos . . . ; or whether intersubjectivity and therefore sociality does not rather belong exclusively to the mundane sphere of our life-world. (Schutz 1962, 167; cf. Schutz 1966, 77–78)

Naturally, this reflection with regard to the possibility of a plurality of transcendental I's—a reflection that Schutz unfortunately advances without any argument—is a decisive one. In order to speak meaningfully of a transcendental intersubjectivity, there must be a plurality of transcendental subjects, or at least the possibility of such a plurality.[38] But although such a plurality must be denied and declared nonsensical by a strict Kantian transcendental philosophy, Husserl's own efforts to grasp a transcendental intersubjectivity—efforts that must really be seen as transformative—amount to precisely the attempt to show that this concept is not only meaningful, but also ultimately necessary.[39]

CHAPTER II

Husserl's Phenomenology of Intersubjectivity

II.1. WORLD AND PRIMORDIALITY

As we have indicated, the task of phenomenology consists in systematically explicating and elucidating the ontic sense of the world by investigating the intentional-constitutive accomplishments of transcendental subjectivity. If we consider the natural attitude more closely, it immediately becomes clear that apprehending the world as a world in common for all subjects belongs among the most basic assumptions of the natural attitude. It is, as Husserl says, experientially obvious that I and the other perceive the same thing, although my perceptions belong to me and the other's perceptions belong to the other (9/389). The world is immediately experienced as one and the same, although it appears to each experiencer in a particular way (3/60[55]). This finding can serve as a leading clue for further investigation.

The world is experienced as our common world. There belongs to its own sense as objective world "the *categorial form*, '*once for all truly existing*', not only for me but *for everyone*" (17/243[236]). True being thus not only means being for an individual I, but points a priori beyond the individual I to the nexus of possible intersubjective verification. However, it is not only on the level of theoretical reason that this holds good; rather, as we shall see later, there is already a reference to intersubjectivity at the purely *pre-predicative* level (9/431, 14/289, 14/390, 17/243[236], 6/469). An explication of the ontological structure of the world therefore leads us, by way of this disclosure of the sense of the world as a world for everyone, to transcendental intersubjectivity, for on account of its intersubjective sense, the world necessarily appeals back to the *transcendental validity and acceptance of others* (15/110). Husserl occasionally even mentions the possibility of an intersubjective reduction that could lead directly from the common world to transcendental intersubjectivity, to the *nos cogitamus* (8/316, 15/69). For the time being, however, it is only important to be clear that in the transition into the transcendental attitude, the world and everything mundane must naturally be maintained as a phenomenon, i.e., as a correlate of consciousness (14/289, 15/110). This is in no way lost by the transcendental reduction. Thus when Husserl introduces the *primordial* reduction (the abstraction to the primordial, which we shall turn to in a moment) in addition to the transcendental reduction, such a further step has precisely the task of suspending this intersubjective acceptance—a further step that naturally would not have been necessary if the transcendental reduction had already taken care of it.

The experience of the world as "existing for everyone" simultaneously means an experience of its transcendence compared to our own subjective experience. We never experience the actual world, and everything actually existing, as a private formation, but rather as existing in itself in contrast to all experiencers and experienced appearances (1/123, 15/5). An explication of the ontic sense of the world therefore requires an examination and a transcendental clarification of this transcendence and this being-in-itself.

The constitutive elucidation of the actual and true being-in-itself of the world that confronts the subjects who experience it is properly only carried out by means of an analysis of the experience of others (15/26). But in Husserl's view, a mode of the object's being-in-itself is already manifested within the experience of the single (solitary) subject. It is thus necessary, for the sake of clarity, to make a fundamental distinction between two types of transcendence—a primordial, subjective, or immanent transcendence on the one hand, and a genuine, true transcendence in the proper sense on the other—and to inquire into the sense of this distinction (1/136, 14/344, 14/442).

Obviously, this differentiation is directly related to the question of the scope or range of subjective and intersubjective constitution respectively. But before we begin our analysis of this difference, it is worthwhile to refer briefly to Husserl's methodic procedure in § 44 of the *Cartesian Meditations,* whose goal is precisely to implement this differentiation. Thus Husserl speaks of a thematic epochē that is effected within the transcendental sphere of experience with the goal of delimiting the sphere of ownness—which means the primordial sphere of what is my own in a distinctive sense, insofar as it does not yet contain anything constituted by way of the constitutive involvement of foreign I's (17/248[241]). Although the primordial reduction is occasionally presented as a radicalized version of the transcendental reduction, this is somewhat misleading. That is to say, it obviously already presupposes the transcendental phenomenological reduction and takes place within it; hence it can more suitably be seen as a thematic restriction (abstraction) to a particular province within the transcendental sphere that has already been opened up by the reduction (cf. 15/530-31). Husserl is therefore quite aware that marking out the boundaries of a primordial sphere of experience, and thereby distinguishing the sphere of what is originally one's own from the sphere of the other, already presupposes the being of the we, of the others (14/387). Moreover, he does explicitly emphasize that it holds for all *deconstructions (Abbaureduktionen), including the primordial reduction,* that the strata focused on in the deconstruction are not each constituted in a genetic sequence that would correspond to the founding-founded sequence of strata (Ms. C 17 36a). Thus Husserl does not seem to advocate the thesis that the primordial level has a temporal priority compared with the intersubjective level.

When one performs this restriction or abstraction to the *primordial,* all constitutive accomplishments of an intentional relatedness to foreign subjects (be it immediate or mediated) are left out of account (1/124).[1] However, this leads not only to a thematization of the sphere of ownness just mentioned, but also to an indirect opening up and thematization of the constitutive performance of transcendental intersubjectivity. And it is precisely this that then makes it possible to take up a position with regard to the relationship of foundation obtaining between subjective and intersubjective constitution:

> It can be asked how far the constitution of ontic sense reaches within primordiality, which I must bring to light abstractly, although I naturally know perfectly well—and can abundantly convince myself through reflection—that the ontic sense of extended nature is not built up purely primordially, and that others are constantly assisting me, as it were, as long as they are experienceable and experienced by me as others. If, however, I want to understand how the ontic validity that is part of the sense, "others,"

is founded—and to what extent primordial validity, and unity of
validity, is founding for making the perception of others possible—
I must at first stubbornly trace out the scope of primordial constitution as a founding of validity arising from the systematic structure,
within the system of possible experience, of fulfilling identification, thought as proceeding in a concordant synthesis of the
verification of something itself. (15/270-71)

Now when Husserl speaks of the relationship of founding involved
in the ontic validity that is part of the sense, "others," this must be understood in conjunction with some of the basic elements of his theory
of intentionality. As we have already mentioned, simply dogmatically
presupposing a plurality of subjects or an *alter ego* is phenomenologically unacceptable. Instead, whether and how I can experience something like a foreign I at all is precisely what I have to investigate (cf. 1/
122). Accordingly, Husserl returned again and again to an analysis of
the hierarchy of foundation of acts of various types, constantly emphasizing that direct intuition is the original consciousness—and is so in
various ways. First, intuition gives us the object as originarily present
in person; second, in comparison with all other types of acts, it is the
most original. Thus any image-consciousness—or for that matter, any
presentification—is characterized, according to its essence, by a certain
mediatedness of intentionality, and necessarily points back to an *earlier*
intuitive presentation. For example, remembering is not a mere consciousness of the past; rather, it is consciousness of a past perception,
and thus as a derived mode of consciousness, it contains within itself a
senseful reference back to the primal mode of perception.[2] Consequently, no presentification, and no making co-present, of a determinate apperceptive type is possible without a prior perception (13/
337). This now also holds for the relation between the originary experience of oneself and the appresenting experience of others, for in
Husserl's view, what is most basic is that the subject experiences itself
in primordially original experience, with the other only experienced
on this basis (15/96, 15/587). The sense, "subjectivity," is primordially
presently given to me in my self-experience and is only then appercep-
tively carried over to the other (9/242, 1/140, 8/62, 14/295). (Note,
however, that this carrying over must not be understood as an inference by analogy, for it is a matter of an apperception on the basis of similarity, of a type of experience with its own specific character, and not

of an "inference" or a conceptual act—1/141.) To put it another way, self-perception is more original than perception of others (13/347). Hence the motivational foundation for the constitution of any genuine transcendence lies within the sphere of original experience (17/248 [241]).

But by proceeding from this point of departure, has Husserl made it impossible to grasp intersubjectivity, i.c., the relation between equivalent subjects? Is it not simply the aporetic character of his starting point that comes to expression here—namely, the attempt to make intersubjectivity understandable on the basis of the accomplishments of a solipsistic subject? Or is Husserl simply describing the initial situation in which phenomenology finds itself, insofar as the phenomenological task is precisely to understand intersubjectivity rather than presupposing it? The way in which this question is to be answered depends on, among other things, what Husserl means by "self" when he speaks of "self-experience" and "self-perception" in the passages just mentioned. Later, we shall have ample occasion to investigate this in detail, and thereby to demonstrate the complexity of the way in which Husserl ultimately grasps the relation between (experience of) the self and (experience of) others. For the time being, however, we can be content with establishing that according to Husserl, there is only experience of others (and intersubjectivity) because there is self-reference (and subjectivity). Here we do not need to trace out the exact way in which Husserl understands the dialectical relationship between self-experience and experience of others, nor do we need to pursue the way in which he analyzes the performances of passive synthesis that he terms *pairing;*[3] at this point, it is sufficient to have shown why he had to perform the abstraction to the primordial.

II.2. IMMANENCE AND TRANSCENDENCE

Let us now attempt to get to the bottom of the two basic types of transcendence mentioned above, beginning with the so-called *primordial transcendence.*

Even as early as the *Logical Investigations,* the question of objective identity leads to the demonstration of its transcendence vis-à-vis the act that intends it. Any theory of intentionality must explain the relation between act and object, and as we have already pointed out, Husserl—in contrast to Brentano—claims that the intentional object is in no way really intrinsically immanently contained in the act (19/385[557-58]). Thus if the categorial distinction between act and object is to be maintained, the intended object must be understood as act-transcendent:

> However we may decide the question of the existence or non-existence of phenomenal external things, we cannot doubt that the reality of each such perceived thing cannot be understood as the reality of a perceived complex of sensations in a perceiving consciousness. (19/764-65[862])

That the intentional object may not be characterized as a mental content can be demonstrated in several ways, first of all by considering the identity of the object intended. The same object can be intended in more than one intentional act. Two perceptions of one tree do not confront us with two trees, and the independence of the identity of the object from that of the act testifies to the object's not being really intrinsically contained in the act. Every experienceable object consequently possesses a certain ideality in contrast to the many temporally individuated acts; its transcendence as something real is a particular form of ideality (17/174[165]), and Husserl occasionally characterizes reality (i.e., the spatiotemporal mode of existence) as an *empirical ideality* (14/278).

Given that what is first of all implied in the being-in-itself of the object is its independence from individual acts—which therefore also points to the possibility of returning to the same object in different acts—it becomes comprehensible why Husserl can claim that the question of the constitution of objectivities *existing in themselves* leads back, in all cases and entirely as a matter of principle, to the problem of recollection (11/110-11). That is to say, the *transcendence* of the object is only constituted at the moment in which its identity across different acts is ascertained. The identification of the object is precisely the noetic correlate of the identity of the object. And it would be impossible to ascertain this without recollection. Thus without the possibility of recollection, and the "synthesis of recognition" linked with it, there would be no lasting and abiding being (11/10, 1/96, 1/155), for if there were no ability to recollect, then talk of one and the same object would be senseless (17/291[285]).

Husserl therefore believes

> that the "one" constituted exclusively in perception itself, just as it is constituted in pure passivity prior to any recollection

and to any active cognition, is still not an "object." An "object" is the correlate of a cognition, and this cognition lies originally in synthetic identification—which presupposes recollection. (11/327)

And it is for this reason that he can conclude that the transcendental synthesis of time performed in original time-consciousness provides the universal and formal framework that conditions any constitution (even any intersubjective constitution) of "identical unity" and of "objectivity" (11/125, 11/128).[4]

On closer observation it is nonetheless clear that the transcendence discussed untll now—the transcendence that is made possible by time-consciousness—is still in no way sufficient for us to be able to speak of objectivity, since even hallucinated or phantasied objects that we normally characterize as being "merely subjective" can be called forth once again in memory. This possibility does indeed testify to their act-transcendence, but by no means to their objectivity.[5] We can therefore consider the possibility of identifying an object in recollection as a necessary but not at all sufficient condition of the constitution of objectivity. Thus the experience of transcendence that is made possible solely through recollection is only worthy of the name "transcendence" in a certain manner, for it is still just a purely *subjective* transcendence. That is to say, although the thing is constituted as an intentional unity—as an identifiable unity of actual and possible perceptions—and therefore reaches beyond this current perception, up to now it is merely an identical unity verified in the intentionality of *my* perceptual appearances, be they actual or possible, present or recollected, etc. (14/344). It is indeed true that the subjective or primordial transcendence discussed until now is not a really intrinsic part of the conscious lived experiences, but has its own specific ideality as an intentional unity. Nevertheless, as a unitary sense and a unitary regularity governing the appearances available to *me,* such transcendence still does not go beyond me in any radical way (14/8; cf. 1/80, 1/136, 6/370[359–60]). To put it another way, the transcendence of the object discussed up to this point is characterized by its independence from my own *currently actual* experience. The object is *primordially transcendent* insofar as it goes beyond my currently actual conscious lived experience and maintains its identity across the acts. But if we are concerned with objectivity as well as identity, then we will have to have recourse to a more genuine transcendence, i.e., one that is transcendent even in relation to my own *possible* acts.

It can thus be recognized that we have not yet taken leave of the primordial sphere. On the primordial level, the identity of the object is precisely nothing other than the intentional unity of my own *possible and actual* acts (8/180, 8/186–87), and Husserl even occasionally defines the real achievement of the abstraction to the primordial as a restriction of the sphere of experience to what is actually perceived, i.e., to the originarily given, since this abstraction refrains from including any constitutive accomplishment traceable to others (15/129). The abstraction to the primordial thereby begins with the world that I experientially accept as valid, in order to come back to that which I experience and can experience of it *originaliter* (15/51). What is or can be originarily perceptually constituted in a subjectivity is thus immanent to it in a certain way, although not really intrinsically immanent (8/495). And while that which is originally experienceable at any time is something that is *proper to me* in a distinctive sense (Husserl speaks in this connection of the *monad,* designating with this term the *ego* in its full concretion, i.e., the *ego* in the streaming multifariousness of its intentional life along with the objects meant in this life and constituted for this ego—1/26, 1/102, 1/135, 14/46), everything that can only be indicated—i.e., that can never be brought to the original givenness of something itself, but only appears through appresentation—is something *foreign* (1/144).

While in Husserl's view, the type of transcendence that we have been discussing in this section is independent of the experience of others and of the *alter ego,* there is also a more authentic sense of transcendence properly speaking, a transcendence that truly goes beyond the primordial sphere in the radical sense of exceeding or transgressing it (17/248[241])—a transcendence that is already implied in any talk of genuine objectivity and in every actual perception. It is a matter here of a transcendence that goes beyond both *my own actual* experience and *my own possible* experience, i.e., of a transcendence that depends on intersubjectivity and is therefore only made possible by the experience of others (14/8, 14/442, 6/371[360]). Thus we can distinguish between a primordial transcendence and an intersubjective transcendence, for it is through the experience of others that we are led beyond our immanent sphere of ownness and arrive at the truly transcendent *inter*-subjective world (14/442).

II.3. THE PERFORMANCE OF OTHERS

As already mentioned, Husserl claims that the foreignness and transcendence of others consists in the other's being inaccessible to me in
her originary being-for-herself, for "if what belongs to the other's own
essence were directly accessible, it would be merely a moment of my
own essence, and ultimately he himself and I myself would be the same"
(1/139). Or as he also puts it, "it is precisely because the foreign subjectivity does not belong to the sphere of my original perceptual possibilities that it is not exhausted in being an intentional correlate of my own
life and its rule-governed structure" (8/189). Husserl now proposes the
radical thesis that the transcendence of objectivity is constitutively
related back to this transcendence of others, i.e., to the peculiar elusive
character of this experience of others. For it is only through the appresentative givenness of a foreign I that something can be constituted as
having a validity-claim that transcends my own existence (14/277), and
it is only because I experience an *alter ego*—an *ego* other than mine—
that I can experience objectivity and transcendence. Thus my constitution of these categories of accepted validity is *mediated* through my
experience of others (1/120):

> The transcendence with which the world <is> constituted con-
> sists in its being constituted by means of others and of the gen-
> eratively constituted co-subjectivity (Ms. C 17 32a).[6]

> For me the world is that which, roughly speaking, is meant in
> me . . . , but meant as it is meant through and across others, re-
> ceiving ontic sense from them as well. (15/114)

Any real transcendence, any actual transgression whereby subjectivity
goes beyond itself, thereby rests upon the experience of an other, an
other that—since it transcends that which is essentially proper to
me—is the source of all transcendence (15/560):

> *Here we have the only transcendence that is genuinely worthy of the*
> *name*—and everything else that is still called transcendence,
> such as the objective world, *rests* on the transcendence of for-
> eign subjectivity. (8/495 n. 2)

Husserl therefore calls the other I *"the intrinsically first other"* (1/137;
cf. 17/248[241]) and writes that only constitutive phenomenology

has given the problem of the experience of others its true sense and scope — namely, by recognizing how "the otherness of 'someone else' becomes extended to the whole world, as its 'Objectivity', giving it this sense in the first place" (1/173).

But why is it that it is through the others that the world and everything mundane are constituted with a new type of transcendence? First and foremost, it is because if the world can also be experienced by another subject, it is not reducible to my acts (be they my actual acts or my possible acts). In other words, the genuine transcendence of reality implies its experienceability for a stream of consciousness transcendent to me. (Naturally, this formulation must not mislead us into interpreting intersubjective experienceability as a mere epistemic criterion for the assumption of a world that is foreign to the subject and exists purely in itself, since this would mean falling back into the objectivism that is suspended or overcome through the epochē.) Reality is intersubjectively experienceable, and my constitutive experience of it is therefore mediated by my experience of its givenness for *another* subject. (It is for just this reason that the other must be really transcendent to me, and not merely an intentional modification or an eidetic variation of me — for otherwise the fact that the other experiences the same thing that I do would have no more importance than finding the same photograph and news item in multiple copies of the same newspaper.)[7] Hence it is only by experiencing that others experience the same objects that I do that I experience these objects as objective. Only then are the intentional objects granted a validity that makes them objective (i.e., intersubjectively valid) intentional objects.

To be sure, two difficulties arise here. In the first place, the following problem must be pointed out. Although there does in fact exist a close connection between intersubjectivity and reality — which, moreover, can be negatively formulated to say that whatever cannot in principle be experienced by others cannot have transcendence and objectivity ascribed to it — under normal circumstances I do also experience as real and objective that which I alone experience *in fact;* indeed, I do so without the other seeming to play any role at all. This is even implicitly admitted by Husserl himself when he writes that the validity structure of being-experienceable-for-everyone that is linked with the sense of objects does not vanish even if I alone were to be spared from a universal plague (1/125, 15/6, 4/81). Here, however, we must make a distinction between two phases in our concrete experience of others: namely, between our original experiences of the primal other, on the one hand—experiences that *permanently* make the constitution of objectivity, reality, and transcendence possible—and, on the other hand, all subsequent experiences of others (cf. Chapter II.5). But although the later experiences of others do come precisely too late to make the constitution of objectivity and transcendence possible, this does not mean that they are transcendentally insignificant. It is indeed the case that they can no longer make the constitution of validity possible—but they can "redeem" it, in the sense of "cashing it in" in experiential evidence. To put it another way, although my individual experience of the tree in the forest is an experience of a real, objective tree, these validity components are at first given merely signitively. It is only when I experience that others experience the same tree that the objective validity claim within my own experience is intuitively cashed in.

And in the second place, one could naturally ask whether Husserl's thesis that it is the other who first makes the constitution of actual transcendence possible is false insofar as any concrete experience of others can turn out to be an illusion, i.e., erroneous or hallucinatory (cf. 14/474-75). Thus it seemingly suffices that I *believe* that I am perceiving others who are experiencing objects; in reality, it is not actually necessary for anyone to be there, and perhaps no one is ever really there. But there is a misunderstanding lying at the basis of this criticism. That is to say, although the concrete experience of others is presumptive, this does not hold for the essentially necessary connection between intersubjectivity and objectivity. To put it another way, even if the validity of my own experience changes when it is a case of a deceptive experience of others, this does not detract from Husserl's thesis that the constitution of objectivity is related, of essential necessity, back to intersubjectivity (to the experience of others); rather, all that it shows is that Husserl's overcoming of solipsism in no way consists of providing an argument for the *factual* existence of others (cf. Chapter II.5).

But let us continue our analysis. When Husserl writes that the experience of the being-in-itself of the world is mediated through the experience of its givenness for a foreign subject, and is therefore founded in my experience of the foreign I, it becomes clear that my experience of the other is always an experience of an experiencing or world-related foreign I. It must thus be emphasized that in the experience of others, it is not solely the foreign I that is given to me; rather, the surrounding world experienced and experienceable for the other I is necessarily given as well (14/140). The validity of my experience of the other (an experience through which I have the other as validly existing for me) already includes my *co-acceptance* of the validity of the other's own experience—and indeed, this is true first of all when it is a matter of the other's own lived body. (Here it must naturally be recalled that every concrete experience of the other is a lived bodily experience of an incarnate other, and this is why intersubjectivity, as a concrete relation between subjects, is a relation between lived bodies.) That is to say, the experience of others involves a positing of identity between the foreign body appearing externally to me and this body as it appears to the one whose body it is (13/252; cf. 14/83). My experience of something as the lived body of another necessarily presupposes that *the same* lived body that I experience externally is also experienced by someone else as his own lived body, which is precisely why Husserl characterizes the foreign lived body as the third term mediating the congruence between my own experience and that of the other (14/485). The foreign lived body (the lived body of the other) is the first intersubjective datum, and my apprehension of it *as* a lived body is the first step on the way toward the constitution of an intersubjective world in common (14/110, 15/18, 15/572):

> That his lived body is not only the physical body I directly perceive it to be, but is a lived body, already includes the co-acceptance of the perception that the other has of his lived body as the same body that I perceive, and likewise for his surrounding world as materially the same as the surrounding world that I experience. I cannot posit others without co-positing, along with their experiencing life, that which they experience—i.e., without positing, in co-acceptance, what I presentify them as experiencing, positing this in the same way as I accept what I experience more originally on my own. (14/388)

In other words, our experience of the other is always an experience of the other as world-experiencing. Thus when I have a concrete experience of others, there is always simultaneously co-posited, along with the posited foreign lived body over there, the appearance that I would have if I myself were perceiving from over there (14/287):

> The perception that the other has, according to my empathiz-
> ing, nevertheless actualizes the same mode of appearance that is
> there for me as well, but that I do not currently actually have.
> (14/288)[8]

This point is central, for if the other experienced an appearance that
belonged to a system of appearances that was unreachable and unexperienceable for me, we could never arrive at the constitution of a
world in common. It is evident, however, that everyone who is there
for me as an other—who is experienceable for me as an other—
experiences a world that is none other than the world that is also experienceable for me (14/384). Thus it is with transcendental necessity
that my experience of the other implies a common world. That is to
say, a foreign I that lived in a completely different world would be
absolutely unexperienceable for me (and therefore also senseless
from the phenomenological standpoint). This consideration ultimately leads Husserl to the claim that there can be only one sole transcendental intersubjectivity; and correlatively, there can be only one
sole objective world, for if there are any structures within the *ego* that
imply the co-existence of others, there must be one sole nature (1/
167; cf. 6/146[143], 6/258[255]). Hence it is transcendental intersubjectivity (and—contra Schutz—not the transcendental I or ego)
that must be a *"singulare tantum."*

It would, however, be a misunderstanding to infer that every dissent would thereby be excluded. On the contrary, in Chapter IV we
shall show how one of the most radical consequences of an intersubjective transformation of transcendental philosophy consists precisely
in opening up the possibility of dissent—indeed, of dissent at the transcendental level. However, any dissent necessarily presupposes a basis
of consensus, since a fundamental stock of common experiences must
be presupposed for reciprocal communication to take place—and it
is only on this basis that any declaration of differences of opinion can
take place as well (4/80, 4/206).[9]

Since any (appresentative) positing of another subjectivity includes within itself the positing of the unity of my perceptual appearances and the other's perceptual appearances as concordant
perceptions of the same thing (14/259), the problem of the relation,
and the coincidence of identity, between my sphere of ownness and
that of the other turns out in a certain way to be a specious one. That

is to say, the problem can only arise when these have already been distinguished—which presupposes precisely that the experience of the other has already done its work (1/150):

> I do not have an appresented second original sphere with a second "Nature" and, in this Nature, a second animate bodily organism (the one belonging to the other ego himself), so that I must then ask how I can apprehend my Nature and this other as modes of appearance of the same Objective Nature. On the contrary, the *identity*-sense of "my" primordial Nature and the presentiated other primordial Nature is *necessarily* produced by the appresentation and the unity that it, *as* appresentation, necessarily has with the presentation co-functioning for it— this appresentation by virtue of which an Other and, consequently, his concrete ego are there for me in the first place. (1/152; cf. 14/10)

Let us attempt to summarize the considerations up to this point. Husserl claims that when I experience an experiencing other, the validity categories of my experience are subjected to a decisive change. By means of these others, the object is provided with a validity that lends it an independence with respect to my own performance. The object (i.e., the object that is experienced by both of us) is no longer exhausted in its being-for-me, but is torn away from me. Through the other, the object is constituted as reaching beyond me, and this must also be understood temporally. The object can continue to exist after my death, when I no longer stand in any possible connection with it.[10] Thus the categories of *transcendence, objectivity,* and *reality* are intersubjectively constituted. They can only be constituted by a subject that has experienced other subjects. Yet Husserl also remarks that the same holds for the categories of *inwardness, appearance,* and *immanence.* What he is thinking of is the following. When I experience that the same object can be experienced by several subjects, and that it is given to us in various profiles (13/9), then I realize that there is a distinction between the object itself and its appearance, its being-for-me. What I previously simply experienced as a perceived thing is now transformed into a mere appearance of "the one objectively existing thing"; on the basis of the concomitant synthesis, it has "taken on . . . the new sense 'appearance of,'" a sense that is "henceforth valid" (6/167[164]; cf. 4/82).[11] Thus Husserl says that the expression "my appearance of the object" is already transcending, for what is subjectively real for me can only be termed an "appearance" precisely when others are already positable for me (9/453, 13/382):

> It is questionable—indeed, more than questionable—whether here, at the level of a thing-constitution that is thought solipsistically, I can designate the appearances as subjective. . . . The introjection of sensations and appearances into a subject, or their apprehension as merely subjective, originates in intersubjectivity. (13/388–89)

> What for an individual subject, prior to any relationship of empathy to other subjects, is "world," becomes "aspect" as soon as a relationship of empathy arises. (13/304)

> For the human being who has not undergone the experience of empathy, or from the standpoint of the abstraction from any empathy, there is no "inwardness" of an "externality"; such a human being would have all of the lived experiences—and all of the objectivities, of whatever sort—that are included under the title of inwardness, but the concept of inwardness would be lost. (13/420)

Hence it only makes sense to speak of something "subjective" when I have already experienced other subjects, and have thereby acquired the concept of intersubjective or objective validity. And it is for precisely this reason that Husserl also denies that I can experience subjective appearances prior to the experience of others—that is to say, this very determination is itself intersubjectively derived.

II.4. HORIZON AND INTERSUBJECTIVITY

We have now offered a provisional presentation of the constitutive implications of the experience of others. In order to be able to make further progress with the analysis, and to disclose the real radicality in Husserl's phenomenology of intersubjectivity, the perspective will now be turned around, as it were. We have previously indicated that with Husserl, one can speak of several sorts of relation to others, and that one of them in particular exists *prior to* any *concrete* experience of others (i.e., prior to any currently actual experience of a particular, lived bodily foreign I) and must be seen as its condition of possibility. Hence we claim that the constitutive performance of transcendental intersubjectivity is in no way exhausted by the concrete experience of others. This claim must now be cashed in through a detailed analysis of *horizon intentionality.*

Let us once again take the analysis of unmodified perception as a point of departure. We have already mentioned that the perceptual object is act-transcendent. However, the object not only transcends the act, but also transcends its current appearance. That is to say, when an (external) object is perceived, one must always distinguish between the "appearance" and "that which appears," insofar as the object is never given in its totality, but only in profiles: "If perception were always the actual, genuine self-presentation of the object that it pretends to be, there could be only a single perception for each object" (19/589[cf. 713]; see also 3/86–89[89–92]). But the same object can always be brought to givenness on multiple occasions and in multiple ways.

This insight—which seems banal at first—has, on closer inspection, a number of extremely far-reaching implications. Husserl often pointed out that in the perceptual performance, I do already have a consciousness of a complete thing. Although only a profile is there "in person" in the perception, I do not see and intend this profile, but rather the thing itself; I am directed through the profile toward the object. Whether I look at a book "from above or below, from inside or outside, I always see [the] book. It is always one and the same thing, and indeed, is the same . . . according to the meaning of the perceptions themselves" (19/677[cf. 789]). What is given through each individual perception is therefore the book itself, though to be sure it is the book as it appears from a particular side.

According to Husserl, it is characteristic of perception that by virtue of a *horizon intentionality* active in it, the absent aspects of the thing are always more or less indeterminately co-intended (6/161[158]). The sense of the given profile obviously depends on its relation to the profiles that are not given, and no perception *of the object* would be possible if we were only conscious of what was actually given. Hence for perception actually to be what it is—namely, a perception of the object itself—other aspects that are absent in the currently present perception must be co-present in some way; without this horizon of what is co-intended, the transcendent perceptual object would not be thinkable, for it is the horizon of anticipations—a horizon that cannot be separated from the object—that gives the concept of transcendence its particular sense (9/183; cf. 3/86–89[89–92]).[12] And it is this very horizonality that attends every transcendent perception. For as Husserl tells us, every spatial-thingly perception is, according to its own sense, so radically anticipatory that "even in the contents of what is itself seized upon in the given perceptual moment," there are "moments of anticipation," which is why "there is at bottom nothing in the perceived that is purely and adequately perceived" (8/45). In other words, "nothing whatsoever can be given without (in the case of actually concrete givenness) the co-consciousness of something beyond what is intuitively given" (9/486).

What is co-intended, however, includes not only the absent determinations of the thing itself, but also further co-given objects (*Mitobjekte*) surrounding it in the background (EU 28[33]). The perception of an object is always a perception of an object in the perceptual field (6/165[162]), and the object could not be an object without a horizon intentionality that ultimately points to the world-horizon and thereby embeds every object in the world (1/21, 6/267[264]), since it is the horizonality of the object that points to its world-belongingness (*Welthaftigkeit*). Thus Husserl distinguishes between *inner horizon* and *outer horizon*, and we can accordingly establish that there is a transcendence of sense accompanying every apperception—indeed, a transcendence with regard to the constantly anticipated surrounding objects in the outer horizon, on the one hand, and, on the other hand, a transcendence pertaining to the inner horizon as well, i.e., to the stock of not yet apperceived features of the intuitively given object (cf. EU §§ 8, 22, and 33; 11/8, 9/433, 6/165[162]).[13]

Moreover, taking the notion of the horizon into consideration can simultaneously help us grasp the concept of the world more precisely. That is to say, until now we have spoken of the world without making it clear that it is not at all a "heap of things," but is rather the all-encompassing horizon and context of sense within which all objects are given. But it is not only this. It is also the universal field toward which all our acts are directed, a standing-streaming field embracing all of our aims and goals. Thus the world does not exist in the way that an entity or an object does, but exists in a uniqueness for which a plural form makes no sense. The difference in the mode of being of the world and that of an object within the world thereby indicates two fundamentally different correlative modes of consciousness

(6/146-47[143-44]). Nevertheless, as we will show later, the paradox is that this emphasis on the distinction between "world" and "thing" only really comes into its own at the very moment when Husserl does speak of a plurality of (home) worlds.

Our previous analysis of the relation between perception, appearance, and horizon must now be supplemented by taking the following important aspects into consideration. When there is talk of an appearance, this naturally not only presupposes something that appears, but also presupposes someone to whom it appears. The appearance is always an appearance *of* something *for* someone. Whatever appears, however, appears spatially, appearing at a certain distance from the observer and in a certain perspective. But this obviously requires that the experiencing subject itself has a relation to space — that by virtue of being a lived bodily subject, the subject itself exists spatially in some way (3/116[124-25], 4/33, 13/239). Accordingly, when it is said that things appear, and that they do so from this or that side, one must not forget that this entails a relation to a "here" that only exists on account of, and through, the lived body (4/159, 9/392). As Husserl puts it, the lived body thus bears within itself the *"zero point of all these orientations"* (4/158). As the absolute "here" in reference to which every other object is a "there," the lived body therefore belongs to every experience. Hence in the immediate experience of space (i.e., prior to the constitution of objective space), our own lived body is the center to which space as a whole is related (11/298). It is for this reason that Husserl writes that the lived body is the condition of possibility for other objects (14/540), and that every experience of the world is mediated by, and made possible by, our lived bodilihood (6/220[216-17], 4/56, 5/124). Spatial objects can thus only be constituted by incarnate subjects.[14]

Moreover, these observations with respect to the lived body as a condition of possibility for perception, or for the constitution of perceptual objects, are radicalized the moment Husserl is no longer satisfied with a mere investigation of the lived body as a center of orientation, but instead makes the transition to an investigation of the constitutive role of lived bodily *movement*. At first, Husserl simply points to the significance of lived bodily movement (the movement of the eye, making contact with the hand, the lived body walking) for spatial experience (11/299); ultimately, however, he claims that the intuition of spatial objects is a process that is made possible by our kinaesthetic "sensation," i.e., our awareness of lived bodily movements and positions.[15]

Thus the entire system of aspects is related to the correlative kinaesthetic system. Each appearance of an aspect is an appearance of an aspect only in relation to a kinaesthetic holding still or to a kinaesthetic movement (Ms. D 13 I 4a), and perception is therefore a unity of achievement that essentially arises from the interplay of two correlatively related functions. On the one hand, we have the kinaesthetic sequences, and, on the other hand, we have the sequence of sensed features correlated with them and motivated by them (4/58). Thus every time a chain of appearances flows off, it is accompanied by a system of "sensations of movement," i.e., by a series of unthematized kinaestheses to which it is related. Without this, the appearances could not continually pass over into one another, and therefore the entire chain could not constitute the unity of a sense (11/14). This is why Husserl can say that the kinaesthetic sequence is the condition of possibility for the currently given appearances having the intentional reference whereby they can be appearances "of" something at all (4/66, 16/159, 6/109[106–107]).

In order to make Husserl's argument clear, let us attempt to turn thematically toward a perceptual object. As we have indicated, the object always transcends its currently actual appearance. What Husserl points out, however, is that my constitutive experience both of the transcendence of the object (relative to the individual profiles) and of the identity of the object (in the multiplicity of profiles) is only possible if I have the ability to observe the object from several sides, just as an experience of the object's transcendence in contrast to the multiplicity of perceptual acts requires recollection. But this shift of profiles or perspectives presupposes movement, and indeed, either my movement or that of the object. In both cases, however, the presupposition for the two different perspectives actually being perspectives of the same object (and for the object actually being transcendent) is that there is a *continuity* between these perspectives, that they can slide over into one another, as it were. The experience of this continuity is exactly what is made possible by the kinaestheses.

It therefore only makes sense to speak of an appearance (in the sense of something different from that which appears) when there are several of them. And this diversity of appearances (i.e., different appearances of one and the same appearing object) can only be experienced through a continual shift of perspectives that is precisely what is rendered possible by the kinaestheses. For this reason, the kinaestheses must be taken as a condition of possibility for the identity of the object in the diversity of its appearances (16/189, 11/14-15).

To put it concisely, spatial experience—perceptual intentionality— is thus a *movement* that can only be performed by an incarnate subject (16/176).[16]

This consideration simultaneously makes it clear that there is also a connection between horizon and kinaesthesis. While the currently actually appearing front side of the bookcase is correlative to a certain position of my lived body, the horizon of co-meant but absent aspects of the bookcase is correlative to my kinaesthetic horizon, i.e., to the system of my possibilities of movement (11/15). That is to say, insofar as these absent aspects are actual aspects of one and the same object, they are included within an intentional "if-then" nexus. If I move in thus and such a way, then this or that aspect must come to appearance (6/164[161-62]):

> All possible profiles of an object, as a spatial object, form a system
> that is coordinated to one kinaesthetic system, and to this kinaes-
> thetic system as a whole, in such a way that "if" some kinaesthesis
> or other runs its course, certain profiles corresponding to it
> must "necessarily" also run their course. (9/390)

Although it is true that the horizonal mode of givenness of the ob-ject (and the implied differentiation between what is presented and what is appresented) is related to a lived bodily here, i.e., to my lived bodily here (4/158), and although it is also true that the object is only given horizonally—since it is impossible in principle for any percep-tual subject whatever to be simultaneously "here" and "there"—it is nevertheless important for the further course of our investigation that this not be misunderstood subjectivistically or anthropologically, as though it were a merely factual limitation arising from the imper-fection of human nature (in this case, from our lived bodilihood). On the contrary, it is the ontological structure of the object (its transcen-dence and its status as belonging within the world) that gives rise to the circumstance that the object can only appear for a subject that is situated in a here. It is thus not by way of some flaw that the spatial ob-ject only appears in profiles; rather, this mode of givenness belongs to the regional essence of this type of object as such (cf.3/321[333]).

Hence even a more perfect intellect could not grasp the thing, in the totality of its aspects and determinations, in a single perceptual act, for as Husserl says in *Ideas I,* it turns out that

> something such as a physical thing in space is only intuitable by means of appearances in which it is and must be given in multiple but determined changing "perspective" modes and, accordingly, in changing "orientations" not just for human beings but also for God—as the ideal representative of absolute cognition. (3/351[362])

At this point it is necessary to bring into view the horizon intentionality already mentioned. Above all, we must ascertain precisely how the absent but co-meant aspects of the object are appresented for us. We must thus analyze the mode of functioning that is proper to horizon intentionality. And the outcome of this analysis will be that horizon intentionality, or the horizonal mode of givenness of the object, is *intersubjective* in its very essence.

If we want to investigate the absent aspects, it is clear, to begin with, that we are not permitted simply to presume their givenness and existence dogmatically, for this step is rendered impossible through the epochē. Instead, we must investigate them in their correlation to consciousness. But what intentional acts have these absent aspects as their correlates?

Husserl occasionally tells us that seen noetically, the horizon is a horizon of my capabilities. That is to say, there is a multifarious "I can" that belongs, evidentially, to the horizon. Guided by the orientational structure already at work within the perceptual present, I can penetrate into multiple horizonal directions of orientation: in the direction of the past, in the direction of the future, or in the direction of what is co-meant (Ms. C 3 7b). It lies in the essence of reality that whatever is still not currently actually experienced *can* come to givenness, for it belongs to the horizon of my current experiential actuality (3/101[106–107], 14/453, 2/25).[17] Such possible intuitive givenness (i.e., an intuitive givenness that is possible in principle) thus points to my horizonal capabilities. To put it another way, Husserl occasionally characterizes absent aspects as noematic correlates of *possible* perceptions. Two different explanations immediately present themselves here.

Either 1) the absent but co-meant aspects are appresented as aspects that were given or could be given as present in my past or future perceptions—e.g., the back side of a bookcase is presentified as a side I have already seen or could subsequently see—or 2) the absent but co-meant aspects are to be taken as correlates of currently actual, co-existing perceptual possibilities. In this case, they would then be the correlates of the fictive perceptual acts I could perform if I were there (instead of here) *now*, with all this understood in the subjunctive mood, contrary to fact. Hence the back side of the bookcase is fictively co-given as the side that I "would" see if I "were" over there at this moment. We emphasize the fictive character of this possibility, which is precisely a possibility that cannot be *actualized* (and thus why in a certain way, it is not really a "possibility" for me at all). That is to say, the front side and the back side of the bookcase cannot, as a matter of principle, be intuitively given to the same consciousness at the same time, since the currently actual intuitive givenness of one aspect excludes in principle any *simultaneous* intuitive givenness of another aspect of the same object for the same subject.[18] To put it another way, the back side of the bookcase is genuinely transcendent to me when I am observing the front side, for it is true in principle that both cannot be simultaneously given as currently actual in my flow of consciousness (i.e., it is impossible for them to be so given).

Although we are going to distinguish between these two explanations, Husserl made more or less undifferentiated use of both of them in the *Logical Investigations,* as well as in later works. On the one hand, he writes that perception is built up partly out of purely perceptual intentions, but partly out of merely imaginative or even signitive intentions as well (19/589[713]). On the other hand, however, he writes in immediate conjunction to this that every "external" perception

> is a mixture of fulfilled and unfulfilled intentions. To the former there corresponds the part of the object that is given as a more or less complete profile within this individual perception, *to the latter the part of the object that is not yet given, the part that would thus come to currently actual and fulfilling presence in new perceptions.* (19/590[cf. 714], emphasis altered; cf. 9/172)[19]

The decisive question is now whether one or the other of these explanations is actually phenomenologically acceptable. In the first case, the object is taken as the principle of unity running through a temporally extended multiplicity of appearances. But this interpretation does not agree with our experience at all. When I perceive a bookcase, I do not perceive something that has a currently actual profile now, had one previously, and will have another one later. The present front side is not a front side with respect to a past or future back side, but is precisely determined as a "front" side by its relation to a *coexisting* "back" side. Thus it lies in the sense of the object itself that at each moment, it possesses a multiplicity of actually coexisting profiles. As Husserl himself says, it is exactly the case that each appresentation makes something *co-present* (1/139, Ms. A VII 12 2b, 28b), and it is only this state of affairs that can be unified with the true transcendence of the object. One should accordingly also take care not to overlook the circumstance that the correlation of an absent aspect with a past or future *perception* in no way gives us a co-present back side, but yields an additional *front side*. Thus it is obviously impossible to understand the peculiar horizonal givenness of non-present, co-meant aspects by means of the first explanation, insofar as it would only give us the aspects as concurrent front sides.[20]

This last objection is also relevant to the second explanation. But beyond this, if the second explanation were true, it would shatter the homogeneity of the perceptual object. Although in perception the object is always only partly intuitively given to us, the *reality* of the object is still a unitary whole—a reality that would be nullified if the object partially consisted of *fictive* aspects (aspects that were the noematic correlates of fictive perceptions). Naturally, we can imaginatively conjure up for ourselves the particular way the non-present sides would look. It is clear, however, that this imaginative activity does not constitute the horizon of the object, but already presupposes the object's reality. Our phantasy is comparatively free with regard to how we imagine the determinations of the back side, the inside, the underside, etc.; its determination and its imaginative filling out nevertheless necessarily take place within the horizon structure. And in contrast to our imaginary projections, which can naturally be demolished by subsequent perceptions, horizonality itself has no hypothetical or irreal character. *How* the back side of the bookcase looks is a contingent question; *that* it has a back side is, on the contrary, an actually effective necessity, and for this reason it cannot be explained by linking it with a fictive possibility. To put it another way, the reality of the perceptual object implies the reality of the perceptual horizon, i.e., the *reality* of the absent aspects—although the particular way these aspects would look is characterized by an (eidetically regulated) determinable indeterminacy, and precisely for this reason remains open to being imaginatively filled out (11/6, 1/83).

As we have already mentioned, Husserl does occasionally use both these explanations. It is interesting, however, that in a research manuscript from 1920–21 he seems to have become aware of their problematic character, for there he himself seeks an alternative clarification of the appresentation that is at work in horizon consciousness. Thus he writes that the "infinite system of 'possible perceptions' and the correlative 'possible looks' of a transcendent object"[21] are neither systems of perceptions that I actually have or could generate, nor systems of imaginations or memories. Rather, it is a matter of unique presentifications (Ms. A III 9 23b) whose particular character he unfortunately fails to specify positively.

Let us therefore turn to a third possibility in order to investigate to what extent it can help us further.

It is certain that the absent but co-meant aspects must be understood as correlates of possible perceptions. However, these possible perceptions must be compatible with my own currently actual perception, for they must be simultaneously actualizable with it; indeed, it is exactly from this circumstance that the absent but co-meant aspects of the thing provided by my horizonal appresentation are to obtain their character as *currently actually coexisting aspects*. It is nevertheless just this compatibility that is lacking both from my fictive perceptions and from my past or future perceptions. And it is precisely for this reason that it is impossible for the absent profile to be a correlate of *my* possible perception.

Now, however, we find the following passages in Husserl:

> One subject cannot simultaneously have two aspects of the orthological manifold. But a plurality of aspects can be simultaneous if they are distributed across various subjects, and they must be simultaneous if these subjects are simultaneously experiencing the same physical thing. (13/377–78)

> I cannot have the appearance that I have from "my standpoint" (the location of my physical body in the now) from another standpoint; with the shift in standpoints, the appearance is altered in a lawfully regulated way, and it is evident that the appear-

ances are incompatible. I can have the incompatible appearance at another time if I take up another location in space. And likewise, an "other" can have that same appearance, now, precisely if that other is now at another location. (13/2-3)

The contradictory observation becomes concordant when I take the doubling as a doubling. A priori, I cannot be simultaneously here and there, but something similar can be here and there—I can be here, and an equivalent (and again also more or less similar) I can be there. (13/264)

. . . to everything alien (as long as it remains within the appresented horizon of concreteness that necessarily goes with it) [there belongs] an appresented Ego who is not I myself but, relative to me, a modificatum: an *other* Ego. (1/145)

In other words, a relation to a foreign subjectivity seems to be in play whenever there is talk of a multiplicity of coexisting profiles! It is through the foreign I that the incompatibility of the coexisting profiles becomes compatible (1/148). That is to say, the foreign I can have, as present, the coexisting profile that is absent for me. Hence the co-present profile can be understood as the noematic correlate of the perception carried out by a foreign I.

We have previously explained how the experience of others, which is an experience of an experiencing foreign subject, simultaneously implies positing, and co-accepting as valid, the appearance that the other would perceive from her position (cf. 13/297, 14/287-88). The appearance available to the other—an appearance that I presentify in the experience of an other—is posited as present, and is not posited as a hypothetical perceptual appearance, but as an actual one. However, it is posited as an appearance that the other has, not as one that I have (14/255).[22] I could only have it if I were now over there.

When there is talk of concrete, currently actual experience of an other—and correlatively, of the currently actual coexisting profile that is thereby granted to the object—we are obviously dealing with an abstraction or construction that still does not lead us to our goal. That is to say, when I perceive a bookcase, I perceive it as a transcendent object that exists in itself and is horizonally given. This acceptance of the object as existing does *not* presuppose that I am *simultaneously* having a concrete experience of an other that would furnish the bookcase with a further, currently actual profile. Moreover, the bookcase naturally does not consist of *two* currently actual profiles. As a transcendent object, it possesses an infinite diversity of coexisting and compatible profiles, and my experience of it naturally does not presuppose that each of its profiles is simultaneously perceptually intended by a subject, which would presuppose an infinite plurality of foreign I's who are currently actually perceiving it (and who are perceived by me as so doing). Although not only the appresentation but also the horizonal givenness of the object (i.e., the *appearance* of the object) seem to presuppose some sort of relation to foreign subjectivity, it is neither a matter of the relation to one foreign I alone, nor a matter of the relation to the factual existence of several I's.

Husserl, was aware of the inadequacy just mentioned, and he therefore conceded that the issue does not rest solely on the *factual* experience of others. When we speak of a genuinely transcendent object, and therefore imply its experienceability for a stream of consciousness that is transcendent to our own (which is why the other cannot simply be an eidetic variation of myself), naturally what we mean is not merely its experienceability for the foreign subject with whom we currently stand in connection, but its experienceability in principle for everyone. To every thing-experience or world-experience there accordingly belongs a reference to the constant co-acceptance of intersubjectivity— even when I have no explicit objectivating intention directed toward others.[23] Thus in every genuine thing-experience, there is always at least an implicit relation to others as co-objectivating or co-cognizing (6/468), and every object therefore points to an *indeterminate* subjectivity or to an open plurality of subjectivities in which it is constituted (13/463, 14/470). Hence the explication of the horizon would seem to lead to *possible* others, and insofar as a single other alone is not sufficient, the explication ultimately leads to an *infinite plurality of possible others,* which Husserl occasionally characterizes as the *open intersubjectivity:*

> Thus anything objective that stands before my eyes in an experience, and first of all in a perception, has an apperceptive horizon—that of possible experience, *my own and foreign.* Expressed ontologically, every appearance that I have is from the very beginning a member of an open, endless (though not ex-

plicitly actualized) range of possible appearances of the same [objective something], and *the subjectivity of these appearances is the open intersubjectivity*. (14/289, emphasis altered; cf. 9/394, 15/497)

The thing is therefore constituted as a synthetic unity of *my actual and possible experiences and the actual and possible experiences of all others*. The "true thing" is the object that is identically maintained in the multiplicity of appearances available to a plurality of subjects (4/82): "The thing is a rule of possible appearances. This means that the thing is a reality as a unity of a manifold of appearances connected according to rules. Moreover, this unity is an intersubjective one" (4/86). Differently formulated, it thus lies in the sense of experience that

> what is experienced as real actually exists with the ontic sense that it has as the correlate of the system of the concordant possible experience of all co-experiencing subjects that can possibly enter into connection with me—or that it has in such a way that what is currently actually experienced points horizonally to a concordance in the ongoing synthesis of possible experience (one's own experience and that of any number of fellow humans that may enter into co-functioning), a synthesis that must moreover always be renewed. (Ms. A VII 2 22b; cf. 15/44, 15/33, 14/274)[24]

Let us attempt to recapitulate the results once more against this background. To every experience of an object, there essentially belongs a reference to further possible experiences, since absent aspects are co-intended through, and beyond, the intuitively given appearance. However, since these possible experiences are incompatible in principle with my *currently actual* experience, it is a matter of the experiences of possible others. Thus both the appresentation and the appearance of the object point to open intersubjectivity.

But what exactly is meant with this concept of possible others? Is it not highly problematic—perhaps even countersensical—to characterize a *possible* subjectivity or a plurality of *possible* subjectivities as "constitutive"? Isn't constitution always carried on by a *factual* stream of consciousness? This is true in a certain way. It is a matter of fact that my perceptual object is constituted by me; I can only do this, however, because my horizonal relatedness to the world contains structural references to the perceptions of possible others, and it is precisely for this reason that my horizon intentionality is incompatible a priori with a transcendental solipsism that would deny in principle any such plurality of streams of consciousness.

With a shift in accent, the same state of affairs can be expressed in such a way as to bring to light a clear parallel between Husserl's analyses of perception and Merleau-Ponty's (cf. Chapter VI.4 below): as a constituting subjectivity, I am directed toward objects whose horizonal givenness and whose transcendence bear witness to their openness for other subjects. The objects are not exhausted in their appearance for me; rather, there are always alternative perspectives, or co-intended aspects, that could be perceived by other subjects. Since the appearing object always leaves open the possibility that it is there for others too, then whether or not such other subjects do in fact appear on the scene, the appearing object refers to other subjects, and for this very reason is intrinsically intersubjective.[25] It is an entity that does not merely exist for a single I, but refers a priori to intersubjectivity. And it is for precisely this reason that its constitution can only be elucidated through a radical implementation of the reduction to transcendental *intersubjectivity*.

II.5. TWO TYPES OF RELATION TO OTHERS

What we have been able to establish up to this point with regard to the constitutive role of intersubjectivity—namely, that within horizon consciousness, there is a constitutively co-functioning reference to open intersubjectivity—now requires a decision with regard to the two types of relation to others that have been differentiated until now, as well as a systematic elaboration of the relationship of founding that obtains between them. Is the concrete experience of the lived bodily foreign I the condition of possibility for a horizonal relatedness to the world, a horizonal world-relatedness that is apparently intersubjectively structured? Or is the converse the case, so that the concrete experience of others is first made possible through an intersubjective openness that is already given with our relatedness to the world? These are questions that ultimately lead to the problem of the reduction to the primordial.

From Husserl's perspective, the answer seems simple at first, for both Husserl's detailed presentation of the concrete experience of others and his observations on primordiality, along with a number of remarks explicitly referring to the issue in question, all support the first possibility—namely, that the concrete experience of the other provides the constitutive foundation for open intersubjectivity (cf. 6/ 246[243], 1/153). Husserl seems to offer two alternative explanations for this: 1) the constitution of the intersubjective horizon is a gradual process that can never be closed off; 2) the constitution of the intersubjective horizon is a sudden and self-contained occurrence motivated by a particular type of concrete experience of the other. Let us consider each of these in turn.

1) In *Zur Phänomenologie der Intersubjektivität III*, Husserl admits that the matter does not end with factual empathy (i.e., concrete experience of others). He emphasizes that it must be shown how an open horizon of co-subjects is motivated on this basis (15/497; cf. 17/ 246[239–40]) and claims that it is a matter of a gradual broadening:

> Everything mundane is constituted intersubjectively. The constitution of intersubjectivity and of an intersubjective world is constantly in progress, and has a corresponding horizon within which this constitution counts for me beforehand as still taking on new intersubjective sense in relation to new I-subjects. (15/45)

Hence it is through access to the others of others that spatial and spatio-temporal constitution is *broadened*—a broadening that then also spreads to past others through the expressions and indications left behind from their having-been-active-there (Ms. A VII 1 15a). Thus each I-subject has his "horizon of empathy," i.e., that of his co-subjectivity—a horizon that is to be opened up "through direct and indirect commerce with the chain of others, who are all others for one another, for whom there can be still others, etc." (6/258[255]; cf. 15/138, 15/176, 15/439).

On closer observation, however, it turns out that here it is not a matter of the constitution of open intersubjectivity, but of the broadening of our experiential knowledge of the plurality of *factual* others, along with their currently actual surrounding worlds (cf. 15/198). Whereas the question of open intersubjectivity relates to a formal structural element of our world-experience per se, what is at stake here is a gradual change in the validity claim of our experiences, depending upon how many subjects we have directly and indirectly included, through constant iteration, in our "circle of acquaintances"—a change

that can be especially dramatic when we encounter members of a foreign world (or of a different cultural sphere).[26] That this explanation
therefore provides no answer to our question regarding the motivation of an open horizon of co-subjects is subsequently also conceded by
Husserl: in connection with the passage cited above from *Zur Phänomenologie der Intersubjektivität III,* he writes that here it is a matter of a
broadening of the formation of the sense, "objective world." But this
broadening is performed within a framework of sense that has always
already been achieved. An open horizon of indeterminate others is already predelineated for this formation of sense, a horizon that is then
filled with others with whom we are newly becoming acquainted (15/45–
46). The broadening of our factual circle of acquaintances expresses a
higher-level *concretization* of our intersubjective relation—which, however, it therefore also already presupposes.

2) An alternative course can be taken (albeit one that still takes
concrete experience of others as foundational) by way of a more precise description of a particular consequence of the concrete experience of others that has not yet been mentioned.[27] A special case of
the experience of others is the case in which I experience another as
experiencing me, so that this mediated experience of an "other" coincides with my own experience of "myself." A very important consequence results from this "most original form of reciprocally existing
for one another" (8/137), to use Husserl's words, i.e., from this special case in which I experience my counterpart as being experientially
directed toward me myself, so that my own self-experience is mediated by the other—and I therefore ultimately experience myself as
foreign:

> The difference between oneself and the foreign I vanishes; the
> other apprehends me as foreign, just as I grasp him as foreign
> for me, and he himself is a "self," etc. Parity thus ensues: a mul-
> tiplicity of feeling, willing I's that are alike in kind and each in-
> dependent in the same sense. (13/243–44; cf. 15/635)

Husserl now points out that the self-objectivation and self-
mundanization occasioned through the other—which "entails an *Objectivating equalization* of my existence with that of all others" (1/
158)—takes place in inseparable unity with the objectivation of nature as nature for everyone (14/87). We will later follow up on these
latter points; for the time being, all we want to make clear is that I am

led to the insight that just as the other is an *alter ego* for me, I am likewise an *alter ego* for the other. I am one among others, and am therefore included in the "everyone" that receives its sense precisely from this experience (17/245[238], 15/645). I experience that I am intentionally enclosed within this external plurality of others, and I thereby gain the self-apperceptive form of "I am a member of a community of I's as a 'we'-community" (14/468). A communal life is thus possible in which many subjects live in such a way that "everyone" knows herself to be a member of a personal community of action stretching out into an indeterminate and boundless distance (8/136-37).

But the becoming-one-among-others is simultaneously a becoming-an-other, and this "alter-ation," to use Theunissen's concept (Theunissen 1986, 88-89), has far-reaching constitutive implications. That is to say, it carries along with itself a unique type of disempowering and decentering of my I, insofar as I can no longer be seen as the sole constitutive center. According to Theunissen, the objective world—with its sense, "there for everyone"—can only be constituted by an I if this I itself is in a certain manner "everyone" (Theunissen 1986, 100). Thus a sense of "everyone" must already be constituted in this I itself, and must already be functioning as its horizon, for this I to be a part of an objective world, since it is only in relation to this "everyone" that the world can be objective. Once again, however, the "everyone" can only be realized as the horizon of the I's experience of the world when the I itself is included in "everyone," and hence is one among the others (17/245-47[239-40]). It is only when I do not merely experience the other as *an* other, but also experience myself as a mere "someone," that the notion of "everyone" attains its full sense.[28] The moment I understand that just as my perspective on the world is only one among many, so also am I only one among many, then in a certain way, the relatedness of the object of my experience to "me" is suspended. A de-perspectivization and de-subjectivation of my experiences occurs because it is immaterial "who" performs the experience; as Waldenfels puts it, the experience of the alien implies that one's own experience has become alien to oneself (Waldenfels 1990, 29).[29]

The question is now whether the constitution of "everyone" founds the constitution of open intersubjectivity. We have established that any talk of the horizonal givenness or the appearance of the object implies structural references to a plurality of compossible subjects. Has the possibility of this plurality now been secured? The "alter-ation" un-doubtedly makes a very important constitutive contribution, for it does relate directly to the shift in our experience of ourselves, and of the world, that is effected by the experience of others, and hence does properly stand in the center of Husserl's analyses of intersubjectivity. Nevertheless, it obviously concerns a different aspect of our constitu-tion of sense and validity than the aspect that emerged in our explica-tion of the intersubjectivity that is the constitutive correlate of the horizon structure. And it then also becomes clear that alter-ation can-not found intersubjectivity, since—like every concrete experience of others—"alter-ation" implies an experience of the horizonally appear-ing foreign lived body, and for this reason it already presupposes, within the horizon intentionality, a constitutively co-functioning refer-ence to open intersubjectivity.

Now if the concrete experience of others does not found open in-tersubjectivity, but on the contrary presupposes it, there are a num-ber of consequences that also affect the possibility of the reduction to the primordial. That is to say, if this is the case, intersubjectivity is ob-viously not first established at the moment when an individuated I (primordially) perceives a foreign I; rather, the experience of others takes place within an already available intersubjective dimension.[30]

As we have previously mentioned, Husserl attempted to delimit a primordial sphere of that which is my own in a distinctive sense, since it does not as yet contain anything constituted by the constitutive par-ticipation of other I's (17/248[241]). If my horizon intentionality a pri-ori implies references to the intentions of others, the attempt to carry out a transcendental aesthetic at the *primordial* level obviously miscar-ries (17/297[292], 1/173). Husserl does indeed claim that the *res ex-tensa* that is at stake in a transcendental aesthetic must be distinguished from the objective physical body existing-for-everyone, and that only the latter is provided with a validity that points to an open totality of co-subjects (15/499–500; cf. 4/55–90). But since every experience of appearing objects already presupposes constitutive references to tran-scendental intersubjectivity, we must reject the claim that there can be a transcendental aesthetic at the primordial level.

We can therefore follow Held with regard to the hierarchy of foundation, and maintain that Husserl (often) committed the error of trying to found the unthematized relation to co-functioning others in a thematic experience of others (Held 1972, 46–47). It is not our thematic experience of the other that makes our experience of the intersubjective world possible; rather, the horizon structure of our relatedness to the world points to open intersubjectivity, and it is the latter (along with our own horizonal openness) that makes our thematic and concrete experience of the other possible. Naturally, this does not preclude the concrete experience of others from being, for its part, the condition of possibility of the *thematization* of the anonymously co-functioning open intersubjectivity. It must be maintained, however, that others are not originally present for me and familiar to me as objects of a particular intentionality, but rather as co-functioning in all intentionality; as a co-present, the foreign present precedes the explicit experience of, and encounter with, others (15/446, 15/455, 15/465, 15/492, 15/645).[31]

These observations need not lead to the (hasty) conclusion that it has therefore turned out to be impossible to carry out the reduction (or abstraction) to the primordial. On the contrary, it may very well be the case that in the domain of passive synthesis, or at the level of self-awareness and time-consciousness, there are indeed primordial realms that are constituted by a single subject alone quite as a matter of principle. If our line of argument is valid, all that is allowed is the limited conclusion that both noetically and noematically, the (present) horizon points to intersubjectivity, so that any experiences that cannot be confined to what is purely given, but rather also co-intend absent aspects, do indeed imply a reference to intersubjectivity for this very reason.

Moreover, this horizonal unity of intuitive presence and appresentatively making co-present can be interpreted as an indication of our perspectival *finitude*. As we will show later, it is no accident that it is precisely horizon intentionality that implies references to others. That is to say, there is a close connection between our finitude and our openness with regard to others (cf. Chapter III.2 and Chapter VI.4).[32]

Hence although we cannot yet exclude the possibility that the constitutive contribution of intersubjectivity is founded and belongs to a higher level (1/69), we have at least provisionally shown that this contribution is not founded in the constitution of the foreign I. And if it is not dependent upon the (contingent) emergence of an other in my perceptual field, one must naturally consider whether intersubjectivity is contingent at all — or whether it does not belong instead to the a priori structure of subjectivity.

The following passage testifies that such an idea is in no way foreign to Husserl:

> Naturally, the world is not cobbled together out of the primordially reduced worlds. Each primordial [sphere] is the product of a reduction from an intersubjectively and generatively constituted sense; the ontic sense stems from the intersubjectively concordant experience of any one of these [primordial spheres], an experience that already has a sense-relation to intersubjectivity. *As mundane experience, my experience (thus already each of my perceptions) not only includes others as mundane objects, but constantly includes them, in existential co-validity, as co-subjects, as co-constituting—and both are inseparably intertwined.* (Ms. C 17 36a, emphasis added)[33]

Thus in Husserl's late writings, there are in fact not only frequent investigations into the performance of co-functioning intersubjectivity, instead of investigations into the concrete experience of others, but also tentative reflections concerning the revision of the hierarchy of foundation—for example, when Husserl asks: "When empathy occurs—is perhaps community, intersubjectivity also already there, and does empathy then merely accomplish the disclosure of it?" (Ms. C 17 84b; cf. Chapter III.2 below).[34] As so often with Husserl, however, what he actually accomplishes in his analyses must be emphasized in contrast to most of his own meta-reflections and programmatic explanations.[35]

In summary, it can be stated that for the time being, we must distinguish between two types of relation to others, and correlatively, between two types of constitutive performance of intersubjectivity. (Later—cf. Chapter IV.3)—we shall have occasion to speak of a third type.) Although the concrete experience of others presupposes the constitutive contribution of open intersubjectivity, and although the former is *founded* in the latter, naturally this in no way means that the entire constitutive contribution of the concrete experience of others has already been accomplished by this anonymously co-functioning intersubjectivity.[36] On the contrary, there are obviously irreducible distinctions between the respective accomplishments. While open intersubjectivity can be situated with respect to the horizon structure, the concrete experience of others (which—and it is precisely this that must be emphasized—is what first opens up the possibility of *dissent,* and thereby inaugurates a heightened experience of transcendental *alterity)* is, as we have indicated, directly linked with a shift in our *categories of validity*. Consequently, it is only the concrete experience of others that permits the self-mundanization of the transcendental I and the thematic experience of validity-for-everyone. It is only the concrete experience of others that makes the intuitive "cashing in" of our validity claims possible; if in addition to this, the categorial determination, *"transcendence,"* is also dependent on the foreignness and the merely appresentational givenness of others, then it too is first made possible by the concrete experience of others. Husserl is entirely justified in emphasizing the central significance of the analyses concerning the concrete experience of others, for the concrete experience of others does indeed play a constitutive role. Thus it must be strongly emphasized that the distinction between these two types of experience of others in no way corresponds to the distinction between "constituting" and "constituted" intersubjectivity mentioned at the beginning of our investigation (cf. Chapter I.4).[37]

Naturally, the emphasis on the importance—and the irreducible variety—of the concrete experience of others does not imply that our focus on open, anonymous intersubjectivity suddenly turns out to be irrelevant. That is to say, although our thematization of open intersubjectivity only bears upon an entirely formal stratum, the investigation has nevertheless brought about an important elucidation of Husserl's investigations. It has not only turned out that *any* experience possessing horizonal references to co-present aspects implies a unique type of a priori relation to intersubjectivity (a finding that has nullified the possibility of a transcendental aesthetic at the primordial level), but also that the possibility of the concrete experience of others can itself be seen to be dependent on this fundamental intersubjectivity. Instead of simply dogmatically presupposing its possibility, we have begun to make this fundamental intersubjectivity transcendentally understandable by pointing to its dependence on the horizonal openness of the subject—on the constant mixture of presence and absence in the subject's structure of experience.[38]

We can turn to a thesis of Carr in immediate connection with these observations. He claims that the *nos cogitamus*—which is supposed to serve as a new foundation after Husserl has introduced transcendental intersubjectivity—is non-apodictic, because the experience of others, which has the same presumptive character as any external perception, possesses no absolute certainty (Carr 1973, 32-35).[39] That is to say, according to Husserl, it would be thinkable that no other ever came forth in the course of original experience, just as it is thinkable that every experience of the other could be canceled (14/474-75). This observation—which is used by other interpreters to accuse Husserl of never actually managing to extricate himself from solipsism, since in contrast to the *cogito sum,* every positing of the other is characterized by an essentially necessary presumptivity—can now be rejected on the basis of our analyses up to this point.

We can take it as demonstrated that a phenomenology of the experience of others leads to an "expansion of the phenomenological reduction into a *reduction to pure intersubjectivity*" (9/246), and it is for this reason that the claim that the phenomenological reduction invalidates any possible positing of a foreign transcendental subjectivity must be regarded as nonsensical (8/497). At the same time, however, it must be emphasized that it belongs to the sense of inter-subjectivity that the *concrete* other always appears in an "evidence of external experience." If the consciousness of an other were given in the same way in which self-consciousness is, this would amount to abolishing alterity and taking the other as part of the self. Yet the foreign I that is experienced in the appresentational experience of others is not a hypothesis, a substruction, or a mere anticipation, but is *experienced,* and can thus itself be verified or canceled in the manner proper to experience (14/352). Consequently, it is misleading to regard the falsifiability of the currently actual positing of others as an expression of solipsism. The other is given to me originally in empathy, for what I see is not a sign, not a mere analogue, but *the other* (14/385, 29/182, 1/153, 15/ 506), even though the other's mode of givenness is fundamentally different from the mode of givenness of an object. For it is not an experience of the "givenness" of something itself: it is an experience in which something itself is "evinced," "manifested," "made known" *(es ist eine selbstbekundende Erfahrung und keine selbstgebende*—cf. 14/354). The other's relation to herself is indeed inaccessible to me. But *that* the other is inaccessible to me *is* accessible to me (1/144, 15/631), and to call for any more would mean to posit the most original mode of givenness of the other as a mode in which it would be precisely an I itself, and not an other, that would appear before me (Boehm 1969, 15). To put it another way, interpreting the falsifiability of the experience of others as "solipsism" can be compared with construing the necessarily horizonal mode of givenness of spatial things (and their constant presumptivity) as a denial of their reality.

On the basis of these discussions, however, we can immediately make fruitful use of our earlier distinction between two types of relation to others: one type is the a posteriori and presumptive character of our currently actual experience of others, while the a priori and apodictic character of open intersubjectivity is something else entirely. As Husserl writes, the explication of my own transcendental present horizon leads to transcendental and currently actually co-present others and to their horizons, and it becomes clear on this basis that there is an *apodictic* universal structure of intersubjectivity predelineated in every *ego* whatsoever (15/192). It would thus be misleading to claim that the contribution supplied by co-functioning open transcendental intersubjectivity could somehow be influenced by any possible mistake in my concrete experience of others. Even if I were to know with certainty that I was the sole survivor of a universal plague, my world-experience would always still be dependent on transcendental intersubjectivity as my irreducible accomplice.[40]

But when we make the claim that even independently from the contingent emergence of a concrete foreign I in my perceptual field, my (pre-predicative) experiences imply a constitutively co-functioning reference to intersubjectivity, naturally this in no way excludes talk of a *solitary* constituting subject, if by this we understand a subject that has still not had any *concrete* experience of the other. Nor are we denying the possibility of cognitive accomplishments performed by this solitary subject, a point that is of decisive importance when it is a question of the relationship of phenomenology to linguistic pragmatics. However, we will defer this problem to Chapter VII.

CHAPTER III

Intersubjective Subjectivity

III.1. THE COMMUNITY OF MONADS

Now that we have concluded our analysis of the intersubjectivity of horizon intentionality, we have three tasks before us. 1) Here in Chapter III, we must continue to analyze the relation between transcendental intersubjectivity and transcendental subjectivity. And this is not just because a thorough investigation must trace out the constitutive contribution of intersubjectivity both to the constitution of objectivity and to the constitution of subjectivity; after all, it still remains open whether intersubjectivity plays any role at the fundamental level of the self-constitution of the I. Rather, it is also because it is only the analysis of this relation that can show whether a philosophy of intersubjectivity signifies a *break with* or a *radicalization of* a philosophy of subjectivity. 2) Then in Chapter IV, we must describe the fundamental alteration of the phenomenological concept of reality that is called forth by Husserl's incorporation of transcendental intersubjectivity. 3) Finally, we must endeavor to show why it is precisely the incorporation of intersubjectivity that makes a new fundamental understanding of phenomenology possible, and why a number of basic phenomenological concepts can only be seen in a correct light when they are seen in terms of Husserl's reflections on transcendental intersubjectivity. This demonstration begins in Chapters III and IV, and culminates in Chapter V in an analysis of Husserl's concept of constitution.

We have arrived at the result that the world is never exclusively the accomplishment of an individual consciousness; rather, the experience and constitution of the world always and necessarily proceeds in the togetherness of a communalization of consciousness (15/546). Its ontic sense is constitutively related back to a sense-bestowing that is not performed by *one* pure I, but by a pure, and universally closed, absolute plurality of monadic I's (14/266). And Husserl himself points out that since what is characterized, within the phenomenological reduction, as "absolute being" is the universe of transcendental subjects that stand in actual and possible community with one another, the phenomenological reduction therefore leads to a *monadology* anticipated in the "brilliant insights" of Leibniz (8/190).

> *A priori,* my ego, given to me apodictically—the only thing I can posit in absolute apodicticity as existing—*can be a world-experiencing ego only by being in communion with others like himself:* a member of a community of monads, which is given orientedly, starting from himself. (1/166, emphasis added)

According to Husserl, the disclosure of the constitutive significance of transcendental intersubjectivity has led to a decisive modification and fine-tuning of his concept of absolute subjectivity. While at first the transcendental subjectivity disclosed through the transcendental reduction is indeterminate, in further reflection it is displayed in its fullness as transcendental *intersubjectivity,* since the deepest and most universal self-meditation of the philosophizing *ego* leads to the discovery of absolute intersubjectivity (6/275[340]). Absolute self-cognition soon leads to we-cognition, to a cognition of the absolute total subjectivity (6/472):

> Thus transcendental subjectivity is broadened to intersubjectivity —or rather, properly speaking, it is not broadened; rather, transcendental subjectivity only understands itself better. It understands itself as the primordial monad that bears other monads intentionally within itself, and must necessarily posit them as transcendental others (with the concordance of experience making the existential certainty necessary as long as experience ongoingly proceeds in a concordant style). (15/17)

Insofar as the others to whom I am necessarily led through the explication and elucidation, within the transcendental reduction, of my own transcendental I are *transcendental* others, the incorporation of intersubjectivity in this connection is justified in a legitimate transcendental phenomenological sense. That is to say, the reduction is not breached, and for this reason the others do not come into play as co-pregiven in a naive way either (15/16). And it is precisely this that

distinguishes Husserl's transcendental approach from the mundane
phenomenology of intersubjectivity pursued by Schutz.

It has thus been shown that the subjective correlate of the world
one arrives at through the transcendental reduction includes not only
my own I, but also the subjectivity pertaining to all "others." We can
therefore state that the "reduction to transcendental subjectivity"
turns out to be ambiguous. On the one hand, the subjectivity positable in the epochē is to be understood as the monadic *subjectivity*
proper to the phenomenologizing I (i.e., to the subjectivity currently
carrying out the concrete analyses concerned). And on the other
hand, it is to be understood as the transcendental *intersubjectivity* that
is opened up and made accessible within this monadic subjectivity
(15/73). The following must therefore be differentiated: on the one
hand, the subject engaged in transcendental phenomenologizing,
and on the other hand, transcendental subjectivity pure and simple—
and the latter turns out to be transcendental intersubjectivity (15/74-
75). At the same time, however, it must be emphasized that included
in the very sense of every "we," there is a centering in me as the I who
has the we-consciousness (15/426). This necessity of an I-centering of
transcendental intersubjectivity is of the greatest significance, and we
shall be returning to it later (see Chapter III.3).

We have already spoken of the way in which the experience of others
motivates a decentering of our own absoluteness. And in connection
with this, it turns out that Husserl not only speaks of an intersubjectivity
opened up and made accessible in transcendental subjectivity, but emphasizes at the same time that this intersubjectivity is the absolute ontological basis. For if there are many monads, then none is self-sufficient in
the full sense, insofar as their own content, within their own being-for-
themselves, is such that it necessarily requires foreign, monadic being.
Hence it is only the totality or cosmos of monads *(Monadenall)* that is actually self-sufficient, i.e., absolute (14/295):

> Concrete, full transcendental subjectivity is the totality of an
> open community of I's—a totality that comes from within, that
> is unified purely transcendentally, and that is concrete only in
> this way. Transcendental intersubjectivity is the absolute and
> only self-sufficient ontological foundation *[Seinsboden]*, out of
> which everything objective (the totality of objectively real enti-
> ties, but also every objective ideal world) draws its sense and its
> validity. (9/344, trans. altered)

The full universality, and the full range, of transcendental subjectivity is thus the transcendental total subjectivity *(Allsubjektivität),* and it is only this that can be designated as the constitutive correlate of the world (8/480). Only thereby is each *ego* what it is—"as *socius* of a sociality, as a 'community member' within a total community" (15/193). It is only the I's in their community that are the absolute bearers of the world (8/505). These reflections finally lead Husserl to the insight that absolute being—the being of a transcendental subject—means being as a member of transcendental intersubjectivity (Ms. C 17 88b). In its full universality, transcendental subjectivity is *inter*-subjectivity (8/480). Or as Husserl puts it in the *Crisis,* "subjectivity is what it is—an ego functioning constitutively—only within intersubjectivity" (6/175[172])—a statement that brings along with it the surprising consequence that it not only makes sense to speak of a plurality of transcendental I's, but is also necessary to do so. And this is not just because a constitutive explication of the world, of transcendence, and of objectivity requires it, but because the transcendental I is necessarily *not* a *"singulare tantum"*! If there is one transcendental I, there is necessarily the possibility of more than one, for it is only in inter-subjectivity that this I is a constitutively functioning I, i.e., a transcendental I. Husserl therefore writes that no absolute can withdraw from this universal coexistence; not only am I not *solus ipse,* but no conceivable absolute is *solus ipse* (15/371). And Husserl even claims that the absolute is disclosed as the *intersubjective interrelatedness of absolute subjectivities* (13/480). The constitutive foundation, the "place" that allows for appearances, would thus seem to be precisely this inter-space *(Zwischenraum)* of interrelationship.

Yet if intersubjectivity is a condition of possibility for constitutive functioning, then it becomes hard to understand how intersubjectivity itself could ever be regarded as constituted (which it is in Husserl's usual train of thought). Here a new interpretation of the concept of constitution could be of inestimable help. We shall return to this in Chapter V.1.

III.2. UNITY AND PLURALITY

We must now confront our clarification of the constitutive performance of transcendental intersubjectivity, and our claim regarding Husserl's intersubjective transformation of transcendental phenomenology, with a number of opposing remarks that could awaken the suspicion that Husserl's incorporation of intersubjectivity can lay no claim to radicality after all, but is merely subsequently canceled once again. This confrontation, which requires the introduction of some thematic regions that have not been mentioned until now, will at the same time permit us to deepen our treatment of the relation between intersubjectivity and subjectivity.

That Husserl's phenomenology culminates in a phenomenology of transcendental intersubjectivity can be thrown into doubt from at least two sides. On the one hand, we find the claim in Fink that although Husserl had indeed formulated the thesis of plural transcendental subjects in the Fifth Cartesian Meditation, one can also find, within Husserl's late philosophy, the notion of a primal life *(Urleben)* prior to the distinction between *ego* and *alter ego*—thus a prior primal life from which the plural can first break forth (Fink 1976, 223). On the other hand, the claim has also been made that Husserl ultimately annuls the plurality in favor of the individual transcendental I, insofar as he seems to persist in seeing the *ego* as the constitutive foundation of intersubjectivity.

Fink has put forth the first interpretation on a number of occasions. For example, in the "Discussion" published along with the English version of Schutz's essay on "The Problem of Transcendental Intersubjectivity in Husserl," Fink mentions that in some manuscripts, Husserl seems to have come to the notion of a "primal subjectivity" that is "prior to the distinction between the primordial subjectivity and the transcendental subjectivity of other monads. He seems to try to some extent, to withdraw the plurality from the dimension of the transcendental," and speaks, in these "very late" manuscripts, of a "primal life" that is "neither one nor many, neither factual nor essential," but is rather "the ultimate ground of all these distinctions": a transcendental primal life that "turns itself into a plurality" and first constitutes the difference between "fact" and "essence" within itself (Schutz 1966, 86). Thus according to Fink's interpretation, what counts as "absolutely ultimately functioning" is pre-egological—prior to any individuation, and consequently also prior to any plurality. But we would like to contest the correctness of this interpretation, since we find it to be in blatant contradiction to Husserl's constant emphasis on the difference of transcendent subjects from one another, as well as his insistence upon the constitutive significance of this difference. This absolute differentiatedness (or transcendence) cannot be maintained if plurality has its foundation in the self-pluralization of an absolute that is prior to all individuation.

Fink has unfortunately not supported his interpretation with textual references.[1] But we can find reflections that may perhaps confirm this interpretation if we turn to the thematic realm of time-constitution. Thus as a consequence of our discussion of Fink's position, we shall have the opportunity of deepening our analysis of transcendental intersubjectivity by introducing the fundamental constitutive level: we must turn to *temporality*.

Husserl does occasionally speak of the constitution of the totality of monads as a *monadization,* a *self-multiplication,* and a *self-unfolding* of the *ego* into a monadic plurality (6/416–17, 15/635, 15/589). These terms immediately seem to support Fink's interpretation. But Husserl unequivocally understands this monadization as the constitution of a monadic universe comprised of monads of equal status and essence (15/636), i.e., here it is exclusively a matter of a new description of the process and results of *"alter-ation."* To be sure, it is new that Husserl explicitly links it with *self-temporalization* (15/589). Self-temporalization is thus regarded as the condition of possibility for the experience of others, as well as for the "self-alienation" (15/634) and monadization that this implies; as he says, "self-temporalization through depresentation *[Ent-Gegenwärtigung]* . . . has its analogue in my self-alienation *[Ent-Fremdung]* (empathy as a depresentation of a higher level—depresentation of my primal presence *[Urpräsenz]* into a merely presentified *[vergegenwärtigte]* primal presence)" (6/189 [185]). Husserl thus seems to indicate that since temporality is constituted with a retentional and protentional structure in which "every moment of the present bears within itself a reference to other moments that precisely escape it in its genuine presence and have their significance only in bursting this presence open from within" (Römpp 1989a, 137), then temporality is of decisive significance for the possibility of relation to others. The distantiation and alienation from itself that the I undergoes in temporalization—the "ekstatic" self-division into future, present, and past I that is brought about by temporalization as a de-presentation on a first level—seems to make possible a type of openness for the other precisely on account of its dissolution of absolute self-presence.[2, 3]

During the many years of his engagement with the question of intersubjectivity, Husserl returned again and again to the analogy between experiencing others and "remembering" or "bringing to mind" *(Erinnerung)*.[4] That is to say, in both cases it is a matter of unique types of appresentations that are simultaneously original modes of given-ness, and modes of givenness of something that eludes us in principle. It is thus said that empathy (self-alienation) is a present modification of remembering my own self (15/642), and Husserl occasionally characterizes the co-presence *(Mitgegenwartsein)* of others as a bringing-to-mind-along-with *(Miterinnerung)* instead of as a recollection, a bringing-to-mind-again *(Wiedererinnerung)* (Ms. C 3 45a). Let us attempt a more precise investigation of this connection between temporality and intersubjectivity.

We have previously shown (Chapter II.3) how the experience of others implies positing an identity between the foreign body that externally appears to me and the same body as it appears to the other concerned. But the experience of others also implies further positings of identity. There is not only a coincidence of what is "there" for me and what is "here" for the other (i.e., the constitution of a common *space*), but also a coincidence of my now and the other's now (i.e., *simultaneity* and a common *present*). What we perceive in common coexists through coincidence — and with this, there is also a coincidence between my constituted time and the other's (15/331). If transcendental others are given to me, this obviously means that they transcendentally coexist with me (15/372; cf. 14/103, 1/166). In other words, the primal mode of my own streaming present "coincides" with that of the other (15/343), who is experienced precisely as someone who is time-constituting—i.e., as someone constituting a mundane present and a mundane temporality, with temporal contents of past and future, starting from her own present (15/42).

However, this coincidence is a specifically peculiar kind of *unity in conflict* (14/143) or *coincidence in difference* (15/642), for the

> time of my streaming life and that of my neighbor is . . . separated by a deep abyss, and even the imagery of this word still doesn't say enough. For if, as this time (with the sense of time that is grounded precisely in the monad as such according to its own essence), the time of my own streaming life were one with that of my neighbor, the two of us would be one I with one life, one stream of lived experience, one capability, and so on. (15/339; cf. 15/577)

Although during the course of empathizing, my present and that of the other are given simultaneously, temporal point for temporal point (which makes possible the constitution of an intermonadic time of a higher level), the other's present is not intuitively present to me perceptually. Rather, it is given in the manner of empathy, which is why the simultaneity of "empathizing" and "empathized" is not intuitively present either (15/332, 13/189). The foreign living present is thus *presentified* in my experience of others (15/331); as Husserl says, what is primally present in stream B can appear only apprehensionally within the primal present of stream A (13/29). There is consequently something specifically peculiar to this simultaneity and common temporality, insofar as it does not imply that a foreign present turns into a present of my own, but rather means positing a *co-present (Mitgegenwart)* alongside mine (cf. 8/134, 14/495, 15/238). Husserl even emphasizes that I can only intuitively find the other, and the other's stream, *in conflict with* my own (14/141, 14/98). Hence the one time constituted through the communalization of monads does not contain the individual monadic temporal processes within itself as parts within a whole; rather, it is a matter of streams that are "partly simultaneous, partly successive, there in disjunction or in overlapping partial coincidence" (15/636). The coexistence is therefore not to be understood as though the temporalizing streams of consciousness were stretches within a common universal time, as though what is formed in one of them—namely, the psychic content in its temporality —could be carried on, in continuity, in the other stream. Rather, the common time of coexistence is a constituted time arising from the intentional coincidence of the psyches in their being-for-one-another, i.e., the co-presence *(Mitgegenwart)* of others is founding with respect to the mundane present (15/334).

> My standing-streaming primal being, and then my self-temporalized present in the temporalized time of my *ego,* as the present for my past and future. Then recapitulation in empathy: foreign standing-streaming primalness, foreign self-temporalized present, past, etc., and self-time as identical in these modalities. Further: intersubjective synthesis, constitution of a simultaneous present. Primal modality of temporal coexistence, all of us in a community of being, in mutual temporal externality, in mutually temporalizing

interpenetration *[im zeitliche Aussereinander, im zeitigenden In-einander].* In this there also lies the retroactive shift of a temporalization of temporalizations, a temporalization of primally temporalizing primalnesses, or an inner communalization of them. Thus it is also possible to speak of the one persisting primal aliveness (the primal present, which is not a temporal modality) as that of the totality of monads. (15/668)

The experience of others can accordingly also be understood as an experience of foreign temporality,[5] and perhaps the appresentative character of the experience of others is even most suggestively demonstrated in this experience of foreign temporality. As Römpp writes, the non-perceivability in principle of that which is to be ascribed to a foreign subject can be reformulated in terms of temporal concepts: the foreign self-temporalized time that is posited in the appresentation is posited as a time that is in principle not perceivable by me (Römpp 1992, 107).[6] This possibility of a temporal reformulation can profitably be applied in another way as well, since the reference to intersubjectivity that we have disclosed within horizon intentionality is temporally to be interpreted in such a way that the mundane present is presented for me, perspectivally, as a field of experience that presently belongs to me—a field whose horizon points not only to the co-presence of the other sides valid for me, but also to the co-subjects and to the modes of appearance of the mundane present that belong to them (Ms. C 17 31a).

We have ascertained that Husserl speaks of an inner communalization of living presents established through monadization. Subsequently, there is a persisting primal aliveness of the totality of monads (15/668; Ms. C 16 104a), a streaming *(strömenseiende)* intersubjectivity (Ms. C 3 45b). But even on the basis of Husserl's observations on time-constitution, it is still possible to ask whether what is absolutely ultimately functioning is not pre-egological, i.e., prior to all individuation, and consequently prior to any plurality as well—an interpretation that seems to be supported *expressis verbis* by the following passage:

> The analysis of the structure of the primal present (the persisting living streaming) leads us to the ego-structure and to the continual substratum of the *egoless streaming* that founds it, and thereby, through a consistently carried out regressive inquiry *[Rückfrage],* back to that which makes even this sedimented ac-

tivity possible and which this sedimented activity presupposes: the *radically pre-egoic.* (15/598, emphasis altered)

Yet upon closer examination of Husserl's description of the essential structure of the living present (i.e., the primal temporalization), what is striking is his recurrent emphasis on the idea that "in a way that is difficult to describe,"[7] the I-center is everywhere in the living present (Ms. C 16 7b, C 16 69b). Thus, correctly seen, talk of egolessness is—as Husserl says—a mere abstraction within world-constituting subjectivity (Ms. D 14 5b), since the stream of consciousness in its primal originality is unthinkable without a primally original I-pole that holds sway even in the anonymous process of consciousness (15/350). Husserl's simultaneous mention of the egolessness and egoicity of consciousness makes it clear that a conceptual equivocation is in play. When Husserl speaks of "egoless streaming," the expression "egoless" does not refer to the lack of an I, but rather to the primal passivity of the streaming, which is beyond egoic influence (cf. Chapter V.1). And when he speaks of a pre-egoic level, this is by no means a reference to an absolute, pre-individuated ground; instead, he is talking about a level prior to the constitution of the I as a thematic *object of reflection.* Although the I is constantly on hand as holding sway and functioning (as the I-pole of affection and action), this does not mean that it is already constituted as an *object* from the very beginning, since the "ontification" of the I is a subsequent accomplishment that is preceded by a non-intentional, pre-reflective self-awareness that is always there. As a constituting, performing I, as the constantly undergoing-achieving center of all constituting affections and actions, I am, as temporalized and temporalizing, always "self-aware"—but I am not aware "of" myself in the customary sense, i.e., I am not an intentional "object" in the natural sense (Ms. C 16 68b, C 16 49a).

Thus according to Husserl, it is necessary to distinguish "between the 'I that I am' on the subject side and the 'I that I am' as Object for myself" (4/253):

Consequently, we continually have the distinction between the I and *cogito* as functioning but not seized upon (operatively functioning subjectivity), and the possibly thematized I and its *cogito,* thematized directly or itself seized upon. To say it straight out, operatively functioning subjectivity and objective subjectivity (objectified, experienced thematically, represented,

thought, predicated) must be distinguished. And whenever I
have myself, and whatever else besides, as an object, I am simultaneously necessarily on hand extra-thematically as an operatively functioning I, accessible to myself, as this operatively
functioning I, through reflection—i.e., through reflection as a
new, and now once again non-thematic, activity of the operatively functioning I. (14/431; cf. 29/183–84)

The I is there objectively as an intentional object in every such
reflection. But as Husserl says, reflection has the remarkably peculiarity that what is "seized upon perceptually" in it is characterized in
principle as something that not only "exists and endures while it is
being regarded perceptually," but "*already existed before* this regard
was turned to it" (3/95[98]; cf. 8/412): "If I say 'I,' I grasp myself in
unqualified reflection; however, like every experience—and above
all, like every perceptual experience—this self-experience is a sheer
directing-myself-toward something that is already there for me,
something that is already in awareness and just not grasped thematically, not attended to" (15/492–93). Hence prior to reflection,
there is already an I-consciousness that is not seized upon, an unthematic and non-objective consciousness, since the being of the I is a
continual being-for-itself through absolute self-appearance—and it
is for precisely this reason that the I can essentially reflect on itself at
any time, making itself thematic (8/412, 17/279–80[273]). Thus in
manuscript C 10, Husserl speaks of constant self-affection as the
condition of possibility for one's own functioning (Ms. C 10 3b, 4b,
10a; cf. Ms. C 16 82a). The making-oneself-into-an-object presupposes a pre-reflective "self"-awareness, i.e., it already presupposes
the I in function (4/318; Ms. C 10 5a). That the ontification of the I
is therefore a subsequent accomplishment also comes to expression
when Husserl points out that it is due to retention that consciousness
can be made into an object (10/119). That is to say, the condition of
possibility for reflection is to be found in the self-splitting and self-
alienation of temporal ekstasis. Temporally seen, reflection is always a
subsequent becoming aware of something that has preceded it. It
presupposes a distance from the living functioning—a distance that
it then bridges.

     What is of even more interest in this context, however, is that Hus-
serl himself brings out an analogy between the thematization of the

anonymously functioning I-subject and the thematization of anonymous intersubjectivity. Neither I (the current I-subject) nor intersubjectivity comes, as functioning, thematically to awareness. However, this does not exclude that we can subsequently be thematized in a self-objectivation. And this in turn presupposes an activity that is already functioning unthematically (15/483). As a functioning I, I am not thematic. But as an I that has "self-awareness," I am nevertheless *potentially thematic* within my own horizon, just as the potential others to be found in my thematic horizon are potentially thematic as well. And I can accordingly make myself thematic, although in thematizing myself, I can never seize upon everything that I am (15/484). Similarly,

> I experience community with others in empathizing appresentation, as a parallel to recollection. When recollection occurs, the continuity of my past—a continuity [stemming] from my continual coincidence with myself, a continuity already there from continual retention—is presupposed, is [its] underlying basis. *When empathy occurs, is perhaps community, intersubjectivity, likewise already there, and does empathy then merely accomplish the disclosure of it?* (Ms. C 17 84b, emphasis added)[8]

This question is then answered in the affirmative, since Husserl characterizes empathy as an unfolding of something that is already there, and rather than taking empathy as primal, he speaks instead of a primal intentionality manifesting the continuity with others—a continuity that belongs to every streaming present, just as retention does (Ms. C 17 84b).

Hence both the ultimately functioning others and one's own primally constant I originally manifest themselves as anonymous; the possibility of an ontification of the I presupposes a prior pre-reflective self-awareness, while the possibility of concrete (objectivating) experience of others rests upon an originary co-present *(Mitgegenwart)* of the other I—a co-present that is inseparable from me in my own living making-myself-present-for-myself (Ms. C 3 45a). But just like one's own ultimately functioning I, the foreign "I function" (which must be co-present in the common world-constitution and the intersubjective relations we factually encounter) remains non-objective; it maintains uncancelable anonymity (Held 1966, 160).[9]

Meanwhile, we can state that when Husserl speaks of a pre-egoic level, he is in no way referring to an absolute pre-individual ground;

rather, seen with more precision, it is a matter of distinguishing between various egoic levels. Thus, for example, he says that when in the
course of genetic inquiry, we construct a pre-I as a starting point, this
does not yet have anything to do with a person, but does already entail
an I-pole as center of affection and action (Ms. C 16 68b). That is to
say, the anonymously functioning I already belongs to primal presentation in I-affection and I-activity, although it is naturally not yet thematic (Ms. C 10 2a). Thus—to express it differently—temporality is
an accomplishment of the I in every way (Ms. C 17 65b), and the "pre-
egoic" level is the level of the anonymously functioning I that has not
yet been objectified through reflection.

Husserl now takes up the notion "that every I, regarded purely as
I, has its individuality in its life of consciousness, and purely as living in
it . . . . The absolute uniqueness lies in the content of every I itself"
(Ms. C 17 15b; cf. 4/299–300).[10] "What is uniquely and *originally* individual is consciousness, taken concretely with its Ego" (4/301, emphasis added). It thus turns out to be even less plausible that Husserl
wanted to defend the thesis of the subsequent self-pluralization of a
pre-individuated absolute.

Let us now turn to the realm of the *intentionality of "drives" (Triebin-
tentionalität)*, where Husserl speaks of instincts that are aroused within
the streaming of "passive," "I-less" temporalization (Ms. E III 9 4a). What
Husserl intimates here is the being on hand of a pre-theoretical, pre-
active interconnectedness *(Verbundensein)* of subjects. The intersubjective
connection arising purely from original passive intentionality—namely,
from the obscure intersubjective instincts that only exhibit their sense
when these instincts are disclosed by being satisfied—stands in contrast
to the sociality instituted through specific activity (9/486):

> Here I can only briefly point out that it is not only through so-
> cial acts that such connectedness can be brought about. Just as
> individual subjects develop their activity on the basis of an ob-
> scure, blind passivity, so the same also holds for social activity.
> But passivity, the instinctive life of drives, can already bring
> about intersubjective connection. Thus at the lowest level, a
> sexual community is already established through the instinc-
> tual sexual life, even though it may only disclose its essential in-
> tersubjectivity when the instinct is fulfilled. (9/514)

Thus alongside a more cognitive approach to the problem of

intersubjectivity—one that is connected with the relation to an open intersubjectivity that is implied in every experience of the world—there is also the possibility of giving a phenomenological account of "being-with" or "being-for-others" through an analysis of drives and emotions. This way to intersubjectivity has chiefly been taken up by Scheler and Sartre, and we will be returning to their contributions later. But the notion that relatedness to the other is present in the sexual drive itself is already found in Husserl (15/593-94; Ms. E III 9 28b). And Husserl remarks that through the manifestation of intersubjective interrelationship within drive-intentionality, it becomes clear that individual I's are dependent, and only the totality of I's is wholly concrete, i.e., self-sufficient (14/374). Because of its instinctual reference to others, the individual monad is not *in se et per se concipitur;* there arises, from within itself, a pointing beyond itself, and it is therefore not self-sufficient (14/257, 14/295).[11] Hence Husserl even speaks of a unity of multiple primordialities established through the interpenetrating drive-fulfillments (15/594) and characterizes the plurality of transcendental I's as an absolute being-together in the mode of a coexisting in interpenetration (15/367-68). Thus what we find within the community of monads is an intentional includedness, a transcendental coexistence, an intermonadic interpenetration of egoic life and operation (15/370, 9/485).[12]

What appears in naive positivity or objectivity as mutual externality is therefore revealed, after radically carrying out the reduction, as an intentional interpenetration (6/259[255]). Thus one can speak of an inseparable being-for-one-another: neither am I, for myself (and I just as I am), separable from the other, nor is the other separable from me. Each is for himself, and yet is for the other. Each, as existing, has its sense as a sense arising from itself, and at the same time has this sense for every other, and this belongs to the essence of each (15/191, 15/194). Each stands in actual intentional community with the other, and this is an essentially unique connectedness—namely, that of intersubjectivity itself (1/157, 6/241[238]).

In view of these considerations, Strasser has concluded that the strict separation of streams of consciousness must be given up because it cannot be reconciled with drive-intentionality. According to Strasser, the intentions pertaining to these drives lead to an interpenetration of fulfillments such that the strict separation of monadic immanences is canceled. And he therefore claims that Husserl speaks of a primally abiding streaming that precedes the separate streams of individual monads (Strasser 1975, 16–17).

However, we must contest this interpretation, for when it is a matter of intersubjective unity (and this, by the way, also concerns Husserl's occasional allusion to the *"Gemeingeist,"* or "communal spirit"), it is always a question of a unity arising from a plurality. The intentional interpenetration by no means signifies a fusion of I's, but rather presupposes their difference:

> In a certain sense, the individuality of psyches means an unbridgeable separation—thus a being-other and a being mutually-external-to (in a logical and not a spatial sense) that can never develop into a continuous connection, into a connection that would be a continuous mutually flowing into one another of the times proper to each monad. On the other hand, this separation does not prevent monads from "coinciding" with one another—in other words, it does not prevent them from being able to be in community with one another—and indeed, the separation is the condition of possibility for this coincidence and community. (15/335; cf. 15/339)

Hence the diversity, difference, and plurality of subjects are precisely a condition of possibility of any community, for fusion and being-one would entail the dissolution of *inter*-subjectivity.[13] Seeing the world as an intersubjective unity—as a unity arising from my communalization with those who are other for me—is precisely what implies that there is no possible continuity between my I-pole and another I-pole, for this would exclude legitimate mention of an (actual) plurality (15/576–77).

We pointed out earlier that Fink offers no proof to substantiate his interpretation of Husserl. However, we can readily find the view referring to the derived character of plurality in Fink's *own* manuscripts from the 1930s. For example, in "The Phenomenological Philosophy of Edmund Husserl and Contemporary Criticism," he denies that transcendental intersubjectivity comprises the ultimate ground (Fink 1970, 132), and writes that the transcendental totality of monads by no means amounts to the sufficient and definitive concept of transcendental subjectivity, but presents only a first level of its elucidation (Fink 1970, 128). In *Conversations with Husserl and Fink,* Cairns reports a conversation from September 23, 1932 in which Fink not only doubts the transcendentality of intersubjectivity but also suggests that the primal ego is the "first emanation of the absolute" rather than counting as the absolute itself (Cairns 1976, 95). Likewise, we find the following declaration in Fink's *Sixth Cartesian Meditation:*

> What perhaps is shown, then, is that the *community of monads* it-self represents one more *constituted stratum* in the constitu-tive becoming of the world. The question is therefore posed whether the *transcendental individuation of plural monads* is a final and reductively irremovable determination of constitut-ing life. What may then be proven is whether the *Absolute* itself is *articulated in the plural* and subjected to an *individuation* — or whether all articulations are only *self-articulations within it,* and it itself can only be thought definitively under the *Idea of the "One."* (Fink 1995, 145)

Although it cannot be excluded that passages that could confirm Fink's interpretation are to be found in Husserl's *Nachlass,*[14] such a train of thought is fundamentally alien to the Husserlian point of departure, and probably derives from Fink's influence.[15] It is no ac-cident that Husserl takes over the notion of "monadology," for what this term testifies to is precisely his sympathy toward a pluralistic ontology.

III.3. THE UNIQUENESS OF THE PRIMAL I

After our critique of Fink's interpretation, we must turn to the second objection — namely, the claim that Husserl cancels plurality in favor of a single transcendental I once again, insofar as he sees the *ego* as the constitutive foundation of intersubjectivity and even emphasizes the uniqueness of the primal I.

In *Phenomenological Psychology,* Husserl remarks — after he has men-tioned the role of intersubjectivity — that to begin with, the others are there for me only within my experiential life, and it is within this life that I must bring them into existence for me for the first time. Thus whenever I experience their beliefs as being in accordance with my be-liefs, this is because I have constituted the others as having these beliefs; whenever I experience something as being valid for others, this is be-cause I have constituted the others as accepting precisely those validi-ties (cf. 9/464). He accordingly writes in the *Crisis* that "it was wrong,

methodically, to jump immediately into transcendental intersubjectivity and to leap over the primal 'I,' . . . which can never lose its uniqueness and personal indeclinability" (6/188[185]). And he further remarks
that although the world does already, and ongoingly, have the ontic
sense, "world-for-everyone," one must never forget that it is I who have
this "everyone"—i.e., all co-subjects—in acceptance, and have posited
them in acceptance precisely in the way that they are valid for me—
determinately or indeterminately, known or unknown (6/416). Finally, he writes in *Zur Phänomenologie der Intersubjektivität III:*

> For what "it is an other" says for me throughout, however, is
> only: it exists by virtue of my constitution. Thus it is evident
> that transcendentally speaking, the being of others depends on
> my being. However, it simultaneously belongs to the sense of
> others who exist for me that the same thing holds for them.
> Thus the world is constituted for me and for others—and by
> means of them, an intersubjective world—in such a way that
> everything that is, depends on my being, yet also on the being
> of others—who exist for me. (15/39)

> Whatever is, is for me and comes from me: anything else is not
> thinkable. And if there is another I, then it is a unity of accept-
> ance constituted from me and in me—and yet it is another I,
> and as that, an I for whom everything is for it and through it
> once again, even I myself. Thus I myself am, from myself and
> through myself, an I that only is what it is through and in the
> other I, which for its part is this other for me and arising from
> me. (15/369–70)

> But I am still I, privileged as the bearer of acceptance of the world
> existing for me. It is true that as a unity of actual and possible ex-
> perience, this world is related to the totality of operatively func-
> tioning subjects, but this totality is the universe of co-functioning
> subjects obtaining their ontic sense for me from out of my own
> primordiality. (15/645)

Against this background, Aguirre has claimed that the constitution of
intersubjectivity in the I is an enduring theme in Husserl, and that
nowhere in his writings does the possibility seem to be indicated that
intersubjectivity is seen as something that would ground my being as

absolute *ego* (Aguirre 1970, 63 n. 78). According to Aguirre, Husserl consequently makes a correction to the apparently definitive result of the transcendental reduction (namely, the laying bare of transcendental intersubjectivity). When Husserl writes in the *Crisis* that it is the primal I who constitutes the horizon of transcendental others as co-subjects within the transcendental intersubjectivity that constitutes the world (6/187[184]), he is just carrying the reflection to its radical conclusion (Aguirre 1982, 43).

Is this tracing of intersubjectivity back to the *ego* a denial of the previous exposition of the transcendental function performed by intersubjectivity? Is the reference to intersubjectivity thus a mere "appearance," while in reality Husserl adheres to a solipsistic starting point? A response to these questions must ultimately lead to an analysis and clarification of the concept of constitution, which we will come to later. But in our opinion, the doubt that has been raised can already be dispelled. That is to say, that Husserl occasionally persists in claiming that the primal I is fundamental does not contradict his intersubjective transformation of the transcendental philosophical project, but is on the contrary a presupposition of it. Hence we must once again bring to mind what is unique about Husserl's phenomenology of intersubjectivity. For Husserl, intersubjectivity is not some relation, within the world, that is to be observed from the outside; it is not something transcendent to consciousness, or some sort of system or structure in which consciousness would be founded. And Husserl's reference to intersubjectivity by no means implies giving up a starting point in a philosophy of consciousness, provided that this starting point is correctly understood in transcendental philosophical terms. The very opposite is the case: intersubjectivity is a relation between me and the other or others, and correspondingly, its treatment and analysis must necessarily take the I's relation to others as the point of departure. Thus intersubjectivity can only be described and elucidated through a radical explication of the I's structures of experience—which naturally not only implies the egoicity of inter-subjectivity but also simultaneously implies the intersubjective structuration of the I. And it is precisely these research results that Husserl is trying to express in the passages mentioned above. Moreover, against this background it becomes clear why Husserl's monadic philosophy of intersubjectivity naturally cannot be seen as a mere resurrection of a Leibnizian conceptual heritage: as we shall see later, it is not only because Husserl does not presuppose a preestablished harmony running through the monadological community, but also because this monadological plurality is only to be regarded from the standpoint of the individual I, rather than from God's view from nowhere.[16] It is only from the standpoint of the individual I that intersubjectivity and the plurality of constitutive centers can be phenomenologically articulated and displayed:

> It is not that first there are several psyches, and the question is under what conditions they are "compatible" with one another in factual existence. Rather, the question is how, when I am certain of one psyche and immerse myself in its own proper essence (in an intuition that gives this itself), can I gather from this that it is merely "a" psyche, and can only be "a" psyche — so that in this very essence it must point to other psyches? How is it that this psyche does indeed exist in and for itself, yet still only has sense within a plurality that is grounded in itself and that is to be articulated and displayed from out of itself? (15/341)

We have mentioned above (Chapter II.5) that it is only possible to hit upon a definitive position pertaining to the justification of the abstractive reduction to the primordial after the role of intersubjectivity in the domains of passive synthesis and of self- and time-constitution has been clarified. In the meantime, we have been able to establish that Husserl has come a long way with this. Transcendental intersubjectivity is obviously of central importance not only with respect to the constitution of objectivity but also when it is a matter of the self-constitution of transcendental subjectivity. Thus, for example, Husserl writes that the personal I has a *relative mode of being* (4/319). For as he says, if there were no Thou for me, there would also be no I in contrast to it (13/6). Hence the I first has its peculiar ownness in the Thou and is only constituted in contrast to it (13/247; cf. 15/603). It therefore holds a priori that "self-consciousness and consciousness of others are inseparable" (6/256[253]). "Experiencing—in general, living as an ego (thinking, valuing, acting) —I am necessarily an 'I' that has its 'thou,' its 'we,' its 'you'—the 'I' of the personal pronouns" (6/270[335-36]).

Naturally, here it is important to distinguish between the mundane and the transcendental I. That in order to apprehend itself with a mundane self-apperception, the I requires a Thou, and hence a counterpart that is itself an I, has already become clear through our presentation of the process of alter-ation (cf. 4/242, 4/319, 6/256[253], 15/342). Thus Husserl also says that the *real* I is a constituted intentional unity—not just in relation to a pure I and a stream of consciousness with its multiplicities of appearances, but in relation to an intersubjective consciousness, i.e., an open multiplicity of monadic pure I's, separate from one another, unified through mutual empathy into a nexus that constitutes intersubjective objectivities (4/111). Even as early as 1910, Husserl was expressing himself in such a way as to indicate that it is only in distinction from others that the mundane I is correctly identified and recognized as a unity (13/244).

But this relationship of dependency does not only obtain when it is a matter of the real, mundane I. Moreover, even if it did only have to do with the mundane I, it would still be a misunderstanding if one were to believe that what concerns the mundane self-apperception has no transcendental implications; on the contrary, as we shall show later (see Chapter V.1), the self-mundanization, or apprehending-itself-as-a-human-being, of the transcendental I is by no means a question of contingency—rather, it is Husserl's view that this is a matter of a transcendental necessity. But in any case, Husserl also expresses himself quite explicitly on this issue, saying that the being of the transcendental subject is a being as a member of transcendental intersubjectivity, and insisting that the I, as transcendentally-constitutively functioning I, is what it is only within intersubjectivity (Ms. C 17 88b; 6/175[172]).

Nevertheless, the problem now arises that in spite of these observations, Husserl comes back to the following thesis:

> The absolute I—which in utterly unbroken constancy is prior
> to every existent and bears every existent within itself, which in
> its own "concretion" is prior to all concretions—this absolute I
> bearing each and every conceivable existent within itself is the
> first *"ego"* of the reduction—an *ego* that is wrongly so called,
> since for it an *alter ego* makes no sense. (15/586)[17]

Hence the absolute I is not *an* I that still has its Thou, along with its "we" and its universal community of co-subjects, in natural acceptance. The "I" that I reach in the epochē can only be named "I" by way of an equivocation (6/188[184]). The concrete *ego* of the reduction is thus unique in such an absolute sense that it cannot meaningfully be multiplied; instead, it excludes any such multiplication as meaning-less (15/589-90).

At first glance, this vacillation between an original plurality and a fundamental uniqueness of the primal I would seem to indicate a fundamental lack of clarity (or even a suggestive contradiction) in Husserl's position. But his train of thought can easily be understood as being free from contradiction if one distinguishes between two different ways of posing the problem. In the first place, the sense of the passages just mentioned can be disclosed with the help of Ms. B I 14. There Husserl says that "I" admits of no plural when the word is spoken in such a way that it is *originarily* significant. Others do indeed experience themselves as I, but I experience *myself*, and not them, as I (Ms. B I 14 127a). Thus I do not have a second exemplar alongside myself of which I could say, "That is I." Accordingly, I cannot speak of *an* I when "I" means precisely *I*. The "I" is absolutely unique and individual (Ms. B I 14 138a). The indeclinability of the I that Husserl mentions (an indeclinability that excludes any multiplication) points to a uniqueness that is obviously one of an *indexical nature*—thus it is emphatically *not* a matter of a substantial uniqueness—and it even readily permits other such uniquenesses! For as Husserl writes, "The unique I—the transcendental. In its uniqueness it posits 'other' unique transcendental I's—as 'others' who themselves posit others in uniqueness once again" (Ms. B I 14 138b; cf. 14/212).[18] This emphasis on indexical uniqueness, which may indeed serve to resolve many of the misunderstandings raised by considering the uniqueness to be a "substantial" one, is by no means to be understood as a merely contingent linguistic fact. The relatedness of sense back to an I-consciousness is not dependent upon the factual availability of linguistic terms such as "I," "ich," "je," "jeg," etc.; rather, it is a matter of a fundamental transcendental relationship that is ultimately linked with the problem of individuation and self-awareness. Hence for the I who says "I am"—and says it in the right sense—the I is the primal intentional ground; it is "the *primal matter-of-fact to which I must hold fast,* which I, as a philosopher, must not disregard for a single instant" (17/243-44[237]; cf. 14/307, 29/165).

In the second place, in order to demonstrate that the contradiction alluded to only appears to be a contradiction, one must point to an equivocation in Husserl's concept of the I—namely, that in his determination of the *transcendental* I, Husserl is operating with *at least* four intersecting characteristics: 1) the I as a unity within the stream, i.e., as the pole of affection and action—and here it is important to emphasize that according to Husserl, the identity of this I is not merely the identity of something that endures, but the identity of something that performs, i.e., the I-pole (Ms. C 10 18b); 2) the I as an object of reflection; 3) the I as that which stands in contrast to a Thou; and 4) the I as person. In its full transcendental concretion and performance, the I cannot be characterized without the Thou (without the co-subject). Yet a certain determination according to strata is quite possible. Thus, for example, with reference to the absolute and original uniqueness of the I mentioned above (which, as original, is not first established by way of a contrast), Husserl writes that it is possible to bring to light the I as an identical I in its peculiar ownness without contrasting it with others (15/351). Moreover, in *Zur Phänomenologie der Intersubjektivität II*, this notion is refined in an interesting way, for here Husserl introduces a distinction between "subject" and "I" (i.e., personal subject):

> The pole of all affections and actions necessarily on hand in the subject imagined as solipsistic, the subject of motivation running throughout the stream of lived experience, which as such is the constant subject of a striving in various modalities, becomes an I—and thereby a personal subject, acquiring personal "self-consciousness"—in the I-Thou relation, in the community of striving and willing that is made possible through communication. (14/170–71)

Husserl thus distinguishes between a subject per se and a personal subject, and writes that the origin of personhood is to be found in social acts. That is to say, it does not suffice for personhood if the subject becomes aware of itself as the pole of its acts; personhood is only constituted by the subject entering into social relation with other subjects, so that it is already objective in practice (14/175; cf. 4/204-205, 15/177, 15/603). To put it another way, one can indeed speak of the I without others when it is a matter of an abstractive determination of strata—when the I under discussion is the I as the pole and functional center for affections and actions. But if one wishes to talk about the full and concrete I, it is simply not possible to speak of an I without others (cf. Chapter III.2).

By now, it should have become clear why Husserl occasionally insists upon the absolute priority of the I—the subjectivity that is always my ownmost *(der je-meinigen Subjektivität)*—and how he can unify this with a demonstration of transcendental intersubjectivity as the absolute basis of being. It is indeed the case that transcendental subjectivity, taken purely and simply, is transcendental intersubjectivity, and that this and this alone is the constitutive correlate of the world. Within it, however, there is predelineated a necessary centering in the I as the I who has we-consciousness (15/426). This in no way means that some "intersubjectivity" that is supposed to exist prior to individuation (a notion that turns out, on closer examination, to be a *contradictio in adjecto*) then subsequently undergoes a "centering"; rather, transcendental intersubjectivity "contains transcendental subjectivity within itself" (15/75) as the place of its unfolding. For as we have shown, transcendental intersubjectivity is indeed nothing other than the relatedness of subjects to one another. In this way we have found a way of explaining Husserl's allusion to the ambiguity of the reduction to transcendental subjectivity (15/73). The complete reduction leads not only to transcendental subjectivity but also to transcendental intersubjectivity. Neither of them can be thought in isolation: transcendental intersubjectivity is precisely the nexus of transcendental subjects, and in its full concretion, transcendental subjectivity is determined a priori by its relation to others (cf. 1/167).

At the same time, however, it must also be maintained that Husserl obviously does hold the view that one can speak of the I as the principle of unity of the stream of consciousness without bringing in the effective performance of others. At this very rudimentary level, there is an operatively functioning accomplishing that is in fact solitary, that is not first brought about by way of others. But Husserl simultaneously emphasizes that although we are not *dependent* upon others at this level, we are, in our primordially temporalizing uniqueness, already *open* toward others in their primally living co-presence. That this position (which retains a legitimate sphere of primordiality) is the very presupposition of a theory of intersubjectivity—and that consequently, one cannot conceive of intersubjectivity independently from a (possible) plurality of individuated subjects—is what we shall attempt to defend in our final chapter, where our exposition must come to terms with the theories of Apel and Habermas.

CHAPTER IV

The Transcendental Consequences

IV.1. THE POSSIBILITY OF DISSENT

In the course of our presentation of the constitutive performance of transcendental intersubjectivity, we have discussed the connection between the constitution of the objective world and our relation to others. Among other things, we have shown how our experience of others co-implies the validity of the others' experiences, for as we have found, the appresentative experienceability of the other implies a common world. Now, however, we must inquire more closely into the previously mentioned possibility of *dissent* arising on the basis of this world in common (see Chapter II.3). Such dissent is only made possible through the concrete experience of others, which once again includes a heightened sensibility with regard to transcendental plurality and alterity. What are the conditions of possibility for the experience of dissent; above all, what consequences does this experience of conflict have for Husserl's theory of the intersubjective constitution of objectivity? Can the experience of conflict be permanently maintained without jeopardizing the positing of objectivity? Closely connected with this complex of problems is the necessity of distinguishing between various types of objectivity. Thus it will turn out that various types of objectivity or truth have to be seen as correlative to the various levels of monadological communities established through the experience of others. And this will ultimately lead to the following distinction: 1) objectivity as related to a limited universe of subjects, i.e., to a certain limited universe of normal subjects (14/68), and 2) objectivity as related to the totality of any cognizing subjects whatsoever who belong to the nexus of subjects in which the knowing subject in question stands (14/111). It is precisely with the incorporation and transcendental treatment of *normality* that the ultimate level of the constitution of objectivity—namely, that of the constitution of scientific truth, together with the third type of relation to others previously mentioned—then becomes understandable.

To treat these lines of inquiry comprehensively and in detail would ultimately lead us too far into the problem of the lifeworld. However, a brief exploration of the terrain of the problem is necessary, for only in this way will it become clear how radical the revolution occasioned by Husserl's intersubjective transformation of transcendental philosophy really is. A decisive *broadening* of the transcendental field of objects has taken place through Husserl's incorporation of transcendental intersubjectivity, and through his new characterization (to be discussed below) of the relationship between subjectivity, intersubjectivity, and world. The traditional framework of themes pertaining to the practice of transcendental philosophy is burst open, making possible a transcendental constitutive investigation of domains previously reserved for disciplines such as psychopathology, sociology, anthropology, and ethnology—domains that a classical (Kantian) transcendental philosophy would relegate to an empirical-mundane province without any transcendental relevance (cf. 15/391).

IV.2. NORMALITY AND OBJECTIVITY

In the concrete experience of others—especially in the concrete experience of the (linguistic) actions of the other (cf. 15/442)—we are occasionally confronted with differences of opinion. The experience of others and the communalization of our experiences do, of course, imply an identification of the objects given in our respective experiences. But by no means are all the mundane objects experienced by the other, along with the entire field of the world in common experienced by the other, given in a mere repetition, as though all the objects showing up in the synthetic unity of my experience and that of the other were completely equivalent (15/46). Rather, the experience of others leaves open the possibility that no complete identity of systems of appearance arises (14/277). From time to time, then, our apprehensions and experiences are not in agreement, and the constitutive implications of this dissent must now be investigated—although it must already be emphasized that the very experienceability of discrepancies and discordances indicates their inherent intersubjectivity (cf. 15/47).

In order to proceed carefully here, we must first distinguish between various types of dissent, for we could indeed readily establish that although our belief in the one world in common presupposes its validity for everyone, that belief is by no means shaken by each and every instance of dissent (9/496). If we pass over the case where one subject is corrected by another,[1] since here it is not a question of a genuine (abiding) dissent, we can distinguish between a dissent (or a difference) pertaining 1) to the orthoaesthetic systems of perception; 2) to physical and psychic normality; and 3) to cultural spheres.

1) In the course of our sensory experience, we can ascertain that this experience is characterized by an inherent relativity. While I experience the water as warm, my *alter ego* experiences it as cool; my perspective on the table is never exactly the same as that of my neighbor. This statement can lead us to establish a distinction between the fundamental components belonging to experiences in common—components that we ascribe to the thing itself—and individual differences, which we regard as being merely subjectively conditioned, i.e., we make a distinction between primary and secondary qualities (4/88, 6/288[309-10).[2] In other words, the moment this relativity comes into view, we have a motivation that legitimizes the natural scientific search for the non-relative, physically determinate thing in itself. Thus what is called for by the differences between our perceptual systems is a constitution at a higher level (13/381). Science (and exact natural science in particular) aims beyond the relativity of intuitive nature—a relativity that is precisely essential to intuitively given nature (6/27[29])—toward just this nature "in itself," and it attempts to determine this in-itself as that which remains "identical throughout all relativities" (6/309[330]). The result of this constitutive achievement is that the nature given in intuitive experience becomes an appearance of an essentially non-intuitive nature "in itself" that can nevertheless be theoretically determined intersubjectively (4/207). Hence experience of this particular type of conflict leads

> to problems of the physical in-itself; to closer observation of
> the presenting appearances in their relation to a *specific lived
> bodilihood* and to *"normal" subjectivity;* and then to the problems
> of a transcendental-reductive theory of the possibility of "objective" natural science. (14/277, emphasis added)

We have spoken earlier of the decisive constitutive significance of the lived body, and Husserl repeatedly emphasizes in this connection how important it is to investigate the distinction between normality and abnormality, a distinction belonging to the essence of operatively functioning lived bodilihood as such. For "what we normally experience simply as the world signifies a world-sense which depends upon the presupposition of a normal body in its normal functioning" (9/ 199).[3] Thus the nature of things as *aistheta* is related to my lived body and to my *normally* functioning sensibility (4/56) — and it is precisely the indeterminateness and relativity of lived bodily experience that science wants to transcend (although science simultaneously presupposes it as the foundation of sense).

When we speak of the constitutive significance of the lived body (cf. Chapter II.4), we must naturally distinguish between the unthematic, operatively functioning lived bodily consciousness, and the thematic, objectivating consciousness that takes the lived body as a physical body. We have to distinguish the lived body as "subject" from the body as an "object," and Husserl emphasizes that the original and immediate lived bodily awareness is not an object-consciousness. On the contrary, the objectivating experience of the lived body as a physical body is a self-objectification that — like every customary perception of an object — is made possible by a previously functioning, unthematic lived bodily consciousness:

> Here it must also be noted that in all experience of things, the lived body is co-experienced as an operatively functioning lived body (thus not as a sheer thing), and that when it is itself experienced as a thing, it is experienced in a double way—i.e., precisely as an experienced thing and as an operatively functioning lived body together in one (14/57; cf. 15/326).

Thus there is obviously a similarity between the relationship of the objectivated lived body to the operatively functioning lived body and the relationship of the I of reflection to the pre-reflective, operatively functioning I (cf. Chapter III.2). This point is essential, for it contributes to a clarification of the relationship between subjectivity and lived body. That is to say, Husserl emphasizes that this relationship cannot be understood as the presence and activity of the subject in a spatial object (13/240). On the contrary, the perceptual functioning of the lived body in original lived bodily consciousness (in concrete self-consciousness) is immediately grasped as my egoic holding sway (14/

540). Hence the constitution of the lived body (as an object) is not an activity that is carried out by a disembodied subject; rather, it is a question of a self-objectification that is carried out precisely by a subjectivity that already exists as a lived body.

Now it is precisely this operatively functioning, lived bodily consciousness that Husserl goes on to characterize as a constitutive *primal norm* that can already be found in the solitary *ego* (14/126), even though it only receives its full determination as "normality" within the intersubjective community.

That Husserl grants this priority to operatively functioning lived bodilihood has certain decisive consequences. Considered in terms of genetic phenomenology (and the mention of normalities has its place in precisely this mode of consideration), operatively functioning lived bodilihood is prior to the experience of non-living materiality. But that the lived body is prior to constituted inanimate "nature" also means that it precedes the experience of a purely physically appearing foreign body of an other (15/637), so that a "body" of this nature is initially experienced as a modification and an abnormality. Perhaps this is just what Husserl is referring to when he speaks of the lived bodily relation between mother and child as the most original of all relations (15/511, 15/582, 15/604-605).

There are various contexts in which Husserl was engaged in a thorough investigation of the significance of what is to count as the typical normality, for he regards it as an essential determination of our life of consciousness. Here, however, it is sufficient to point out that it is closely bound up with the temporal structure of our experience, and that the establishment and specification of normality can therefore be traced back to our acquired experiences (which are, in part, experiences we have in common). That is to say, according to the essential laws of passive constitution, our intentional life takes up within itself, as a habitual acquisition, what has already been constituted, in order to apperceive the new in a similar manner. Our current acts pass over into possessions for the I, and with this, they become that which is pregiven for new acts of the I (4/214). Hence my expectation of normality is founded on my past: "in accordance with what is retentionally given to consciousness as having already happened, something new coming along in the same style is 'to be expected'" (11/186). But since I have always already been in connection with others for as long as I can remember, whatever emerges newly is apperceived according to sedimented and habitualized patterns of apprehension stemming from an *intersubjective* sense-history (cf. 14/117, 14/125, 15/136). And if there is no agreement—i.e., if the protentional anticipations of normality are disappointed—we have an experience of (primal) anomaly or abnormality, the constitution of which begins precisely through the interruption in the transfer of sense that occurs when the protention of normality is not fulfilled (Ms. D 13 234b). To be sure, this experience then leads to the subsequent modification and specification of normality itself, for we subject everything to the requirement of reintegrating the anomaly, as a breach of the originally concordant unity of appearance, back into a new normality at a higher level (15/438). Nevertheless, we usually do not speak of "abnormality" when it is a question of the experience of orthoaesthetic differences, for here there is the possibility in principle of exchanging apprehensions.

2) With more radical dissent, however—e.g., a seeing person coming to understanding with a blind person—this is not the case, and the categories of *normality* and *abnormality* then become used thematically for the first time. That is to say, as previously mentioned, they only receive their full content within intersubjectivity (cf. 6/166[163]). As Brand puts it, normality is precisely also a *conventionality* that goes beyond the individual and has a *"one* does it this way" attached to it (Brand 1979, 118; cf. 15/611). I learn what counts as normal from others—initially and for the most part from those closest to me, hence from those I grow up with, those who teach me, and those belonging to the most intimate sphere of my life (15/428-29, 15/569, 15/602-604). And it is in this way that I participate in a communal *tradition*. Thus the system of normality ultimately points to the chain of generations receding into the past and thereby bears witness to the constitutive significance of tradition and generativity.

What is now decisive is that only the apprehensions of those fellow members of the monadic community who are characterized as "normal" are relevant for the possibility of our own constitutive performance. When we speak of "everyone," what we are talking about is ultimately a certain (idealized) *average* (15/141, 15/231, 15/629). "Everyone" designates those who belong to a group of normal fellow human beings; normality exists in and by virtue of the community (15/142). And only a normal person can enter into conflict with us concerning the truth and falsehood, the being and non-being, of the surrounding world of our communal life, precisely because only normal persons are apprehended as co-constituting it (15/162, 15/166, 9/497), while the apprehensions of abnormal persons have (at least immediately) no implications for our understanding of the world.[4] To put it another way, what is important for the theory of constitution about the use of these categories is exactly that a differentiation of entire strata of systems of appearance can be allowed without any further constitutive implications as long as the conflicting apprehensions are "canceled," precisely *as abnormalities.*

3) Now, however, we must distinguish between two basic types of (ab)normality. On the one hand, we speak of normality with reference to a mature, healthy, and rational human being. On the other hand, we speak of normality with reference to everyone who belongs to our home world or cultural sphere, where "cultural sphere" has many forms and levels; there are not only European and Chinese cultural spheres, but also (sub)cultural spheres of the family, of a social class, of phenomenologists, of mercenaries, etc. Hence when we speak of *abnormality,* we are not merely referring to (enduring) lived bodily and psychic distinctions (cf. 15/159),[5] but also to cultural distinctions pertaining to various life-communities and surrounding worlds.

As we have mentioned, it is beyond the scope of this presentation to analyze the encounter between home world and foreign world in any detail. At first, it is only important to emphasize that under certain circumstances, our experience of an abnormality can be changed into an experience of a foreign normality—especially, of course, when the abnormality is experienced as shared by many.[6] A peculiar type of shift of validity thus takes place at one stroke, for as we have already pointed out, what counts for us as "abnormality" is to be seen as a modification of what counts for us as "normality." Yet the moment that a concordant apprehensional system is apprehended as a new and foreign normality, it breaks off from our own normality, for it turns out to be a self-sufficient normality with abnormalities of its own. Hence what is implied in our apprehension of a foreign normality is precisely its independence from our own: what is peculiar to the "foreign" is precisely that it breaks through the total style of our own normality (15/431).

But if a plurality of normal worlds (in relation to various communities) has already been constituted—a plurality that cannot, of course, be observed from the outside, but only by a subject experiencing the foreign world from within his own normality (1/162, 15/627) — we will be confronted with a difficulty, insofar as this plurality of worlds must still ultimately have a constitutive relation to the one world in common. That is to say, anyone can come to an understanding with anyone from any life-community, apprehending the other precisely as an other of a foreign normality. This would not be possible if we lived in two fundamentally different worlds (14/134).[7] Hence we must investigate how far the common world grounded by way of experience of others reaches, and to what extent abnormality and divergence are possible at all (15/159). There is, however, no absolute abnormality, for it is constituted exclusively as a modification of normality, and then also subsequently flows back into the reigning normality (Ms. B IV 5 5a). Everything — no matter how foreign or incomprehensible it may be — has, as Husserl says, a core of familiarity, without which it could not be experienced at all, even as foreign (15/432).[8] And it is now a matter of zeroing in on the "familiarity" that serves as a form of access to the surrounding-worldly variations and pluralities. Thus what must be worked out is

> the absolute objective world-structure — the absolute structure running through every surrounding world that is held in common by any self-contained, constituted life-community (or better, any particular human group) — as that objectivity which everyone can and must grasp, in unconditioned universality, for human beings to be there for one another and for a community to be able to be constituted, be it ever so loose (even merely that of existing for one another and understanding one another, or being able to understand one another at all). Since this absolute objectivity is the universal, while as a member of a particular human group each human being still has his concrete surrounding world (and this is the only one he can have concretely), it is clear that this absolute objectivity is only thinkable as an abstract formal structure in all surrounding worlds — and at the same time, it is that which makes necessary or possible an experience of identity in contrast to their difference. (9/498-99)

Thus just as with the experience of the relativity of our sensory experience, so too the experience of the relativity of our cultural-historical normality can serve as the motivation legitimizing the search for an absolute scientific truth (15/169). That is to say, "if we set up the goal of a truth . . . which is unconditionally valid for all subjects, beginning with that on which normal Europeans, normal Hindus, Chinese, etc., agree in spite of all relativity," we are on the way to an objective science (6/142[139]). The objectivity that is constituted as the correlate of a home world, or of a delimited community of persons who reciprocally consider each other to be normal, is now itself taken as a mere appearance of a true objectivity, for it is precisely the aim of science to establish the truly existing—not determining it as that which is experienced by particular persons and peoples, but rather as that which exists in unconditioned validity for everyone (cf. 6/324[278]). Hence we must make a distinction between the following (a distinction that will simultaneously fine-tune the question of the constitution of objectivity):

> 1) objectivity as intersubjectivity, apprehensionally related to a "universe" of subjects, although the universe can be a limited one, e.g., that of the community of normal subjects; 2) "strict" objectivity related to the actual unlimited "universe," the totality of all knowing subjects, of whatever sort, who stand in relationship to the knower. (14/111)

Thus the being that we understand as "objective" in the absolute sense is an intersubjectively constituted being conceived as experienceable and determinable as the same for the broadest possible intersubjectivity (namely, for every possible subject entering into the nexus of communication), while any being that is only valid in relation to a delimited intersubjectivity is merely subjective-relative (Ms. D 4 12b; cf. 15/176).

Husserl now claims that the difference between various surrounding worlds of life and culture is given on the basis of a spatiotemporal world-form that they hold in common and that must be functioning precisely for the multiplicities of cultural formations to be *accessible* (1/161-62). Thus he speaks of *nature* as that which is accessible for everyone in unconditioned universality, as that which is unconditionally held in common and identically experienceable (Ms. C 17 45a). If the world is to be one, in itself in contrast to all subjective experiences, and if it is to be possible to speak of objectively valid truths extricated from the relativism of subjectivity—that is, truths that must necessarily be acknowledged by anyone *rational*—then among the determinations of the thing, there must be components that are accessible to every subject in the same manner, and hence are necessarily common to all subjects. In other words, such components are free in principle from any "contingent" relation to the subject, since if they pertain to one subject, they pertain to all subjects. Husserl includes space, time, and all purely logical concepts in this category (13/384).

Although it can scarcely be denied that "the basic form of all identification of the intersubjective givennesses of a sensuous content is of such a kind that they necessarily belong to one and the same *system of location*" (4/83), these types of *formal* ontological conditions do not at all seem to be enough to make communication and agreement possible. However, this is also implicitly conceded by Husserl, for he characterizes operatively functioning lived bodilihood as a primal norm and emphasizes that even in the case of the "incomprehensible" other, we do at least comprehend the lowest stratum of the other's holding sway in her own lived body. Thus Husserl also seems, at least on occasion, to take into consideration certain *"material"* conditions such as a similarly functioning lived bodilihood or a similar instinctual life as the condition of possibility for agreement (15/433).[9]

Meanwhile, a more precise articulation of the levels of constitution has become possible. Previously, we distinguished between the first sensuously intuitable thing (which is perceivable by the solitary subject, and has the objectivity of something in itself in contrast to the contingency of this subject's perceptions and memories of it), and the intersubjective thing (which has the objectivity of something in itself in the sense of something that exists objectively, that exists in itself even if it is not actually grasped by anyone, while being graspable by everyone as being the same thing that every possible other could grasp perceptually). The former is then merely subjectively "in itself," while the latter is unqualifiedly objective. But now it has become possible to differentiate this "unqualifiedly objective" thing further. We can distinguish between the object held in common by the color blind, on the one hand, and the intuitable object for any normal human being on the other, with the latter then counting as the true object. Nevertheless, even this relation to a normal human community is itself ultimately still something contingent. The ultimate "exact" objectivity, which has no contingent relativity at all, is that of the physical thing (the thing of natural scientific description), which is absolute because its truth is a truth experienceable by any subject whatsoever of possible experience, and thus the only relativity it has is one that is ultimately necessary—namely, being relative to a subjectivity, of whatever sort (Ms. D 4 12a-b).

Husserl now links the latter level of constitution—the constitution of theoretical scientific truth—with reflections on the constitution of linguistic ideality. (In the current context, this has little to do with the relationship of founding obtaining between pre-predicative and linguistic experience, insofar as what Husserl is interested in at this point is an epistemological goal, i.e., in furthering the work of judgment through a suitable *scientific language,* so that the results receive lasting objective documentation in the shared cultural world—17/31[27].) That is to say, the objectivity of the ideal formation is only completely constituted when its persisting existence, its continuing being, is secured during times when the inventor and her companions are out of contact with the communicative community, or no longer alive at all. Hence the formation of a written language does not merely serve the purposes of communication but also helps to secure an objective acquisition accessible to everyone and verifiable by everyone (15/175):

> The important function of written, documenting linguistic expression is that it makes communications possible without immediate or mediate personal address; it is, so to speak, communication become virtual. Through this, the communalization of man is lifted to a new level. (6/371[360-61]; cf. 17/349)

It is through linguistic embodiment that ideality attains its true ideal objectivity, receiving, in its documented form, an objective existence reaching beyond the currently actually cognizing subjectivity and its acts (6/369[358], 17/38[35]). It is only in this way that the ideality escapes its intrapersonal origin and loses its occasional connection to place, time, and persons.[10]

With this true constitutive accomplishment of language, we are spared the necessity of always having to start over from the beginning (15/224); instead, we can proceed on the basis of a stock of already constituted sense and build upon it. Without this documenting, conserving, and preserving function of written language, complicated scientific theories, for instance, would hardly be possible (6/373[363]). But there are two dangers that go hand in hand with this. First, Husserl observes that instead of leading a life based on consulting the experiential evidence for ourselves, we fall victim—"very quickly and in increasing measure"—to the *"seduction of language"* (6/372[362]). That is to say, as subjects brought up within language, we are exposed to the obscure intentions and apperceptions that have been sedimented and handed down in linguistic usage. Language is indeed intersubjective from the very beginning (17/349), for words bear the stamp of "everyone." Everyone can speak in this way and understand it; "I, like everyone," express this in such and such a way (14/108). And Husserl already pointed out in *Ideas II* that in addition to tendencies proceeding from other persons, there are also demands and requirements arising, "in the intentional form of indeterminate generality," from the customs, usage, and tradition of the cultural milieu: "one" judges this way, "one" holds the fork this way, and so on (4/269). It is thus a matter of being seduced into a life that is not genuinely an ethical life, for a life of self-responsibility—a life lived in freedom and rational autonomy—consists precisely in making my own decisions for myself, not passively yielding to the influence of others (4/269).[11] Second, there is the well-known danger of objectivism, which Husserl addresses at some length in the *Crisis*. The separating of idealities from their subjective origin—a separation that is itself, of course, a subjective achievement—easily leads to an abstraction from their subjective sources, so that these sources themselves are forgotten. And it is precisely this (forgotten) abstraction that is implied in the scientific inadequacy of the mundane sciences sketched at the beginning of our investigations (see Chapter I.2).

What is thereby brought to light in our differentiation of levels of constitution is that Husserl in no way wants to limit the notion of truth to ideal, exact truth. On the contrary, his critique of objectivism implies a restriction of the scope of the objectivistic concept of truth. Husserl's own position accordingly promotes an openness toward a plurality of various modes of apprehension and description that are each related to various "normalities":

> What if the relativity of truth and of evidence of truth, on the
> one hand, and, on the other hand, the infinitely distant, ideal,

absolute, truth beyond all relativity—what if each of these has its legitimacy and each demands the other? The trader in the market has his market-truth. In the relationship in which it stands, is his truth not a good one, and the best that a trader can use? Is it a pseudo-truth, merely because the scientist, involved in a different relativity and judging with other aims and ideas, looks for other truths—with which a great many more things can be done, but not the one thing that has to be done in a market? It is high time that people got over being dazzled, particularly in philosophy and logic, by the ideal and regulative ideas and methods of the "exact" sciences—as though the In-itself of such sciences were actually an absolute norm for objective being and for truth. (17/284[278])

Although that which is discovered by physics is not a new "physical object," but rather the true "logical"-objective concept of the perceived (Ms. A III 9 8b), it must also be emphasized that this idea of the absolute thing—the thing in its full truth satisfying all possible "relations"—is not at all the guiding idea of practical life. That is to say, for the human being who is living extra-scientifically, what is understood under the title of a "thing" is always a thing in a certain "relation," and what one wants to become acquainted with is the thing in precisely this delimitation of sense, i.e., the thing precisely as it appears within the horizon belonging to the situation in question (8/244). Hence in our customary life, we are not at all concerned with natural scientific objects, but with valuable and useful objects of the most varied sort. As Husserl says, what we call "things" are paintings, statues, gardens, houses, clothes, table, tools, etc. (4/27), and in everyday, extra-scientific life, our interest in things is guided by practical concerns: whatever satisfies our practical interest counts as the thing itself (11/23).

Thus although natural science tries to overcome all relativity, the "subjective-relative" does not simply function as an irrelevant moment of transition toward the non-relative, but rather as "that which ultimately grounds the theoretical-logical ontic validity for all objective verification," and therefore as the source of evidence and of verification (6/129 [126]). For even the (pre-scientific) lifeworld itself has, in all its relativities, its own universal structure—a structure that objective science itself depends upon and must, after all, presuppose (6/142[139]).

IV.3. HISTORICITY AND GENERATIVITY

In the meantime, it has turned out that the levels of normality and abnormality correspond to the levels of the constitution of being, from relative being in relative appearances all the way to the objective true being of the truly existing world (15/155). Insofar as reason, which is the correlate of true being, is also a structure of normality— namely, that of rational subjects (15/36) —then the being and truth of absolute objectivity also correspond to a subject-relative normality (cf. 15/35). And its constitution can accordingly be understood as the culmination of the development of transcendental intersubjectivity, which is to be conceived precisely as an ongoing unified process of cultivating an ever newer system of norms at ever higher levels (15/421).

This bears witness to Husserl's historical-philosophical orientation, for both the development of higher systems of norms and my own home-worldly normality are historical—namely, both are instituted through tradition and generativity. For as Husserl says, in the succession of generations sharing the communal unity of a tradition, each new generation inherits what was constituted through the labor of previous generations, and now itself reshapes this heritage once again (9/410, 15/164, 15/218-19). Hence ever new generations cooperate in transcendentally building up the structures of validity pertaining to the objective world, which is precisely a world handed down in tradition (15/463). Husserl refers to *normal life* as *generative life* and states that every (normal) human being is therefore *historical* by virtue of being constituted as a member of a historically enduring community (15/138-39, 15/431). Thus community and communalization inherently point beyond themselves to the open endlessness of the chain of generations, and this in turn to the historicity of human existence itself.

With this reference to *generative intersubjectivity* (15/199), however, one must simultaneously raise the question concerning the transcendental relevance of the incarnation and mundanization (or "humanization") of the transcendental I; one must inquire into the transcendental significance of birth and death. We shall return to this question in Chapter V.1, but it is necessary to realize from the beginning that Husserl does not regard birth and death as contingent facts. Rather, he sees birth, death, and generativity as constitutive events making the constitution of the world possible (15/171). As he puts it, the transcendence of the world consists in its being constituted by means of others, by means of the *generatively constituted co-subjectivity* (Ms. C 17 32a). Being embedded in "the unitary flow of a historical development"—in a generative nexus of birth and death— belongs as indissolubly to the I as does its temporal form (6/ 256[253]; cf. Ms. K III 12 27a). That Husserl ascribes constitutive implications to this being embedded in a living tradition cannot be denied. And one might now be inclined to claim that this ultimately points to the possibility of an exchange of monads (cf., e.g., 15/195, 15/609). Hence it is quite conceivable that "it is not always the same individual monad that contributes—in the same manner, in the same typical style, and at the same level—to the total constitutive achievement" (Strasser 1975, 27-28). It would therefore be the total transcendental achievement of the totality of monads—an achievement realized through communication and in the course of history—that would have to count as the "absolutely constituting" achievement. On the one hand, this is quite correct: transcendental subjectivity as such *is* transcendental intersubjectivity, and it is this alone that is the constitutive correlate of the world. On the other hand, however, one should not forget that a necessary centering in an individual I, as the I who has we-consciousness, is predelineated within this transcendental intersubjectivity itself (15/426). According to Husserl, this "us" or "we" ultimately extends "from me to present and past and future others" (15/61; cf. 15/38, 15/139, 15/142, 15/499): what is "historically primary in itself" is our own present (6/382[373]). But from the phenomenological point of view, it is clear that the past, previous generations, and any valid sense reaching beyond my own finitude cannot be treated from the perspective of an outsider.[12] Thus one must not succumb to the abstraction according to which one could speak exclusively of the totality of monads and of generative intersubjectivity, without simultaneously taking into consideration the transcendental primal I as the place where they are unfolded and displayed (15/667). Intersubjectivity and subjectivity cannot be treated separately. Hence one cannot assume—as sometimes mistakenly happens in treatments of Husserl's *Crisis*—that all the difficulties connected with examining the relation between subjectivity and intersubjectivity simply vanish if one merely takes the shared, generatively handed down lifeworld as one's point of departure. The lifeworld is by no means a field that transcends consciousness and can simply be described and analyzed in a naive ontological fashion; rather, the lifeworld is a structural moment of the fully grasped (inter)subjectivity that is opened up by the transcendental reduction. The radicality of Husserlian phenomenology consists precisely in thinking historicity, world-analysis, *and* transcendental philosophy together. Of course, it can scarcely be denied that Husserl did not manage to think this synthesis through to the end in a satisfactory manner. But whenever it is a matter of evaluating the scope and the claims of his thought, we must at least pay attention to his attempt in this regard.

Our observations until now can finally allow us to turn to the third type of transcendental intersubjectivity or relation to others. In addition to the anonymously co-functioning open intersubjectivity that is at work in the horizon structure and the concrete experience of others that is directly linked with the exchange of our categories of validity, there is also a type of intersubjectivity that is founded on the latter, but is different from it and irreducible to it. This third type of intersubjectivity operates at the level of handed down normality, and it is of constitutive significance as a realm of that which is anonymously public. Wherever I turn, the world in which I live (as the world that is the correlate of normality) presents me with references to others. I am in the midst of a world that has already been provided with sense by others, and my formation of judgments, my self-apprehension, my evaluations, and my interpretation of the world are guided by a linguistically articulated pre-understanding. Thus I understand the world—and through it, myself—by virtue of a handed down linguistic conventionality (15/224-25). It would therefore seem that it is not only the transcendence and foreignness of others that is of constitutive importance, since the commonality of the us and the we—i.e., the background (linguistic) being-together-with-one-another in averageness, normality, and everydayness that provides the operative basis of agreement—is also a condition of possibility for forms of constitution at a higher level. For example, the category of "historical reality" implies a type of transcendence that I can only constitute by taking over a handed down sense that I myself am not the author of.[13]

The consequences that are to be drawn from our reflections upon normality thereby testify in all clarity to the decisive implications of an intersubjective transformation of the foundation of transcendental phenomenology. Quite apart from the decisive shift in the way of understanding the relationship between subjectivity and world that comes to expression in this transformation (a shift we shall come back to in Chapter V.1), it is also through this transformation that the objective world comes to be understood as a historical world. That is to say, the constitution of an *objective* world in common is the result of a constantly progressing mutual process that is always under way. The transcendental constitution of the world that exists for me has its stages, beginning with the constitution of a concordant home world— a home world that lies within my own horizon and is accessible to me precisely for this reason: I am at home there (15/629-30). Subsequently, there follows the critique of my own home world within the horizon of foreign "home worlds," in order to establish the unity of all the home worlds that can be synthetically connected, i.e., in order to constitute the one true world (15/235). The communal experience that gives us the world-for-everybody is thus not something that is completed in a single act, but is a historical process of becoming, a developing achievement of fusion of horizons and communalization (15/209, 15/220). There is no *fixed world;* rather, it is what it is for us only in the relativity of normalities and abnormalities (15/212, 15/ 381, 6/270[336]; Ms. C 17 31a). Its being only has the appearance of being fixed; in truth, what is fixed is a form of normality that can break down (15/214). Thus the intersubjectively valid world has the status of an intersubjective presumption that can only be cashed out in continual correction. Concordance is not simply a given, but has to be established though the play of mutual discordances and discrepancies. And this is a concordance that can always be ruptured by further conflict, only to be restored once again in a correcting concordance at a higher level. But absolute concordance—i.e., the world in itself— is nowhere to be found; rather, it is always pending, always undecided, always "suspended between relative truth and relative untruth, between being and seeming" (15/614).

On the whole, then, the actual and ultimately valid true world is an idea of the world as it would be experienced in an ultimately valid concordance that would be established *idealiter* (8/47). As the ideal correlate of an intersubjective experience—and ideally, of one that can always be (and indeed is) ongoingly carried out concordantly—the objective world is essentially related to the intersubjectivity that is itself constituted in the ideality of an endless openness (1/138, 15/33).

Hence absolute truth (objectivity) is the expression of an idealization, just as the "in itself" is an ideal of approximation, a regulative idea that guides our experience of the foreign (world). And this is an ideal that one can approach in progressive and ever more complete correction, even though it can never be reached, since each factually attained correction leaves open in principle the possibility of further corrections (8/52; cf. 3/331[342–43], 6/282[304]). (But this certainly does not imply that there are no apodictic truths at all; rather, it implies that whatever *can* be corrected is open in principle for further corrections.) The following citations can confirm that this is not merely a matter of an epistemic question:

> Naturally, this question must not be posed in a perverse way, as though a being-in-itself of the world were already absolutely certain, as though an absolute guarantee for it were accomplished or were to be accomplished for it from who knows where—perhaps even by a deity and divine cognition—and as though now the question is merely how far our experiential knowledge reaches, and how much of the true being of the world can be attained on its basis through the method of freely chosen experiments and rational thinking. (Ms. B I 12 IV 76a–b)[14]

> The indeterminateness is not an imperfection of our cognition in relation to an existing world established in complete determinateness in advance; rather, the indeterminateness belongs to the ontic sense of the world itself, purely as a world of experience. (Ms. B I 12 IV 77a)[15]

Thus reality or objectivity, as valid for everyone, is naturally not something merely lying before us in itself; instead, it is a structure of validity that gains acceptance in an infinite movement of relative achievements that are carried out intersubjectively (29/188). The world (or the truth) that subjects hold in common is not imposed upon these subjects from the outside, but arises from a process of reciprocal interaction.[16] Thus—in contrast to Leibniz—the harmony of the inter-monadic relationship is not simply presupposed, for it comes about through the reciprocal constitution of a world in common that the experience of others makes possible. But neither is it a rule established from above (14/266), for as we have previously shown in detail, every monad fundamentally stands in essential passive and active connection with every other monad.[17] Hence there is a constitutive "unity of influencing and being influenced by one another, such that in all this, a common product is achieved: nature as that which is first in itself" (14/271).

Earlier, we asked to what extent abnormality (and dissent) is possible at all. This question does, of course, present a real problem for a theory of transcendental intersubjectivity. That is to say, the question basically has to do with why a pluralization of constitutive centers does not lead to absolute disparity. How can this looming consequence be avoided? It must be pointed out, however, that plurality cannot be regarded from the outside, but only from the experiencing I, and it is precisely the experienceability of this plurality by the I that guarantees its incorporation into the one world in common. The possibility of agreement is thus ensured in principle, and Husserl would obviously deny the possibility of a radical incommensurability.[18] All that can be at stake is a "merely" factual incommensurability that can in principle be overcome.[19] This formalistic transcendental philosophical argument — which Husserl also attempts to support through *teleological* considerations, since he points out that monads are only compossible as a monadic whole "governed" and determined by laws of development striving toward the constitution of one and the same world and of objective truth (14/271) — can, however, also be supplemented by *meta-eidetic* considerations.

And this is precisely because the compossibility of monads is made possible by essential laws (14/271). In *Phenomenological Psychology*, Husserl writes that the eidetic structures of the *ego* — structures without which an *ego* as such is unthinkable — are for this very reason valid not only for my own *ego*, but for any *ego* whatsoever. The other (any other) necessarily has the same essential style as I do (9/324, 15/382, 1/169). Hence although every I, considered purely as an I, has its individuality and absolute uniqueness, there is a universal form, a universal essence, through which every I is exactly this — an I (Ms. C 17 15b). At the same time, however, this means that whatever I find pertaining, in essential necessity, to the style of a world experienceable by me must also hold good for the style of a world experienceable by anyone else — or in any case, for any other that would be experienceable for me *as* an other (14/385, 15/162). Thus the individual subjects of transcendental intersubjectivity are furnished with "mutually corresponding and harmonious constitutive systems" (1/138). "The intersubjective (universally subjective) validity of essential phenomenological truths is indubitable, and is predelineated in principle within the purely phenomenological sphere" (14/307). In other words, it is a transcendental *logos* running through the community of monads that restricts the range of abnormality and supports the possibility of reciprocal commerce and of the one common world (cf. 15/161 and 1/181).

CHAPTER V

A New Characterization of Phenomenology

V.1. BEYOND IDEALISM AND REALISM

We indicated at the beginning that a presentation of the constitutive contribution of transcendental intersubjectivity would make a new understanding of phenomenology possible. Now that some of the decisive implications of the intersubjective transformation of transcendental phenomenology have been presented in Chapter IV, we shall attempt to analyze the concept of constitution. Two related problems must nevertheless be distinguished: establishing to what extent the incorporation of transcendental intersubjectivity can elucidate the genuine sense of every type of constitution; and displaying the specific sense of the constitution of others or of intersubjectivity.

Let us begin with a recapitulation of Husserl's pre-transcendental reflections on the concept of constitution, which we can find in the *Logical Investigations*. There Husserl puts forth the thesis that our being directed toward an object is of "constitutive" nature. Our "intentionality" is simultaneously an "accomplishment" or "achievement"— namely, a building up of the object in its objective identity. As we have already mentioned, however (cf. Chapter I, n. 7), the question of objective reality was still excluded in this inaugural, "breakthrough" phenomenological work; for this reason, the concept of constitution was characterized by a metaphysical neutrality. Constitution meant neither realistic restitution nor idealistic production, but was simply a formal description of the building up of the intentional object.[1]

But this statement does not preclude some more detailed observations. Husserl writes, for instance, that it is first of all our apperceptive

interpretation that goes to make up the *existence of the object for us* (19/
397[566]), and in connection with categorial objects, he emphasizes
that it is a matter of a sphere of objectivities that can only "themselves"
come to appearance in founded acts (19/675[788]). From this it is
obvious that when Husserl speaks of constitution, he is thinking of certain acts of consciousness that must be on hand for the givenness (appearance) of the intentional objects in question to be possible. He
explicitly repeats this description of constitution in his lectures on *The
Idea of Phenomenology,* where he says that objects come to givenness in
acts of thought (which is where they are constituted); only here do
they show themselves for what they are (2/72). Now it is characteristic
of the *early* Husserl that he understands the constituting act *eidetically.*
It is not this individual, *factually* extant act that is constitutive for an objectivity, but rather the act *in specie.*[2] Thus Husserl can link the existence of the intentional object with the question of it cognizability *in
principle* (and not that of its factually being cognized). This descriptive
finding (without any further considerations concerning the existence
or non-existence of mind-independent objects) — a finding that does
not in itself imply any idealistic thesis — is ultimately all that can be
established with regard to the formal concept of constitution in the
Logical Investigations.[3]

But after the transcendental turn, the same type of metaphysical
neutrality can no longer be maintained. And as previously mentioned
(Chapter I, n. 32), Husserl's phenomenology of intersubjectivity is
often rejected on account of a *creationistic* interpretation of his concept of constitution. Two alternatives now present themselves. Either
one could simply argumentatively deny that the concept of constitution as such has to be construed creationistically, or one can bring out
its equivocity, as Tugendhat, for example, has done (1970, 222). Tugendhat claims that when it is a matter of the constitution of others, we
can speak only of an epistemic priority of the constituting consciousness,
whereas we can establish both an epistemic and an ontological priority for the constituting consciousness in the case of thing-constitution.
Although the others are *epistemologically* constituted for me in my own
acts, and they attain sense and validity for me only in this way, they are
not dependent upon me *in their being,* for this type of dependence
would make their transcendentality (i.e., their co-constituting performance) impossible once and for all (Tugendhat 1970, 222). Though
Tugendhat's proposal presents an attractive possibility on account of

its simplicity, it seems to us that his suggestion misses the point. For as Husserl writes in *Zur Phänomenologie der Intersubjektivität III:*

> But in my being and being-accepted-for-myself, I am still prior to everything else: everything accepted stems from my own validity, and I do see this at once through reflection. Perhaps one will say that this "merely" signifies the trivial point that from the standpoint of knowledge, I am the earlier; if I were not, then I could naturally not know the other. But doesn't this word, "merely," testify to an entirely insufficient grasp of the transcendental state of affairs obtaining here? Does it not lie in this state of affairs that the being of all others depends upon my own being? In, of course, the transcendental sense. . . . To be sure, it simultaneously belongs to the sense of the others existing for me that the same holds true for them. (15/39)

The difficulty obviously consists in understanding exactly what Husserl means by this "transcendental state of affairs." However, one must also ask the fundamental question of whether the old opposition that Tugendhat calls upon—the opposition between epistemic and ontological priority, or between (realistic) *restitution* and (idealistic) *production/ creation*—is at all useful in actually grasping the sense of constitution. Do not these alternatives remain within an objectivism that is precisely what has been overcome once and for all through the transcendental reduction? It does not appear possible to maintain a strict distinction between the "order of being" and the "order of constitution" after objectivism has been transcended.[4] Although Husserl is often reproached for never having given a definitive answer to the question of whether constitution means "restitution" or "production," perhaps this reproach is ultimately unjust insofar as the question is posed from the wrong angle. It is worthy of notice in this context that proponents of a creationistic interpretation, who often call upon Fink's "The Phenomenological Philosophy of Edmund Husserl and Contemporary Criticism"—an essay approved by Husserl—seem never to have read this essay with care. Fink's interpretation of the productive character of transcendental intentionality—i.e., his claim that the essence of constitution must be defined as *productive creation*—continues with the notion that this characterization is chiefly meant to highlight its contrast to a receptive, mundane-ontic characterization of constitution. He then remarks in conclusion that ultimately, what the term "constituting" designates is neither a receptive nor a productive occurrence; rather, it is a relationship that is not attainable with ontic concepts at all, but "can be indicated solely through the enactment of constitutive investigations" (Fink 1970, 134).

By no means should it be denied that Husserl's concept of constitution is in fact marked by an ambiguity and lack of clarity, and that Husserl never treated it systematically or clarified it sufficiently (cf. Fink 1981b). This ambiguity is predominantly related to distinctions lying within that which is to be constituted—distinctions that have to do with the relationship between affectivity and activity. For example, the constitution that is at work in the self-temporalization of the I and in pre-predicative experience, on the one hand, and the constitution that is at work in categorial experience and in the construction of cultural objects, on the other, have different structural moments that must be analyzed separately and on their own in order to come up with a careful and comprehensive clarification of the concept of constitution. And in this connection we must take note of the following asymmetry: although the constitution of categorial objects implies a greater measure of activity (and more of an optional character, as it were), their constitution is ultimately *founded* in sensibility, and thereby possesses a certain character of articulation *(Explikation)*. In contrast, the primal impressions, which are passively constituted, have no further grounding or foundation, and hence their constitution cannot be understood merely in terms of an articulation of something pregiven.

However, these distinctions chiefly concern the manner of constitution, while in this context our interest is directed precisely toward a clarification of the status of its achievement, or toward the status of that which is constituted. What does it signify as such to say that something is "constituted"?

First of all, let us attempt to give a general reply to this question. Husserl has often emphasized that it is a decisive misunderstanding to interpret the constitutive correlation as a traditional subject-object correlation (6/265[262]). That is to say, one must observe the central change in the concept of the subject that is determined through the epoché and the reduction. Being and consciousness essentially belong together and, as belonging together, are also concretely one: transcendental subjectivity (1/117). Thus the monad (as the title for subjectivity in its full concretion) encompasses both the *ego* in the flowing multiplicity of its intentional life and the objects meant in this intentional life and constituted for it (1/26, 1/102, 1/135, 14/46). We can only agree with Brand when he writes that all talk of subject and object, I and world, can only draw its sense from the originality of operatively functioning intentionality, and can only be measured in its terms (Brand 1955, 28). Although Husserl did not always express himself in this way, it cannot be denied that the traditional concept of the subject has been fundamentally broadened, and thereby also fundamentally modified: it is not only the customary subject-object dichotomy that has been overcome (or perhaps undermined), but also the notion that the correlation between subject and object is a strict and static one. Or to put it another way, two concepts of subjectivity are in play, concepts that ought not to be confused: a narrower and more abstract one that designates precisely what we usually understand under the title of "consciousness," and a more encompassing, more concrete one that includes both consciousness and world—since as Husserl admits, subjectivity in the full and complete sense is a world-experiencing life, and the I-pole is merely an abstraction (15/287). Perhaps the clearest way to illustrate this terminologically is to point out that the concepts of "lifeworld" and "life of world-consciousness" ("Weltbewußtseinsleben"—cf. 15/539) are quite closely linked and can only be understood in their interconnection.

In what follows, let us put forth two closely linked theses. First, it is a central element in Husserl's later reflections on constitution that the constitutive process is characterized by a *reciprocity* and *mutuality*, insofar as the constitutive agents are themselves constituted through the constitutive process. Second, Husserl understands constitution as a process that unfolds in a tripartite structure of I-intersubjectivity-world, a process that cannot be grasped either as production or as restitution.

1) As we have previously mentioned, the constitution of space and of spatial objects presupposes a functioning lived bodilihood, and it should also be pointed out in this connection that the constitution of objective space implies a lived bodily self-objectification (cf. Chapter II, n. 15; and see also 16/162). As Husserl says, it is crucial not to overlook the "constant reciprocal relation" between the constitution of I and lived body, on the one hand, and the constitution of real things, on the other (5/128). This observation seems to us to be of great importance, insofar as it unequivocally contradicts the ideal of an isolated and worldless constitutive subject and can also be thoroughly substantiated. Thus, for example, Husserl writes:

In the transcendental *ego*, in the universality of its transcendental, operatively functioning life of consciousness, the world is constituted as existing for it in such a way that this entire life of consciousness emerges as itself in the world. The constituting consciousness constitutes itself, the objectivating consciousness objectivates itself— and indeed, in such a way that it brings about an objective nature with the form of spatiotemporality; within this nature, my own lived body; and, psychophysically one with the latter (and thereby localized in natural spatiotemporality, in terms of spatial location and of temporal position and duration), the entire constituting life, the entire *ego*, with its stream of consciousness, its I-pole and habitualities. (15/546)

Thus—to put it another way—in his later reflections, to a certain extent Husserl seems to abandon thinking of the correlation between world and subjectivity in terms of a strict separation, in order to emphasize instead the processual interconnection between self-mundanization (corporealization), communalization, and having a world:

Thus I, the *ego*, have the world as the result of an achievement in which I constitute myself on the one hand, and [then also] my horizon of others—and thereby the homogeneous we-community—together in one. And this constitution is *not world-constitution*, but rather is the achievement of what can be designated as the *monadization of the ego*—as the achievement of personal monadization, of monadic pluralization. (6/416-17, from May 1937; cf. 15/639, 15/368)

The same conception is expressed when Husserl writes that world-constitution as such implies a mundanization of the constituting subject (1/130, 15/287), and when he points out that the world is to be seen as the transcendental achievement of the *mundanization* of transcendental intersubjectivity (15/403).[5] We can also find this emphasis on the extremely close relationship between (inter)subjectivity and world in Fink, who tells us that the true theme of phenomenology is neither the world nor a subjectivity standing in opposition to it, but rather the becoming of the world in the constitution of transcendental subjectivity (Fink 1970, 130). Hence there is no strict relationship of correlation between transcendental subjectivity and world; rather, "the genesis of constitution is the *self-actualization* of constituting subjectivity in *world-actualization*" (Fink 1995, 45).

These observations make it possible to clarify certain surprising statements that one can occasionally find in Husserl's writings. From time to time he claims that the constitution of a world in common is the condition of possibility for separate subjects to exist for one another (14/100), and that reciprocal understanding is only possible through the constitution of transcendent objectivity (14/105-106). At first glance, this seems to contradict our earlier interpretation completely. But here Husserl's thought has to be interpreted in terms of this thesis of the self-mundanization of transcendental intersubjectivity as the condition of possibility for the experience of others and for transcendental coexistence (Ms. C 17 32a). That is to say, we can hardly conceive the relation between subjects—i.e., intersubjectivity—without simultaneously also thinking of the world as the place of their encounter. Hence intersubjectivity cannot be conceived in any other way

> than as explicitly or implicitly in communion. This involves being a plurality of monads that constitutes in itself an Objective world and that spatializes, temporalizes, realizes itself—psychophysically and, in particular, as human beings— within that world. (1/166)

Thus the transcendental subjects can only exist concretely for one another through a mundanizing and "substantializing sense-bestowing that they mutually impose upon one another and then, within this reciprocal relation, upon themselves—in the substantialization or realization of animality and humanity" (8/505-506; cf. 15/373, 13/480).

Here two fields of problems are indicated. First, the seeming circularity in the argumentation has to be pointed out (4/80).[6] Second we have to inquire whether this substantialization is a necessary moment in the self-unfolding of the constituting I—whether it takes place with transcendental necessity.

The following difficulties therefore arise here in principle. How can one claim that it is the concrete experience of a foreign transcendental I that first makes world-constitution possible, if one must concede that my encounter with concrete others within the world always precedes it? Perhaps a simple example can illustrate this. If we are investigating the constitutive relation between operatively functioning lived bodilihood and objective space, it becomes obvious that this relation is not a simple one. The constitution of objective space as a homogeneous system of coordinates presupposes a self-mundanization of the operatively functioning lived bodilihood in such a way that the indexical reference back to my absolute here is suspended, as it were. But I am not able to carry out this self-mundanization all by myself; rather, it only becomes possible through the process of "alter-ation," i.e., only when I experience someone who experiences me—and only when I take over the other's apprehension of me:

> It is only through the experience of others and the establishment of an intersubjectivity that a homogeneous nature is constituted —homogeneous in that given inwardly, all lived bodies have the character of lived bodies for the subjects concerned, and given externally, they take on the character of things given to everyone. Each human being now simultaneously apprehends his lived body as a physical thing insofar as he apprehends it as apprehensible by anyone else as a physical thing. (14/413-14; cf. 15/489)

But how can I have a concrete experience of others without already pre-supposing an intersubjective space that I and others have in common? In order to resolve this seeming circularity, first we need to refer to the co-originality previously mentioned—namely, the equiprimordiality of communalization, having a world, and self-mundanization (1/130)—for regarded genetically, these cannot be separated from one another. And second, it must simply be realized that there is a pre-objective or pre-theoretical spatiality and nature (17/247[240]) that is already intersubjective.[7]

Whether the transcendental I's becoming a human being is or is not to be seen as a mere empirical fact is a question whose answer has already been indicated. That is to say, as previously mentioned, birth, death, and generativity are to be seen as constitutive events making the constitution of the world possible (15/171). And it is precisely this that comes to expression in Husserl's claim that the lived body is the condition of possibility for the experience of others; for communication; and for the constitution of any objectivity (8/186-87). Although Husserl (in contradistinction, for example, to Merleau-Ponty) insists that as the source of temporality, the I-pole can neither arise nor pass away, and can therefore exist independently of the lived body, he emphasizes at the same time that death is to be understood as a withdrawal from the world and from the community, a withdrawal that can be compared to a dreamless sleep (13/399, 13/464-65, 11/379-81, 3/119 [127-28], 15/609). But a sleeping, dreamless I—an I without an operatively functioning lived body—is undoubtedly a limit concept. If we want to grasp the I in its full concretion, then naturally we must consider the world-constituting I, which is at the same time mundanized, humanized, and embodied. Thus if it belongs to the essence of subjectivity to be constituting, then embodiment and self-mundanization are just as essential to it.

This exposition now clarifies why the relationship between the transcendental I and the empirical I has to be rethought. As Husserl already justifiably emphasizes in the *Encyclopaedia Britannica* article, there are not two I's:

> My transcendental ego is thus evidently "different" from the natural ego, but by no means as a second, as one separated from it in the natural sense of the word, just as on the contrary it is by no means bound up with it or intertwined with it, in the usual sense of these words. It is just the field of transcendental self-experience (conceived in full concreteness) which can in every case, through mere alteration of attitude, be changed into psychological self-experience. In this transition, an identity of the I is necessarily brought about; in transcendental reflection on this transition the psychological Objectivation becomes visible as self-objectivation of the transcendental ego, and so it is as if in every moment of the natural attitude the I finds itself with an apperception imposed upon it. (9/294[173])

It has thus become clear that the empirical I—i.e., the mundanization of the transcendental I—is not some contingent addition to the transcendental I. And for this reason, it by no means lies outside the scope of transcendental philosophy to thematize this mundanization. Quite the contrary, it is an essential task of transcendental phenomenology to thematize the empirical I precisely as a necessary mundanization of the transcendental I. For as Husserl even writes, it is apodictically certain that the I must be found in the world as a human being (29/260), because without this mundanizing self-apprehension, which takes place precisely in reciprocal communication, no objective world could be constituted (29/265-66, 15/368).

To be sure, it is one thing to establish that the subject is constituting, embodied, and communalized, in order subsequently to analyze the constitutive implications of this, and it is something else entirely to ask for an answer to the metaphysical question of *why* the subject is constituting, embodied, and communalized. A truly thorough answer to this question would require a systematic investigation of the teleological structure of temporalization, a task that is, of course, impossible within the framework of the present study. (Whether such a task could succeed at all without violating the phenomenological principle of all principles—i.e., without making use of speculative modes of thought—is, however, open to doubt.)

Nevertheless, against the background of the reflections we have already carried out, we can state that when Husserl says that the existence of a world in common for subjects presupposes the objective psychophysical existence of subjects in the world—as well as when he conversely claims that the coexistence of multiple subjects presupposes that they have a world in common within which they exist psychophysically (14/129)—he is neither denying his previous presentation of the intersubjective constitution of the world nor falling back into dogmatism. Instead, for him it is ultimately a matter of emphasizing the complex, processual character of constitution.

Thus to all appearances, Husserl is by no means talking about a transcendental subjectivity that could abstain from constitution, nor is it a matter for him of a subject that is clearly and distinctly separate from the constitutive process. In reality, constitution is the self-realization of constituting subjectivity—i.e., transcendental (intersubjective) subjectivity is constituted in the process of constitution, in the process of bringing the world to appearance. And this is a self-constitution that precisely implies the constitution of others (both as *genitivus objectivus* and as *genitivus subjectivus*) as well, insofar as the I needs the others in order to be able to develop as a constituting I.

Yet these observations should not be allowed to mislead us into denying that there is any distinction between the transcendental and the mundane, between the constituting and the constituted. That is to say, it is something very different to investigate the empirical I as an object within the world and to analyze the I as constituting, i.e., as transcendental (an analysis performed through the reduction). Thus if the transcendental I were to be absorbed without residue into the products of its constitution, then any type of transcendental self-reflection —even that which has been carried out in the present study so far— would be impossible. There are nevertheless two reasons why we are emphasizing the connection between the transcendental and the mundane. First, it allows us to bring to light a dimension of Husserl's argument to which, in our opinion, sufficient attention has not yet been paid. Second, it is precisely because we have claimed that any interpretation that does *not* take into account the connection between constitution, on the one hand, and mundanization, having a world, and communalization, on the other, not only finds itself confronted with a number of paradoxical statements made by Husserl but is ultimately unable to solve the problem of intersubjectivity.

Consequently, although it has been shown that world-constitution implies a self-mundanization (and not merely as a subsequent outcome, but as a co-constitutive condition of possibility), this does not thereby mean that the constitutive agent is completely absorbed into its world-constitution. The constitutive agent is indeed only realized and actualized in this mundanization (which is why any analysis that wants to investigate transcendental subjectivity in its full concretion has to include this dimension). But there is a level at which this agent remains *non-mundane (unweltlich)*. That this stratum of constitutive subjectivity is nevertheless not *worldless (weltlos)*, even though it is non-mundane, will be shown shortly.

2) We can now proceed to our claim with reference to the tripartite structure of constitution, and thereby answer the question concerning the genuine sense of constitution.

As a bringing to givenness (14/47),[8] neither does constitution mean a mere epistemic re-production of something that already exists, nor does it express a receptivity understood as though constitution is influenced by an *external* impulse (whether this is supposed to stem from an unknowable thing in itself or from physicalistic entities). Both of these explanatory models are incompatible with the radicality of the transcendental phenomenological mode of inquiry, and they are therefore unsuitable for contributing to the clarification of the concept of constitution. As Husserl has already explained in the *Logical Investigations,* the concepts of *inner* and *outer* have their origin in the *naive* metaphysics of everyday life (19/673[786], 19/708[815]), and for this reason these concepts cannot be decisive for a phenomenological clarification of the relationship between subjectivity and world. On the other hand, however, neither is constitution to be understood as though intentional contents could be deduced from transcendental subjectivity,[9] nor is it the expression of an *arbitrary productivity* on the part of a worldless transcendental subject, as though the constitutive process could be arbitrarily guided or controlled by such a subject. That is to say, every constitution includes a moment of facticity (i.e., every constitution refers to the primal fact of the hyle—15/385). Or in other words, every activity of the I presupposes affection (4/337), a point that Husserl brings to expression in the following way in a passage from 1931:

> The constitution of entities on various levels, of worlds, of times, has two primal presuppositions, two primal sources that—temporally speaking (in each of these temporalities)—continually "lie at the basis of" such constitution: 1) my primordial I as an operatively functioning primal I in its affections and actions, with all its essential structures in the modes pertaining to them; 2) my primordial non-I as a primordial stream of temporalization, and even as the primal form of temporalization, constituting a temporal field—that of primal concrete materiality [Ur-Sachlichkeit]. *But both primal foundations are inseparably one, and thus are abstract if regarded on their own.* (Ms. C 10 15b, emphasis added)[10]

And Husserl further speaks of the primally flowing non-I that has constituted the hyletic universe within itself, a primal streaming whose primal temporalizing constitution does *not* have the I as its source, and hence happens without the participation of the I, although the latter is always "there" *("dabei")* (Ms. C 10 16a). Now in our opinion, hyletic affection is to be understood as the most original world-relation (although to be sure, "world" is here to be understood neither as a cultural world nor as an objective reality, but rather simply as the non-egoic source of intersubjective sense, a line of thought culminating in Brand's remark that a worldless I is sense-less—see Brand 1955, 47; cf. 15/131, 15/287, 14/378-79). And if this is indeed the case, then we are well on the way toward understanding sensing as a structure of being-in-the-world.[11] But if every constitution points to the primal fact of the hyletic, and if this hyletic affection is to be understood precisely as a relation to the world, we can then point out that a *worldless* constituting I is unthinkable. (On the other hand, however, if this is *not* understood as a relation to the world, then it becomes quite difficult, if not impossible, subsequently to establish intersubjective sense.) Thus when Husserl characterizes transcendental subjectivity (which, let us emphasize once again, includes, in its full concretion, the world as well) as sense-bestowing (8/457, 17/ 251[244], 15/366), he is pointing out that sense is and makes sense only insofar as it appears. If we are talking about constitutive sense-bestowing, what this says is that subjectivity is the place where (nex-uses of) sense can manifest themselves, develop, and appear, i.e., can come to *self-actualization* (15/434) — which is why constitution can be regarded as the genesis of the world in the constitution of transcen-dental subjectivity.

So far, we have mentioned only two elements, subjectivity and world. But Husserl's statement in *Ideas II* must be emphatically re-called here: I, we, and world belong together (4/288). Even if not ev-ery constitution seems to imply transcendental intersubjectivity—we have already pointed out (Chapter III.3), for example, that in primal temporalization, there is an operatively functioning production that seems to be a solitary performance — the moment we have to do with appearances, there is always (on account of horizonality) a reference to intersubjectivity. Therefore in order to designate the *complete* con-stitutive foundation, we have had to speak of the tripartite structure of I-we-world—an interpretation that can be supported to a certain ex-tent by Husserl's later but frequent mention of the *intersubjective life of world-consciousness* (e.g., 29/192, 29/247). At the same time, we must also refer to the passage previously mentioned where Husserl writes that it is only his reflections on intersubjectivity that have made the complete and genuine sense of transcendental phenomenological idealism understandable (1/176). The constitutive relation between subjectivity and world cannot be understood without intersubjectivity, for the world is intersubjective, or intersubjectively experienced, from the start (cf. Chapter II, n. 40). Otherwise it would hardly be un-derstandable how Husserl could ever characterize it as a unity of in-tersubjective experience (14/350, 1/138, 15/33).

Naturally, the emphasis placed upon the interconnection of the three elements must not be mistaken for an obliteration of the distinc-tion between them. Although I, we, and world ultimately form a unity, and are abstract if regarded on their own, none of the three elements can be reduced to any one of the others.

This interpretation might recall Hegel's absolute idealism. But as Fink has stressed, no matter how speculative this conception may sound, it is still not some "metaphysical construction," but rather "the simple formulation of the basic knowledge won by the phenomenological

reduction" (Fink 1970, 139) — a claim that can be confirmed by emphasizing the many similarities between Husserl's reflections and those of
later phenomenologists.[12]

If this interpretation is correct, a whole series of reproaches that
are customarily leveled against Husserl are automatically weakened.
It has become clear, for example, that Husserl's transcendental phenomenological idealism lies beyond the distinction between idealism
and realism (cf. Fink 1995, 159) — at least if realism is defined as a theory that argues for the existence of objects independent from consciousness, thus claiming that the being and essence of reality subsist,
in principle, entirely without relation to an experiencing subject (cf.,
e.g., Rescher 1992, 255), and if idealism is defined as a theory that argues for the absolute character of subjectivity by claiming either that
every object is a really intrinsic (immanent) part of consciousness or
that a worldless consciousness is the sole ground and the sole source
of the ontic sense of the world. That Husserl's phenomenology is a variety of phenomenalism must likewise be denied, for as we have seen,
the *Logical Investigations* already tells us that "however we may decide
the question of the existence or non-existence of phenomenal external things, we cannot doubt that the reality of each such perceived
thing cannot be understood as the reality of a perceived complex of
sensations in [the] perceiving consciousness" (19/764-65[862]).
Again and again, Husserl emphasized that "the transcendent world;
human beings; their intercourse with one another, and with me, as
human beings; their experiencing, thinking, doing, and making, with
one another: these are not annulled by my phenomenological reflection, not devalued, not altered, but only understood" (17/282[275];
cf. 9/254[101-102], 6/191[187]). Hence it must be stressed once
again that Husserl's position stands in accord with the positions of
later phenomenologists to a considerably greater extent than is customarily claimed.

Finally, let us turn against this background to the specific sense of
the constitution of others, beginning with a summary of our findings
thus far.

In our presentation of Husserl's analyses of the experience of
others, it has turned out that I cannot bring the foreign subjectivity to
originary givenness. For as we have already mentioned, "if what belongs to the other's own essence were directly accessible, it would be

merely a moment of my own essence, and ultimately he himself and I myself would be the same" (1/139). In other words, if the consciousness of others were given in the same way as self-consciousness is given, this would mean annulling alterity and taking the other as part of the self. And as we have seen, Husserl even emphasizes that it is precisely because the foreign subjectivity does not belong to the sphere of my original perceptual possibilities that it also cannot be "exhausted in being an intentional correlate of my own life" (8/189). But this does not mean that there is no experience of others at all. That is to say, the foreign I is given in an appresentative experience—and not merely as a hypothesis or substruction, or as a mere anticipation, but rather as something *experienced*, and therefore as something that can itself be confirmed or canceled in the manner proper to experience (1/153, 14/352). What I experience in the experience of others is neither a sign nor a mere analogue, but rather *the other* (14/385, 29/182, 1/153, 15/506), although the other's mode of givenness is fundamentally distinct from the mode of givenness of an object. That is to say, it is an appearance in which something is itself evinced, indicated, or manifested, not one in which something is itself "*given*" (*eine selbstbekundende und keine selbstgebende Erscheinung*—14/354). The I that is indicated in the experience of others is, as Husserl says, not something transcendent that is constituted, but something that is indicated through the transcendence of the indication (13/445).The other is inaccessible to me in her own self-relatedness. But *that* the other is inaccessible to me *is* accessible to me (1/144, 15/631). And to ask for more than this would be to posit, as the most original mode of givenness of the other, the very mode in which an I is given for itself, which is precisely *not* the mode in which an other stands before me. Thus it is a matter above all of respecting the uniquely specific character of the mode of givenness of the other—namely, the "verifiable accessibility of what is not originally accessible" (1/144). And in spite of the misleading yet constantly repeated criticism leveled against Husserl, this respect was something he always demanded.

This assertion, however, does not answer *per se* the question of how Husserl's talk of the "constitution" of foreign subjectivity should be understood. Is the other dependent upon me in her being? In the meantime, however, we have gained the necessary means to offer an answer. First of all, we must point out the peculiar character pertaining to any talk of the other or of the foreign I. It is obviously a matter here of a *relational concept* that presupposes a reference back to the current (own) I. The *foreign* I is precisely foreign *for me* (it is I who am different from it), not for itself, and when the constitution of the other is discussed in terms of a constitution of being, it is obviously a matter of the constitution of the foreign I's being for me (and not its own being for itself).[13] Were this not the case, it would actually be an annulment or denial of *foreign* subjectivity. That this is also Husserl's own interpretation can be supported by the following pair of references. First, Husserl writes that the "I am" prescribes whether, and which, other monads *are others for me,* as well as prescribing that it is to me that the "other" stands in an originary relation, and he insists that the constitution of the *alter ego* by no means entails that I invent, make, or create this transcendence (1/168, 17/244[237-38], 17/258[251], 15/13). Second, he also consistently emphasizes that the presumptivity and fallibility of the experience of others concerns precisely the otherness of the foreign I (i.e., its otherness for me), and not its own being for itself. Naturally the *cogito sum* of the foreign I is characterized by the same apodicticity as mine is (15/43; cf. 8/504, 14/155, 1/157).

But these observations must now be corrected in one respect. That is to say, the foreign I's own being for itself does actually depend on me in a certain way, insofar as the other's being for me is indeed central to the other's own being for himself. We mentioned earlier (Chapter III.1 and III.3) that inter-subjectivity is of importance precisely when it is a question of the self-constitution of transcendental subjectivity. The I without a Thou is not a complete I, for the I is what it is only as *socius* of a sociality (13/6, 13/247, 15/603, 15/193). Naturally, this holds for every I—not only for me, but also for any foreign I (experienceable by me). If we transform our previous findings in accordance with this, we can now make the following claim. It is indeed possible to speak of the other's own being for himself as independent from me if it is a matter of an abstractive determination of strata, and if we are talking about the other as a pole and center of functioning for affections and actions. But if we are talking about the full and complete other, it is not possible to assert such independence: in his full transcendental concretion and performance, the other (experienced by me) cannot be characterized without me (as co-subject). And the interdependence of subjects naturally concerns not only my own being as a subject but that of every subject.

V.2. META-PHENOMENOLOGY

Husserl often referred to the necessity of a second stage of phenomenological research that would take the form of a critique of transcendental experience and cognition (1/68, 8/252, 17/295[289]). If phenomenology is to succeed in securing its total horizon, a phenomenology of phenomenological reduction will also be required (6/250 [247]). Hence phenomenology would also have to become reflexively related to itself (1/178), for where

> something culturally new emerges, the doing is always first, and only afterwards the self-explication of what has been done—which is by no means an easy matter, all the more so in that the sense of something still ongoingly emerging can only be fully manifested when it has been fully accomplished. The many subsequent reflections upon what is proper to the phenomenological method used, and upon its scope, later led to essential broadenings and deepenings of the method itself. (9/366)

Husserl is sometimes reproached for never having carried out this phenomenological self-reflection. We are not questioning the fact that he never completely accomplished it. But it seems to us that his intersubjective transformation of phenomenology must be seen precisely as such a higher-level critique of naive, straightforward phenomenology (8/478). That is to say, if we bear in mind the transformative reformulation of his thinking, so that such themes as generativity, historicity, and normality are incorporated into transcendental phenomenology —a reshaping that in our opinion, is surprisingly far-reaching and radical—then we can begin to see intersubjectivity as the key to this transformation, or as the connecting thread that ties it all together. If Husserl had not been striving to understand intersubjectivity as a fundamental transcendental concept, the transformation we are talking about could scarcely have occurred.

Now it is striking how early Husserl actually did arrive at this insight. It is indeed lacking in the *Logical Investigations,* but Husserl himself often pointed toward his 1910/11 lectures on "Basic Problems of Phenomenology" (see 13/77-194 for the first part of these lectures) as the place where the main points concerning the solution to the problem of intersubjectivity and the overcoming of transcendental solipsism were developed (17/250[243], 5/150, 13/245, 8/433, 14/307). Thus Husserl was already aware of the transcendental importance of intersubjectivity at the time of *Ideas I,* even though the latter is still predominantly conceived in terms of a "solitary," egological approach. For as he writes in the *"Nachwort"* to the *Ideas* (1930), the second volume of the *Ideas,* which was drafted at the same time as the first, was to have supplied the complementary accounts of intersubjectivity (5/150). Our thesis can accordingly be stated in this way: the moment that Husserl realized that the descriptions and the province of objects belonging to phenomenology could not be restricted to the really intrinsic contents of lived experience—and that instead, the intentional correlate must also be seen as a phenomenological theme[14] —he necessarily had to come across transcendental intersubjectivity, since a clarification of the sense of the object (or of the world) as valid for everyone necessarily leads to the transcendental validity of others (15/110). Hence an expansion of egological phenomenology was obviously necessary as well, and this subsequently led to a far-reaching modification—or better, to a decisive *clarification*—of the real sense of the core themes of transcendental phenomenology.

CHAPTER VI

The Further Development of the Phenomenological Theory of Intersubjectivity

VI.1. HOMOGENEITY AND PERSPECTIVIZATION

We have now completed our interpretation of Husserl. But before we turn to the proposed critical engagement with the linguistic-pragmatic conception of intersubjectivity, let us first take a look at post-Husserlian phenomenology.[1] As previously mentioned, what is really at stake here is assessing to what extent a specifically *phenomenological* treatment of transcendental intersubjectivity can contribute to the current state of research and discussion. The fact that we have devoted the main part of our discussion to Husserl's analyses reflects our conviction that his analyses of intersubjectivity contain unnoticed riches whose radicality has hitherto been underestimated. This holds true even when one compares Husserl to later phenomenologists. But it should not be denied that these later thinkers too have made fundamental contributions to the development of a phenomenological theory of intersubjectivity. In what follows, we shall present important aspects of these very contributions.

However, it is unfortunately not possible to go into the work of Heidegger, Sartre, and Merleau-Ponty in as much detail as we did in our treatment of Husserl. Thus in what follows, we are not claiming to make an exhaustive presentation of the positions of the post-Husserlian phenomenologists. Instead, it is a matter of a careful *selection* of themes—a selection that is nevertheless meant to serve several ends. First of all, we want to offer a range of investigations of intersubjectivity that in our

opinion complement Husserl's analyses in a systematic fashion, lending
them a new perspective in the following ways: by providing specific analyses of the various types of relation to others and by offering reflections on
the interrelatedness of subjectivity, intersubjectivity, and world. But in
addition, we also want to display what the various phenomenological
analyses have in common, for it will turn out that there are certain aspects of the problem of intersubjectivity that are indeed continually being taken up and addressed within the phenomenological tradition as a
whole.[2]

VI.2. HEIDEGGER—DA-SEIN'S BEING-WITH

At the beginning of his analysis of being-with in *Being and Time,* Heidegger writes (in the context of referring to Scheler's *The Nature of Sympathy*) that a clarification of being-in-the-world leads us to the insight that
a subject is never given without a world and without others (SuZ 116).
Thus Heidegger indicates at the outset that it is within the context of
an existential-ontological analysis of Da-sein's being-in-the-world that he
comes across intersubjectivity. We shall now pursue this clue, although
in the following analysis we shall be restricting ourselves to Heidegger's
position around the time of *Being and Time,* and will refer only to this
work, to *History of the Concept of Time: Prolegomena,* and to *The Basic Problems of Phenomenology.*

In both the *History of the Concept of Time* and *Being and Time,*
Heidegger comes across others in connection with his analyses of the
everyday surrounding world. If we investigate the phenomenal structure of the world, just as it shows itself in "everyday preoccupation,"
then in this preoccupation with the world, it is not a matter of a world
that is "anyone's own particular world"; rather, from the very beginning, we are moving within a common *public* "totality of surround-
ings" (PZ 255). Moreover, according to Heidegger, we are not first
and foremost occupied with perceptual objects in a theoretical way,
but with "handling, using, and taking care of things" (SuZ 67; 68–69).
But the entities we encounter in this "taking care of things"—entities
that Heidegger calls *"useful things,"* "gear," or "equipment" (each of
these expressions has been used to translate *Zeug*), and whose unique
mode of being he characterizes as *handiness*—point, in accordance
with their ontological structure, to other persons. That is to say, if we
consider a totality of useful things—for example, the surrounding or

environing world of a craftsperson—then in the work one is taking care of, as well as in the materials and the tools that are being used, others are there too, not only as others for whom the work is done, but as others by whom the tools themselves have been produced in the first place. Thus in the world of matters to be taken care of, we encounter others again and again (PZ 326, SuZ 117). And here it must be emphasized that the useful thing's implicit references to others can also be references to *indeterminate* others (cf. PZ 260–61). As Heidegger writes, in utilizing useful things, Da-sein is already coordinated with the *Mitda-sein* of others, i.e., with the "innerworldly being-in-itself" of these others (SuZ 118). In utilizing a useful thing, Da-sein is indeed already *being-with* others, and here it is "completely indifferent" whether or not an other is factually present (GP 414). That is to say, even if they are not objectively present and on hand in person, others are "there too" *(mit da)* in the world in which everyone dwells. Just as Da-sein is not at all first a worldless subject, an "inwardness," to which a "world" would then be added, Da-sein likewise does not at all first become being-with when an other does in fact turn up. Hence when being-with is spoken of as a being-character that is co-original with being-in-the-world, it is a matter of an existential-ontological character that determines Da-sein even when no other Da-sein is factually on hand (PZ 328–29). If the other is lacking, this simply means that Da-sein's constitution of being *(Seinsverfassung)* as being-with does not attain its factual fulfillment (or unfolding).[3] That is to say, one can ultimately only speak of the other as "lacking" precisely because Da-sein is being-with (PZ 328, SuZ 120). Against this background, Heidegger stresses that being-with (as being open in principle to others) is "the formal condition of possibility of the *co-disclosure* of the Dasein of others for the Dasein which is in each instance one's own" (PZ 328; cf. SuZ 124). Concrete experience of others is only possible on this basis (SuZ 125):

> The disclosedness of the *Mitda-sein* of others which belongs to being-with means that the understanding of others already lies in the understanding of being of Da-sein because its being is being-with. This understanding, like all understanding, is not a knowledge derived from cognition, but a primordially existential kind of being which first makes knowledge and cognition possible. Knowing oneself is grounded in primordially

> understanding being-with. It operates initially in accordance
> with the nearest kind of being of being-together-in-the-world
> in the understanding knowledge of what Da-sein circumspectly
> finds and takes care of with the others. Concernful taking care
> of things is understood in terms of what is taken care of and
> with an understanding of them. Thus the other is initially dis-
> closed in the taking care of concern. (SuZ 123–24)

The problem of empathy—how an initially isolated subject can come
upon an other—thereby turns out to be an illusory problem when Da-
sein is first characterized as being-in and being-with.[4] I do not first
have to establish an empathic connection with the other; rather, I
understand the other immediately from the world that I share with
her (PZ 334–35). As factually existing being-in-the-world, Da-sein is at
the same time being-among *(Sein bei)* entities within the world, and
being-with *(Mitsein)* other Da-sein. Even when the others "are not to
be found there in immediately tangible proximity," the manner in
which they are there too is co-understood "via things" (GP 409–10).
This means that the Mitda-sein of others is already co-understood in
our using things to take care of matters (GP 419).[5] We are constantly
relying upon others. "But when the others become, so to speak, thematic in their Da-sein, they are not encountered as objectively present
thing-persons, but we meet them 'at work,' that is, primarily in their
being-in-the-world" (SuZ 120). Thus Heidegger emphatically holds
fast to the character of our encounter with them within the surrounding world. The others are encountered from the world within which
"Da-sein, heedful and circumspect, essentially dwells" (SuZ 119):

> Because being-in-the-world belongs to the basic constitution of
> the Dasein, the existent Dasein is essentially *being-with* others *as
> being-among* intraworldly beings. As being-in-the-world it is
> never first merely being among things extant within the world,
> then subsequently to uncover other human beings as also be-
> ing among them. Instead, as being-in-the-world it is being with
> others, apart from whether and how others are factically there
> with it themselves. On the other hand, however, the Dasein is
> also not first merely being-with others, only then later to run
> up against intraworldly things in its being-with-others; instead,
> being-with-others means being-with other being-in-the-world—
> being-with-in-the-world. . . . Put otherwise, being-in-the-world is

with equal originality both being-with and being-among. (GP 394; cf. GP 421)

We can stipulate that in his description of being-with as an essential component of the structure of the everyday surrounding world, Heidegger is by no means occupied with a merely *mundane* analysis of everyday *being-with-one-another* (which brings together the being-structure of one's own Da-sein as being-with and the mode of being of others as Mitda-sein or fellow Da-sein). Instead, everyday life serves Heidegger as a point of departure for his *analytic of Da-sein,* and he ultimately claims that being-with is an existential constituent of Da-sein's being-in-the-world (SuZ 125). Thus in § 18 of *Being and Time,* he interprets the worldliness of the world as the referential totality of significance—a referential totality (horizon-structure) that is precisely also established by the disclosedness of others that is constituted together with being-with (SuZ 123). The worldliness of Da-sein's being-in-the-world accordingly implies structural references to the Mitda-sein of others. When it is said that *being-with is a structure of Da-sein* that is equiprimordial with being-in-the-world (SuZ 114), this is thus a matter of Da-sein's being-in-the-world being essentially co-constituted by being-with (SuZ 120).

Since Heidegger characterizes Da-sein as an existence that makes use of things to take care of matters, and that is, in doing so, open to the other—so that Da-sein's being-with is characterized as an existential being-open (SuZ 163)—then the task arises of providing a more detailed characterization of this being-open. It is interesting that like Husserl (cf. Chapter III.2), Heidegger attempts to provide such a characterization by referring to the original connection between openness, transcendence, and temporality. In *The Basic Problems of Phenomenology,* he writes that temporality as transcendence—as what is originally outside itself—is (in a word) openness (GP 360, 377). It is precisely the transcendence grounded in temporality (as the transcendence of Da-sein's being out-beyond-itself) that is the presupposition of Da-sein's being-with others (GP 426). At this juncture, it is naturally important to stress that Da-sein does not first exist, and then make the step beyond itself to the others or to what is extant. Rather, to exist always already means to step beyond—or better, to have stepped beyond. In short, Da-sein as such is "open for . . . ," and the openness "belongs to its being" (GP 426):

> Transcendence is not instituted by an object coming together
> with a subject, or a thou with an I, but the Dasein itself, as
> "being-a-subject," transcends. The Dasein as such is being-
> toward-itself, being-with others, and being-among entities handy
> and extant. In the structural moments of *toward-itself, with-others,*
> and *among-the-extant* there is implicit throughout the *character of
> overstepping,* of transcendence. (GP 427–28)

Hence Da-sein's being-in-the-world is interpreted in terms of an
understanding of the equiprimordiality of the being of Da-sein, the being of Mitda-sein (the others), and the being of the entities—be they
objectively present and on hand, or else "handy" things—that are "always encountered in a disclosed world" (GP 417). Hence just as with
Husserl, being-in-the-world is interpreted as a tripartite structure. As
world-experiencing, Da-sein is always already being-with. Therefore when
Heidegger explains that world-understanding is self-understanding;
that in self-understanding as being-able-to-be-in-the-world, world too is
equiprimordially understood; and that "self" and "world" are not two
separate entities, but are the basic determination of Da-sein itself in the
unity of the structure of being-in-the-world (GP 394, 422), then it must
merely be recalled that being-with is also co-entailed, within the structure of being-in-the-world, as a formal condition of possibility for both
world- and self-understanding. Heidegger accordingly emphasizes that
Da-sein is not at first merely a being-with others, so that it is only on the
basis of this being-with-one-another that Da-sein can subsequently
come to an objective world and to things (GP 421):

> . . . just as the Dasein is originally being with others, so it is origi-
> nally being with the handy and the extant. Similarly, the Dasein
> is just as little at first merely a dwelling among things so as then
> occasionally to discover among these things beings with its own
> kind of being; instead, as the being which is occupied with it-
> self, the Dasein is with equal originality being-with others *and*
> being-among intraworldly beings. (GP 421)

But it is not completely clear whether we can compare what
Heidegger designates with the concept of "being-with" with that
which we have characterized with the term "open intersubjectivity" in
our analyses of Husserl's transcendental theory of intersubjectivity, or
whether it should rather be compared with what we have summed up

under the concept of "anonymous publicness." In other words, it is not yet fully clear whether Heidegger's being-with belongs to the first or to the third level of intersubjectivity. To be sure, the answer would immediately seem to be easy: it must of course belong to the first level, since Heidegger explicitly stresses that it is a matter of an a priori, existential-ontological determination of Da-sein. The problem, however, is that Heidegger's argumentation is based almost exclusively on an analysis of the utilization of "useful things," "equipment," or "gear," which would seem to place being-with on the third level. Nevertheless, the decisive question is whether his argument holds water. Does it really belong, with a priori necessity, to the structure of Da-sein that it makes use of "equipment" or "gear"?[6]

After this general overview, we must now enter into the question of the constitutive implications of being-with—both when it is a matter of self-understanding and when it is a matter of world-understanding. We must accordingly turn to Heidegger's treatment of the *publicness of the they,* of "just anyone."[7]

We have ascertained that initially and for the most part, Da-sein is busy in the surrounding world, where things are utilized and taken care of. In everyday life, Da-sein, is absorbed in the world and understands itself and the others from this world. Against the background of this "being-lost-in-the-world," Heidegger now demands an answer to the following question: "*Who* is it who is in the everydayness of Da-sein?" (SuZ 113–14; cf. 125). It is true that it belongs to Da-sein, that it is what I myself am at any particular time, i.e., that the structure of "temporal particularity" (*Jeweiligkeit*)—and likewise of "mineness," or of "always being my own being" (*Jemeinigkeit*)—is constitutive for the being-character of Da-sein; nevertheless, insofar as there is no Da-sein that would not, in accordance with its very sense, be temporally particular (PZ 206, 325), it can indeed be that "the who of everyday Da-sein is precisely *not* I myself" (SuZ 115): "We must not succumb to the deception that when we say, 'Dasein is in each instance mine'—the being which I myself am—, the answer to the question of the who of Dasein in its everydayness is also already given" (PZ 336). Hence Heidegger claims that in being absorbed in the world and in being-with, Da-sein is not itself. Being-in-the-world—which encompasses, in equal originality, being with things at hand and being-with others—is always for the sake of itself. "But the self is initially and for the most part inauthentic" (SuZ 181):

By investigating in the direction of the phenomenon which allows us to answer the question of the who, we are led to structures of Da-sein which are equiprimordial with being-in-the-world: being-with and *Mitda-sein*. In this kind of being, the mode of everyday being a self is grounded whose explicitation makes visible what we might call the "subject" of everydayness, the *they*. (SuZ 114)

"The others" are not first of all "everybody else but me," as a whole from which the I would stand out; rather, the others are those among whom one also is, but from whom "one mostly does *not* distinguish oneself" (SuZ 118). Da-sein is first of all something that can also be—and is—others. Hence in everyday experience, there is at first neither an experience of the self nor an experience of others. We do not experience ourselves in contradistinction to some sort of inaccessible foreign subjects; rather, our being-with-one-another is characterized by replaceability and interchangeability (PZ 428). We are there in the world together with others. Thus Da-sein is not first of all itself, but as being-with, it is lived by the others with whom it coexists. The "who" of the Da-sein who is living in everydayness is therefore *"anyone,"* is the *"they."* Everyday being-with-one-another completely dissolves one's own Da-sein into the mode of being of the others, relieving Da-sein of its responsibility (PZ 336-38; SuZ 126-27). In other words, Da-sein allows itself to be carried along by the others, and its formation of judgment, its estimation of values, its self-apprehension, and its interpretation of the world are determined, dictated, and controlled by the publicness of being-with-one-another (PZ 340-42; SuZ 127). As a being-in-the-world that is at the same time a being-with-one-another, our experience is interpreted, articulated, and prescribed by others from the very beginning. Hence living in the mode of the "they" is characterized by an "averageness" that leads to a leveling down of Da-sein's possibilities of being and to a leveling of differences. That is to say, not only is each completely equivalent to the other with regard to its possibilities of being, but even distinguishable "others" disappear. And it is first in this inconspicuousness that the peculiar "who" of everydayness—the they—"has its total domination" (PZ 338-39; cf. SuZ 126-27).

Since Da-sein primarily understands itself from entities it encounters within the world—i.e., from things—and lets itself be determined by others, Heidegger speaks of an *inauthentic understanding* (GP 395).

Da-sein is initially and for the most part in the world of matters to be taken care of. This "absorption in" the world has the character of a *being lost* in the *publicness of the they*—i.e., Da-sein "has initially always already fallen away from itself and fallen prey to the 'world'" (SuZ 175). That is to say, insofar as—unlike things—Da-sein does not possess a merely formal-ontological self-identity, but rather has a peculiar self-sameness with itself, it has to appropriate itself, and for this reason it can also lose itself. Da-sein's selfhood is not some objectively present entity, but is precisely a *manner* of existing (SuZ 267). Yet if Da-sein allows itself to be determined in its being by others, then in this forgetfulness of itself, it is existing *inauthentically* (GP 242–43). The self of everyday Da-sein is a they-self, and this has to be distinguished from the authentic self, i.e., the self that has grasped itself as its own (SuZ 129). To put it another way, it is only because Da-sein is determined as such by mineness that there can be such modes as *authenticity* and *inauthenticity* (SuZ 43). And insofar as Heidegger constantly advocates the thesis that the structure of mineness belongs to Da-sein as such, one must not understand the question as to "who" Da-sein is as a question concerning its formal individuation, but rather as a question concerning its qualitative self-identity.

As a they-self, then, Da-sein is absorbed in the world it encounters as closest to it, and its world-interpretation is precisely the one prescribed by the they: at first "I" do not "exist," in the sense of being my own self, but instead "am the others in the mode of the they" (SuZ 129). Thus Da-sein does not initially live in what is own and nearest; rather, these modes of being are precisely that which is most distant from Da-sein. The they provide the world in which one lives in being-with-one-another, and it is from out of this world "that one can first more or less genuinely grow into his own world" (PZ 339–40). Initially and for the most part, the self is lost in the they, understanding itself "in terms of the possibilities of existence that 'circulate' in the actual 'average' public interpretedness of Da-sein today" (SuZ 383). And this means that the interpretation of Da-sein is initially and for the most part guided by a linguistically articulated pre-understanding.

We have already established that being-with is co-constitutive for Da-sein's being-in-the-world. This constitutive accomplishment of our relation to others is granted by Heidegger throughout. For example, he writes that it is in speaking with one another that the world "becomes manifest" (PZ 363). Nevertheless, in connection with his analysis of Da-sein's being lost in the publicness of the they, Heidegger stresses that the *uncovering* accomplished in being-with-one-another is in reality a kind of *covering up* (PZ 377). Heidegger even occasionally characterizes inauthentic understanding and inauthentic existence as a covering up of the full being-in-the-world (PZ 377; SuZ 256, 311). Hence it is not merely a matter of the public interpretation holding sway over Da-sein's possibilities of being in such a way that Da-sein cannot understand itself authentically. Rather, the point is that Da-sein cannot even disclose or uncover either itself or the world at all when it allows itself to be led by the average understanding dominated by the they, for it is then "cut off from the primary and primordially genuine relations of being toward the world, toward *Mitda-sein,* toward being-in itself" (SuZ 170).[8] Thus inauthenticity must be interpreted as a mode of existence in which Da-sein is closed off from a genuine understanding of the self, of others, and of the world, for it has let itself be guided by possibilities of interpretation that have been leveled down to the average. In contrast, what is meant by authenticity is precisely the mode of existence in which Da-sein understandingly makes use of the factual multiplicity and the entire spectrum of possibilities of interpretation and of being, all in order to disclose, uncover, and display self, others, and world in a way that is as suitable as possible to their respective plenitude (and this of course concerns not only their ontic aspects but also their true existential-ontological sense).[9]

In his analysis of *anxiety* and of *death,* Heidegger now attempts to lay open two phenomena that can, according to him, tear Da-sein loose from its falling prey to the everyday being-with-one-another where we are all replaceable. That is to say, anxiety deprives Da-sein of the possibility of falling prey to the public way of interpreting itself. It pulls Da-sein out of the "tranquilized self-assurance" of "being-at-home," in average everydayness, in order to throw Da-sein back upon "its authentic potentiality-for-being-in-the-world"; everyday familiarity "collapses," and, Heidegger writes, the anxiety discloses Da-sein as an individualized possibility-of-being, as an *existential "solus ipse"* (SuZ 187–89). Thus there lies within anxiety the possibility of a distinctive kind of disclosure, because it *individualizes:* it "fetches Da-sein back from its falling prey" and reveals to it the basic possibilities of its being, which are no longer disguised by the "innerworldly" entities "to which Da-sein, initially and for the most part, clings" (SuZ 191). This character of individualizing—which terminologically reveals the original predominance of commonality, and which Heidegger seems to regard as an essential determination of an authentic and genuine understanding of being—also appears in his analyses of being toward death. That is to say, each Da-sein must take dying upon itself in each case; insofar as death "is," it is "always essentially my own" (SuZ 240). But this means that death is "a peculiar possibility of being in which it is absolutely a matter of the being of my own Da-sein" (SuZ 240). The possibility of replaceability and interchangeability—a possibility that characterizes being-with-one-another—fails completely when it is a question of dying (PZ 428–29). Heidegger therefore emphasizes that "with death, Da-sein stand before itself in its *ownmost* potentiality-of-being" (SuZ 250, emphasis added):

> When Da-sein is imminent to itself as this possibility, it is *completely* thrown back upon its ownmost potentiality-of-being. Thus imminent to itself, *all relations to other Da-sein are dissolved in it.* This nonrelational ownmost possibility is at the same time the most extreme one. As a potentiality of being, Da-sein is unable to bypass the possibility of death. Death is the possibility of the absolute impossibility of Da-sein. Thus *death* reveals itself as the *ownmost nonrelational possibility not to be bypassed.* (SuZ 250, emphasis altered)

We can thus establish that according to Heidegger, ownmost (authentic) possibilities of being are *non-relational.* The non-relationality of death "individualizes Da-sein down to itself"; when what is at stake is one's ownmost potentiality-of-being, then "any being-together-with what is taken care of and any being-with the others fails" (SuZ 263). Now this failure should not be misunderstood. It is naturally not a matter of annulling Da-sein's being-in-the-world, and hence it is also not a matter of denying Da-sein's fundamental being-with. As essential structures pertaining to the composition of Da-sein, both "taking care of things" and "being concerned" belong to the condition of possibility-of-existence as such: "Da-sein is authentically itself only if it projects itself, *as* being-together with things taken care of and concernful being-with . . . , primarily upon its ownmost potentiality-of-being, rather than upon the possibility of the they-self" (SuZ 263; cf. 298). This bringing of Da-sein before its authentic being-in-the-world nevertheless implies that Da-sein is so radically thrown back upon itself that the concretion of being-with becomes *irrelevant* (PZ 439–

40). To be sure, it is doubtful whether this could ever succeed at all, for Heidegger emphasizes that it belongs to Da-sein's facticity that as long as it is what it is, it is pulled into the vortex of the inauthenticity of the they. The thrownness in which facticity can be phenomenally seen is not some sort of self-contained fact, but "belongs to Da-sein, which is concerned in its being about that being" (SuZ 179). Da-sein "exists factically" (SuZ 179), and Da-sein's authentic possibilities of being are thus also *factical*, handed down possibilities that Da-sein, as thrown, takes over from the (intersubjective) heritage (SuZ 383).

Hence a certain tension seems to be present in Heidegger's deliberations.[10] On the one hand, he clings to the *formal* structural description of Da-sein as being-with: seen formally, being-with is constitutive for the possibility of world- and self-experience. And Heidegger even stresses that authentic being-one's-self does not depend upon some "exceptional" state of the subject, i.e., a state in which one would be "detached from the they"; rather, authentically being-one's-self is an existentiell *modification* of the they considered as an *"essential existential"* (SuZ 130).[11] On the other hand, however, he emphasizes again and again that in being-with-one-another with the others, Da-sein is guided by the average interpretation stemming from publicness —and guided in such a way that Da-sein is thereby "cut off from the primary and primordially genuine relations of being toward the world, toward *Mitda-sein,* toward being-in itself" (SuZ 170). It is only by being individualized—by being torn loose from all relations to other Da-sein in order to take up for itself its ownmost, non-relational possibilities of being—that Da-sein can attain its genuine and authentic relation to being. Hence it seems that Heidegger is advocating the position that there is no way for others to contribute in any positive fashion to Da-sein's world- and self-experience. This tension seems to be a genuine problem. A possible solution (linked with the passage just mentioned concerning being-one's-self as an existentiell modification of the they) is offered in the following distinction. On the one hand, there is the being-with or being-with-one-another that is always functioning as a formal structure that permeates and co-constitutes every nexus of sense. On the other hand, there is the appropriation of this nexus of sense by the actual Da-sein in each case—an appropriation of intersubjective sense that must be accomplished in and through a process of individualization, so that it is not guided by the public interpretation that covers up the sense in question.

In addition to this, it could be objected that Heidegger does in fact speak of a genuine and authentic relation of being toward others. That is to say, in *Being and Time*, he mentions a type of concernful solicitude (*Fürsorge* has been rendered as both "solicitude" and "concern" in English) that leaps ahead of the other in his existentiell potentiality-to-be, in order first to give "care" as such back to this other, thus helping the other "to become transparent to himself *in* his care and *free for* it " (SuZ 122; cf. PZ 399, 436). Thus it is genuine and authentic being-with-one-another that makes Da-sein, as being-with, open to understanding the other's own potentiality-of-being, and thereby helps the other to understand his own (non-relational) possibilities of being. However, Heidegger stresses that this authentically existing being-with-one-another is primarily determined from the authentic existence of individuals. "Only from and in its resolute individuation is the Dasein authentically free and open for the thou" (GP 408). At first glance, a contradiction seems to be in play here. If Dasein is first free for the Thou by individualization, how can this authentic relation to the other be the very relation that helps Da-sein become individualized? The contradiction disappears, however, when one sees that for Heidegger, authentic being-with-one-another is *not* a reciprocal relation. If I am already individualized, I can help the other to confront himself with his own possibilities of being. But this help is a merely negative kind of help. I cannot individualize the other; I can only help the other by not confirming the other in his *inauthentic* existence. Thus at best, the only way I can help is by *not* taking the other's care away from him, but simply leaving the other in his own potentiality-of-being (SuZ 298). It is therefore not at all the case that genuine being-with-one-another as such could somehow help the Da-sein who is living in everydayness make the transition to a genuine relation to being: Da-sein cannot profit *positively* from being in some specific relation to me; it must attain its authentic self non-relationally.

Hence although Heidegger's position is seemingly free from contradiction, it is noteworthy that authentic being-with-one-another is characterized by the circumstance that only a Da-sein that is already individualized can enter into authentic being-with-one-another, while the Da-sein that is still caught in everydayness (and for this reason can still be helped, albeit indirectly, by the concern that leaps ahead of this Da-sein) cannot be with others authentically precisely because it is not yet individualized. Heidegger thus rules out, first, that it is indeed possible to attain a genuine self- and world-relation together by way of a genuinely reciprocal being-with-one-another. In addition, he denies that the authentically existing Da-sein *needs* any further relations to others (except for the formal determination of Da-sein as being-with); "even being-with in its concretion of 'to be with others' becomes irrelevant" (PZ 439–40). Accordingly, Da-sein also remains untouched in its own existence by the concern for the other that can leap ahead of this Da-sein.

Against this background, one must inquire whether Heidegger's description of authentic concern is not a merely formal allusion that is not worked out within his own theory.

Heidegger was frequently criticized for his pessimistic observations about being-with-one-another, often with the argument that his analysis did not take into consideration the variety of possible modes of being related to one another.[12] At the same time, it is often emphasized that in his investigation, he never draws attention to the actual transcendence and alterity of the other, for once being-with is introduced as a structural element of Da-sein's being-in-the-world, the radical otherness of the other is ignored (cf. Chapter VI.3). We can now attempt to refute this reproach against Heidegger by pointing out that his analyses of being-with and Mitda-sein are situated within an existential-ontological analysis of being-in-the-world and are not at all trying to be analyses of concrete experience of others and of sociality (which Heidegger characterizes precisely as questions of concrete anthropology—GP 394).[13] However, if it were to be demonstrated that the otherness, foreignness, and transcendence of the other are of constitutive significance for being-in-the-world after all, then this attempt to save Heidegger's position would fail, and his analyses would be inadequate. And that the transcendence of the other is indeed of constitutive significance is precisely Husserl's view. We must therefore ask whether being-in-the-world is predominantly dependent upon the *replaceability* and *interchangeability* of others, or upon their *foreignness* and *transcendence*. We shall attempt to answer this question in Chapter VI.5.

If by way of a conclusion we want to single out Heidegger's most essential contribution to a phenomenological theory of intersubjectivity—i.e., if we want to identify what element in his investigation has, in our opinion, systematically supplemented Husserl's analyses—we might point, perhaps somewhat surprisingly, chiefly to the conceptual (and terminological) keenness of his analysis. Heidegger's analysis of being-with as an existential constituent of Da-sein's being-in-the-world is enlightening, as is the resulting thematization of the distinction between an a priori and a factual-contingent intersubjectivity. Nevertheless, what is really new in Heidegger (and here we are completely setting aside the complicated question of to what extent *Being and Time* was influenced by Husserl's analyses) does not lie in this presentation. Nor does it lie in Heidegger's emphasis on the intersubjective characterization of the utilization of useful things, or in his characterization of Da-sein's everyday, public, and average being-with-one-another. That is to say, all of these themes have already been treated by Husserl (in greater or lesser detail). Thus apart from certain individual analyses — e.g., those of anxiety and of death — the essential contribution of Heiddeger does not lie in the factual contents of his analyses but in the conceptual precision with which he is able to formulate his way of posing the problem and to go about answering it. And this conceptual precision is also the origin of the reflective problem-consciousness with which he could begin to work out a phenomenological analysis of intersubjectivity.

VI.3. SARTRE — THE TRANSCENDENCE OF THE OTHER

Sartre's analysis of intersubjectivity in *Being and Nothingness* is guided by two main motives. First, he is concerned with developing his ontological analysis of the essence of the for-itself *(pour-soi)* and the in-itself *(en-soi)*, along with their relation. For as he explains at the beginning of Part Three (which has to do with being-for-others), I need the other in order fully to lay hold of all of the structures of my own being, since the for-itself refers to the for-others (EN 267/303, 260/298); later he points out that the treatment of the relation to the in-itself must necessarily include an analysis of the other precisely because this relation is played out in the presence of the other (EN 410/472). Second, Sartre wants to supply a concrete solution to the problem of solipsism (EN 289/329, 296/337), a problem he was already occupied with in *The Transcendence of the Ego*. More specifically, he claimed at that time that solipsism could indeed be avoided within a non-egological theory of consciousness, since within such a theory — which sees the transcendental field of consciousness as non-personal and the I as a transcendent object and as a product of reflection (TE 36/52–53,

63/80–81) — I no longer have any privileged status vis-à-vis the other (TE 85/104; cf. Chapter I, n. 38, above). In *Being and Nothingness,* however, Sartre concedes that dropping the notion of the transcendental I was of no use in solving the question of the existence of others (EN 280/318). He nevertheless continues to place the problem of solipsism in the center of his reflections. But for him, it is not a question of proving the existence of others; rather, he wants to reveal the foundation of our "pre-ontological" certainty with regard to the existence of the other (EN 297/338). Sartre begins his investigation with a survey of previous accounts — accounts he considers unsuccessful — and he too refers to Husserl and Heidegger. A short summary of his evaluation of Heidegger's contribution will facilitate the transition to Sartre's own theory.[14]

At first, Sartre seems to accept Heidegger's observations regarding the publicness of useful things, for he explains that a useful thing incontestably does refer to a plurality of *bodily* others by whom the instrument has been manufactured and/or by whom it is used (EN 278/316, 389/446, 391/448). And as with Heidegger, the coexistence of others is already co-implied in our activities of taking care of matters and utilizing things. As existing-in-the-world we are constantly dependent upon others:

> To live in a world haunted by my fellowman is not only to be
> able to encounter the Other at every turn of the road; it is also
> to find myself engaged in a world in which instrumental-
> complexes can have a meaning which my free project has not
> first given to them. It means also that in the midst of this world
> *already* provided with meaning, I meet with a meaning which is
> *mine* and which I have not given to myself, which I discover that
> I "possess already." (EN 567/654)

Hence the existence of objects of use in the world indicates our membership in a community of subjects. In my commerce with the equipment or instruments I am using, my most immediate goals are those of the they: I grasp myself as interchangeable with any of my neighbors and do not distinguish myself from them. Ultimately, whenever I make use of an instrument that was manufactured by others for an anonymous consumer, i.e., for a sheer "someone," I forfeit my own individuality. Thus whenever I try on a pair of shoes, or uncork a bottle, or step into an elevator, or laugh in a theatre, I am making myself into "anyone." Certain particular circumstances, arising from the world, can therefore give me the impression of being a part of a *we* (EN 475-77/548-51). In other words, where Heidegger referred to the they-self, Sartre speaks of the we-subject.

Although Sartre does take over an important part of Heidegger's reflections—and praises him for interpreting the relationship to the other as a relationship of being (and not as a mere relationship of knowing)—Sartre's presentation also turns into a pointed critique. That is to say, he denies that Heidegger's concept of being-with describes an original and ontologically relevant relationship of being with regard to the other at all.

According to Sartre, an object can only appear to me as a useful item of equipment when I have a prior experience of others. If I were not already aware of the existence of others, then it would never occur to me to make a distinction between a manufactured piece of equipment and a merely natural object; I would never use a piece of equipment as *"they"* do. Hence the references wherein the equipment points to others are *derived* references that presuppose a more original (concrete) experience of others. For this reason Sartre claims that I can only experience myself as a member of a community of subjects if I already have prior concrete (bodily) experience of others (EN 478-79/551-53). (However, this critique does not affect the analysis of open intersubjectivity on the basis of the formal structure of horizon intentionality.) As a "lateral" relation to the other, being-with can only be established subsequently. Therefore Sartre writes: "The 'we' is a certain particular experience which is produced in special cases on the foundation of being-for-others in general. The being-for-others precedes and founds the *being-with-others*" (EN 465/536-37). Heidegger accordingly made the mistake of interpreting our original relation to the other as an "*oblique* interdependence" and not as a "*frontal* opposition" (EN 291/331), since for Sartre, the essence of the intersubjective relation is ultimately conflict, and not being-with (EN 481/555). As a consequence, Sartre even denies that the experience of myself as part of a we-subject has any kind of ontological relevance: that is to say, correctly seen, there is no intersubjective consciousness, i.e., no collective consciousness that would surpass the individual elements and subsume them into a synthetic whole. The experience of the we-subject is a purely psychological and subjective process within an individual consciousness; it does not establish any ontological connection with the other and does not realize any true being-with (EN 465/536, 477/550). Of course, with this Sartre is identifying "intersubjective" consciousness with a "collective" consciousness—and it is by no means clear that this identification is valid (cf. Chapter VI.4).

Now Heidegger claims that Da-sein is essentially being-with along with others. Hence what is at stake is an a priori structure of being—not a contingent determination that shows up only after concrete encounter with others. But this is precisely the conception that Sartre is criticizing (EN 293/333): Sartre thinks that an a priori being-with would make any concrete relation to *the other as absolute transcendence* impossible (EN 295/335). In other words, the encounter with a truly transcendent other would be impossible if the relation to the other were an a priori element of my own ontological structure. A "theory of intersubjectivity" that emphasizes the undifferentiatedness of I and other, instead of persevering in recognizing the other's transcendence and alterity, is in danger of falling back into a monism that in the end would be comparable to a solipsism (EN 293/333). Sartre therefore explains that if solipsism is to be overcome, the relation to the other—being-for-others—cannot be an element of the *ontological* structure of the for-itself (EN 295/335-36, 330/376). The existence of others is a *contingent* fact, and being-for-others is a mode of being of the for-itself that only arises through concrete encounter with the other. The other cannot be deduced from an a priori for-itself (EN 412/474).[15]

Our treatment of Husserl has already demonstrated that Sartre is justified when he says that our relation to the other is not at all exhausted through the formal determination of "being-with," insofar as one must distinguish between (at least) two entirely different levels (EN 293/334). The question of whether Sartre is justified in categorically denying any apriorism must be provisionally postponed; later it will turn out that, paradoxically, Sartre himself makes use of an apriorism.

Now let us turn to Sartre's own position. Like Husserl (cf. Chapter I.4), Sartre too is convinced that being-with-one-another cannot be observed and described from the external perspective of a third party; rather, it must be elucidated through penetrating self-interpretation. For this reason, he explicitly takes the *cogito* as his point of departure (EN 289/329, 314/358). That is to say, modes of consciousness that intrinsically refer to my being-for-others can be disclosed without leaving the terrain of reflective description (EN 265/301). Thus it is precisely radical *cogito*-reflection that can bring our (contingent) ontological relationship with others to light:

> Just as my consciousness apprehended by the *cogito* bears indubitable witness of itself and of its own existence, so certain particular consciousnesses—for example, "shame-consciousness"—bear indubitable witness to the *cogito* both of themselves and of the existence of the Other.(EN 319/364-65)

The attempt to analyze concrete experiences in order to expose a reference to the other within their intentional structure has already been previously undertaken by Scheler. Scheler claims that we can learn from the intentional analyses of a number of our emotions that we are related to others with a priori essential necessity even prior to, and independent of, any concrete experience of others.[16]

However, the decisive difference between Sartre and Scheler consists in the fact that it is precisely this *a priori* relatedness of subjects to one another that Sartre rejects. According to Sartre, the experiences are in each case only made possible *in and by means of* concrete encounter with the other.[17] The *cogito* does indeed cast me toward the other, as it were. However, this is not because the *cogito* discloses an a priori structure within me, myself, that would be directed toward an equally a priori other; rather, it is because what the *cogito* reveals to me is the concrete and indubitable presence of *this* or *that* concrete other (EN 297/338):

> What the *cogito* reveals to us here is just factual necessity: it is found—and this is indisputable—that our being along with its being-for-itself is also for-others; the being which is revealed to the reflective consciousness is for-itself-for-others. The Cartesian *cogito* only makes an affirmation of the absolute truth of a *fact*— that of my existence. In the same way the *cogito*, a little expanded as we are using it here, reveals to us as a fact the existence of the Other and my existence for the Other. (EN 329/376)

Whereas the problem of the existence of others is traditionally treated in such a way that the original relation to the other is interpreted as a special case of the customary intentional relation to an object (as though the other first appears as a particular perceptual object, that is, as a *cogitatum cogitans*—cf. EN 299/340), the radicalized analysis of the *cogito* discloses a different type of relation between me and the other. That is to say, the other is not only someone I perceive: the other is also someone who perceives me, i.e., someone who radically negates my subjectivity in a certain way, determining me as an object (EN 273/310). The other is thus also the being for and before which I attain my objectivity (EN 317/361). Sartre therefore distinguishes between two types of relation to others, i.e., he holds that one does indeed have to make this very distinction between the other whom I perceive and the other who perceives me, between the other-as-object and the other-as-subject (EN 302-303/344-45). Hence Sartre's original insight consists in reversing the usual perspective. Instead of grasping the other as an intentional object—which would lead precisely to losing the foreign *subjectivity*—Sartre thinks that when I experience my own objectivity (for and before a foreign subject), I also have experiential evidence for the presence of an other-as-subject:

> . . . if the Other-as-object is defined in connection with the world as the object which sees what I see, then my fundamental connection with the Other-as-subject must be able to be referred back to my permanent possibility of *being seen* by the Other. It is in and through the revelation of my being-as-object for the Other that I must be able to apprehend the presence of his being-as-subject. (EN 302/344-45)

Sartre now attempts to use the differentiation between the other-as-object and the other-as-subject to overcome the problem of solipsism. He claims that it would be impossible to explain my everyday (pre-ontological) certainty about the existence of others if my *original* relationship to the other were an experience of the other-as-object. That is to say, like every experience of an object, my experience of the other-as-object is presumptive, referring me to sheer probability; for this reason, if the relationship to the other-as-object were the fundamental relationship to the other, then any claim concerning the existence of others would be purely presumptive as well (EN 297-98/338-39). On the contrary, what my experience of being looked at gives me is precisely an *apodictic evidence* for the presence of the subject-as-other.

Sartre now stresses that it is impossible to transfer my certainty with regard to the presence of the other-as-subject to my experience of the other-as-object, since the experience of being looked at does not depend upon the object that is doing the looking. Thus the look that is directed toward me is not linked with any particular shape or form (EN 303/346). It is not a property of the object that is acting as an I, and if certain objects enter the field of my experience—and in particular, the convergence of the eyes of the other in my direction— this must therefore merely be seen as a sheer occasion that realizes my being looked at (EN 323/369). Ultimately, what the look of the other implies is precisely the "disappearance" of the other's eyes considered as objects that manifest the look (EN 315/359)—an observation that recalls that of Levinas (1982, 89-90).

These reflections now gradually push Sartre toward a suggestive contradiction. I grasp my being seen—which refers me to the real existence of the other—by means of certain appearances in the world that seem to make the glance known to me. But it is possible that I can be mistaken about my experience of being seen: I am bending over the keyhole, and suddenly I hear steps. Someone has seen me. I am ashamed and I get up, scour the corridor with my eyes, and realize that it was a false alarm. In reality, there is nobody there at all (EN 324/369-70). Sartre now comes to the conclusion that the false alarm in no way turns the presence of the other-as-subject into an illusion. Rather, what is revealed as illusion is merely the other's *facticity,* i.e., what falls away is the "contingent connection" between the other and an "object-being," so that what is doubtful is not the other himself, but the other's actually being-there, i.e., what is in doubt is "that concrete, historical event which we can express by the words, 'There is someone in this room'" (EN 324/370).

> We are able now to apprehend the nature of the look. In every look there is the appearance of an Other-as-object as a concrete and probable presence in my perceptive field; on the occasion of certain attitudes of that Other I determine myself to apprehend— through shame, anguish, *etc.*—my being-looked-at. This "being-looked-at" is presented as the pure probability that I am at present this concrete *this*—a probability which can derive its meaning and its very nature as probable, only from a fundamental certainty that the Other is *always* present to me inasmuch as I am *always for-others.* (EN 327-28/374, emphasis altered)

When Sartre advances the claims that the look is merely the concrete manifestation of my original being-for-others (EN 471/543); that the other is present everywhere as that through which I become an object;

and that this fundamental relation to the other is the condition of possibility for my particular experience of the concrete other (which is why the concrete encounter with a particular other would be a merely empirical variation of my fundamental being-for-others—EN 327/373), we can hardly avoid reproaching him for having fallen back into an apriorism.[18] The concrete and factually present other is the other belonging to the realm of facticity, while the indubitable other-as-subject forfeits its non-repeatability and individuality. That this critique is warranted is further confirmed when we note that Sartre even claims that what our experience of being looked at indicates to us is the presence of a *pre-numerical* other-as-subject that Sartre equates directly with the undifferentiated *they*. Thus the other is individuated (and concretized) for the first time in and through our objectification of the other (EN 328–29/375–76).

We can completely accept Sartre's emphasis on the importance of taking the transcendence of the other into consideration. And we can likewise accept his warning that a theory of intersubjectivity is exposed to the danger of monism if it focuses on undifferentiatedness rather than on alterity. But his critique of apriorism seems to us to be mistaken, since embedding the other (i.e., embedding an openness toward the other) in the ontological structure of the for-itself does not at all have to imply that the other is neutralized or rendered harmless. Rather, and quite apart from the fact that the claim of a structural openness toward the other is indeed motivated by the matters concerned, linking the other to the structure of the for-itself can express precisely the "potentiated" consideration of the other as "raised to a higher power" (as is the case in Merleau-Ponty—see Chapter VI.4). Above and beyond this, however, it must also be asked whether demonstrating the factual existence of others can be a philosophical task at all. Is not what is at stake here an empirical way of posing the question, a way that is ultimately not to be confused with the fundamental problem of solipsism—i.e., with the question in principle concerning the intersubjectivity, or the possible plurality, of subjects?

After these introductory observations, now let us pursue the genuine problem: what are, according to Sartre, the constitutive implications of our relation to others? The answer to this question branches out in two directions. For one aspect of the answer, self-experience serves as the point of reference; world-experience is the point of reference for the other aspect.

As we have indicated, it is through the other that I gain my objectivity or objectification (EN 317/361). Sartre accordingly understands the original relation to the other as the experience of my own objecthood, and he says that with the emergence of the other, the for-itself is seen as a being-in-itself-in-the-midst-of-the-world, like a thing among things (EN 481/555). Thus at bottom, his observations can be understood as developing the concept of "alter-ation," since for Sartre what is at stake is precisely that the other endows me with a new ontological dimension.[19]

We have already mentioned that the certainty of the presence of foreign subjectivity does not imply an objectification of this subject. Thus I never truly grasp the other-as-subject (i.e., grasp this subject-other as an object), and the fundamental distinction between the other-as-subject (i.e., the other as she is for herself) and the other-as-object consists in the fact that the other-as-subject "can in no way be known nor even conceived as such" (EN 340/389–90). This fundamental transcendence of the other—which indicates, according to Sartre, the other's being "beyond the world," the other's "trans-mundaneity"—also means that one cannot first of all look for the other within the world. That is to say, the other is not separated from me by any distance or by any body located within the world, but rather only through her transcendence (EN 316/361). Although my original relation to the other is an extra-mundane one, it is nevertheless the occasion for the mundanization of my being that we have already alluded to. In order to illustrate this observation, let us turn to Sartre's well-known analysis of shame, for the experience of shame not only implies the presence of the other-as-subject but also expresses a modification of my own being. Theunissen has formulated this concisely:

> As long as I remain alone, shame cannot arise in me because not only is the one before whom I am ashamed lacking but also the one I can be ashamed of. I must be seen by the Other in order to experience shame, that is, be ashamed of the one whom the Other sees. This is the peculiarity of the phenomenon: that the object of my shame is not I as existing for myself but I insofar as I am *for the Other,* and therefore am constituted by him. The Other "constitutes me in a new type of being"; he conditions me in the very being that he brings to light. In that he, in contrast with my earlier being, makes me into an Other

in this way, the experience of shame serves, in the third place, as a guarantor for the absolute evidence of the alien personal presence. (Theunissen 1986, 220–21)

Hence shame expresses a recognition of my being-for-others. In being ashamed, I accept the judgment of the other. I *am* the way the other sees me (EN 266/302, 307/350):

But the Other is the indispensable mediator between myself and me. I am ashamed of myself *as I appear* to the Other. By the mere appearance of the Other, I am put in the position of passing judgment on myself as on an object, for it is as an object that I appear to the Other. (EN 266/302)

Sartre now points to the peculiar structure of this recognition. That is to say, although in the lived experience of shame I recognize the other's apprehension of me immediately and pre-reflectively, I have no *cognitive knowledge* of this I that I am (EN 334/381). I do indeed accept that I am as the other apprehends me, but *how* the other apprehends me (and how I accordingly am) are precisely matters that pertain to the other and therefore escape me (EN 309/351, 314/358, 412/473). Thus the presence of the other (the other's glance) does not allow the I-as-object to "appear"; on the contrary, it grants me a dimension of being that is "ekstatic" insofar as it lies outside my reach, beyond my knowledge. I am separated from this dimension of being by a radical nothingness that is the freedom of the other (EN 308/351, 314/359, 321/367). Hence the being that is granted to me by the other is inaccessible to me, and Sartre therefore calls my being-for-others my "being-outside" (EN 333/380).[20]

According to Sartre, what is expressed when I involuntarily assume the standpoint of the other—thereby suddenly supplying myself with a self-identity that paralyzes my transcendence, coagulating and petrifying my possible projects and abruptly plunging me into a predicament in which I am what I am, like an object—is the *original fall* (EN 309/352, 336/384, 481/555.[21] That is to say, recognizing my objectification has wide-ranging implications, ultimately effecting an existential alienation (EN 321/367). This alienation is manifested in, among other things, my attempt to grasp my own being by way of what can be revealed in language, i.e., once more attempting to grasp myself through the eyes of the other. That is to say, language is not just something added on to being-for-others, but expresses my being-for-others in an original way, because it confers a significance upon me that others have already found words for (EN 404/463-64, 422-23/485-87). At the same time, however, it is significant that my fallenness into the world comes about through the other's objectification of me. The other's look thrusts me into the world, since to grasp myself as "seen" means grasping myself as being seen in and from the world (EN 309/353). And by objectifying, mundanizing, and reifying me—i.e., by forcing a mundane self-apperception upon me—the other simultaneously spatializes and temporalizes me (EN 313/357). Thus what is implied by the experience of being seen is precisely a modification of my own temporality: I am thrown into the universal, objective time of objects (EN 313/357, 317/362).

Sartre now also come to speak of the *body,* since the two ontological modalities, "being-an-object-for-others" and "being-a-body," are equivalent expressions for the for-itself's being-for-others (EN 396/454). He therefore claims that knowledge of the nature of the body is indispensable in getting to the bottom of the particular connections between my being and that of the other (EN 410/471). It would take us too far afield to pursue Sartre's extensive analysis of the various ontological dimensions of the body in any detail. Of particular interest, however, are his observations about the distinction between pre-reflectively existing my own lived body and the alienating apprehension of my own body as a physical organism, an apprehension that arises when I attempt to seize my own body as an object by assuming the point of view of the other (EN 352/403, 401-409/460-70). And we can only mention in passing that the analysis of concrete relations to the other gradually leads Sartre toward the theme of sexuality, for he holds the view that sexuality belongs to the basic structure of being-for-others (EN 433/498-99). Every concrete connection with others (be it collaboration, conflict, rivalry, obedience, etc.) includes sexual relations, for according to Sartre, sexuality is the fundamental project in which the for-itself realizes its being-for-others and tries to transcend it (EN 457/527).

Let us now turn to world-experience, for Sartre once again uses his distinction between the other-as-object and the other-as-subject in his description of the constitutive implications of our experience of others. When I have an experience of an other-as-object who is observing the objects in my world, my relationship to these very objects undergoes a change. That is to say, Sartre claims that the object *"flees from me"* when it is observed by an other, for the object is then no longer exhausted in being-an-object-for-me (EN 300/341–42). This transcendence of the object is manifested not only by the object's being disclosed to the other in a way that is inaccessible to me (at the moment) but also by its being endowed with a significance that was not initially conferred upon it by *my* own free project. As soon as the other appears as an other-as-object, the world appears to me as alienated, for it is given to me as already looked at—indeed, as "furrowed, explored, worked over" on all fronts. In this way the presence of the other as an other-as-object has the function of revealing complexes of sense that are already *"given"* (EN 577–78/666–67). But at the same time, when the world centered on me is experienced by an other, it is decentered as well, since the other lends the instrumental things of my world an order that points back to the other as a new center of reference (EN 301/342–43, 388–89/446):

> Thus suddenly an object has appeared which has stolen the world from me. Everything is in place; everything still exists for me; but everything is traversed by an invisible flight and fixed in the direction of a new object. The appearance of the Other in the world corresponds therefore to a fixed sliding of the whole universe, to a decentralization of the world which undermines the centralization which I am simultaneously effecting. (EN 301/343)

While my world is eroded and alienated by the other-as-object, the consequences of the presence of the other-as-subject are much more radical: according to Sartre, we cannot simultaneously perceive the world and apprehend a look that is fastened upon us (EN 304/347). Hence the alienation from myself brought about by being looked at also simultaneously includes "the alienation of the world which I organize" (EN 309/353). When I am posited and mundanized as an object, I can no longer constitute and maintain a world. Under the look of the other, the situation retreats from my grasp (EN 311/355).

At first glance, Sartre's reflections seem to follow Husserl's. With Husserl too, it is the experienceability of the world by others that convinces me that the world is transcendent to me. When the world is experienced by an other, it is severed from me. But although for Husserl, the severing from the world that is occasioned by the transcendent other is what first makes the actual constitution of the objective worldliness of the world possible, Sartre claims that the other-as-subject *deprives me of the world*. The presence of the other in his looking look does not contribute to reinforcing the world, but "undoes" the world and makes it escape me (EN 318-19/363-64):

> First, the *Other's look* as the necessary condition of my objectivity is the destruction of all objectivity for me. The Other's look touches me across the world and is not only a transformation of myself but a total metamorphosis of the *world*. (EN 316/360)

Sartre does indeed concede that the ontological structure of my world also includes its worldliness for the other. But he emphasizes that what is at stake here is an empty, formal, and derived concept of the (intramundane) other that does not at all take into consideration, phenomenologically, the actual consequence of my encounter with the other. To hold, with Husserl, the view that the objectivity of the world is co-constituted by the transcendence of the other is for Sartre to misunderstand the nature of the encounter with the other completely.

Thus we are confronted with the following problem once again: which of the two—the *transcendence* of the other, or the *replaceability* of the other—has constitutive implications?

If by way of a summary we want to single out Sartre's most important contribution to the development of a phenomenological theory of intersubjectivity, it undoubtedly lies in his radical emphasis on the transcendence and alterity of the other. Through his critique of undifferentiated intersubjectivity; through his analysis of the other-as-subject (which in some respects is very similar to Levinas's position); through his development of the concept of "alter-ation," and through his introduction of the emotional dimension, Sartre has clearly supplemented Husserl's own analyses. To be sure, it is not the case that the themes just mentioned cannot be found in Husserl at all (indeed, the contrary is true). However, Sartre's treatment has shifted the accent, and for precisely this reason it has opened up a new perspective on some important aspects of the problem of intersubjectivity.

VI.4. MERLEAU-PONTY—FINITUDE AND OPENNESS

Finally, let us turn to Merleau-Ponty, who has addressed the problem of intersubjectivity in nearly all his works. We shall, however, chiefly take our bearings from *Phenomenology of Perception, Signs,* and *The Visible and the Invisible.*

The focal point of his investigation lies in an analysis of the conditions of possibility in principle for intersubjectivity, and not in a description of concrete experience of others—i.e., the aim of his investigation is to answer the question of how the relationship between subjects is possible at all. His handling of the problem is guided by the insight that a treatment of intersubjectivity simultaneously requires an analysis of the relationship between subjectivity and world. It is not possible simply to insert intersubjectivity somewhere within an already established ontology; rather, the three regions "I," "others," and "world" belong together and can only be explicated side by side. To put Merleau-Ponty's account in a nutshell, the subject must be seen as a worldly incarnate existence, and the world must be seen as a common field of experience (VI 322/269), if intersubjectivity is to be possible at all.

Let us begin with his critique of the idealistic concept of the subject. According to Merleau-Ponty, it is impossible ever to bring intersubjectivity into play if one understands constituting consciousness as a pure being-for-itself. If I, as a constituting consciousness, were in absolute coincidence with myself; if I were defined as absolute self-possession; and if I could never find anything outside of myself that I myself had not put there, then a second I and a plurality of subjects would be impossible. First, an absolute constituting consciousness of this nature could not tolerate an equal: it could not constitute any equiprimordial other and would therefore necessarily be unique (PP 428/373; VI 90/62). That is to say, if the other were merely an immanent sense-formation of my constituting consciousness, its status as a true *alter ego,* as an equivalent equiprimordial subject, would naturally be lost (RC 150/106-107).[22] Second, for such an I there would not be the rupture within self-coincidence that—according to Merleau-Ponty—first makes possible the openness to, and advertence to, the other:

> If the sole experience of the subject is the one which I gain by coinciding with it, if the mind, by definition, eludes the 'outside spectator' and can be recognized only from within, my *cogito* is necessarily unique, and cannot be 'shared in' by another. . . . Unless I learn within myself to recognize the junction of the *for itself* and the *in itself,* none of these mechanisms called other bodies will ever be able to come to life; unless I have an exterior others

have no interior. The plurality of consciousness is impossible if I have an absolute consciousness of myself. . . . If it is perfect, the contact of my thought with itself seals me within myself, and prevents me from ever feeling that anything eludes my grasp . . . (PP 427–28/373; cf. Chapter III.2)

But Merleau-Ponty stresses that subjectivity is not "motionless identity with itself"; rather, it is essential to subjectivity to open itself to an other and "to go forth from itself" (PP 487/426). As he tells us, it is precisely my own experience as such that makes me open for what I am not, be it the world or the other (SNS 164–65/94). Subjectivity is not hermetically sealed up within itself, remote from the world and inaccessible to the other. Instead, it is above all a relation to the world, and Merleau-Ponty accordingly writes that openness toward others is secured the moment that I define both myself and the other as respective relations to the world, relations that coexist within a common system (VI 114/82; Merleau-Ponty 1960, 30/PrP 118). For the subject in each case is not a being that is enclosed in its own immanence; rather, it is open to the world, and this is exactly why it can also be open to the other. In other words, I am never so utterly self-contained that the other is completely alien and inaccessible to me. Instead, it is because I am beyond myself from the beginning—because I am always already other to myself—that I can encounter the other (VI 74/49; S 215/170).

This being-beyond-oneself, which is so very central in making intersubjectivity possible, is particularly accentuated in Merleau-Ponty's analyses of *temporality* and *corporeality*. Like Husserl and Heidegger, Merleau-Ponty understands the temporality of the subject as a movement of transcendence that ruptures absolute self-transparency and self-presence from the very beginning. This also comes to expression in the reflective relationship to oneself, for on account of temporal extension, there is, as Merleau-Ponty says, a "thickness of duration" interposed between the reflecting I and the I that is reflected upon, thereby making their identity problematic (PP 397/344). Merleau-Ponty further characterizes the subject's corporeality as a third mode of being between that of a pure subject and that of a pure object—a mode that "liberates" the subject from its purity and transparence (PP 402/350) and thereby makes the openness toward the other possible: "The possibility of another person's being self-evident is owed to the fact that I am not transparent for myself, and that my subjectivity draws its body in its wake" (PP 405/352). As Merleau-Ponty writes, intersubjectivity offers no difficulties once we first grasp the subject as "existence," i.e., as an *incarnate* being-toward-the-world (PP 403–404/351; PM 192/138). If the perceptual subject is always already situated; always directly inserted, by virtue of being born, into an intersubjective nexus of sense; and always already transcending—endowed with a structure that refers to the world and characterized by a constant being-beyond-oneself—then coexistence is thinkable, for then the other too would be experienceable in her being-beyond-oneself, in her corporeality (PP 403/350–51, 413/360, 427/373; S 140/112). We experience one another in the course of our active life within the world that we hold in common, and I can experience an other because the other is behaving in a way that is also a possible way for me to relate to the world (PM 198/142). But if I can understand the existence of the other on the basis of my own body, it is because the "I can" and the "the other exists" already belong to the same world. Hence Merleau-Ponty characterizes one's own body as a presentiment of the other, and experience of others as an echo of our own bodily composition (S 221/175), pointing to the correlation that obtains between my consciousness of my own body and my experience of others. In both cases what is at stake is the experience of incarnation (Merleau-Ponty 1960, 35/PrP 123). I am given to myself "as a certain hold upon the world," and it is my body that perceives the body of the other, finding in this body something like "a miraculous prolongation of my own intentions, a familiar way of dealing with the world" (PP 406/354). Thus by virtue of their structural similarity, the foreign body and my own body form a single whole, an *intercorporeity* (S 213/168).

Merleau-Ponty now attempts to confirm and extend these reflections through analyses of perceptual experience and of the structure of the sensuous world. That is to say, once we first understand the world as an intersubjective field of experience, understanding the possibility of intersubjectivity will be far easier.

I experience the world as being real for any subject who shares my situation with me (PP 464–65/405–406; Merleau-Ponty 1947, 124–25/PrP 17–18; PM 189/136). Hence the world is not only experienced as my world, as the correlate of my own consciousness, but is also experienced as the correlate of any consciousness I may ever encounter (PP 390/338; S 216/171). If I enter into conversation with someone else, I am not conversing with "a flow of private sensations indirectly related to mine through the medium of interposed signs"; rather, I am speaking with someone who "has a living experience of the same world as mine," who is present together with me in this world, and "with whom I am in communication through that world" (PP 464/405). Hence it is not the case that each of us has her own private world. Instead, if I were over there where the other is, then I would experience what the other experiences; conversely, the other would experience what I experience if she were here at this moment. Thus my own perspective on the world does not have determinate boundaries, but spontaneously slips into and overlaps that of the other (VI 187/142, 89/61; PP 406/353). This observation eventually leads Merleau-Ponty to the insight that it is the openness of the subject toward the world—an openness that represents a dispossession rather than a taking possession—that leaves room for the other, holding open a place for the other within the subject's own horizonal structure of presence and absence. That is to say, I have no perceptual monopoly on being; rather, the objects only display themselves to me partially and thus have a right to "many other witnesses besides me" (S 215/170, 22–23/15–16). In other words, both the transcendence and the inexhaustible richness of the perceptual object bear witness to its intersubjective ontic validity and its openness with regard to other perceiving subjects (VI 188/143). Since the appearing object already leaves open the possibility of also being there for others (whether or not such others do in fact show up), it refers to others, and for that reason it is intersubjective.

Hence according to Merleau-Ponty, a phenomenological description does not disclose subjectivities that are inaccessible and self-sufficient but reveals a continuity between intersubjective life and the world. The subject is an "intersubjective field" that realizes itself in its presence to the world and to others—not in spite of, but precisely *by way of* its corporeality and historicity (PP 515/452):

> There is therefore no occasion to ask ourselves why the thinking subject or consciousness perceives itself as a man, or an incarnate or historical subject, nor must we treat this apperception as a second order operation which it somehow performs starting from its absolute existence: the absolute flow takes shape beneath its own gaze as '*a* consciousness', or a man, or an incarnate subject, because it is a field of presence—to itself, to others

and to the world—and because this presence throws it into the
natural and cultural world from which it arrives at an understanding of itself. (PP 515/451)

As we can already see, Merleau-Ponty's position is not in agreement
with Sartre's description of being-for-the-other. One of Merleau-
Ponty's basic insights is that I can only have an experience of the other
if I am already a possible other in my own relation to myself, i.e., if I can
appear to myself as an other. "If the other people who empirically exist
are to be, for me, other people, I must have a means of recognizing
them," and the structure of being-for-the-other must therefore already
belong to the dimension of being-for-oneself (PP 511/448). Thus the
other is not a mere fact, but a possibility of my own being. And in reality,
"the mystery of the other is nothing but the mystery of myself," precisely
since it is only possible to understand the experience of the other—of
the one who is foreign to me—when it is understood that I am foreign
to myself (PM 188/135). Hence my encounter with the other is predelineated in my encounter with myself as an object, for then I am already
an other to myself. If I perceive a part of my own body in an objectifying
way, then I am perceiving myself in my being for-others—and it is within
the horizon of this experience that the other appears to me as well (VI
278/225; PM 186/134). Moreover, not only am I able to experience myself, but I can also be experienced by the other. To put it another way,
in my corporeal existence I am intersubjective and social from the start;
the concrete encounter with the other is not experienced as an alienation, as Sartre claims, but only makes it clear that I was *always already open
for this.*

Thus instead of seeing the basis for my objectification in the
other, as Sartre does, Merleau-Ponty emphasizes, first, that the look of
the other can only objectify me when I experience the other, and for
that reason, my objectification does not take place entirely without my
help. Second, however, he points out that the other can only look at
me because I am visible, i.e., because we are both inhabitants of the
same world. Consequently, we are not at all two incompatible nihila-
tions but already find ourselves—prior to any deliberate adoption of
a position—situated within an intersubjective world, and any struggle
or conflict would be impossible and unthinkable if there were not already a common ground and a peaceful coexistence (PP 408/355; cf.
VI 114-15/82-83, 298/244-45). Thus the other-as-object is merely an

inauthentic modality of the other, and my objectification by the look of the other is only painful and unpleasant because it takes the place of a possible and more natural communication. Sartre's error therefore lay in failing to pursue his analyses of being-for-the-other far enough to reveal the primordial intersubjectivity that makes alienation, conflict, and objectification possible. Hence like our relation to the world as a whole, our relation to the social is a constant dimension of existence: "I may well turn away from it, but not cease to be situated relatively to it" (PP 415/362).

Merleau-Ponty now ultimately understands the problem of the social as a special case of the general problem of transcendence, just as he also sees the problem of my relation to others and the problem of my relation to things as a single basic problem (VI 115–16/83). (Thus he does not attribute any particular constitutive or world-opening function to the transcendence and inaccessibility of the other, which is perhaps the greatest weakness of his theory. That is to say, Merleau-Ponty lays such enormous stress on the presence of alterity that one occasionally gets the impression that there is no decisive difference between my relationship to myself, my relationship to the world, and my relationship to the other.) The decisive question (a question pertaining to any constitution) is therefore how I can be open to phenomena that transcend me, yet at the same time "exist only to the extent that I take them up and live them" (PP 417/363). And this is not merely a question that reveals Merleau-Ponty's understanding of the concept of constitution (cf. Chapter V, note 12); it is a question whose solution is already announced in *Phenomenology of Perception* when he writes that the solution to all problems of transcendence lies in the pre-objective present (PP 495/422). It is accordingly a matter of tracing out the relation between me, the other, and the world at the most fundamental level of experience. For if we begin with an initial situation in which the distinction between these three elements has already crystallized, so that I and the others are already furnished with a (supposedly) fixed self-identity, then we have lost the possibility of understanding intersubjectivity. Thus it is worth going back to "the social with which we are in contact by the mere fact of existing," already prior to any objectification (PP 415/362).

This is exactly what Merleau-Ponty attempts to do through analyses drawn from theoretical accounts of perception and from developmental psychology. Hence he claims that acts of perceiving have a pre-personal

or pre-egological structure that is characterized by a fundamental anonymity. That is to say, every perception takes place in an atmosphere of
generality; it remains, as he says, "in the mode of the impersonal 'One'"
(PP 277/240; cf. 249/215).[23] It is not truly *I* who perceive; rather, perception "happens" and something "is perceived." Consequently, perception includes a moment of depersonalization, and insofar as the
perceptual subject is permeated by this anonymity (PP 408/356), the experience of others (the access to the other) presents no problem. There
is no problem of the *alter ego,* because it is neither I nor the other who perceives, but an "anonymous visibility" that inhabits us both (VI 187/142).
It is only if I forget that I belong to a common perceptual field and "reduce myself to what reflection will make of me" that the experience of
others becomes problematic (S 221/175).

Merleau-Ponty arrives at similar results in his studies of child psychology; as he says, the experience of others and the experience of the
intersubjective world are only a problem for adults (PP 407/355).
Thus he claims that at the first developmental stage, we cannot speak
either of the child's self-experience or of the child's experience of
others, even saying that at this stage there is a common, anonymous
life without differentiation. To be sure, there is also no real communication, for communication presupposes a distinction between the
subjects. Merleau-Ponty nevertheless speaks, with Scheler, of an original state of corporeal *pre-communication* (Merleau-Ponty 1960, 32–33/
PrP 119; cf. PP 406/354).[24]

Merleau-Ponty is well aware of the danger of this solution. It is
burdened with the same problem as Fink's assumption of a primal life
prior to the distinction between *ego* and *alter ego,* i.e., a primal life that
is the basis for the subsequent emergence of a plurality of subjects. If
the perceiving subject is anonymous, the perceived subject is likewise
anonymous. Merleau-Ponty consequently concedes that the attempt
to bring a plurality of consciousnesses out of this single collective consciousness runs up against difficulties (PP 408–409/356). As we also
saw in conjunction with Sartre, we must hold fast to the distinction between an anonymous collective consciousness and a pluralistic intersubjectivity (SNS 157/90; Merleau-Ponty 1947, 125/PrP 17). Hence it
is not a matter of advocating (as Scheler had done, in Merleau-Ponty's
opinion)[25] a panpsychism that destroys the distinction between I and
other in order to make the experience of others possible (Merleau-
Ponty 1988, 42–44/Merleau-Ponty 1973b, 46–48; S 220–21/174–75).

However, there is a distinction between a theory that denies or cancels the subject's individuality and a theory that introduces something impersonal into the heart of subjectivity. And as Merleau-Ponty writes in *Phenomenology of Perception,* solitude and communication, individuality and generality, are not two possible conceptions of the subject between which philosophy has to choose, but rather two moments of a unique structure that is the concrete subject itself (PP 412/359, 514/450–51).[26] Thus an emphasis on the solitude and individuality of the subject remains justified despite the existence of a fundamental sociality. And Merleau-Ponty even speaks in this connection of a *lived solipsism* that remains insurmountable (PP 411/358, 413/360). That is to say, I can never live the presence of an other in the way in which the other lives this presence, i.e., I can never experience the other in the same way in which I experience myself and the other in turn experiences herself (VI 89/61). The other's sorrow is a situation that the other lives through; for me, it is merely appresented. Even if the self-awareness of thought is incorporated into a pre-thetic and pre-reflective life, this does not cancel the distinction between subjects that makes intersubjectivity a true inter-subjectivity.

The last aspect of Merleau-Ponty's analysis of intersubjectivity that we want to mention briefly here has to do with his observations concerning the intersubjective character of language. For as he maintains, in a way that anticipates Apel's argument (see Chapter VII.2), it is indeed possible to construct a solipsistic philosophy. But in so doing, one presupposes a linguistic community that one is addressing. Thus one is never speaking for oneself alone, but for all (PP 414/360; VI 111/79), and it is for this reason that the formulation of the thesis of solipsism implies a performative contradiction.

If one observes *dialogue* in more detail, it turns out that it furnishes a common ground between me and the other — that in its own peculiar way, it recapitulates the corporeal-perceptual coexistence at a higher level. That is to say, both my own words and those of my partner in the conversation are called forth from us by the state of the discussion, and are moments in a joint venture of which neither of us is the author. The objection raised by my partner "draws from me thoughts which I had no idea I possessed, so that at the same time that I lend him thoughts, he reciprocates by making me think too"; we are collaborators, and our perspectives "merge into each other," forming "a single fabric" (PP 407/354). Insofar as the other's words call forth foreign thoughts within me (VI 277–78/224), what I experience when I speak or understand is the presence of the other within me, or my own presence within the other. When I speak, I am an other to myself, and when I understand, "I no longer know who is speaking and who is listening" (S 121/97).[27] Thus what we run into once again in the case of language is a shared anonymity. Things are articulated by a speech that is not the work of any of us, by a speech that we are not the master of, but are mastered by (S 27/19; SNS 154/88). According to Merleau-Ponty, it is against this background that the sense of Husserl's statement that transcendental subjectivity is intersubjectivity can finally be understood (S 121/97; PM 202/145).[28]

Can we say in conclusion something more detailed about transcendental intersubjectivity? On more than one occasion, Merleau-Ponty has referred with approval to Husserl's intersubjective transformation of transcendental philosophy (see, e.g., S 121/97; PP 415/361; SNS 237/134). And he writes that being does not display itself somewhere "before me," in front of me, but rather at the intersection of my perspectives and those of the other; the sensible world and the historical world are "intermundane spaces" *(intermondes)*. For as a relation to the world, my own life is, as we have seen, always enveloped in an atmosphere provided by meaning held in common and by a common history—an atmosphere that makes this very life possible (VI 116–17/84). Hence according to Merleau-Ponty, "only the philosophical consciousness of intersubjectivity enables us to understand scientific knowledge" (S 140/111), and the incorporation of intersubjectivity ultimately replaces dogmatic objectivism with an appropriate phenomenological account according to which the concepts of "truth" and "reality" are understood in correlation to a community of subjects (RC 121/87).

As we have indicated, Merleau-Ponty also critically addressed earlier phenomenological accounts, and in distinction to Heidegger and Sartre, he rates Husserl's analyses surprisingly positively. Thus of the three phenomenologists considered in this chapter, he was the only one to have taken Husserl's phenomenology of intersubjectivity seriously— perhaps because out of the three of them, he was the most familiar with Husserl's late research manuscripts.[29] In any case, his view is undoubtedly the one that most resembles Husserl's; moreover, Merleau-Ponty too grasped the far-reaching and radical consequences of the turn to transcendental intersubjectivity:

Now if the transcendental is intersubjectivity, how can the borders of the transcendental and the empirical help becoming indistinct? For along with the other person, all the other person sees of me—all my facticity—is reintegrated into subjectivity, or at least posited as an indispensable element of its definition. Thus the transcendental descends into history. Or as we might put it, the historical is no longer an external relation between two or more absolutely autonomous subjects but has an interior and is an inherent aspect of their very definition. They no longer know themselves to be subjects simply in relation to their individual selves, but in relation to one another as well. (S 134/107)

Interestingly, Merleau-Ponty was of the opinion that Husserl attempted to integrate historicity and temporality into his philosophy much more decisively and radically than was the case with Heidegger, in part because he sees Husserl as trying to overcome the strict separation between ontic investigation and ontological investigation (Merleau-Ponty 1988, 421-22/PiP 93-94)—an interpretation that fits particularly well with our analyses in Chapters IV and V.

Although Merleau-Ponty has contributed to the phenomenological discussion of intersubjectivity with an entire series of striking analyses devoted to particular themes (here we could give special prominence to his discussions of incarnation, perception, and speech), his most decisive contribution nevertheless seems to consist in bringing to light the interconnection between intra-subjective and inter-subjective alterity. In other words, what is crucial is his emphasis on the importance that the rupture in self-coincidence has for the possibility of intersubjectivity: I can only encounter the other if I am beyond myself from the very beginning; thus I can only experience the other if I am already a possible other in relation to myself, and could always appear to myself as an other. Although one can already find inceptions along these lines in Husserl, Merleau-Ponty pursued these key ideas with unsurpassable emphasis.

VI.5. I, WE, AND WORLD: A SYSTEMATIC SUMMARY

In our presentation so far, we have attempted to substantiate the thesis that one can speak of a transcendental phenomenological treatment of intersubjectivity—of an incorporation of intersubjectivity into that which can legitimately be termed transcendental. Before we turn to our critical engagement with the pragmatics of language, let us offer a brief systematic, topical summary of our results. This summary will simultaneously enable us to respond to the question posed earlier. Is it the transcendence or alterity of the other, or is it the anonymous being-with-others that is of constitutive significance?

A central result of our analysis has been to establish that a treatment of intersubjectivity simultaneously requires an analysis of subjectivity and of the world. One cannot accommodate intersubjectivity within a fixed dualism between subject and world; rather, all three belong together—they reciprocally illuminate one another and can only be understood in their interconnection. It doesn't matter which of the three we take as a starting point, for we will inevitably be led to the other two: the subjectivity that is related to the world gains its full relation to itself, and to the world, only in relation to the other, i.e., in inter-subjectivity; intersubjectivity exists and develops only in the mutual interrelationship between subjects that are related to the world; and the world is realized only in the inter-subjective intermundane space *(intermonde, Zwischenraum)*.

In what follows, we shall attempt to set forth the ways in which intersubjectivity appears within the relationship of the subject to itself and to the world in each of the three levels that we have brought to light in our interpretation of Husserl.

1.1) In order to understand how it is *possible* for the subject to encounter and relate to the other and the world, we must first understand that the subject is neither a static self-identity nor a self-enclosed self-reference; rather, it is essential to the subject to be able to open up to an other (be this an object or a fellow subject).The subject is never so self-contained that the subject is closed off from the foreign, but is beyond itself from the beginning, and it is for this reason that the subject can also be open for the other and for the world.

This transcendence of the subject is most fundamentally expressed in its temporality. Within the streaming present, there is no stillpoint of self-presence; rather, each moment, each present instant, bears absence within itself. Self-temporalization is an original being-beyond-oneself, an ecstatic self-splitting and a constant self-alienation and de-presentation that ruptures self-coincidence and makes the openness toward the foreign possible. To put it another way, it is the intra-subjective alterity that makes the experience of inter-subjective alterity possible.

Being-beyond-oneself also comes to expression when one's relation to oneself becomes thematic. In reflective self-consciousness, I am never wholly one with myself; rather, temporality drives a wedge between myself as subject and myself as object. That I in principle can apprehend myself as an object (and can always do so) is indicated by my self-alienation. That is to say, as an object, I am other to myself. Thus my relationship to the other is not some external relation but it concerns my own being as a subject. I exist for others, even when I am merely reflecting upon myself. (Of course, this does not preclude a pre-reflective self-acquaintance; on the contrary, such pre-reflective self-acquaintance must already be in play in order for any talk of *self-alienation* to be meaningful.)

That my objectifying relationship to myself is indicative of my own alterity can also be seen in my corporeality. When I observe a part of my own body, I perceive myself in my being-for-others. Just as I experience myself, so also can I be experienced by others. Hence what is manifested in my corporeality is precisely the external dimension of my subjectivity.

However, it is not only my relation to myself, but also my relation to the world that leaves room for the other. My horizon intentionality contains structural references to perceptions carried out by possible others. No appearing object is thinkable in principle without the horizon of what is co-meant, and what this horizonal co-presence of non-given aspects refers to is precisely open intersubjectivity. Thus my being as a relation to the world is intimately linked with my openness to others. I am directed toward objects whose horizonal givenness and transcendence testify to their openness to other subjects. They are not exhausted in their appearance for me and do not exist solely for me. Rather, there are always alternative perspectives; there are always co-meant aspects that could be perceived by other subjects. Since in its constant mixture of presence and absence, the appearing object always leaves open the possibility for others to be there too, then whether or not such others do in fact appear, the object itself refers to others, and for this reason it is intrinsically intersubjective.

Up to this point, the role of intersubjectivity has been described merely formally. The structure of the subject is such that, first, a relation to the other is not excluded a priori, and second, the relation to the other—or to possible others—is always already there as a permanent possibility. But what consequences does the concrete encounter with a factual other have?

1.2) If I have a concrete experience of an embodied foreign I who experiences the objects that I experience, and if I experience that the other experiences me as well, then both my experience of objects and my experience of myself are altered.

When I discover that the object I am experiencing is also accessible to the other—that the object offers and discloses, to others, aspects of its being that are inaccessible to me (at the moment)—then my own relationship to the object undergoes a shift. When I experience that it can also be experienced by others, the object withdraws from me, tears itself away from me, and is no longer exhausted in being an object-for-me. Thanks to the other, the object is constituted with a validity that endows it with an independence vis-à-vis my own experience. Thus my experience of the object's intersubjective experienceability convinces me of its transcendence.

My differentiation of the merely subjective (the hallucinatory) and the objective is therefore made possible by *concrete* intersubjectivity, by my *factual* encounter with the other. My constitution of the validity category of *objectivity* or *reality* is mediated by the fact that I experience such objectivity by way of the other, and it is this alone that makes it possible to cash in these validities intuitively. Such a category is intersubjectively constituted and can only be constituted by a subject who experiences other subjects.

However, my concrete encounter with the other does not only bring about a change in my experience of objects; my experience of myself is correspondingly changed as well. When I experience that my counterpart is directed toward me, then my experience of myself is mediated by the other, and, ultimately, I experience myself as the other experiences me—as someone foreign. I am led to the insight that I am an *alter ego* for the other, as the other is for me; I am one among others. The other objectifies and mundanizes me, and as a result, my existence is put on a par with that of all others.

But although the other mundanizes me (whereas self-reflection only objectivates me—15/289), it would be a misunderstanding to believe that it is exclusively my status as an object in the world that I achieve by way of the other. Even aspects of my subjectivity are first constituted by way of the other, for it is only in the I-Thou relation, when I enter into social relations with other subjects, that I acquire my consciousness of myself as a person.

1.3) Finally, in addition to the a priori intersubjectivity that is active in the horizonal structure and to the concrete experience of others that is directly linked with the shift in our categories of validity, there is a type of intersubjectivity that is founded in the latter, although distinct from it and irreducible to it—a type of intersubjectivity that is effective at the level of handed down normality and that is of constitutive significance as the realm of anonymous publicness.

As an incarnate subject, I am always already situated, already inserted—by virtue of my birth—directly into an intersubjective, historical nexus of sense. And as an educated person, I am a member of a historical community, learning from others what counts as "normal" and thereby, as a communalized subject, participating in an intersubjective tradition.

Hence I find myself in a historical-cultural world that is already provided with sense furnished by others and that constantly refers to these others. Every cultural object has been produced by someone and for someone, and when I make use of it, what I am doing has always already been prescribed in advance by others.

Moreover, as a communalized and educated cultural-historical subject, I am endowed with language, and exactly here am I intersubjective in an eminent way. First, I am continually making use of thoughts foreign to me, and both my self- and my world-understanding are guided by an anonymous inherited sense-history. Second, in speaking I turn toward others and coexist in dialogue with them.

Thus I understand the world—and through it, myself—by virtue of a handed down linguistic conventionality. It is therefore not only the transcendence and foreignness of the other that would seem to be of constitutive importance; the commonality of the "us" and the "we"—i.e., the horizonal (linguistic) being-with-one-another in the averageness of normality and the everyday—is, as the operative basis for agreement, a condition of possibility for the constitution of the historical world.

2) We can now recognize that the presentation thus far has made it possible to answer the question posed earlier—namely, is it the transcendence of the other or the replaceability of the other that has constitutive implications? In contrast to Sartre (cf. Chapter VI.3), we should want to claim that both of these characteristics are indispensable—

i.e., instead of excluding one another, they complement each other—and that a satisfactory theory of intersubjectivity must therefore allow for and embrace both of them.

Furthermore, we can now see that while Sartre has denied the existence of the first level of intersubjectivity and misunderstood the implications of the second and third levels, Heidegger has confused the first and third levels and neglected the second level of intersubjectivity, i.e., that which is accomplished by means of the transcendence of the other. In contrast, Husserl escapes both types of one-sidedness because he approaches the relation to others in terms of all three of these strata. That he assigns constitutive significance to the transcendence of the other does not need to be repeated here. At the same time, however, his analysis of *normality* allows him to disclose an average and everyday community that as a realm of public being-with-one-another is itself of constitutive significance. Thus Husserl in no way contests the importance of agreement and consensus, but treats them thematically in his analysis. And it is characteristic of his reflections that, on the whole, he rates the constitutive contribution of the other or of others more positively than do either Sartre or Heidegger, who have both ignored the genuinely horizon-opening aspect of being-with-one-another. That is to say, although Husserl is not blind to the objectifying, mundanizing, and "concealing" character of intersubjectivity, at the same time, he does indeed claim that both subjectivity and world can only fully be realized through the contribution of the other.

In our analysis of the further development of the phenomenological theory of intersubjectivity in the work of Heidegger, Sartre, and Merleau-Ponty, we have attempted to give special prominence to the elements that can systematically complement Husserl's theory. Hence it has not been a matter of comparing the positions of the later phenomenologists with that of Husserl in order to set forth the latter's strength, and we shall forgo any further such defense of Husserl here as well. However, on the basis of our analyses so far, the following remark would seem to be appropriate.

And that is to point to the exemplary caution and reserve that characterize Husserl's analyses. Although Heidegger, Sartre, and Merleau-Ponty must be praised in general for the clarity and directness of their analyses—analyses that often lead to the same results that Husserl reaches only after many laborious studies delving into the most minute details—this directness also has its price, for something is lost by it. When one cuts the Gordian knot instead of untying it, one loses the chance of becoming intimately acquainted with the rope. And it is precisely because Husserl always hesitated, rather than falling prey to hasty decision or choosing some easy solution, that he never underestimated the difficulties and complexities of this field of problems, but rather devoted an attention to them that is truly worthy of the founder of phenomenology. For this reason Husserl's phenomenology of intersubjectivity is characterized throughout by a greater range and systematic complexity than the analyses of his followers. Or to put it another way, this is exactly why we have been able to establish that the decisive contributions of Heidegger, Sartre, and Merleau-Ponty have seldom consisted in revealing entirely new dimensions of the problem of intersubjectivity—for, as a rule Husserl has anticipated them—but have consisted in the further development of existing dimensions and in shifts of accent or emphasis that wind up clarifying the problem itself. Of course, this should not be understood as denying the worth of these later thinkers' contributions, for there is naturally a decisive difference between an initial rough understanding that lays out a structure, and a thematic elaboration that works it all out.

3) Instead of highlighting further differences, then, let us briefly point once more in conclusion to the homogeneity, in method and in results, of the specifically phenomenological treatment of intersubjectivity.

First, we have established that intersubjectivity is never conceived as an autonomous structure or relation in the world that is to be observed from the outside. Intersubjectivity is a relation between subjects, which is why the point of departure for a phenomenological treatment of this theme must be an investigation of a subject that is related to the world and to others. In other words, it is precisely a careful analysis of such a subject's ontological composition and its structures of experience that can reveal the fundamental significance of intersubjectivity. But it also follows from this that intersubjectivity can by no means be understood as a category that transcends subjectivity. The turn to intersubjectivity in no way serves to refute a philosophy of the subject; on the contrary, it makes a genuine understanding of such a philosophy possible for the very first time.

Second, it should also have become clear that the intersubjective character of the subject can in no way be understood as a contingent feature (once we disregard Sartre's problematic and ultimately contradictory conception). It does not arise only at the moment when a factual and concrete encounter between a number of subjects first exists, but is (at least in part) a matter of an a priori determination.

Third, it is characteristic of the phenomenological analyses that we have presented that without ever denying the eminently intersubjective character of language in any way, they have chiefly (if not exclusively) endeavored to demonstrate the role of intersubjectivity in the pre- or extra-linguistic structures of subjective experience—be it in simple perception or tool-use, in emotions and drives, or in temporality, corporeality, or self-awareness.

CHAPTER VII

Phenomenology and
the Pragmatics of Language

VII.1. THE LINGUISTIC-PRAGMATIC CHALLENGE

We have shown in detail how a transcendental significance is ascribed to intersubjectivity within phenomenology, specifying how we can speak of a phenomenology of transcendental intersubjectivity or of an intersubjective transcendental phenomenology. We wish to conclude our work with a discussion of the current relevance of the phenomenological treatment of intersubjectivity. We have chosen to focus on Apel and Habermas because they are prominent representatives of a contemporary non-phenomenological approach to intersubjectivity. Moreover, it is chiefly through their works that the idea of the real necessity of an intersubjective transformation of transcendental philosophy (and in recent years, of an already accomplished—and irreversible—paradigm shift as well) has become widespread. That is to say, both Apel and Habermas have criticized the classical, "monological" or "methodologically solipsistic" mode of thought from a *linguistic-pragmatic* point of view. Hence in this chapter we shall present the basic features of their critique of the traditional philosophy of consciousness, along with their arguments for an intersubjective paradigm shift.

Although strictly speaking, Apel and Habermas advocate two different philosophical positions (Apel characterizes his position as a *transcendental pragmatism,* while Habermas occasionally speaks of his position as a *universal pragmatism*),[1] their arguments for the necessity of an intersubjective paradigm shift are quite similar, and it is this commonality that will be analyzed in what follows. However, certain elements of their own positions must be omitted in this context. This is true for

Apel's deliberations on an ultimate reflective grounding; for the theory of discourse ethics worked out by both thinkers (which Apel sees as a direct consequence of his intersubjective transcendental pragmatics — TP II 357); and for the complex theory of communication developed by Habermas. (In fact, in Habermas's own opinion, the latter ought to be seen in any case as the foundation for a critical *social theory,* rather than as a contribution to a philosophical discussion of foundations — TCA I xxxix, xli; cf. PDM 76).[2]

Among Apel's writings, we are mainly concerned with *Toward a Transformation of Philosophy;* "The Question of Grounding: Philosophy and Transcendental Pragmatics of Language"; *Understanding and Explanation;* and *Diskurs und Verantwortung;* and among Habermas's writings *Knowledge and Human Interests; On the Logic of the Social Sciences; The Theory of Communicative Action; Vorstudien und Ergänzungen zur Theorie des kommunikativen Handelns; Postmetaphysical Thinking;* and *The Philosophical Discourse of Modernity.* Additional works will be cited as needed.

VII.2. APEL'S FUNDAMENTAL THESES

According to Dallmayr (1978, 1), Apel's *Transformation der Philosophie I–II,* which includes essays from 1955 through 1972, can be read as a kind of position statement for contemporary thought. Thus we can turn to Apel's critique of the philosophy of consciousness, along with his plea for a new appraisal of intersubjectivity in terms of linguistic philosophy, for an articulation of the paradigm shift that has taken place in the 20th century.

To a great extent, Apel's reflections can be understood as an ongoing discussion with the tradition. His observations about the need for an intersubjective transformation of transcendental philosophy rest principally on two accounts — on the later Wittgenstein's conception of language games, and on the concept that Peirce developed of the infinite interpretative community (TrP 139). And these observations are unfolded in conjunction with an explicit critique of classic transcendental philosophy (or philosophy of consciousness) and of its three main representatives: Descartes, Kant, and Husserl.

Apel's critique is by no means formulated from the standpoint of a relativism, objectivism, or naturalism. Rather, Apel repeatedly emphasizes that what is at stake for him is a *transformation* or *renewal* of transcendental philosophy. The transcendental philosophical manner of inquiry should not at all be abandoned; Kant's question concerning the transcendental conditions of possibility and validity for science must still be answered (TrP 136). What Apel advocates, however, is the thesis that the answer to this question today must be guided by insights into the transcendental status of language and thus of the linguistic community. Transcendental philosophy must accordingly undergo a linguistic-philosophical or linguistic-pragmatic transformation, for according to Apel, the account provided by the classic philosophy of consciousness miscarries because of a series of aporetic assumptions—chiefly because of its *methodological solipsism,* which Apel understands as the final consequence of the Cartesian metaphysics of subject and object (TP II 83). For him, such solipsism simply consists in the claim that the possibility and validity of knowledge can in principle be understood without the transcendental-logical presupposition of a communicative community, i.e., it is understood as the constitutive accomplishment of an individual consciousness (TrP 287 n. 6).[3]

We shall be returning to Apel's concept of the communicative community shortly. First, however, we shall point out his main linguistic-philosophical arguments against methodological solipsism.

In Apel's view, it is language, understood in the most universal sense, that is the condition of possibility for intersubjectively valid experience (TP I 311)—a thesis principally upheld by two arguments. First, Apel stresses the distinction between private evidence given to consciousness and intersubjectively valid, linguistically formulated arguments (QG 83). Second, he claims that a single individual cannot recognize something *as* something without already being a participant in an intersubjective process of linguistic communication and understanding (TP I 59-60).

1) The background to Apel's claim that the pre-linguistic and pre-communicative evidence given to consciousness cannot sufficiently ground linguistically conditioned, intersubjective validity (DV 97) must ultimately be sought in his appeal to Wittgenstein: namely, Apel claims that the solipsistic position can be definitively refuted by proving that the assumption of a *private language* is nonsensical (TP I 326).[4] That is to say, if this were a meaningful assumption—if it were possible for a single individual alone to follow a rule, exclusively on the basis of the evidence given to her own consciousness and without the possibility of intersubjective verification—then the question concerning the criteria

for validity could no longer be answered (TrP 158). For how could evident convictions be put in question or criticized at all (QG 82)? Hence Apel does not merely want to claim that the subject lacks any guarantee that her own private evidence of truth is intersubjectively valid. Rather, he is insisting that it cannot even meaningfully be claimed that a lone subject could privately possess any evidence what-soever of *truth:*

> Anyone who wished to introduce a language for empirical data accessible only to himself (e.g. pains) that was intelligible only to himself (one not consistently connected with standard usage and consequently untranslatable) would not possess any criteria for the correct use of language. He would be unable to distinguish between the arbitrary and the norm, since every operative norm which provides criteria for such distinctions is dependent, among other things, upon the fact that other people can check whether the norm is being followed. (TrP 32)

One can only meaningfully speak of following a rule on the basis of a public language game within which "rule-following can, *in principle,* be checked by every participant by virtue of publicly available criteria" (TrP 197). For this reason the problem of the validity of truth can no longer be seen as a problem of evidence given to a solitary consciousness—which would imply an unacceptable immunization against criticizability—but must primarily be seen as a problem of the intersubjective formation of consensus on the basis of linguistic (argumentative) communication and understanding (TP II 312). It is only because someone's "evidence for consciousness" can be mediated through "linguistic agreement" that it can count as valid, binding knowledge (TrP 137). As we know, the consequence of this view is that the subject can only identify and recognize his sensations and lived experiences as such by means of their connection to external criteria such as expressions and publicly valid words. The experiencer's lived experiences are comprehensible only when they are mediated by public language (TP I 266–67; TrP 12). Hence they are by no means unstructured private qualities, but are interwoven through and through with the structure of one's native language (TP I 122–23).

Although—seen empirically—each one thinks for herself alone, this thinking claims to have intersubjective validity—not only with respect to the truth of the thoughts, but even before this, with respect to their sense. That is to say, the thinker must be able in principle to share these thoughts with others, as linguistically articulated sense, and to that extent it is a matter of principle that no one can think alone (DV 199). Thus Apel claims that the very possibility of meaningful thinking is always already mediated by a *real* communicative community whose existence must still be logically presupposed even if the thinker is its last surviving representative (TP II 340, TrP 258). My own evidence must accordingly be confirmed by a communicative community, and this insight would be valid in principle even for the final solitary empirical human being: even this individual must presuppose 1) that there had indeed been a real communicative community and 2) that an unlimited ideal communicative community *would have to* be able to confirm her evidential insight (QG 92).

Thus in our terminology (see Chapter II.5), Apel seems to exclude not only the cognitive achievements of a *solipsistic* subject but also the cognitive achievements of a *solitary* subject, to the extent that he postulates the relation to a real—i.e., concrete—community as a necessary condition of possibility for sense and truth.

2) Apel's second main argument now consists in the thesis that the intersubjectively valid interpretability of the evidence of a given phenomenon is dependent upon the propositional sentence with which the state of affairs in question can be linguistically described. That is to say, if one abstracts from the linguistic a priori—and according to Apel, this means from any interpretation and explication of the phenomenon in question—one could indeed establish the sheer existence of the phenomenon perceptually, but could not establish its what-content by perception alone (Apel 1990a, 27–28). In other words, no one can recognize something *as* something without using linguistically mediated conceptual determinations, i.e., without already being a participant in an interpersonal process of linguistic agreement and understanding (TP I 59–60). One person alone cannot recognize something *as* something on the basis of the accomplishments of his own consciousness, since at the level of the subject-object relation, knowledge already presupposes the acquisition of language, the application of language, and the mediation of tradition that enables sense to be understood and communicated at the level of the subject-subject relation (TrP 111, 147–48; TP II 314). Apel therefore emphasizes that one is compelled in principle to bring all significative

intentions to explicit linguistic expression if the validity claim pertaining to the significative intention—its claim to being intersubjectively understandable—is going to be able to be cashed in. Thus insofar as the intersubjective *validity* of the signification is first constituted at the level of linguistic expressibility, and insofar as the intersubjective *comprehensibility* is dependent upon this linguistic expressibility, then there is a priority of linguistic *conventions* of signification over significative *intentions* (Apel 1990a, 31–32).

This position naturally evokes the question of language acquisition, i.e., of acquiring linguistic competence. Apel has also dealt with this, and he claims (in an explicit confrontation with Chomsky) that this competence—which is both a grammatical competence and a communicative competence—can be acquired only on the basis of an *internalization* of public linguistic norms within the process of socialization: only the disposition to acquire competence is innate (TrP 206). To be sure, Apel stresses that language acquisition is not a mere matter of being "trained" or "drilled" (TP II 323); rather, it is already a matter of an intersubjective process of communication. And as preconditions for this process of communication, he singles out innate dispositions such as the child's ability for pre-linguistic communication and interaction (TrP 211). However, despite the obvious necessity of ascribing certain competences to potential communicative participants, it is not necessary, according to Apel, to trace these back to an egological basis as the condition of possibility for learning a language and for being able to be socialized. That is to say, the child is not an "ego-subject" from the very beginning, but "first attains this ego-subjectivity" through "identification with a role which falls to it in the community of interaction and linguistic communication" (TrP 118-19). It is only in the socialization process itself that the acquisition of an ego-identity becomes possible through communication with others, and through the understanding of the "me" from the perspective of the others that such understanding implies (DV 446–47).

Against the background of these considerations, it is obvious that the attempt by the traditional philosophy of the subject—i.e., by methodological solipsism—to use radical self-investigation to "reflect" its way out of entanglement with language (and the form of life acquired with it) is not only factually impossible, but fundamentally nonsensical, since intentionality is conditioned and made possible a priori by the deep grammatical structure of language (TP II 314–15). It is interesting to notice that Apel explicitly turns against Husserl in this context, reproaching him for having ignored the linguistic, sociocultural, and historical conditions of sense-constitution by offering an account of constitution that traces it back to the intentional achievements of a solitary transcendental consciousness (Apel 1989b, 164). That is to say, the impossibility of a monologically (i.e., solipsistically) conceived transcendental philosophy would also show up in the failure of the epochē and of the reduction to the primordial, although Apel does not at all observe the distinction between them.[5] For if one conceptually suspends language and the life relations involved in it—relations that connect the ego not only to the external world but also to the social world *(Mitwelt)*, i.e., to the "Thou" and the others as potential communication partners—then the very sense of the "I think" will be suspended at the same time (UE 56–57; cf. QG 91). That is to say, the publicly understandable sense of the "I think" already presupposes the linguistic a priori and the communicative community (Apel 1979a, 40; 1974, 292). To put it another way, the methodological solipsist already presupposes a public language game even in stating the very arguments that are supposed to be valid for the solipsist himself (TP II 315). And according to Apel, it is for this reason that Husserl could never have brought the indubitability of his own I-consciousness to awareness in a form that was understandable and valid for him if he had not already formulated it linguistically (QG 92).

It should have become clear in the meantime that for Apel, the classic concept of transcendental philosophy must undergo a radical transformation inasmuch as it can no longer be grounded in a pre-linguistic and pre-communicative synthetic achievement performed by an individual. It is no longer possible to proceed from the transcendental I as the guarantee for the intersubjective validity of knowledge; rather, as intersubjectively valid, knowledge and world-constitution are always already linguistically mediated, and to this extent they are always already mediated by the synthesis established in public communication (UE 238–39).

As mentioned, Apel by no means wants to relegate the problematic of sense-constitution and the validity of knowledge to the realm of empirical psychology. Rather, he claims that this problematic must be thematized anew in accordance with the semiotic transformation of transcendental philosophy, i.e., it must be recast as a problem of the *formation of consensus* within the transcendental communicative community

(TP I 29–30). Instead of continuing to speak of the conditions of possibility or validity of representations, it is a matter of posing the Kantian question afresh as a question concerning the possibility of argumentation and of intersubjective communication about the sense and truth of propositions or systems of propositions, for the real achievement of 20th-century philosophy is "the insight into the transcendental importance of language and, thereby, of the language community" (TrP 136; cf. TrP 138 and TP II 163, 333).

It is against this background that Apel now introduces his concept of a transformed transcendental philosophy. For him, the "highest point" of transcendental reflection is no longer the "unity of consciousness of the object and self-consciousness" but the sought for intersubjective unity of interpretation (TP II 164; TrP 266–67). The transcendental synthesis of apperception is replaced by the agreement between language users, and the transcendental subject by a community of interpretation (TrP 87–88, 104). And this is why Apel can write that knowledge is not to be understood exclusively as a function of consciousness, but must primarily be understood as a real historical process of interpretation (TrP 104, 140).

Hence the agreement of other subjects is no longer to be regarded merely as a *criterion* for the correctness of our judgments (as Apel formulates it in allusion to Kant); rather, the possibility of forming a consensus belongs to the constitutive *conditions of possibility* of truth, and Apel therefore characterizes consensus as the ground and guarantee of the objectivity and truth of knowledge (TrP 104–105; UE 239). Hence the relation to the other is not a subject-object relation; rather it is a unique type of subject-subject relation that does not merely supplement the epistemological subject-object relation, but ultimately makes it possible (TP I 27; TrP 112–13).

Now one could naturally inquire how intersubjective agreement can ever serve as a guarantee of truth and as a foundation of validity, given, first of all, that there is no *one* universal agreement, but a plurality of agreements that mutually contradict one another, and second, that there are many intersubjective agreements that are factually false.

But Apel's view must be specified with more precision. First, in no way does Apel define reality, objectivity, and truth by calling on the notion of a factual consensus; rather, the consensus that is at stake here is a convergence of processes of interpretation within an unlimited, ideal community, and this convergence is to be postulated as normative (TrP 104-105). Thus he naturally does not proceed simply to define truth in terms of consensus, for only a sufficiently grounded or rational consensus (with rational consensus defined as a consensus reached through ideal discussion), and not a merely contingently reached consensus, can serve as a guarantee of truth. The claim that our sense-constitution has intersubjective validity can only be cashed in—if it can be cashed in at all—by the consensus of an unlimited, ideal community of communication and interpretation (Apel 1989b, 165; TrP 109-10):

> In place of Kant's metaphysically presupposed "consciousness as such" always already guaranteeing the intersubjective validity of knowledge, we now have the *regulative principle* of critical *consensus*-formation in an ideal communicative community that must first of all be established within the real communicative community. (TP II 354-55)

Second, Apel emphasizes that this *ideal* communicative community is "always already counterfactually anticipated" in every *real* community that "comes to an understanding about meaning and truth" (UE 239). This does not only mean that anyone involved in argumentation as such must necessarily presuppose the regulative ideal of an absolute truth arrived at by communication among members of an unlimited community of interpretation as a principle of recourse (TrP 79-80, 123). Rather, because the linguistic a priori is already postulated with every argument, every word, and every action that claims to be intelligible (TrP 140), there is already some factual agreement as well, a factual acknowledgment of pragmatic-semantic rules held in common, which not only make further agreement and dissent possible but can also serve as an irreducible ultimate grounding. That is to say, Apel claims that anyone who is arguing meaningfully has already implicitly acknowledged a number of transcendental epistemological presuppositions serving as norms of the transcendental language game (TrP 138). He therefore claims to have found an irreducible foundation, an "Archimedean point," for a transcendental-pragmatic ultimate grounding of philosophy (Apel 1989a, 51-52). That which cannot be denied without actual self-contradiction, and at the same time cannot be deductively grounded without a formal-logical *petitio principii,* must be counted among those transcendental-pragmatic presuppositions of argumentation that are always already acknowledged if the language game of argumentation is to retain its sense. Apel calls these transcendental-pragmatic modes of argumentation a sense-critical form of ultimate grounding (QG 90):

> With this, I think, we have reached—through *transcendental reflection* on the *conditions of possibility and validity for understanding* —something like a Cartesian point of *ultimate grounding* for philosophy. That is to say, anyone whatsoever who takes part in philosophical argumentation has already implicitly acknowledged the presuppositions just mentioned as the *a priori of argumentation,* and cannot contest them without simultaneously raising doubts about his own argumentative competence. (TP I 62; cf. QG 89–90)[6]

Thus although Apel has allowed himself to be guided in no small measure by Wittgenstein's conception of language games, and understands the language game in terms of a historically developed framework serving as the condition for the understanding of meaning, he does distance himself from its relativistic implications. It is of course true that transcendental philosophy is concretized in the concept of the language game (TrP 33); indeed, this is the case precisely because the language game mediates between the abstract alternatives of apriorism and empiricism (TP I 25; TrP 27; TP II 323). Hence we are referred both to the contingent condition of the convention-laden realization of intersubjectively valid significations in particular languages, and to the contingent condition of being a member of a historical community of language, culture, and tradition (DV 113).[7] However, it is a misunderstanding to believe that the various language games simply stand side by side like separate monads with no connection between them (TP I 174; TP II 350), which would make reciprocal communication impossible. Rather, there is a commonality to all language games—a commonality to which we gain access when we learn a language. Consequently, the competence both for reflection on one's own language and for communication with all other language games is also acquired in the process of socialization (TP II 347; TP I 247). Apel thus wants to sail between the "Scylla" of a "relativistic" hermeneutics that sacrifices its own conditions of possibility to the pluralism of monadic language games and the "Charybdis" of a "dogmatic-objectivistic" critique of the other, a critique that "no longer admits of any real discourse" (TrP 172). In other words, for him there is an a priori of language that is at the same time the guarantee for the possibility of intersubjective communication; the conditions of possibility for intercultural understanding are not merely certain similarities in such human situations as birth, death, sexuality, work, and conflict, but also certain transcendental-pragmatic universals (TrP 166-67). And Apel's point is exactly that the possibility of consensus itself is guaranteed by this transcendental language game (TP I 64).

In this connection, Apel alludes (as does Husserl) to the possibility of dissent, emphasizing that creative dissent is only possible within the framework of a consensus-forming discourse (DV 158-59). Dissent already presupposes communication, and in this sense it is privative. Thus it is a matter of utmost importance that the concept of consensus not be misunderstood as if it stood in service of some sort of repressive agenda whose goal is utter uniformity. Rather, as a principle of communicative understanding, the concept of consensus presents the condition of possibility for a maximal development of different, but equally legitimate, forms of life (DV 178).

At this point, let us note that Apel is operating with an ambiguous notion of consensus. On the one hand, there is the intersubjective unity of interpretation that is yet to be attained, but functions as an anticipated regulative ideal, and concerns, as it were, the *material* content of truth. On the other hand, there is the formal linguistic a priori that is always already recognized (including, according to Apel, not only a minimal logic but a minimal ethics—QG 93; TrP 144; TP II 357). And it is consensus in the latter sense of a linguistic a priori that is the irreducible condition of possibility for any intelligible argumentation.

Yet although Apel is completely convinced of the transcendental significance of language, he is simultaneously aware of the danger arising from simply identifying the transcendental subject with the logical form of language. That is to say, this strategy—which is to be found, in different versions, in both analytic philosophy of language and structuralism—attempts to replace the transcendental-pragmatic dimension of intersubjective communication with the establishment of an ideal, anonymous-objective system of linguistic symbols, so that it would be this alone that would permit, a priori, intersubjective meaning (TP I 242; TrP 11, 150-52, 186; TP II 314). But what Apel sees in this is a paradoxical elimination of the entire problem of subjectivity and of intersubjective communication (TP II 342). He writes that "the system of language—which at one and the same time bears the community and founds it—and the intersubjective validity of the rules for using this language" cannot be explained either by a "methodologically solipsistic" model, or by a "system" model that is assumed to be intersubjectively valid a priori in a way that is "completely independent from the communicative *use* of language" and from the subjective accomplishments of the user of language (TP II 344). It will not do to eliminate completely the entire subject-related, pragmatic dimension of language from the transcendental horizon of inquiry, treating it objectivistically as a region of empirical psychology in order to guarantee intersubjectivity through the logical form of language in a way that is entirely independent from communication and from the experiential interchange between the users of language. That is to say, it is unalterably necessary to incorporate the *pragmatic* dimension of language into linguistic analysis along with the *syntactic* and *semantic* dimensions, for it is necessary to take into account the *use* of language, the *interpretation* of signs—and thus ultimately the user and interpreter of language as well (TrP 78).

Hence intersubjectivity must not be brought into play as a merely postulated category of validity. Rather, despite his sharp critique of the philosophy of the subject, Apel holds fast to an intersubjectivity that is historically realized through communication and interaction (TrP 14); it is ultimately a unique relation *between language-using subjects.*

VII.3. HABERMAS'S CRITIQUE

Like Apel, Habermas is convinced of the necessity of an intersubjective paradigm shift, and the critique of the philosophy of the subject is a recurring theme in his writings as well. Habermas's usual assumption is that the philosophy of consciousness is burdened with a number of insurmountable aporias (PT 8), chiefly because it obstinately remains blind to *linguistic intersubjectivity* (ND 88). In what follows, let us attempt to explicate the sense of this critique.[8]

A. Introspective evidence and linguistic consensus

Habermas has formulated an emphatic critique of the theory of intentionality provided by the philosophy of the subject. Thus he claims 1) that its model of knowledge is incapable in principle of grasping the subject-subject relation, and 2) that the understanding of meaning and truth linked with this model is misleading.

1) In Habermas's view, the concept of intentionality, and the entire architectonic of the philosophy of consciousness, is determined by a model of knowledge that is oriented toward the representation of objects (Habermas 1992a, 16-17). The subject-subject relation, however, cannot be reconstructed according to the model of a consciousness directed toward intentional objects (PDM 169). And for this reason the theory of intentionality remains focused on the relation of a solitary, worldless, disembodied subject to something in the objective world that can be represented and manipulated (PT 44-45).

What is even more interesting is that Habermas explicitly refers to Husserl's phenomenology of intersubjectivity in this connection, writing in *Vorstudien und Ergänzungen zur Theorie des kommunikativen Handelns* that it is precisely an analysis of the phenomenological attempt to ground intersubjectivity that can show why it is necessary to take a linguistic philosophy, rather than a philosophy of consciousness, as the point of departure (VTH 50). For in contrast to the theory of communication, which takes an intersubjectivity already provided by language as its starting point, the difficulty with the transcendental philosophy of consciousness is that it attempts to derive intersubjective relationships from a monological point of departure (cf. VTH 30; PT 43).

Habermas knows that in contrast to Kant, Husserl was reckoning with a plurality of transcendental I's, and was confronted with the problem of transcendental communalization for this very reason (VTH 38; LSW 401). However, because Habermas refers almost exclusively to the Fifth Cartesian Meditation, he characterizes Husserl's phenomenology of intersubjectivity as an attempt to derive intersubjectivity from the monological accomplishments of the ego, and—citing Schutz, Theunissen, Carr, and Hutcheson in support—Habermas rejects this attempt as a failure (TCA I 424 n. 24; TCA II 129; LSW 401). It is precisely because the phenomenological account proceeds from the I,[9] with egoic subjectivity constantly counting as the final possible horizon of legitimization, that there is a persisting asymmetry between myself and the other in each case. Thus Husserl's account cannot accommodate full reciprocity between subjects (VTH 56), which is why the monadological production of intersubjectivity miscarries (TCA II 129; PDM 149-50; VTH 27):

> This fundamental methodological requirement of a philosophy
> of consciousness, which begins in each case with the solitary

reflection upon the performances of one's own subjectivity, excludes in principle any possibility that the others constituted through me and for me could simultaneously enter into precisely the same relationship toward me as I do toward them as my intentional objects. Rather, I am methodologically compelled to assert my preeminence, as the founding primal I, over all the other I's who guarantee the intersubjectivity of my world. (VTH 58)

The theory of intentionality's focus on the subject-object relation —which Habermas sees not merely as a historically contingent circumstance, but as an essential characteristic of the philosophy of consciousness (ND 141)—must therefore be replaced by the paradigm of intersubjective understanding and communication (TCA I 390, 391–92; PDM 295–96). As Habermas puts it, the monads do not first "spin linguistic intersubjectivity out of themselves," and intersubjectivity is not first produced by the reciprocal interlacing of subjective but interchangeable perspectives; rather, intersubjectivity is already given along with the "grammatical rules of symbolically regulated interactions" and processes of communication (LSS 117; LSW 401). Every form of interaction and communicative understanding between subjects is mediated by an intersubjectively binding use of symbols that ultimately refers to *ordinary language*. Thus just like Apel, Habermas too claims that language is the basis of intersubjectivity (KHI 157).

2) The critique by Habermas of the concept of intentionality is deepened when he refers to Wittgenstein's reflections on private language and rule-following. Thus he claims that the identity of the signification must be traced back to the intersubjective acknowledgment of rules (LSW 412), since the possibility of a private or monological rule-following is excluded. That is to say, a solitary subject cannot follow a rule alone—for as Wittgenstein has put it in § 202 of his *Philosophical Investigations,* "to *think* one is obeying a rule is not to obey a rule. Hence it is not possible to obey a rule 'privately': otherwise thinking one was obeying a rule would be the same thing as obeying it" (Wittgenstein 1958, 81e). Thus the identity of the rule rests on its intersubjective validity, and without the possibility of *reciprocal critique* and of reciprocal advice and instruction leading to agreement, this identity of the rule would not be ensured. Person A can thus not be certain of following a rule at all if the rule-following in question is not exposed to the judg-

ment of a critic, person B, who can ascertain deviations from the rule. A rule is thereby intersubjective by definition, for it must have validity for at least two subjects if a subject is to be able to follow "a" rule, i.e., one and the same rule (LSS 128; LSW 413; TCA II 17–18; VTH 65; PT 68). If one accepts this notion, it implies that understanding identical significations presupposes having the ability to participate in a public practice with at least one other subject (VTH 66).

Habermas accordingly denies that identical significations can be formed within the intentional structure of a solitary subject. There simply are no "pure" or "prior" intentions of the speaker; rather, psychic "states" are only transformed into intentional "contents" when and if they are inserted into the structures of linguistic intersubjectivity (EI 390; VTH 11–12). Hence there is no "pre-linguistic" meaning, and meaning must be understood instead as linguistic signification:

> Meaning is unthinkable without intersubjective validity; that is why it must always be expressed in symbols—there is no such thing as pre-linguistic meaning, in the strict understanding of an identical signification   Meaning is primarily bound up with communication in an everyday language, not with "experiences." Meaning may well be expressed in intentions—in expectations and fears, in wishes and opinions—but intentions can only be accorded intersubjective validity to the extent that they are understandable; they must be expressed, and can never be merely private. (LSW 417)

Thus Habermas explicitly wants to replace the primacy of intentionality with that of linguistic communication and understanding (VTH 50, 58), and he stresses that insofar as the concept of a "rule" is introduced from the start with reference to a relationship between subjects, this concept avoids the problem of a private consciousness that only subsequently comes into contact with others. The advantage of the theory of communication lies in proceeding directly from the intersubjective relationship, which the theory of constitution tried in vain to derive from the accomplishments of monadic consciousness (VTH 58–59). But that it proceeds from the intersubjective relationship means that it always already presupposes the system of linguistic rules without analyzing the origin of this system, a point that Habermas himself also concedes (ND 137).

Although he denies the idea of meaning or truth independent from language, Habermas is also confronted with the question of the development of linguistic ability. Here he refers to theories of signification developed by Piaget and Mead (VTH 414) and writes that the genetic theory of knowledge has shown that language merely "rests on" the *pre*-linguistic foundations provided by such categories as space, time, causality, and substance, as well as by rules for the formal-logical combination of symbols (LSW 340). Although these pre-linguistic ways of organizing *symbols*—ways that are formed in nexuses of interaction—do function as the basis for the intersubjectivity of living together and acting with one another, they do not permit any public communication in the strict sense, for it is only by virtue of being integrated into the linguistic system of rules that they can guarantee the intersubjectively binding identity of significations (LSW 352–54). However, it is important that Habermas does acknowledge that there are pre-linguistic roots of cognitive development in early ontogeny, without, however, seeing his own theory as in need of supplementation on that account (PT 27 n. 18; TCA II 46).

In connection with his critique of the concept of intentionality, Habermas now also reproaches phenomenology for continuing to refer to a private methodology, instead of entering into communication and linguistic expressions as the pragmatics of language does (LSS 111; PT 45, 134). Thus phenomenological descriptions cannot be intersubjectively tested at all, but only checked in individually performed meditations. Habermas's claim is therefore that the philosophy of the subject appeals in general to an introspective access to facts of consciousness, which is why it is methodologically dependent upon a kind of introspection that is not only difficult to verify but ultimately refers to entities that still bear the stigma of being "merely subjective" (PT 7, 23, 45).

These observations quite naturally lead to a critique of the concept of truth that is based on evidence (VTH 48), for what Habermas emphasizes is the difference between the subjective "experience of certainty" and the intersubjective, linguistically expressed "validity claims":

> Validity claims are distinguished from experiences of certainty by their intersubjectivity; one cannot meaningfully claim that a statement is true only for one particular individual or that a person's expressions are only truthful for some individuals. In

contrast, the certainty of a perception — the paradigm for certainty as such — exists only for the perceiving subject and for no one else. To be sure, a number of subjects can share the certainty that they have had a particular perception. But to do this, they must say so, i.e., they must make the same claim. A validity claim announces itself as something that is intersubjectively verifiable, whereas I can only express a certainty as something subjective, although it may serve as an occasion to place "dissonant" validity claims in question. Whereas I "have" a certainty, I "make" a validity claim. This distinction is important for the fact that it is exactly these two sorts of discursive validity claims (truth and correctness) that are only *mediately* founded in experiences. (VTH 140-41)

Hence truth ought not to be sought in the private evidence of consciousness, but rather in the possibility of argumentatively grounding a criticizable validity claim (EI 383). "Truth" means that *everyone* can justifiably be prevailed upon to recognize the validity claim of assertions as legitimate, and it can therefore only be demonstrated in the successful argumentation through which the claim to validity is cashed in (EI 388-89; VTH 153).[10] Thus it is by reason of principle that validity claims cannot be cashed in intuitively but only discursively. And it is accordingly only linguistically formulated arguments that induce us to acknowledge the legitimacy of any validity claims that have been put in question (VTH 48).

Habermas further claims that the condition of the truth of statements is the potential agreement of all others. Each would have to be able to be convinced that I am justifiably attributing a predicate to the object, and would then have to be able to agree with me. To put it another way, I may attribute a predicate to an object if and only if anyone who could enter into argumentation with me would attribute the same predicate to this same object.

Although the sense of truth must measure up to the requirement of achieving a consensus, and although truth claims function precisely as claims that must be taken in light of the possibility that they could be cashed in discursively if need be (VTH 109, 137, 139; PDM 322-23), Habermas stresses that not all consensus that factually is or can be reached can be a sufficient criterion for truth. Otherwise we could no longer distinguish a false consensus from a true one. Truth may only be ascribed to those propositions we counterfactually assume any sane subject would have to agree with if such a subject could only examine its views long enough in unlimited and unconstrained argumentation (LSW 440). It is only a sufficiently grounded, rational, or reasonable consensus, and not a merely contingently reached consensus, that can serve as a criterion, and hence the consensus that can serve as a criterion is defined as a consensus that has been reached through an ideal discussion.[11]

However, the communicative participants "cannot avoid supposing, in a reciprocal way, that the conditions for an ideal speech situation have been sufficiently met" (PDM 323). It belongs to the structure of possible speech that in performing speech acts, we counterfactually suppose that the ideal speech situation—where the only compulsion that is allowed is that of the better argument, and the only motive that is permitted is that of the cooperative search for truth—is not a mere fiction, but is real. Hence the normative foundation of linguistic understanding is constantly effective as an anticipated basis. That is to say, it guarantees the counterfactual agreement that must unite every potential speaker and listener in advance if communication is to be possible at all (EI 386; VTH 125, 177).

Habermas is thus in agreement with Apel that there are a number of universal conditions of possibility for communication, and he claims that every natural language contains within itself a universal structure that is acquired when we learn to speak and that enables us to step out of our own language in order to interpret a foreign language and make it understandable (LSS 145, 147–48; LSW 350). Because of this common linguisticality, the possibility of consensus and of restoring disturbed communication always exists (LSW 274; VTH 131).

Although Habermas writes that the horizons of various communicative communities work out their differences from one another by linguistic communication until these horizons fuse with one another (PDM 359; TCA I 70, 100; PT 16–17), this should not be misunderstood. Habermas often characterizes the intersubjectivity of communication in ordinary language as "porous" and "refracted," and we shall return to this. Moreover, he claims that any consensus that may actually appear is only a transitory unity that supports and furthers the pluralization and individualization of forms of life and lifestyles. Hence—like Apel—Habermas defends himself against the interpretation of the requirement of consensus as a requirement of repressive uniformization. For this reason, he finally declares, against his neo-structuralist critics, that "more discourse means more contradiction and difference" (PT 140).[12]

B. Self-consciousness and intersubjectivity

Habermas's attack on the philosophy of the subject is also supported by observations from developmental theory and from the theory of socialization. Let us attempt to present this side of his critique.

His theory of ego development combines the classic investigations of Piaget, Mead, and Freud (VTH 471), and Habermas denies that the type of self-consciousness presupposed by the philosophy of the subject as the "supreme point of reference" (PDM 374) is an original phenomenon (PT 44; Habermas 1969, 13). On the contrary, the identity, the individuality, and the self-consciousness of the subject are all first formed on the level of intersubjectivity, in relationship to other subjects (LSW 349, 434).

Habermas especially praises the *symbolic interactionism* developed by Mead because it succeeds in mediating between the two moments of *socialization* and *individuation*. That is to say, it is necessary to understand that in the process of socialization, the growing child is simultaneously building up its own identity and constructing the social world. Socialization must be understood precisely as individuation, and individuation as socialization (VTH 582; PT 26, 48; PDM 347). Habermas had insisted earlier on the connection between these two elements, and in *Technik und Wissenschaft als Ideologie,* he writes, for example, that individuation could only be conceived as a process of socialization. It must therefore be emphasized that socialization may not merely be conceived as the socialization of an (already) given individual; rather, it is the process of socialization that first produces this individual itself (Habermas 1969, 15–16). It is thus evident that for Habermas, individuation is to be grasped as "a socially produced phenomenon that is a result of the socialization process itself and not an expression of residual, natural needs that escape that process" (TCA II 58).

Although the identity of the individual is first formed in the process of socialization (TCA II 97), Habermas stresses that it is necessary to distinguish three concepts of identity. First, we have the generic identity of a person who is, qua person, capable of speech and action. This abstract

generality of "any ego whatsoever" is secured precisely by the universality
of the structures of the capabilities for cognition, language, and action.
Second, we have the numerical identity of a single, individual person.
This particularity, which physically separates the subject from all other
subjects, is guaranteed by the contingent organic substrate of the ego in-
carnated in its body. Thirdly, we have the qualitative identity of a specific
person with an individual life history, a particular character, and so on.
This individuality is ensured by the circumstance that the ego is formed
under concrete life circumstances — in particular, under the influence of
language as the medium of socialization that founds the intersubjectivity of the lifeworld (VTH 192; TCA II 101-102; cf. Habermas 1986, 334).[13]

Habermas now attempts to link this conception with the thesis that
a pressure toward individuation is built into the interaction that produces socialization through the communicatively oriented use of language, with its system of personal pronouns (PDM 347; TCA II 60) — in
all likelihood, because it is this system that enables the child to play "social roles in the first person" (TCA II 90). Following Mead, Habermas
thus identifies the principle of individuation with the structure of perspectives established by the communicative roles of first, second, and
third person (TCA II 58-59; PT 24). It is within these perspectives that we
first encounter "the *pronominal* meaning of the expression 'I'" (TCA II
104), and — speaking polemically against Dieter Henrich — Habermas
explicitly emphasizes that the relationship to oneself posited through
the structure of linguistic intersubjectivity does not need any prior, pre-
linguistic subjectivity, for "everything that earns the name of subjectivity,
even if it is a being-familiar-with-oneself, no matter how preliminary, is
indebted to the unrelentingly individuating force possessed by the linguistic mediation of formative processes" (PT 25).

Finally, in order to assess correctly Habermas's conception of the
relation between self-consciousness, individuality, and intersubjectivity,
it is necessary to address his emphasis upon the importance of reciprocal recognition for the formation of self-consciousness. Although it is especially in his earlier writings that Habermas takes his bearings from
this Hegelian model — for example, when he says that self-consciousness can only arise on the basis of the reciprocal recognition between
subjects (KHI 32; Habermas 1969, 19) — this model remains in the background as an important component of his overall conception even in
his later work.

The process of recognition alluded to is of a linguistic nature, and Habermas stresses that the identity-guaranteeing relation among individuals who recognize one another is formed and maintained within normal conversation in ordinary language (LSW 349). The linguistically structured community is characterized precisely by the circumstance that the communalized subjects in each case identify themselves with one another, reciprocally both recognizing and acknowledging one another as "homogeneous subjects" and as non-interchangeable individuals (KHI 157; cf. 138). At bottom, Habermas understands *intersubjectivity* as this relationship of recognition, and he himself highlights its paradoxical character. That is to say, the subjects must on the one hand see themselves as identical; both of them are, precisely, subjects. On the other hand, the reciprocity of the recognition also requires the non-identity of the one and the other subject: both must claim absolute difference, for as Habermas says, to be a subject includes the claim of complete individuation (LSW 350, 415; VTH 77).

Although Habermas claims both that intersubjectivity is given with the linguistic system of rules (LSS 117; LSW 401) and that subjectivity's self-understanding is first made possible through the structure of linguistic intersubjectivity (PT 25), at the same time, he also wants to advocate the idea that intersubjectivity is established in communication between subjects (LSW 556), that it is inaugurated only in the relation between the equiprimordial *ego* and *alter ego* (Habermas 1986, 332). Habermas therefore criticizes the priority that Taylor claims for the we over the I (Habermas 1986, 330). That is to say, to speak of consensus (and, we may add, of intersubjectivity) presupposes the autonomy and non-interchangeability of the subjects concerned:

> The communicatively achieved consensus is indebted not only to the idealizing assumption of the identity of linguistic significations, but to the force of negation and the autonomy of non-interchangeable subjects, among whom intersubjective agreement concerning criticizable validity claims must be *attained*. (Habermas 1986, 331)

In a similar way, Habermas warns against the temptation to ascribe to society attributes that have been borrowed from the individual subject in order then to integrate individuals as parts subordinated to this "higher-level" subject (LSW 403; PDM 376). This would lead not only to

an illegitimate personalization of society but also—and this is even more
important—to a destruction of intersubjectivity, for *ego* and *alter ego* can
maintain an intersubjective relation only as long as they can recognize
each other in their identity *and* difference, i.e., as long as they are not dissolved into a collective identity (TCA II 50; Habermas 1992a, 32).

Habermas often mentions in this connection that the intersubjectivity of linguistic understanding is the result of constructive accomplishments "achieved in the form of a refracted intersubjectivity" (PT
47), i.e., a "discontinuous," "interrupted" intersubjectivity (LSS 150).
What is meant is that communication between subjects is always incomplete, diffuse, and fragile (LSS 149–50; TCA I 100–101). Understanding could indeed be guaranteed by the type of theory of signification
put forth in systems theory or structuralism, where it would be fixed
analytically that all the language-users would have the same code and
the same stock of signs at their disposal. Habermas, however, is in
agreement with Apel's critique of this "solution," and writes that with
this type of theory of signification, the very problem of communication
itself simply dissolves (LSS 150, VTH 360).

Thus the stress that Habermas puts on the priority of communication must be understood in conjunction with his discussions of
ego-identity. He writes that fixed and rigid linguistic systems would
"eradicate the breaks in intersubjectivity and at the same time the
hermeneutic distance of individuals from one another"; they would
precisely fail to make possible that "delicate balance between separation and union in which the identity of every self must engage"—for
the problem of ego-identity is precisely and simultaneously the problem of a linguistic communication that "makes possible the crucial
balance between . . . the sacrifice of individuality and the isolation of
the solitary individual" (LSS 150; cf. LSW 73–74).

VII.4. A PHENOMENOLOGICAL REJOINDER

Through our presentation of the positions of Apel and Habermas,
we have gained a number of further arguments for the transcendental relevance of intersubjectivity. But it has also become clear that the
linguistic-pragmatic argument cannot be unified with the phenomenological account without further ado, and we have even established
that Apel and Habermas have been quite explicit in their critique of
phenomenology and its treatment of intersubjectivity.

In what follows, we shall attempt to refute this critique, and by doing so, we shall finally be able to answer the question concerning to what extent phenomenology can contribute to the current discussion of intersubjectivity.

Our reply will have four parts. First, we shall point out in general that the linguistic-pragmatic interpretation of phenomenology—and thereby also its critique of phenomenology—is extremely problematic. Second, we shall claim, that the linguistic-pragmatic attempt to keep its distance from the philosophy of the subject is inconsistent with its own observations on the relationship between subjectivity and intersubjectivity. Third, we shall subject its sharp separation between the private evidence of experience and public linguistic consensus to a phenomenological critique. Fourth, we shall claim that although the linguistic-pragmatic argument for the intersubjectivity of language—or the linguisticality of intersubjectivity—is correct, it cannot serve as the foundation for a theory of intersubjectivity, since it comes too late and, paradoxically presupposes precisely the same solipsistic theory of consciousness that it wants to criticize.

1) Our presentation has made it clear that Habermas and Apel take phenomenology to be burdened with a number of weighty aporias. Thus they have reproached phenomenology (and the Husserlian version in particular) with being solipsistic; with having attempted to derive intersubjectivity from the monological achievements of an isolated *ego;* with focusing on the manipulative relation of a solitary, worldless, disembodied subject to things in the objective world; with ignoring the sociocultural and historical conditions of constitution and with overlooking the connection between socialization and identity-formation; and so on. We shall address some of these points shortly, but it should already be clear from our detailed presentation—in particular, from our presentation of Husserl's phenomenology of intersubjectivity—that this critique is fundamentally mistaken and is based on an insufficient acquaintance with phenomenology.

This also holds true for a further critical point raised by Habermas, a point we have not yet mentioned. According to Habermas, the paradigm of a philosophy of consciousness is intimately linked with the search for ultimate grounding (cf. TCA I 2; PDM 104, 178-79; PT 33; MC 118-19). However, he emphasizes that the claim put forth by such a philosophy to be a "comprehensive, closed, and final" science (one that needs no further commentary and permits no improvement and no innovation) is incompatible with the "unprejudiced openness" characterizing current fallibilistic scientific theories (PT 36). Yet it is particularly problematic to reproach Husserl for claiming to possess this kind of closed and final knowledge, as is shown, for example, in the following passage from *Formal and Transcendental Logic:*

> And to stick to tradition—which, for motives long forgotten and, in any case, never clarified, reduces evidence to an insight that is apodictic, absolutely indubitable, and, so to speak, absolutely finished in itself—is to bar oneself from an understanding of any scientific production. (17/169[161])

Thus Husserl denies, quite explicitly, that he sees the *cogito* (or transcendental intersubjectivity) as an absolutely "secured" foundation that would serve as the highest *principle* of a *transcendental deduction* (6/193[189]). As Husserl often said, it is precisely the case that transcendental phenomenology belongs to a fundamental class of eidetic sciences that is entirely different from that of mathematics (3/158[169-70]). Hence he too regards the idea of absolute truth as a regulative idea, and he therefore characterizes philosophy—as a science that is built on an ultimate foundation and based on ultimate self-responsibility—as an *idea* that can only be realized "by way of relative and temporary validities and in an infinite historical process" (5/139; cf. 1/53, 6/171[168]).

That transcendental phenomenology does not defend any sort of rigid and absolute concept of truth or reality is also expressed in Husserl's discussions of the correlation between objectivity and normality. As has been mentioned, Husserl characterizes the intersubjectively valid world as an intersubjective presumption that can only be cashed out in a process of constant correction. We can therefore only reiterate that absolute concordance—i.e., the world "in itself"—is never given but is always pending, "suspended between relative truth and relative untruth, between being and seeming" (15/614). Thus for Husserl there is no *fixed world.* Rather, the world exists for us only in the relativity of normalities and abnormalities. Its being has only the appearance of being firmly fixed; in reality, this is the merely provisional solidity of a structure of normality whose stability can break down and collapse.

Hence in reality there are greater similarities between transcendental phenomenology and linguistic pragmatics than Apel and Habermas believe. Phenomenology too has taken note of the interconnection between intersubjectivity, truth, and reality. This can be illustrated by the following three passages—passages that (apart from certain terminological idiosyncrasies) could easily be ascribed to Apel or to (early) Habermas, although they actually come from Husserl:

> Of course, as long as one interprets transcendental subjectivity as an isolated ego and—like the Kantian tradition—ignores the whole task of establishing the legitimacy of the transcendental community of subjects, any prospect of a transcendental knowledge of self and world is lost. (29/120)

> Concrete, full transcendental subjectivity is the totality of an open community of I's—a totality that comes from within, that is unified purely transcendentally, and that is concrete only in this way. Transcendental intersubjectivity is the absolute and only self-sufficient ontological foundation *[Seinsboden]*, out of which everything objective (the totality of objectively real entities, but also every objective ideal world) draws its sense and its validity. (9/344, trans. altered)

> [It lies in the sense of mundane experience that] what is experienced as real actually exists with the ontic sense that it has as the correlate of the system of concordant possible experience of all co-experiencing subjects that can possibly enter into connection with me—or that it has in such a way that what is currently actually experienced points horizonally to a concordance in the ongoing synthesis of possible experience (one's own experience and that of any number of fellow humans that may enter into co-functioning), a synthesis that must moreover always be renewed. It is precisely this that implies the construction of an idea of the total system of possible experiences of all subjects possibly co-functioning with one another within the horizon of the currently possible modalizations and corrections. (Ms. A VII 2 22b).[14]

One ought not overestimate how far this rejoinder reaches. It would make it too easy if one were to attempt to reject the arguments of Apel and Habermas simply by demonstrating weaknesses in their Husserl interpretation.[15] What is at stake for them is not at all producing a careful interpretation of Husserl, but making certain systematic points. For this reason, the truly decisive question must be this: is it at all possible to develop a theory of intersubjectivity, such as that of Husserl, within the paradigm of a philosophy of the subject—or is any attempt that does not begin from a linguistic philosophy condemned to fail, as Apel claims (TrP II 175 n. 37)?

2) As has been mentioned on several occasions, Apel and Habermas understand the shift to a paradigm of intersubjectivity as a final and definitive break with a philosophy of the subject or of consciousness. In what follows, we want not only to bring the sense of this assumption into question but also to point out a number of ways in which their own theories transgress it.

That is to say, there is a contradiction between the way in which Apel and Habermas (verbally) distance themselves from the paradigm of a philosophy of the subject, on the one hand, and their use of elements from this very tradition, on the other. Put another way, both Apel and Habermas make use of the "instrumentarium" of this tradition over and over again—indeed, too often to be able to speak of an actual break with the philosophy of the subject, yet too infrequently to make their own accounts really plausible. Let us turn to some examples.

Apel writes that the emancipation of the thinking subject in modern epistemology is irreversible, and that the rational autonomy of the human being that was won by the Enlightenment cannot be abandoned; rather, it is the subject of knowledge that must remain the final critical court of appeal for reflection upon validity (TP I 41; TP II 317). Habermas claims that when linguistic analysis becomes linguistic pragmatics, dimensions of the philosophy of the subject that had been "given up for lost" are won back (PT 46). Both thinkers criticize the attempt to establish comprehension or intersubjective sense through structuralism or systems theory because, in their view, it is impossible to conceive linguistic intersubjectivity independently from the subject's communicative use of language and exchange of experiences. "Intersubjectivity" designates precisely this commonality and community between subjects (VTH 206), and Habermas even criticizes Taylor for claiming the priority of the we over the I. Hence the difference between subjects is not to be dissolved into a collective identity, for intersubjective consensus, comprehension, and agreement presuppose the autonomy and the non-interchangeability of the subjects concerned.

Against this background, it is, as we have indicated, somewhat difficult to understand how Apel and Habermas are able to write that their own accounts represent a radical break with the philosophy of the subject.[16] Above and beyond this, Habermas in particular seems to be confronted with a further problem. How can he claim that individuality is the result of a process of socialization—that it is first produced by socialization, by the relationship to other subjects—and at the same time write that intersubjectivity and consensus presuppose the autonomy and absolute difference of the subjects concerned?

Let us turn briefly to Husserl's position in order to clarify the problem. That the I, as person, requires a Thou is also recognized by Husserl; he explicitly states that the origin of personhood or personal unity lies in social acts, and that it is first of all in the I-Thou relation that the I attains personal "self-consciousness" and thereby becomes a personal subject (14/171-75). It is, however, extremely important to note that Husserl differentiates between various levels of I-structure. Thus there is a distinction between the subject as such (or the I as a unity in the stream, i.e., as pole of affection and action) and the personal subject. When Husserl writes that it is true a priori that "self-consciousness and consciousness of others are inseparable" (6/256 [253]); that there is no I without Thou (13/6, 13/244, 13/247, 15/603); and that each I is what it is only as "socius" of a sociality, as a member of a community (15/191-94), this concerns precisely the I as a person, and not the I as a pole of affection and action. Hence Husserl is in no way defending the thesis that socialization is the source of every type of self-consciousness, subjective identity, and individuation. Quite the contrary, he would even claim that every concrete relation between subjects presupposes a prior plurality of different (i.e., individual) streams of consciousness.

While Husserl sees this rudimentary identity of consciousness as irreducibly lying at the basis not only of personal identity but also of the relation to others (i.e., intersubjectivity), Habermas claims that there is no pre-linguistic subjectivity that precedes the relationship to myself that is posited in and through the structure of linguistic intersubjectivity. It is only when the child learns to say "I"—i.e., it is only when the child learns the system of personal pronouns and the perspectival structures linked with them—that it is individuated.

But, what is really behind this difference in conception is more of a shift in accent or a conceptual equivocation than a really fundamental disagreement.[17] That is to say, despite his own differentiation of various concepts of identity, Habermas seems to be exclusively interested in exploring *personal identity* (understood as the qualitative identity of a specific person with an individual life history, a particular character, etc.) in terms of a theory of socialization (TCA II 100–101). In contrast, he has hardly dealt with the problem of the individuation of the *numerical self-identity* of the stream of consciousness, and his few remarks with reference to this seem to indicate that he understands it exclusively as a physical difference that is ensured by the contingency of the organic substrate.

In order to make our critique more precise, then, we would in no way want to deny that personal identity (in the sense indicated above) is dependent on social relations and that both the acquisition of individual characteristics and the representation of who one wants to be (cf. TCA II 101, 106) go hand in hand with socialization (on the contrary, what is incomprehensible is how Habermas can understand this as an attack on the philosophy of the subject). We would, however, want to claim that his reflections are insufficient and of limited validity, since Habermas has not paid enough attention to certain aspects of the structure of consciousness. To include and acknowledge the individuality of the stream of consciousness seems to us not only to be called for philosophically but also to be unconditionally necessary if the consistency of his own theory is to be salvaged. That is to say, as long as Habermas sees individuation exclusively as a product of socialization, he does not have the means at his disposal simultaneously to understand intersubjectivity as a relationship of recognition between non-interchangeable and absolutely different individuals.[18]

Finally, this critique must be made still more pointed. The very idea that a philosophy of intersubjectivity would not be a philosophy of the subject makes no sense in principle, for intersubjectivity is a relation between subjects. It presupposes a (possible) plurality of subjects, and for that reason it can neither precede the difference between subjects nor explain or deny this difference. To put it another way, if one wants to get rid of any residue of the philosophy of the subject, one would necessarily also have to distance oneself from the concept of intersubjectivity.

Within phenomenology, what we find is that instead of conceiving of subjectivity and intersubjectivity as irreconcilable alternatives, there is an attempt to think them together. Thus according to Husserl, the introduction of the intersubjective dimension does not imply any refutation of the philosophy of the subject or any break with it, but merely a better understanding of it. However, this introduction of an intersubjective dimension remains meaningful only within such a philosophy of the subject. Thinking intersubjectivity phenomenologically in this manner naturally remains unacceptable for anyone who holds from the start the misguided conviction that on account of its starting point in a philosophy of the subject, phenomenology is determined by an object-oriented or idealistic architectonic that makes it impossible a priori for it to understand intersubjectivity.[19] In reading Apel and Habermas, however, one gets the impression that precisely this sort of defining statement is in play. Habermas in particular seems to persist in interpreting the philosophy of the subject as a homogeneous tradition that consists of *foundationalism, phenomenalism,* and *solipsism*—a characterization that has leveled the tradition down and, as Matthiesen too has pointed out, has made it impossible for Habermas to gain an adequate understanding of phenomenology (Matthiesen 1985, 32, 63).

One could, of course, simply deny that phenomenology can still be designated as a philosophy of the subject at all. (Although this strategy is customary when it is a question of Heidegger or Merleau-Ponty, it seems to us to be necessary only if one has committed oneself from the start to a very narrow and limited concept of subjectivity.) But at bottom, what is at stake is more than a mere matter of a terminological conflict. Thus it would not help the situation even if a proponent of linguistic pragmatics were to concede that the latter is in reality still to be characterized as a philosophy of the subject. For whether or not one interprets either phenomenology or linguistic pragmatics as a philosophy of the subject, their respective treatments of intersubjectivity are still essentially different (e.g., in choosing a first-person or a third-person perspective), and thus they represent alternative accounts.

3) A central point in the linguistic-pragmatic argument against the philosophy of consciousness is the claim that calling upon the evidence of consciousness and the "experience of certainty" presupposes a misleading understanding of meaning and truth. But it can be questioned whether this critique hits its target, for the concept of evidence that is questioned seems to have little to do with the phenomenological concept of evidence. In addition, the notion implied here of a sharp separation between experiential evidence and linguistic consensus seems highly problematical.

Let us now attempt to elucidate these two critical points, beginning with some remarks concerning the reproach that phenomenological analyses cannot be intersubjectively tested because they are dependent upon "introspection."

If I phantasize something and then reflectively ascertain that I have done so, I am making use of an introspection. Thus the remark, "Now I am imagining a hot air balloon," is based on introspection, and although someone can interrogate me in order to establish to what extent I am using the term "hot air balloon" correctly, my statement does in fact elude intersubjective verification. But the assumption that phenomenological analyses (e.g., analyses of correlation) consist of such introspective descriptions of experience is preposterous; it rests on a misunderstanding of intentional analyses as well as of the epochē and the reduction. As we have set forth at the beginning, the epochē does not imply any cancellation of the object-directedness of my intentional acts. These acts retain their relation to something in the world—indeed, to something worldly that possesses intersubjective ontic validity. Thus the analysis of intentionality is in no way at first directed toward entities within the stream of experiences (or as Husserl would say, to really intrinsic contents), as Habermas seems to assume (PT 45),[20] but rather to the purely and simply given intersubjective life-world. The latter serves as the point of departure for the investigation of correlations, and it functions as a leading clue for "inquiring back into the multiplicities of manners of appearing and their intentional structures" (6/175[172]). Of course, what is at stake then is an exploration of such a (world-related) subjectivity. But this research is not "introspection" when what we understand by that word is a reference to private experiences, for the analysis claims to be investigating universal structures. Thus what is at stake is not merely my own consciousness but any possible consciousness, and it is for this reason precisely that my own analyses and my own descriptions can be checked and criticized by any co-subject who has adopted the appropriate phenomenological attitude. In a certain way, this corroboration does indeed presuppose an individual re-performance of the analysis. But it makes no sense to conclude from this that it cannot be intersubjectively tested (LSS 111), since every such corroborative review, be it of mathematical models, archaeological discoveries, or philosophical theses, presupposes a corresponding subjective procedure.

A similar misunderstanding arises in connection with the critique of evidence offered by Habermas and Apel: namely, it occasionally sounds as though Husserl is being reproached for identifying evidence with an experience of feeling certain. However, from the beginning Husserl criticized as incomprehensible any theory that equates evidence with a "feeling," since it cannot answer the question of why certain lived experiences are accompanied by a feeling of evidence and others are not (2/159, 18/183[187]). At the same time, he reproaches this theory for being phenomenologically untenable, and he even characterizes the so-called feelings of evidence as psychological fictions (3/46[40]). For Husserl, evidence is not some feeling of certainty; rather, it distinguishes a specific mode of givenness of the meant object—namely, the originary mode of givenness. When the object itself is given (be it a sensuous object or a categorial object), i.e., when the object is itself present, then it is given with evidence:

> Evidence . . . designates *that performance on the part of intentionality which consists in the giving of something-itself [die intentionale Leistung der Selbstgebung].* More precisely, it is the universal pre-eminent form of "intentionality", of "consciousness of something", in which there is consciousness of the intended-to objective affair in the mode itself-seized-upon, itself-seen—correlatively, in the mode: being with it itself in the manner peculiar to consciousness. (17/166[157–58])

Here evidence is not some private feeling; rather it characterizes the mode of givenness of intersubjective objects. It is precisely for this reason, however, that it also implies an intersubjective validity claim and is accordingly open for critique. Thus we are naturally also reminded of our presentation of Husserl's phenomenology of intersubjectivity. It is precisely our experience of others that makes possible the constitution, and "cashing in," of objective validity. Husserl's analysis is indeed guided by the insight that in communalization, our insights are subject to constant correction and legitimization (6/166[163]).[21]

The notion that the appeal to evidence would imply an immunization against criticizability, as Apel claims, must also be rejected. In *Formal and Transcendental Logic,* Husserl describes the way in which the scientist, who is guided by the idea of an evidence reached by *critique*—i.e., "an evidence that is perfect or perfectible by systematic stages, and attainable by means of criticism, an evidence having as its correlate an attainable, or approachable, true being"—must again and again go back critically to insights already won in order to check them and submit them to criticism (17/130[125]). That is to say, evidence not only has its degrees of clarity, but it can be deceptive. To be sure, this does not imply any kind of skepticism, for the ostensibly apodictic evidence that is revealed to be an illusion presupposes a similar evidence that "shatters" it:

> The *possibility of deception* is inherent in the evidence of experience and does not annul either its fundamental character or its effect; though becoming evidentially aware of <actual> deception "annuls" the deceptive experience or evidence itself. The evidence of a new experience is what makes the previously uncontested experience undergo that modification of believing called "annulment" or "cancellation"; and it alone can do so (17/164[156]).[22]

These discussions gradually lead to the question of whether the sharp distinction between the evidence of experience and linguistic consensus is justified at all.

Before we present our objections, however, let us briefly point out that the reflections of Apel and Habermas are somewhat indecisive. That is to say, it would be a misunderstanding if one were to believe that they want to abandon the role of evidence completely. Apel does indeed write that traditional epistemology cannot show how the evidence of consciousness can be carried over into the intersubjective validity of linguistically formulated statements—yet at the same time, he emphasizes that this evidence of consciousness is indispensable (QG 59; see also Apel 1974, 290)! The validity of knowledge must therefore always be *simultaneously* grounded on the possible evidence of consciousness available to individual, competent subjects of knowledge (as "autonomous representatives" of the transcendental subject of knowledge as such) and on the a priori, intersubjective rules governing argumentative discourse (QG 78). Thus Apel himself must deny that it is possible meaningfully to think of an argumentative grounding discourse without presupposing specific knowledge based on evidence, and vice versa (QG 78). With regard to the problem of truth, the evidence of consciousness and the intersubjective validity of linguistically formulated arguments are thus two courts of appeal that cannot be reduced to one another (QG 82–83), and evidence must therefore be recognized as being at least a necessary criterion for truth. It is an epistemologically relevant ground for the intersubjective acceptance of truth (Apel 1990a, 22); as Apel himself concedes, the formation of consensus within the community of interpretation can in no way be thought without such epistemological recourse to knowledge based on evidence (QG 84):

> Although the consciousness-evidence which is always mine does not guarantee the inter-subjective validity of knowledge, still, the *argumentative grounding of validity* in a scientific language game must refer back ultimately to that *evidence* which can, in principle, be ultimately testified to by every single member of the interpretation-community by means of the (empirical or *a priori*) consciousness-*evidence*. (QG 84; cf. Apel 1989c)

In a similar way, Apel acknowledges the consciousness of perceptual evidence (and hence not language) as the irreducible a priori of experience when it is a matter of a verifying identification of a given phenomenon (Apel 1990a, 21–24). Hence we must necessarily rely on the perceptual identification of the meant object when it is a question of securing the real referent of the subject of a proposition. Whether our significative intention is fulfilled can only be decided by perceptual evidence. Here the propositional-linguistic representation of the world of experience can in fact be transcended.

Against this background, it is hard to understand how Apel could use the term "anti-evidence-theory" to characterize his own position (QG 84).

A similar consideration can also be found in Habermas: namely, he occasionally admits that the truth of a statement is dependent upon *two* conditions. It must be founded in experience (which is thus obviously a necessary, although not a sufficient, condition for the possibility of truth); and it must be able to be cashed in discursively (VTH 109).[23]

By and large, however, the distinction that Apel and Habermas have come up with between experiential evidence and linguistic consensus has a distinctly Kantian sound (and here we are thinking of the thesis that "intuitions without concepts are blind"— *Critique of Pure Reason* B 75). Hence both thinkers are vulnerable to the classic phenomenological critique of the Kantian position as found, for example, in

Analysen zur passiven Synthesis, in *Experience and Judgment,* and in *Phenome-nology of Perception*—a critique that we can summarize as follows.

Meaning and validity do not first occur at the level of language; rather, they are already present in perception. To reduce pre-predicative experience to the fact of being affected, and to interpret sensibility as being in itself senseless, is to perform an intellectualistic abstraction that makes it incomprehensible how what is perceived could ever serve as a leading clue for our interpretation. There must on the contrary be a continuity between the pre-predicative experience of objects and features, on the one hand, and the predicative articulation of this experience on the other.[24] But severing meaning or sense from sensibility not only means making the connection between conceptual thinking and sensory perceiving incomprehensible and arbitrary (which occasionally seems to lead linguistic pragmatics into the dead end of linguistic idealism, insofar as it pays far less attention to the world about which we communicate than to this communication itself); it also means that the central problem concerning the possibility of learning a language is left unsolved. When the claim is made that every similarity, and every classification and identification of some-thing "as" something (be it ever so unthematic), is linguistic—that one cannot pre-linguistically experience something *as* something (TP I 59-60)—then (as Cobb-Stevens points out) it becomes impossible to explain the origin and genesis of the linguistic system. One seems to have to presuppose that the linguistic community has always already possessed the linguistic system and that its new members are acquired through their being (blindly) drilled in something they do not com-prehend (Cobb-Stevens 1990a, 43):

> Indeed, the task of learning how language works would be insurmountable, were it not for the fact that predication's struc-ture (identification-description) closely resembles perception's structure (this-such). Moreover, recognition of sounds as repeat-able tokens of a type is clearly a condition of taking things as signs, and therefore of acquiring linguistic competence. The discern-ment of phonemes, morphemes, and words within a sequence of sounds is just as intuitive a procedure as the discernment of any other this-such structure. Of course, the acquisition of linguistic categories and distinctions also makes for more nuanced percep-tions. Aristotle calls attention to the complementarity of perception

and speech in the elaboration of progressively more sophisticated sorting procedures. We understand one another's use of sortal predicates, because we make progress together in relating linguistic articulations to perceptual discriminations. Surely this is a more convincing description of the interplay between saying and seeing, than the reductive theory that institutionalized practices incline us to associate the same perceptual stimuli with the same linguistic routines. (Cobb-Stevens 1990a, 45)

Apel and Habermas would surely deny that their theories imply the model of language learning mentioned above; they definitely don't understand themselves as behaviorists (cf. TP II 323). But they cannot avoid this consequence as long as they continue to maintain that acts of consciousness only become intentional acts (i.e., acts bearing intentional contents) when such acts are inserted into the structure of linguistic intersubjectivity, and that pre-linguistically, no understanding of a given phenomenon is possible (EI 390; VTH 11–12; Apel 1990a, 27–28).

Finally, these observations make it possible to refute the arguments against the possibility of private language and monological rule-following.[25] That is to say, if there is no extra- or pre-linguistic rule-following, then we are once again confronted with the problem of language learning. If the subject does not already have pre-linguistic cognitive competence, and if the subject could not already perform rudimentary syntheses of identity on its own, then it could neither be socialized nor learn language or rule-following. In other words, one must not forget that socialization and language acquisition—i.e., interaction with others—presupposes a successful experience of others. As Husserl says, "Actuality becomes warranted, illusion rectified, in my concourse with others—who likewise are, for me," given in "actual and possible experience" (17/240[233]). In order for me to be corrected, I must already be able to grasp the others as subjects and their statements as statements of correction—hence I must already be able to perform syntheses of identity (cf. Chapter II.2). To put it another way, if one denies that the solitary subject can follow rules alone, then one must also deny that this subject can meaningfully interact with other subjects. It is precisely for this reason that doubting the possibility in principle of solitary rule-following ultimately leads to skepticism, for the subsequent introduction of intersubjectivity can by no means solve the problem. Finally, as

Düsing (1986, 72–73) has remarked, it is still unclear where the others—whose linguisticality and role-identity are what we are supposed to be taking over—have acquired their own capabilities in the first place. An infinite regress seems to be unavoidable if we do not ascribe a minimal independence (individuality), along with the pertinent cognitive competences, to the participants in the socialization process. Paradoxically, Habermas himself draws attention to this problem in his own interpretation of Mead. He writes that Mead has to presuppose that the parents have "the competences for speech and interaction that the child is to acquire"—but he claims that this maneuver is legitimate as long as it is only a matter of an ontogenetic explanation (TCA II 43).

These observations allow us to discern the fundamental weakness of the linguistic-pragmatic position. Although it is a central and important task of transcendental philosophy to investigate consensus in the (scientific) linguistic community, this undertaking can never *replace* the analysis of the subject's experiential evidence but can only *complement* it.

The individual's relation to evidence is also indispensable on other grounds, as emerges from the criticisms repeatedly leveled against the discourse theory of truth that Apel and Habermas have formulated. On the one hand, the objection that has been raised against the notion of the ideal speech situation that is to serve as the criterion for the distinction between a true and a false consensus is that one could never completely reach it or ever unequivocally identify it (Höffe 1976, 329; Skirbekk 1982, 60, 68). On the other hand, it has been pointed out that the problem of validity cannot be solved by anticipation, for we would have no way of knowing what the counterfactually introduced communicative community would decide. Either one already knows right now what is rational, independently from the decisions of the ideal communicative community—and then one would not have to have recourse to it—or else one doesn't know, in which case referring to the communicative community still cannot help us out (Hösle 1986, 247; Baumgartner 1982). To put it another way, it is not only factual consensus that proves inadequate for the theory of validity; a purely ideal consensus, taken strictly as an anticipation, is of no use as a criterion for truth either (Skirbekk 1982, 55). For this reason it is necessary for the individual language user herself to have the capability of transcending factual consensus in order to determine to what extent something could be the result of an ideal discourse. The very notion of ideal communication thus presupposes that the individual subject already has a capability for normative-rational anticipation (Nagl 1988, 367). Naturally, the subject can make a mistake, but on account of the melioristic character of this fallibility (see Chapter VII, n. 22), no skepticism is implied.

However, although we are claiming that both consensus and mastery of language are founded in pre- or extra-linguistic experiential evidence, this does not imply that they can be reduced without residue to such evidence (for it is precisely a matter of a relationship of founding), nor does it imply that pre-linguistic evidence is infallible, or that we should be satisfied with it in our search for truth—let alone that it ought to be regarded as a standard for knowledge. Thus one should not forget that only that evidence about which consensus can be reached is actually worthy of the name of evidence. True being does indeed mean that it is not just being for an individual; instead it points a priori beyond the individual to the nexus of possible intersubjective corroboration—and indeed, already at the pre-predicative level (9/431, 14/289, 14/390, 17/243[236], 6/469).

4) Apel and Habermas have attempted to construct a theory of intersubjectivity based on a linguistic philosophy, and the merit of their effort lies precisely in that, among other things, they have given us a detailed demonstration of the intersubjectivity of language (or the linguisticality of intersubjectivity). This undertaking has brought an important aspect of the problem of intersubjectivity to light—an aspect not already thematized as systematically, or to the same extent, by Husserl, Scheler, Heidegger, Sartre, or Merleau-Ponty. What nevertheless still remains problematic is that the level of intersubjectivity thematized by a linguistic philosophy is itself a founded stratum. That is to say, from the phenomenological side, one would insist that a still more fundamental type of intersubjectivity precedes this—that the subject is already pre-linguistically intersubjective.

Instead of claiming that intersubjectivity can develop only linguistically, and that only a linguistic philosophy "can integrate the *a priori of intersubjective understanding*" (TrP 175 n. 37),[26] phenomenology in no way wants to limit intersubjectivity to the linguistic level. Communication and dialogue are specific, unique, and highly important forms of intersubjective relation, but they are not the only forms of it, or even the most fundamental forms. In other words, linguistic intersubjectivity has a number of pre-linguistic roots. These cannot be dealt with simply by making a few references to developmental psychology (as Habermas has done—cf., e.g., LSW 340; VTH 192, 414, 471), but must be thematically subjected to philosophical analysis. Correctly understood, communication does not exist either prior to or apart from subjects; rather, it consists in an openness of subjects toward one another. Understanding communication will accordingly require an analysis of the pre-linguistic intersubjectivity of the subject, for the relation to others is exhibited in and across the registers of temporality, corporeality, intentionality, and emotionality. Phenomenology has performed such analyses, and for this reason phenomenology can also make it comprehensible how and why subjects can communicate linguistically, instead of simply presupposing such communication.

But our critique of the linguistic-pragmatic theory of intersubjectivity should not be misunderstood. For us, what is at stake is not a defense of a solipsistic subject. On the contrary, what we wish to claim is that in their emphasis on the subject's intersubjectivity, Apel and Habermas have not been radical enough! Both of them want to overcome solipsism. And both of them attempt to do so by arguing, from the point of view of linguistic philosophy, that the subject is a product of socialization, and for exactly this reason it is inseparably linked with others—a solution we have shown to be aporetic. But why does solipsism emerge as a problem for them, and why must it be overcome? Because both Apel and Habermas conceive the pre-linguistic status of the subject as solipsistic! And on this basis it is then claimed that pre-linguistic consciousness is non-intentional and lacks any grasp of meaning, so that intersubjectivity comes into play only through language. The paradoxical consequence is that the subject (or perhaps better, the proto-subjective organism) would remain without intentionality, without a relation to the world, and without intersubjective relations if—for contingent reasons—it never learned a language. It is precisely here that the difference from the phenomenological view is quite striking. That is to say, a phenomenological account would claim, first, that a thoroughgoing analysis of the structures of experience, and of the ontological nature of the subject, would show that already at the pre-linguistic level, the subject transcends itself and is open to the world and to others. And second, from the phenomenological side it is not sufficient to introduce intersubjectivity through contingent and external measures; rather, it can be shown that the subject has an a priori reference to intersubjectivity—a relation that is there whether or not the subject has ever learned a language, and whether or not the subject has had a concrete experience of others. In fact, we can even see the phenomenological account of the interconnection between horizon intentionality and intersubjectivity as a counterpart to the argument against a private language. Thus all we want to claim is that the attempt to demonstrate the intersubjectivity of consciousness by way of a theory of constitution or perception avoids the problems that are linked with the line of reasoning pursued by Apel and Habermas.

VII.5. CONCLUSION

What consequences can be drawn from our critical examination of linguistic pragmatics and from the present work? Above all, we have provided a systematic interpretation of Husserl's phenomenology of intersubjectivity that has made obvious what a fundamental role Husserl assigned to intersubjectivity and how the incorporation of intersubjectivity led to a decisive clarification of his phenomenology. Our attempt to demonstrate that he did in fact subject transcendental philosophy to an intersubjective transformation seems to us not only to have been a successful attempt but also a very fruitful one when it is a question of gaining a new perspective on Husserl's phenomenology.[27]

However, our analysis of Heidegger, Sartre, and Merleau-Ponty has also made it possible to demonstrate a homogeneity, both of method and of results, in the specifically phenomenological treatment of intersubjectivity. Against this background a confrontation with the non-phenomenological approach to intersubjectivity found in linguistic pragmatics has become possible as well—a confrontation yielding the result that the phenomenological treatment of intersubjectivity (cf. Chapter VI.5) has at least three distinct advantages over the linguistic-pragmatic theory of intersubjectivity. First, it avoids conceiving subjectivity and intersubjectivity as irreconcilable alternatives, and for this reason, it does not have to understand their relation as one of mutual opposition or contradiction. Second, it does not limit intersubjectivity to linguisticality, and for this reason, it can fully take the decisive pre- and extra-linguistic manifestations of intersubjectivity into account. Finally, it does not reduce intersubjectivity to a factual—i.e., contingent—relation between subjects; rather, through analyses of the structure of experience and of the mode of being of the subject, it establishes the a priori relation of the subject to intersubjectivity.

Despite this statement, we do not want to claim that there is no merit to what the proponents of the pragmatics of language have accomplished. Perhaps the reading of Husserl that we have offered here would not even have been possible had we not been guided by the focus on the intersubjective transformation of transcendental philosophy that the works of Apel and Habermas provide. In addition, it cannot be contested that agreement and consensus-forming are in fact intimately linked with communication; and although Apel and Habermas have wrongly conceived the connection between language and sensibility, one has to admit that a detailed analysis of language is indispensable if one wants to understand the relationship between intersubjectivity and truth in depth. Whether this analysis of language should be a linguistic-pragmatic one, or whether one should turn instead to a hermeneutical-phenomenological theory of language, is a question that has to remain open here.

We can, however, conclude that phenomenology can in fact contribute to the current discussion of intersubjectivity. For this reason, our book can conclude with the following, only seemingly paradoxical remark. If one wants not merely to presuppose the intersubjectivity that so often serves as the starting point today, but to understand it philosophically, there is every reason to turn once again to the phenomenological philosophy of the subject.

ABBREVIATIONS

DV   Apel, *Diskurs und Verantwortung*
EI   Habermas, *Erkenntnis und Interesse*
EM   Scheler, *On the Eternal in Man*
EN   Sartre, *L'être et le néant/Being and Nothingness*
EU   Husserl, *Erfahrung und Urteil*
FE   Scheler, *Formalism in Ethics and Non-Formal Ethics of Values*
GP   Heidegger, *Die Grundprobleme der Phänomenologie*
KHI   Habermas, *Knowledge and Human Interests*
LSS   Habermas, *On the Logic of the Social Sciences*
LSW   Habermas, *Zur Logik der Sozialwissenschaften*
MC   Habermas, *Moral Consciousness and Communicative Action*
ND   Habermas, *Nachmetaphysisches Denken*
NS   Scheler, *The Nature of Sympathy*
PDM   Habermas, *The Philosophical Discourse of Modernity*
PM   Merleau-Ponty, *La prose du monde/The Prose of the World*
PP   Merleau-Ponty, *Phénoménologie de la perception/Phenomenology of Perception*
PrP   Merleau-Ponty, *The Primacy of Perception*
PT   Habermas, *Postmetaphysical Thinking*
PZ   Heidegger, *Prolegomena zur Geschichte des Zeitbegriffs*
QG   Apel, "The Question of Grounding: Philosophy and Transcendental Pragmatics of Language"
RC   Merleau-Ponty, *Résumés de cours/Themes from the Lectures*
S   Merleau-Ponty, *Signes/Signs*
SNS   Merleau-Ponty, *Sens et non-sens/Sense and Non-Sense*
SuZ   Heidegger, *Sein und Zeit*
TCA   Habermas, *The Theory of Communicative Action, I–II*
TE   Sartre, *La transcendance de l'ego/The Transcendence of the Ego*
TP   Apel, *Transformation der Philosophie, I–II*
TrP   Apel, *Towards a Transformation of Philosophy*
UE   Apel, *Understanding and Explanation*
VI   Merleau-Ponty, *Le visible et l'invisible/The Visible and the Invisible*
VTH   Habermas, *Vorstudien und Ergänzungen zur Theorie des kommunikativen Handelns*

NOTES

INTRODUCTION

1. In citations of Husserl's works, the first number refers to the volume number in the *Husserliana* series, and the number(s) after the slash to the page number(s). Where there is an existing English translation that does not have the corresponding *Husserliana* volume's page numbers printed in the margins, the appropriate page numbers are added within square brackets. (See References at the end of the book, for full information on each volume cited and on currently available English translations.) In citations referring to Husserl's unpublished manuscripts, the final number always refers to the page number in the stenographic original. (For more on the treatment of citations in general, see the Translator's Preface above and the list of abbreviations preceding the Notes.)

2. On the course of development of Husserl's phenomenology of intersubjectivity, see Kern's introductions to *Husserliana* volumes 13, 14, and 15; see also Depraz 1992.

CHAPTER 1

1. Hence Strasser can justifiably write that the publication of Husserl's writings on intersubjectivity has both brought some surprising material to light and demonstrated that all current conceptions of Husserl's phenomenology are inadequate (Strasser 1975, 33). It must be added, however, that this is not so much the case because one can find radically new points of departure in the manuscripts; rather, it is because they provide us with material that illustrates and complements themes and passages in the works already published and does so in such a way as to make these themes and passages truly understandable for the first time.

2. Here we cannot provide any more precise analysis of the question of what motivation for the epoché and reduction could arise within the natural attitude—a question that must be posed because of Husserl's own occasional insistence upon the radical distinction between the natural attitude and the transcendental attitude. See, however, the essays by Lenkowski (1978) and Fink (1981a).

3. We shall not be explicitly investigating the concept of the noema in this context; however, see the careful presentation by Drummond (1990), with whose interpretation and critique of the "Fregean approach" we agree.

4. In *Die Fundamentalbetrachtung der Phänomenologie*, Schuhmann, referring to a remark by Fink, claims that the primary and most fundamental problem of constitution is precisely the problem of world-constitution, while the question of intersubjectivity would be secondary: "What takes priority, then, is

the question of the sense of the being in itself of the *world;* we shall accordingly pass over the question of intersubjectivity, or, as Husserl calls it, of the 'totality of monads.' The reason is because the structure and the problematic of the *alter ego* are the same in principle as that of one's own *ego.* The I and the we are 'taken up into' the eidos *'ego.'* That is to say, even the *alter ego* is faced with the fundamental problem of the world, since for the *alter ego*—just as for the *ego*— the possibility of other I's, and of communication with them, can be more readily given in insight than can the possibility of relating oneself to any being whose mode of being is different in principle from that of the I" (Schuhmann 1971, xxxviii–xxxix). Naturally, we are not denying the importance of clarifying the constitution of the world. Nevertheless, Schuhmann's assessment of what should take priority senems problematic. That is to say, the analysis of transcendental intersubjectivity serves to make this very goal—the transcendence of the world—understandable, and therefore intersubjectivity cannot simply be seen as a problem that can only be explored after an analysis of the world has been achieved. Rather—as will later become obvious—the two spheres of problems go hand in hand.

5.   That it is precisely this correlation that is central to Husserl's thought is demonstrated in the following passage: "The first breakthrough of the universal a priori of correlation between experienced object and manners of givenness (which occurred during work on my *Logical Investigations* around 1898) affected me so deeply that my whole subsequent life-work has been dominated by the task of systematically elaborating on this a priori of correlation" (6/169[166]; cf. 17/253[246]).

6.   Cf. Zahavi 1992a, Ch. V.2 and Ch. VIII.1.

7.   This conception is ultimately quite revealing when it comes to a more precise characterization of Husserl's pre-transcendental, merely descriptive phenomenology. That is to say, in his *Logical Investigations,* Husserl holds the view that any question with regard to the existence and the essential nature of the objective world is a metaphysical question that has no place in his phenomenology (19/26[264]).Thus, for example, it is irrelevant for the phenomenological description of perception whether the latter is ultimately accurate or illusory (19/358[537]), since it is exclusively a matter of investigating the phenomenon as phenomenon. Hence when Husserl occasionally characterizes the perceptual givenness of the object—more correctly, the intuitive fulfillment of the intention—as the givenness of the object itself, this says nothing about the relations of the perceived object to an "objective reality"; rather, this exclusively concerns descriptive traits of the phenomenal mode of givenness of the object. It is precisely when it comes presentively to appearance that the object *appears* as real. Since the question of the objective existence of whatever object is intended is methodologically excluded, this leaves a decided lack in the conception of phenomenology in the *Logical Investigations;* later, Husserl even emphasizes, over and over again, the fragmentary and incomplete nature of this "breakthrough" work (e.g., in Husserl 1939, 110, 117[1975, 17, 24]; however, see also the detailed presentation in Zahavi 1992a and 1992b). But the moment Husserl made the move to a transcenden-

tal philosophy, the conception of the task and scope of phenomenology shifted accordingly, and in the last part of *Ideas I*, entitled "Reason and Actuality," the problem of reality—and correlatively, the problem of the rational consciousness that legitimates this reality within itself—is mentioned and treated (e.g., 3/313[325]). It is this treatment of the question of reality or actuality that gradually led Husserl to *transcendental intersubjectivity*.

8. A theory that attempted to explain the intentional directedness of consciousness in such a way that it presupposed a (causal) effect of an object existing in itself would additionally imply that we could only be directed toward really existing objects; if we consider, for example, the variety of possible hallucinations and phantasy images, along with our directedness toward ideal objects and future events, this implication is immediately refuted. We *can* be directed toward non-existent objects (both universal and individual), and in these cases it is naturally not their non-existence that "really causes" our intentional directedness toward them.

9. Cf. Zahavi 1992a, Ch. II.1 and Ch. III.6, and Zahavi 1994a.

10. A careful investigation of Husserl's concept of sensation and a presentation of the manner in which it is gradually purified from its sensualistic tinge can be found both in Sokolowski 1970 and in Holenstein 1972.

11. This, of course, can once again serve to elucidate the genuine region of objects proper to phenomenology. We accordingly also agree with the following remark by Held: "The phenomenological reduction is not some 'reductionistic' abridgment. To refrain from going along with the natural attitude's belief in the independence of the being of objects from consciousness does not mean to fail to give the objects any attention at all. On the contrary, it is only through reflection that the contents of the objects can be analyzed in accordance with the originary and unabridged way in which these contents present themselves to consciousness. And it is only through epoché and phenomenological reduction that reflection is open without reservation for the analysis of originary modes of givenness. Transcendental phenomenology does not refrain from the world in favor of consciousness; rather, its interest lies precisely *in* illuminating the world as a phenomenon for consciousness. Ultimately, consciousness is of interest for the transcendental phenomenologist only as the place where the world appears" (Held 1985, 41).

12. Aguirre has shown how it is not only the ontological way, but also the Cartesian way to the reduction that is indirect, insofar as they both enter into the transcendental sphere only by way of a critique of world-experience (Aguirre 1970, 33–34; cf. 8/293), with the Cartesian way doing so precisely by demonstrating the inadequacy of world-experience. On the theme of the "ways to the reduction," see also—in addition to Aguirre—Kern (1962) and Drummond (1975). The latter convincingly claims that the so-called second way—the way via psychology—is in reality an important special case of the ontological way (Drummond 1975, 64).

13. Cf. Husserl's remark in Fink 1988b, 78.

14. Cf. Tugendhat 1970, 263.

15. Similarly, Heidegger writes: "It is phenomenologically absurd to speak

of the phenomenon as if it were something behind which there would be something else of which it would be a phenomenon in the sense of the appearance which represents and expresses [this something else]. A phenomenon is nothing behind which there would be something else. More accurately stated, one cannot ask for something behind the phenomenon at all, since what the phenomenon gives is precisely that something in itself" (PZ 118).

16. Here cf. the observations in Fink 1970, 94-95, 135-36.

17. We find the following description in Kern's classic presentation: "the transcendental reduction appears here as *breaking through limitations,* namely, the limitations of natural objective cognition, which is shown to be 'one-sided,' 'abstract,' 'superficial,' and 'shallow.' To use words which hark back to Hegel, it is the transition *(Übergang)* from the limited character of natural consciousness, which sees objects only positively as static, fixed, foreign things standing over against, to philosophical thinking, which recognizes the world as the proper achievement of consciousness, changing and developing throughout various forms" (Kern 1977, 144).

18. For some examples of this mode of interpretation—one that is particularly widespread among Anglo-Saxon Husserl scholars—see Holmes 1975a, Hall 1982, and Hutcheson 1980 and 1981b.

19. In Fink's words, the misunderstanding of the distinction that must be made in principle, within the concept of "phenomenology," between a "philosophy" and a "specific science" leads "to the almost inveterate error in the repeatedly formulated objection that Husserl's phenomenology is uninterested in the 'question of reality,' in the problem of being. It is objected that phenomenology thematized the existent merely as a subjective formation of meaning, as a moment of sense in the intentional life of consciousness" (Fink 1981a, 44). But "if the psychological noema is the *meaning* of an actual intentionality which is to be distinguished from the being itself to which it is related, then by contrast the transcendental noema is this being itself" (Fink 1970, 124).

20. Naturally, this does not mean that every senseful object also exists. To speak of an "existing" object means to speak of an object that is given in a distinctive way—namely, given intuitively *in propria persona.* To put it another way, only that which is intuitively given (i.e., perceptual sense in the broadest meaning of the term) permits us to speak of the existence of the object. Cf. Zahavi 1992a, 109.

21. Up to this point, we have been using the concepts of "ontology" and "metaphysics" as though they were more or less equivalent. However, if one understands "ontology" as the a priori theory of objects, then—as will be shown later (cf. Ch. V.I) —under the title of "metaphysics" Husserl occasionally understands something fundamentally different. Hence the question concerning the possible limitation of phenomenological analysis will emerge again later, but in an entirely different context.

22. Here it is rewarding to turn to the *Sixth Cartesian Meditation,* where Fink writes that no conflict between the truths of the mundane sphere and those of the transcendental sphere is possible, since these truths do not lie on the same

level. In this way the transcendental elucidation of the world "does not in any way deny and disparage truths known in the natural attitude," but rather "makes them radically, i.e., *constitutively,* understandable" for the first time (Fink 1995, 117). Later, however, it will turn out that the relation between the mundane and the transcendental sphere is much closer than Fink seems to indicate here.

23. Cf. also Husserl's letter of June 8, 1934, to Abbé Baudin: "No 'realist' in the usual sense has been as realistic and as concrete as I, the phenomenological 'idealist' (a word, by the way, that I no longer use)" (Briefwechsel, Vol. 7, 16).

24. Cf. Fichte's remarks on the mediation between a higher realism and idealism (Fichte 1986, 121, 148), along with Fink's reflections (Fink 1995, 152–59), which end with the following statement: "Insight into these connections allows clear recognition of how transcendental idealism is *beyond idealism and realism*" (Fink 1995, 159).

25. Cf. Wallner 1987.

26. Schutz sees the question of intersubjectivity as the crux of transcendental phenomenology (Schutz 1962, 165), and ultimately claims that Husserl's theory of intersubjectivity fails on account of his phenomenologically unfounded shift in the concept of constitution "from a clarification of sense-structure, from an explication of the sense of being, into the foundation of the structure of being; it has changed from explication into creation *(Kreation)*" (Schutz 1966, 83; cf. Ch. I.5 of the present work). And Aguirre (1970, 63) characterizes the incorporation of intersubjectivity as the highest consummation of idealism insofar as the being of others is included within my own absolute being. On the contrary, however, Boehm finds—and our position is closer to his views—that it is precisely the theory of the experience of others that can most suitably elucidate the genuine sense of constitution—a sense that is ultimately incompatible with the traditional categories of idealism and realism (Boehm 1969, 2).

27. Here we do not wish by any means to cast doubt upon the philosophical quality of the *Cartesian Meditations,* but only to emphasize that this work's true sense can hardly be understood without referring to the research manuscripts that are now published in *Husserliana* volumes 13, 14, and 15. For an early and well-informed interpretation of Husserl's phenomenology of community based almost exclusively on *Ideas I* and *Cartesian Meditations,* see Boehm 1969.

28. Cf., e.g., Kozlowski 1991, 15.

29. Schuhmann (1988, 56) cites a passage from the English syllabus of Husserl's London lectures of 1922: "In the proper line of its explication lies the development of the originally 'egological' . . . phenomenology into a transcendental sociological phenomenology."

30. Thus Zeltner (1959, 310) speaks of a fundamental aporia in Husserl's phenomenology of intersubjectivity, since the structures of transcendental intersubjectivity worked out by Husserl can only help us to grasp the phenomenon of commonality in relatively empty, vague, and formal universality. A similar reproach can be found in Theunissen (1986, 109–23). With regard to

Husserl's reflections on sociality as a mode of relationship with others at a higher level, cf. Text Nr. 29 in *Zur Phänomenologie der Intersubjektivität III*, as well as Toulemont's classic presentation (Toulemont 1962).

31. Thus Husserl distinguishes between acts in which I simply experience others without necessarily becoming explicitly aware of them, and *communicative* acts in which I turn toward others and the others understand this as a turning-toward (13/98, 4/194, 15/472-75).

32. It is worthy of note that both Husserl's transcendental idealism and his concept of constitution are almost always interpreted *creationistically* by his critics (cf. Schutz 1966, 83; Ricoeur 1981, 124-25; and Ch. V.I). In Ch. V we shall attempt to clarify the sense of the concept of constitution on the basis of the incorporation of transcendental intersubjectivity. But it must already be indicated at this point that if one understands the concept of constitution as a *creatio ex nihilo*, one is likely to miss the entire sense of Husserl's account. It should be obvious, however, that an alternative interpretation of the concept would make the notion of the constitution of an *alter ego* considerably easier. Moreover, the relevance of the earlier sketch of Husserl's fundamental project becomes clear the moment one is confronted with the narrower semantic interpretations of the problem of intersubjectivity. For example, Hutcheson writes that Husserl could never reject solipsism phenomenologically, "for an answer to the solipsist in this way would constitute ontological commitment to the existence of other subjects. But performing the phenomenological reduction amounts to abstention from ontological commitment." In contrast, "Husserl wants to explicate the concept 'existing others', rather than establish the existence of others" (Hutcheson 1980, 146, 150). Cf. Hall 1979, 15, but see also Schroeder 1984, 35–36, whose presentation of Husserl is based exclusively on the *Cartesian Meditations*, and can serve as an example of how readily such a manner of reading one text of Husserl's in isolation can miss Husserl's actual position.

33. Similarly, Fink writes that the transcendental reduction only comes to completion "in the full unfolding of co-constituting *intersubjectivity*, which is *implied* in the transcendental ego" (Fink 1995, 5; cf. 5-6).

34. This is especially the case in Theunissen 1986, Ch. 4. However, see also Schutz 1966, 51-91, and Rohr-Dietschi 1974, 144-50.

35. Husserl already says in *Ideas I* (3/60-61[55-57]) that the unproblematic assumption of the existence of others is a basic component of the natural attitude.

36. In a letter of May 1, 1956, from Schutz to Gurwitsch, this preference for a non-transcendental phenomenology is clearly expressed: "I think, and have always thought, that the phenomenology of the natural attitude is much more pressing and also much more fruitful" (Schutz and Gurwitsch 1989, 255); see also Srubar's essay in Grathoff and Waldenfels 1983. In a work guided by presentations of the positions of Mead, Gurwitsch, and Schutz, Vaitkus (1991) consistently advocates a mundane investigation of intersubjectivity as well. Unfortunately, Vaitkus simply takes over Schutz's critique of the transcendental treatment of intersubjectivity without supporting it through further argumentation.

37. Cf. similar observations in Meist 1980, 582.

38. In a similar way, a transcendental theory of intersubjectivity presupposes an egological theory of consciousness, which is why Gurwitsch can claim that a non-egological conception of consciousness makes the problem of transcendental intersubjectivity superfluous. For if there is no transcendental I and every I is an empirical one, then the question of the relationship between "I" and "others" is an empirical-mundane problem (Schutz and Gurwitsch 1989, 238; cf. Gurwitsch 1966, 290–91, 297). As Marbach has shown, however, Husserl actually abandoned the non-egological theory of consciousness that he had advocated in the *Logical Investigations,* and began to speak instead of the pure I, precisely because he wanted to treat intersubjectivity transcendentally (Marbach 1974, Ch. 5). That is to say, the reason it was necessary to introduce the I as a principle of unity was in order to make possible the delimitation between "one's own" lived experiences and the "foreign" lived experiences presentified in empathy (Marbach 1974, 117). And it is this very delimitation that would not be possible if the essential relation of the lived experiences to the pure I were to be denied, i.e., if one were to advocate a non-egological conception of consciousness according to which we could really only talk about "nobody's" lived experiences (Marbach 1974, 100). See also Bernet 1994, 303.

39. Thus, for example, Husserl writes that there are as many pure I's as there are real ones (4/110)—a conception that Kant would never have accepted, and that points to the fundamental difference between their respective concepts of the transcendental *ego.* Although Husserl's account of intersubjectivity must be seen as transformative in comparison to the Kantian account, the question is more difficult when one also brings into play the transcendental philosophical conceptions of Fichte, Schelling, and Hegel, for they too have attempted a transcendental philosophical elucidation of intersubjectivity. Thus Schelling writes, for instance, that "a rational being in isolation could not only not arrive at a consciousness of freedom, but would be equally unable to attain to consciousness of the objective world as such; and hence ... intelligences outside the individual, and a never-ceasing interaction with them, alone make complete the whole of consciousness with all its determinations" (Schelling 1978, 174). Like Theunissen (1986, 5) and Held (1966, 170), we too must unfortunately limit ourselves to this hint and forgo a more comprehensive presentation. However, we can point to the work of Düsing (1986), although unfortunately her interpretation of Husserl uncritically follows that of Schutz.

CHAPTER II

1. In connection with the performance of the abstraction to the primordial, Husserl mentions that it suspends this validity-for-everyone, and he writes that within the province of the most fundamental, "purely egological" phenomenology, truth is no longer truth "in itself" in any normal sense—not even in a sense where it would be related to a transcendental "everyone" (17/276

[269]; cf. 1/128). Does this claim make sense? Does not any mention of truth require, according to the sense proper to this notion, that it be true once and for all, and indeed, for everyone (8/380)? However, there is a possibility of interpreting Husserl in such a way that although the truths of the primordial sphere are indeed subjective, in accordance with their sense—i.e., insofar as they cannot be asserted by any other subject (14/106) — their objective truth content does not need to be denied on this account. That is to say, the abstraction to the primordial can also be interpreted in such a way that it is a matter of excluding all elements of signification other than occasional expressions referring to the I. The latter sort of significations or truths are nevertheless subjective in a certain legitimate sense, for when I see a tree, neither the perception as a temporally individuated act nor the true statement "I see a tree" can be repeated without modification by another subject. The other can indeed see the same tree, as well as asserting for his own part, "I see a tree." In both cases, however, there would be indexical alterations. The perception would no longer be mine, but the other's, and a shift of I-referents would have taken place. Yet the significations or truths found in occasional expressions referring to the I are indeed objective insofar as they allow an objectivation. The expression "I see a tree" is only true when it allows the modification "She sees a tree." Hence what our analysis is aiming at is that primordial truths are subjective (or private) with respect to their *mode of givenness,* without thereby excluding the objectivity of the *content* of the truth or signification concerned. That is why Husserl is not advocating a nonsensical solipsism of truth or signification, and he can therefore write: "What I myself have as immanent, and grasp in immanent experiencing, can only be grasped *in this way* by me (which is, to be sure, an insight that itself has an objective character insofar as I think of it as a true statement that everyone would have to acknowledge)" (14/107, emphasis altered).

2. Cf. Fink 1981a, 39. Fink is fully justified in adding the following: "The continuous chain of 'perceptual acts,' acts almost constantly given in the flow of conscious processes, is not that to which the implicit sense of memory genuinely refers back. If we inquire into their intentional sense, such *de facto,* concretely occurring perceptions are always more than *pure* perceptions. They are acts in which the existent is present, but in such a way that the existent is completely permeated and saturated by what has been inherited from previous perception and by knowledge that has been acquired individually or through education. What is perceived in such a perception has innumerable, already known characteristics and superimposed layers of sense, both of which cover the core of that which is actually perceived originarily. We do not first begin to perceive, but have always already perceived. Actual perceiving is not originary consciousness, because sedimented acquisitions of knowledge which are traditional and taken over are involved in the perceiving" (Fink 1981a, 40).

3. A detailed presentation of the relationships between passivity, activity, and experience of others, along with an attempt to show on this basis how we

can escape certain aporias in Husserl's analysis of empathy, can be found in Yamaguchi 1982.

4. A more precise characterization of the connection between (thematic) recollection and retention—a connection that is, of course, also of importance with respect to the constitution of the object—can be left out of consideration in this context.

5. Hence it is important to underline that the phantasied Pegasus always transcends my current act of apprehension, just as any perceived table does: what is meant is indeed neither a really intrinsic content, nor this or that imaginatively appearing side of Pegasus, but rather Pegasus itself (cf. 2/72). Thus even in cases of hallucination or phantasy, we are not confronted with intentional objects that would exist *in* consciousness. (Here cf. Husserl's critique of Twardowski's *Zur Lehre vom Inhalt und Gegenstand der Vorstellungen*—see 22/ 309-10).

6. "Die Transzendenz, in der die Welt konstituiert <ist>, besteht darin, daß sie sich mittels der Anderen und der generativ konstituierten Mitsubjektivität konstituiert" (Ms. C 17 32a.)

7. Cf. Wittgenstein 1958, § 265.

8. To be sure, this must not be misunderstood as though Husserl was claiming that in the experience of others, we are always also performing an actual *presentification* of the perceptual profile available to the other (an interpretation that Arp, for instance, proposes, then subsequently criticizes—see Arp 1991, 91). Instead, Husserl's idea is that with the experience of others, we simultaneously have that which the other experiences in *co-acceptance*. This co-acceptance lends validity to our own perceptual object precisely by making it an object for a second I—i.e., this object is an object that is transcendent to me. But it is by no means the case that such co-acceptance has to be intuitively fulfilled for it to exert this effect. In other words, it does not have to be supported by any explicit presentification of the specific contents drawn from the experience and apprehension of the other, although such a presentification can naturally be performed at any time—and often is performed, e.g., in communication: "We already have a certain 'community' in being mutually 'there' for one another in the surrounding world (the other in my surrounding world)—and this always means being physically, bodily 'there.' We experience one another as seeing the same objects—or in part the same—in the same world, which is a world for us. For the most part, as regards this common seeing, this is inauthentic experience, the empty understanding of the others and their experiential situation. But the community of persons, as a community of personal life and possibly as a lasting personal interrelation, is something special. A first step is explicitly to be vitally at one with the other person in the intuitive understanding of his experiencing, his life-situation, his activity, etc. From there one proceeds to communication through expression and language, which is already an interrelation of egos. Every sort of communication naturally presupposes the commonality of the surrounding world, which is established as

soon as we are persons for one another at all—though this can be completely empty, inactive" (6/307-308[328-29]; cf. 13/469, 15/83-84).

9. In a precisely analogous way, it also only makes sense to speak of a pathologically and a normally functioning lived bodilihood of a solitary subject if this subject already has a system of orthological experiences, i.e., experiences running a normal course (cf. 13/368), since it is only on the basis of a concordance of experience that one can speak of abnormality or anomaly (cf. 13/394 and 15/34; see also Ch. IV.2 below).

10. Even my own mortality is concealed until the coexistence of others is brought into play: "Here is the place for the possibility of death—which, however, cannot be objectivated in egological self-observation; it cannot have any lived experiential intuitability, for it can only obtain a sense for me by way of an understanding of others" (15/452; cf. Ms. A VI 14A 5a, Ms. C 17 32a).

11. What comes into view here is the relativity of our current modes of givenness—and as we shall see later (Ch. IV.2), this relativity becomes the motivational foundation for the natural scientific search for the non-relative, physically determinable thing in itself.

12. In *Zur Phänomenologie der Intersubjektivität II*, Husserl makes the following remarks concerning the concept of transcendence: "It already follows from this that the transcendence of the thing of experience cannot have the significance of something that is not experienced; rather, it is the transcendence of the experienced itself, as experienced. As experienced, as itself-perceived, it is immanent insofar as the one perceiving grasps the thing itself, but it is transcendent insofar as the experience, in accordance with its essence, is always anticipatory. It is transcendent in the sense introduced by Leibniz whereby an infinity is called transcendent, yet remains an infinity that can be grasped in immanence. . . . The immanence concerns the nexuses of currently actual experience of that which is experienced. The transcendence, however, consists in the circumstance that the experienced—as intentional, and as what is given, itself, in experience—is experienced 'incompletely,' one-sidedly: the experience leaves open infinities of possible further experiencing of the same object (in syntheses of identification)—and with this, ever-open possibilities of non-confirmation" (14/349).

13. Of course, horizonality should not merely be understood as the mode of givenness of spatiotemporal realities. Depending on the context, a tree does not merely point toward a cluster of more or less determinate aspects within the ontological region, "nature"; the tree, as an object of nature, simultaneously points toward its useful aspects, toward its aesthetic aspects, toward aspect that can be further displayed and explained scientifically, etc. As Husserl says, there are not only horizons of being, but moral horizons, value horizons, practical horizons, etc. (Ms. A VII 2 9a). See also the detailed analyses in Gurwitsch 1966, 175-286, and Gurwitsch 1964.

14. As a matter of fact, here Husserl (in contrast to Heidegger, who contents himself in *Being and Time* with the remark that he will *not* be dealing with "the spatialization of Da-sein in its 'corporeality'"—SuZ 108) anticipates discussions in *Being and Nothingness* where Sartre writes that our being-in-the-

world is literally a bodily being-in-the-midst-of-the-world. It is only because one has "entered" the world that one can constitute it; as Sartre puts it, to say that I have "come to the world" and to say that I "have a body" are equivalent expressions (EN 366/419). And as both Sartre and Merleau-Ponty point out, the structures of the world imply that one cannot see without being visible oneself (EN 365/419; cf. VI 152-53/113-14).

15. It must be emphasized that the constitutive kinaestheses are not to be confused with movement in objective space or with the movement of objectivated body parts. Thus when Husserl speaks of the constitutive significance of the movement and the position of the lived body, this must not be identified with the position and movement of our physical body in objective space, since objective space is precisely a space constituted as "independent from my own movement." That is to say, one can only speak of an "objective" space if its coordinates are no longer related to my indexical here, which is already the case when I experience myself moving *through* "space." Hence the kinaesthetic system (the system of my free possibilities of movement) is originally lived as a free "I can" (11/14). It is only in conjunction with the objectivation of the lived body that the kinaestheses are apprehended as a system arranged into particular objective bodily members. This *localization* of sensations pertaining to kinaesthesis is investigated by Husserl in detail, since it is a condition of possibility for the constitution of the lived body as an object (4/56, 5/118) — an objectivation that is in turn closely linked with the constitution of objective space. That is to say, what is implied when I objectivate my own lived body (i.e., when I apprehend it as one object among others) is precisely a suspension of the indexicality pertaining to my own lived body (cf. Ch. IV.2). The significance of kinaesthesis for the constitution of spatial objects is a recurring theme in Husserl's work. Particularly comprehensive treatments will be found in Section IV of *Thing and Space* (with the title "The significance of the kinaesthetic systems for the constitution of the perceived object"); in Section One, Chapter 3 of *Ideas 2* (with the title "The aestheta in their relation to the aesthetic body"); and in Beilage XVIII of *Zur Phänomenologie der Intersubjektivität III* (with the title "The manner in which the lived body is constituted as a physical body and as a lived body, as well as the ways in which its <constitution> and the constitution of external things are intimately united throughout"). The following presentation cannot do full justice to the complexity of these analyses; see, however, Claesges 1964 and Becker 1973, as well as Zahavi 1994b. For a more recent treatment of kinaesthesis, see, e.g., Lakoff 1987, Ch. 17.

16. Cf. Merleau-Ponty, VI 284/230-31. In addition to this, Landgrebe has pointed out that Husserl's reflections on kinaesthesis as the condition of possibility for the experience of objects must lead to a revision of the way the relationship between receptivity and spontaneity—and, ultimately, the relation between sensibility and reason—is usually conceived (Landgrebe 1963, 117).

17. Thus we must also be sure to avoid understanding the correlation between act and object in such a way as to imply that the existence of the object is linked with its factual givenness; rather, each object is something in itself, i.e., something that exists without its being currently actually perceived.

18. Here one could, of course, point out that it would be possible to see the back side of the perceptual object intuitively in the mirror. However, we would still have to reply that in this case, one would not be looking at the back side of the perceptual object but at a reflection of it.

19. To be sure, even in the *Logical Investigations* this does not imply that our perception of sensuous objects is brought about in multi-leveled acts, as is the case with the perception of categorial objects (cf. 19/676-77[788-89]). As we have pointed out, what we see from the start is the object, not merely one side of it. It is for this reason that in the end, the object also cannot be considered as the *mere* sum or totality of all its profiles, for this would imply that we would have to run through all the profiles before we could add them together in order to see the object itself; rather, the object must be understood as a principle of unity and identity pervading all these profiles. Cf. Bernet 1979b.

20. For this point and some other stimulating suggestions I am indebted to Kojima 1978. In addition, Held 1972 and Sallis 1971 have independently pursued the connection between horizon and intersubjectivity.

21. "unendliche System 'möglicher Wahrnehmungen' und des korrelativen 'möglichen Aussehens' eines transzendenten Objektes" (Ms. A III 9 23b).

22. However, cf. note 8 above.

23. One aspect of Sartre's Husserl interpretation in *Being and Nothingness* is very much to the point here—namely, when he writes: "Thus each object far from being constituted as for Kant, by a simple relation to the *subject*, appears in my concrete experience as polyvalent; it is given originally as possessing systems of reference to an indefinite plurality of consciousnesses; it is *on* the table, *on* the wall that the Other is revealed to me as that to which the object under consideration is perpetually referred—as well as on the occasion of the concrete appearances of Pierre or Paul" (EN 278/316).

24. "das erfahrene Reale wirklich ist mit dem Seinssinn, den es als Korrelat des Systems einstimmiger möglicher Erfahrung aller mit mir möglicherweise in Konnex tretenden miterfahrenden Subjekte hat, oder den es in der Weise hat, daß das jeweils wirklich Erfahrene horizonthaft verweist auf eine Einstimmigkeit in der fortgehenden und immer wieder herzustellenden Synthesis möglicher Erfahrung, eigener und beliebig in Mitfunktion tretender Erfahrung von Mitmenschen" (Ms. A VII 2 22b).

25. This formulation has the advantage of bringing to light the irrelevance of the kind of counter-argument that is at stake in the following sort of objection to our analysis of horizon intentionality. Let us imagine that there is a book lying on a table; the underside of the book is obviously co-intended, but how can this be correlative to the perception that some possible other would have of the book? As long as the book is lying on the table, it is indeed impossible for any subject (and thus not just for me) to perceive its underside.

26. Cf. 15/214 and 15/428-37, as well as Ch. IV.2 below; see also Lohmar 1994.

27. It is above all Theunissen who has pursued this explanatory endeavor, an effort that he presents in detail in Ch. 3 of *The Other*, where he attempts to interpret Husserl's theory by way of his own concept of "alter-ation."

28. Cf. Held 1972, 26.

29. It must be emphasized that the reference to "everyone" only seems to represent a shift in direction toward a meta-subjective standpoint. For as we have previously stated (Ch. I.4), intersubjectivity can only be manifested within each individual conscious life, just as what is performed by transcendental intersubjectivity is only manifested in the performance of the individual subject; hence the term "everyone" refers to everyone who is or can be appresented within *my* subjectivity (8/494, 15/645).

30. It is precisely this manner of posing the problem that Waldenfels addresses in the following remarks: "One might object that in its finitude, my world always already leaves open the *possibility* that it is also there for others whether or not these others factually appear, and hence that it points *eo ipso* to others. However illuminating and fruitful this notion may be, nowhere do I see any indication that Husserl actually worked it out. That is to say, he would have had to place in question the assumption of a primordial sphere of ownness, which forms not merely a sector, but the foundational stratum of the world in common, and thereby absorbs everything foreign into itself from the very beginning. But for him, the possibility of other subjects only means a possible constitution established within my world and thereby within me" (Waldenfels 1971a, 32–33). Although we agree in this context with Waldenfels' critique of Husserl's keeping to the primordial sphere, we have to insist that Husserl did accomplish a broadening of the phenomenological sphere to transcendental intersubjectivity, and we therefore take issue with the claim that he never seriously saw open intersubjectivity as the noetic correlate of the world. This is not only because there is more than enough textual material to demonstrate this but also because Husserl's entire account goes in exactly this direction. It is, of course, a pity that Husserl himself never drew the full consequences from this line of development—but here it would be precisely a case of reading Husserl against himself.

31. Cf. Waldenfels 1971a, 135.

32. To be sure, the connection between horizon and finitude raises a question, for we have already seen that according to Husserl, even God's experience of the world is perspectival (3/351[362]). Hence one cannot trace the perspectivity of the givenness of things back to the finite character of our structure of consciousness; rather, the thing's perspectival mode of appearance is determined by its own regional essence. However, this in no way excludes that our horizonality is, as a matter of fact, an indication of our finitude; moreover, one can also ask here whether the concept of the cognition of an object by an infinite intellect is not a *contradictio in adjecto,* insofar as the very opposition between knowing subject and known object already indicates the finitude of the subject.

33. "Natürlich stückt sich die Welt nicht aus den primordial reduzierten Welten zusammen. Jedes Primordiale ist Reduktionsprodukt von einem intersubjektiv und generativ konstituierten Sinn, der Seinsinn ist aus der intersubjektiv zusammenstimmenden Erfahrung eines jeden, einer Erfahrung, die schon auf die Intersubjektivität Sinnbeziehung hat. Meine Erfahrung als Welterfahrung

(also jede meiner Wahrnehmungen schon) schließt nicht nur Andere als Weltobjekte ein, sondern beständig in seinsmäßiger Mitgeltung als Mitsubjekte, als Mitkonstituierende, und beides ist untrennbar verflochten" (Ms. C 17 36a).

34. "Wenn Einfühlung eintritt—ist etwa auch schon die Gemeinschaft, die Intersubjektivität da und Einfühlung dann bloß enthüllendes Leisten?" (Ms. C 17 84b).

35. Fink has seen this quite clearly: "The problem of a philosophy need not be identical with the particular questions with which its literature begins, with, therefore, the situation which belongs to a philosophy when it begins, or with the predominant, motivating questions which remain with a philosophy throughout its development. The problem need not even be properly formulated. It can have an effect prior to its reflective formulation *in* all of the particular questions, it can stand *behind* all of the individual motivations of thought as the driving motive. If provisional, later reworked stages of a philosopher's development are involved in his own understanding of his thought, uncertainty regarding the fundamental problem of his philosophy remains even where the author formulates this problem" (Fink 1981a, 21).

36. Here we might point to the original sense of "foundation" as it is defined by Husserl in the Third Logical Investigation. That something is "founded on" something else does not mean that it can be derived from it or reduced to it, but only that it cannot exist unless that which it is founded upon also exists (19/281-82[475]).

37. Dauenhauer too has argued that it is possible to demonstrate the possibility a priori of a plurality of I's through an analysis of perceptual intentionality and of horizon intentionality: "Once this a priori possibility is established, then the detection of actual other egos is simply an empirical question. It is then only a matter of verifying that this possibility is indeed actualized in some particular instances" (Dauenhauer 1975, 189). In addition, Arp has stressed the distinction between the concrete other that we experience as existing in the world, on the one hand, and on the other hand, the anonymously co-functioning other embedded in the horizonal structure of intentionality; she then claims that the transcendental constitutive other can never be the other that we experience concretely, since this other—as a mundane subject—presupposes the prior constitution of the world (Arp 1987, 33-34; cf. Arp 1991, 98-99). To be sure, the latter interpretation is disputed by Husserl in *Formal and Transcendental Logic,* for he tells us there that the physical body of the other that I encounter in concrete experience of others can have a significance that is not yet an objective-mundane significance (17/247[240]). If, however, we understand the "mundane" or the "worldly" simply as the "horizonal" in this context, it is difficult to accept Husserl's statement, and Arp's account therefore seems to be justified. It must nevertheless be emphasized—and this can be argued against both Dauenhauer and Arp—that even the concrete experience of others (or of the concrete other) is the condition of possibility for certain extremely important constitutive accomplishments, and for this reason it

cannot be characterized as "merely" mundane, empirical, or constituted, but on the contrary must be characterized as transcendental.

38. Of course, this last formulation should not lead us to think that our demonstration of the existence of an a priori intersubjectivity is the result of a regressive or deductive (and ultimately unphenomenological) search for conditions of possibility. That is to say, the thesis of open, anonymous intersubjectivity is exclusively motivated by, and corroborated through, a concrete analysis of horizon intentionality—i.e., nowhere are we arguing that there *"must be"* an a priori intersubjectivity because the concrete experience of others would be impossible without it.

39. Carr even claims that although it is the foreign I that makes transcendence in the proper sense possible, this foreign I must itself be characterized as an immanent transcendence (Carr 1973, 27). However, this interpretation stands in opposition to Husserl's repeated statements concerning the way in which "the otherness of 'someone else' becomes extended to the whole world, as its 'Objectivity', giving it this sense in the first place" (1/173), so that everything else that receives the title of transcendence "rests upon the transcendence of foreign subjectivity" (8/495 n. 2; cf. Ch. II.3 above).

40. This interpretation finds a kind of confirmation in Cairns's rendering of a conversation with Husserl on June 4, 1932, in which Husserl said as follows; "it is an apodictic transcendental fact that my subjectivity constitutes for itself a world as intersubjective. The other self is therefore a necessary intentional 'object' of the absolutely evident structure of my awareness. Furthermore this other self is necessarily coequal with my self. My transcendental self, by virtue of its evident structure, perceives itself as without any superiority over the other self. (I am an intentional object for him, as he is for me; he is an absolute constitutive consciousness, as I am.) This is all part of the apodictic facticity of my transcendental subjectivity. It does not depend on the fortuitous constitution of a particular object of valid *Einfühlung* <empathy> in perception, but is simply an explication of the fact that I do intend a world as necessarily intersubjective. (That is what I mean by calling it a world. If it were not intersubjective, it would not be a world.) Strictly it is an (open?) infinity of other subjects which is required by the apodictic factual structure of my transcendental consciousness, not *one* other subject" (Cairns 1976, 82–83).

Chapter III

1. Fink's thesis is taken up by Mensch (1988, 1, 394, 405), who attempts to support it in detail by referring to a number of unpublished manuscripts. In our further examination of Fink's interpretation, we shall be guided in part by Mensch's choice of manuscripts, although this in no way means that we agree with his interpretation.

2. We shall return to these ideas (see Chapter VI.4), which we also find in Merleau-Ponty's *Phenomenology of Perception* (see PP 428/373).

3. Sommer quite correctly characterizes temporalization as an objectivation and ontification (cf. Ms. C 16 61a), and claims that the subject's (constitutively) overextending itself points, in and of itself, to an alliance of many subjects (Sommer 1984, 3). Constitution as bringing-transcendence-to-givenness consequently implies a constant self-alienation and self-dispossession, and thereby leads the subject to experience moments of the foreign within itself (Sommer 1984, 5). My constitutive effort to overcome my own finitude and perspectivity reveals, according to Sommer (1984, 6), a moment of foreignness within myself—a view that we have already attempted to present in another manner (cf. Chapter II.5). However, Sommer also speaks of that which is prior even to my earliest memory as a past that on account of its experiential emptiness, was never my present (Sommer 1984, 15), and he claims that this prior consciousness is not my own, but a consciousness foreign to me: "Only when I perceive—thus grasping reality within my restricted perspective and from my contingent place—only then am I myself; it is only then that I can borrow this foreign past in order to lend it to my own I, and in this way appropriate it for myself. Thus my own past arises from the past foreign to me: it is that which is foreign within me, and since it is also an I, it is a foreigner within me" (Sommer 1984, 15–16). But how can Sommer characterize the past that is not my own as a "foreign I within me" when at the same time, he also characterizes this prior past that is empty of content as a "non-individual" past (Sommer 1984, 16)? Can there ever be such a thing? Is not the very concept of a non-individual foreign I absurd? Regarding the possibility of treating the phase of ego-development shortly after birth in a transcendental phenomenological manner, cf. Rohr-Dietschi 1974, 101–12.

4. Cf., e.g., 1/144, 3/325[336], 8/175, 6/189[185], 13/188, 15/447, 15/641.

5. Römpp has justifiably written that Husserl attempted to interpret the relationship of one being-for-itself to another being-for-itself as the being-for-one-another of two temporalities (Römpp 1992, 100). Indeed, it is precisely this notion of a foreign present presentified within my own present that can make the experienceability of a foreign being-for-itself understandable (Römpp 1992, 103; see also Ch. V of that work, as well as Römpp 1989a).

6. Meist has shown how it is the reciprocal transcendence characterizing the relation between one's own "present" and the foreign "present" that first reveals, by way of the resulting decentralization of the communal temporal relationship, the complete non-availability of this temporal relationship, i.e., the historical dimension of factual consciousness (Meist 1983, 99). Thus as Husserl also writes, it is the radical shift accomplished by the transcendental epoché that discloses transcendental historicity (Ms. K III 6 88b). The coexistence of my temporal being and that of the other is, of course, transmitted through others to further others who are others for the first others, thus reaching, through mediated empathizing, even to past subjects with whom I now have scarcely any connection. Nevertheless, I do have some experience of them by way of others who did experience them at one time, with this past experiencing itself handed down in mediated transmission through genera-

tions, i.e., *historically* (15/333; cf. 6/191[188], 6/256[253], 6/381[372], and Landgrebe 1974). In a later essay, Meist claims that only the kind of generative teleology of the totality of monads that Husserl presupposes can salvage the unity of the historical nexus (Meist 1991, 299; cf. our presentation in Ch. IV.2 of the present work).

7. "schwer zu beschreibender Weise" (Ms. C 16 7b).

8. "Gemeinschaft mit dem Anderen erfahre ich in einfühlender Appräsentation, als Parallele der Wiedererinnerung. Wenn Wiedererinnerung einsetzt, so ist die Kontinuität meiner Vergangenheit aus meiner ständigen Selbstdeckung, aus ständiger Retention schon da, vorausgesetz, Untergrund. Wenn Einfühlung eintritt—ist etwa auch schon die Gemeinschaft, die Intersubjektivität da und Einfühlung dann bloß enthüllendes Leisten?" (Ms. C 17 84b).

9. This statement, however, points at the same time to the problems entailed in a *phenomenological* description of this anonymous life; as Husserl says, "The 'pre-being' of the streaming being is precisely something that can be made objective 'at any time,' and is only to be transcendentally described in this way" ("Das 'Vor-Sein' des strömenden Seins ist eben 'jederzeit' gegenständlich zu machen und ist nur so transzendental zu beschreiben"—Ms. C 16 59a). Consequently, the "primal phenomenal present" that is supposed to be the primal existent *(Urseiendes)* is not ultimate after all, precisely because it is a phenomenon (Ms. C 2 10b). Thus since any thematization always already, and continually, implies an ontification (cf. Ms. C 10 5a), the non-objective primal level can only be revealed through a regressive peeling off of the layers concerned—i.e., through a procedure that is basically unphenomenological. This way of posing the problem is treated in detail in Held 1966.

10. "daß jedes Ich, rein als Ich betrachtet, in seinem Bewußtseinsleben und rein darin lebend seine Individualität hat. . . . Im Gehalt jedes Ich selbst liegt die absolute Einzigkeit" (Ms. C 17 15b).

11. A comprehensive treatment of this thematic domain can be found in Lee 1993.

12. It is not only at the level of drive-intentionality that this interpenetration takes place; Husserl also takes up the case of communication, describing how the intentionality of one monad enters into the intentionality of another monad, and how in functioning as poles of intentional performances, two I's can coincide and penetrate one another in such a way that a purely inward mental or spiritual unity of intersubjective intentionality arises. When, for example, I fulfill the wish of another, "it is not just that the other wishes and that what I accomplish in my activities brings about what he wishes. Rather, the wish announced by the other and addressed to me enters into my life—not the other's wish as a moment of his life, from which it is indeed inseparable, and from which it remains inseparable; rather, the intentional correlate of his wishing—his wish—becomes empathically known to me as his wish through his announcement and is taken over by me, becoming at the same time my wish, in a coincidence of identity—but in such a way that it is precisely the other's wish that I am taking over, so that I am fulfilling the intention that

the other is addressing to me, voluntarily doing what the other wants 'from me.' Acting thus, it is I who act, but the other's I—as the I who wishes and addresses my I—is now in coincidence with mine, precisely insofar as the other's wish, and his wish that I fulfill this wish, is one with 'my' wish—but, as I have said, 'mine' only in the other's service, in a consciousness in which his intentionality is unified with my own regardless of the separateness of the lived experiences concerned" (9/485; cf. 14/170, 14/219, 14/269).

13. A related line of argument is found in Scheler, who saw the existence of others confirmed precisely through his analysis of the sphere of emotional acts. For instance, if one takes genuine fellow feeling, love, or sympathy, it is a matter of a true reaching out to, and reaching into, an individuality differing in content and existence from the one that is reaching out. What is under consideration here is an actual intentional transcendence, and it is for this reason that in Scheler's view, our experience of fellow feeling or sympathy can serve as an immediate argument against solipsism (NS 46, 60, 70). Insofar as a number of emotions indicate a (possible) plurality of subjects, Scheler criticizes any monistic metaphysical claim for the existence of a unified supra-individual consciousness. That is to say, considered phenomenologically, intentions exist whose structure is incompatible with the abolition of the substantial diversity of concrete act-centers in favor of a metaphysical principle of unity (NS 64-65): "Hence sympathy does not proclaim the essential identity of persons, as Schopenhauer and von Hartmann allege, but actually presupposes a pure essential *difference* between them (this being also the ultimate basis of their difference in actual fact). The occurrence of a feeling in some sort of supra-individual spirit or universal consciousness, in which the two persons merely participate together, coalescing therein, as it were, would not be sympathy at all. And if, as we saw, it is the very office of true sympathy to dissipate the solipsistic illusion by apprehending the equivalent status of the other person *as* such, it cannot be at the same time a dim perception of the fact that neither of us really exists, but only some third party, of whom we are merely the functions" (NS 65-66, trans. altered).

14. As a matter of fact, there are several passages in Husserl's manuscripts of 1921-22 that could be used to support Fink's interpretation (cf. 14/129, 14/266). However, Husserl himself remarks that these are experimental accounts based on an arbitrary supposition (14/130). And it is even more important to see that here it is essentially a question of earlier deliberations that can in no way be viewed as the culmination of his reflections; on the contrary, they were—in our opinion—abandoned by him once again.

15. It is interesting that Biemel expresses the same surmise in her remarks to the transcription of pp. 47-63 of the E III 4 manuscript: "There seems to be an influence of Fink in this" ("Es scheint ein Einfluß von Fink darin zu sein"—Ms. E III 4, xviii). That is to say, within these pages—and it is not possible to say for sure whether this actually confirms Fink's interpretation—Husserl speaks of an absolute Logos (God) in the new, supra-transcendental-subjective sense, as a highest ultimate unity of ideas that bears ontological uniqueness within itself, and that first gives any transcendental-monadic

being whatsoever its true sense (Ms. E III 4 36b–37a). Strasser remarks that through Husserl's endeavors to exclude any plurality from pre-being, we arrive at the sphere of a phenomenological inquiry into the divine (Strasser 1975, 22). To be sure, we do not share Strasser's views about Husserl's concept of pre-being. But it must be conceded that if Husserl had spoken of a pre-individuated absolute, he would have been taking a step into phenomenological theology. Husserl's other reflections on the concept of God cannot be covered in the present investigation (but cf. 15/610).

16. Ricoeur remarks in this connection: "But in Leibniz all perspectives are integrated into a higher point of view, that of God, by an operation of overviewing *(survol)* which allows passing from the monad to the monadology. No such view from above is permitted in Husserl. It is always from the side, and not from above, that each of us discovers that the same world is grasped from different points of view. For the other perspectives are appresented within one originary perspective, mine, as being different perspectives upon the same object and the same world" (Ricoeur 1967, 133). See also the presentation in Strasser 1975.

17. At first glance, this passage seems to confirm Fink's account after all. Is not Husserl claiming that the absolute is neither *ego* nor *alter ego*, but is prior to this distinction? Our previous deliberations have already indicated that there is a misunderstanding at work here, and in what follows, this will be clearly demonstrated.

18. "Das einzige Ich—das transzendentale. In seiner Einzigkeit setzt es 'andere' einzige transzendentale Ich—als 'andere', die selbst wieder in Einzigkeit Andere setzen" (Ms. B I 14 138b).

Chapter IV

1. In this case, what takes place in communalization is a continual change of validity in mutual correction. "In reciprocal understanding, my experiences and experiential acquisitions enter into contact with those of others, similar to the contact between individual series of experiences within my (one's own) experiential life" (6/166[163]): "Through linguistic communication, the surrounding world—which is already communal, at least in the lower levels—is expanded, in part corrected, or else ongoingly determined, leading to greater determinateness. And this linguistic communication is always involved in building up the experienced sense of the world in which we live in acting, in which—especially when we are acting in the service of theoretical scientific interests—we generate a form of knowledge of a particular type that we then term scientific statements, 'propositions,' axioms, conclusions, scientific 'facts of experience,' and the like" (15/220). The following discussion by Löwith is also of interest in this context: "Something is properly known when it is known as it is in itself, when the knowledge corresponds to the matter in question. . . . However, the question of whether or not the manner and mode in which one individual has brought it to linguistic and conceptual expression actually does correspond to the matter at stake is not a

question that the individual himself can answer, for whatever he answers, he is always still only answering his own question. *The individual in question needs someone else in order to experience whether or not the answer corresponds to the matter at stake.* Only someone else can possibly show the individual anything in the matter in question that speaks against the answer initially proposed. *It is in the discussion between the two parties, and only there, that the 'matter itself' can be given the exposition appropriate to it.* The matter comes to expression by the one individual hearing what the other has to say about the matter. What the other has to say 'about' it does not only augment the first individual's point of view, and thereby the corresponding aspect of the matter, by supplying the other's point of view; rather, one person corrects the other: they correct one another, and in this correction, that which they are talking about—the matter itself— is rectified. Thus when one individual brings the outlook and view of the other into question and says so, he is saying something 'about' the matter in the mode of someone speaking 'for' or 'against' the other's view. And in this way, the possible correctness and objectivity of what can be said about the matter in question is heightened. It is only when the objectivity of a cognition of something can be demonstrated within a free encounter between the individuals concerned—an encounter where the cognition of the one 'corresponds' to the cognition of the other—that this cognition's claim to objectivity is fulfilled, since one individual's knowledge about something is made accessible to another knower. *One cannot attain true objectivity for oneself about anything purely by oneself. Were one to think something through purely by talking it over by oneself, one would not really be in uninterrupted communication with the matter itself, but only with oneself"* (Löwith 1928, 66–67, emphasis added).

2. In *Ideas II,* Husserl claims that this distinction can already be made by the solitary subject (4/77, 4/90).

3. Husserl now poses the extremely important question of whether one can infer from the psychophysical dependency of perceptual appearances 1) that things are not as they appear to be and 2) that non-orthological appearances are as legitimate as orthological ones. However, he denies that the relation to psychophysical conditions should offer any reason for an epistemological relativization of the appearances, and he emphasizes that the appearances concerned are not "orthological" *because* they are psychophysically related to a certain organization of the lived body that is to be termed "normal." Rather, the world, as a really actual world, is constituted in such a way that the system of orthological appearances is associated with the co-constituting lived bodilihood in a way that is governed by psychophysical regularities (13/369). This answer, which also points to the genuine sense of Husserl's concept of constitution, nevertheless also illustrates the problem of anthropocentrism (but cf. Ch. V.1 below). That is to say, if Husserl apprehends reality as constitutively referring back to empirically contingent peculiarities of the human organism, he would wind up with an anthropocentric relativism. Here, however, it is also worth noticing to which lived bodily features Husserl ascribes constitutive relevance. It is obviously a question of determinations such as spatiality, motility, and capability for expression, and not, for example, of the precise number or formation

of our physical bodily members. Thus Husserl also writes in the first *Kaizo* article: "For fundamental considerations such as, for instance, those of pure reason, matters such as whether man's senses, eyes, ears, etc., are formed empirically in this or that way, whether he has two or more eyes, whether he has this or that organ for locomotion, be it legs or wings, etc., are entirely extraneous questions that always remain open. *Only certain forms of corporeality* and psychical spirituality are presupposed and are under consideration; to bring these matters to light as being necessary a priori, and to fix them conceptually, is the task for essential scientific investigation which is consciously worked out" (27/11-12[331], emphasis added). Hence there is a decisive difference between Husserl's observations, and a theory that would conclude, for example, that there cannot be any colors in the ultraviolet spectrum because no such colors can be seen by human beings. However, see also Merleau-Ponty's divergent answer to a similar problem in *Phenomenology of Perception* (PP 455/397).

4. On this entire way of setting up the problem, see, e.g., *Zur Phänomenologie der Intersubjektivität I*, Text Nr. 14, "Solipsistic and intersubjective normality and constitution of objectivity," *Zur Phänomenologie der Intersubjektivität III*, Text Nr. 10, "The world of the normal and the problem of the participation of the abnormal in world-constitution," and Text Nr. 11, "Apodictic structure of transcendental subjectivity. Problem of the transcendental constitution of the world starting from normality."

5. To give a simple example, our constitution of colors is not impaired by there being blind persons who are not able to participate in this constitution (1/154, 15/48). Thus Husserl also emphasizes that in comparing various orthological systems, one can find distinctions of better and poorer. The optimal system has an advantage — namely, it presents the most of the "true thing," the greatest wealth of differences belonging to it (13/379, 14/133).

6. Here cf. *Zur Phänomenologie der Intersubjektivität III*, Beilage XI and Text Nr. 27; see also Held 1991.

7. What comes to the fore here is the structural parallelism between Husserl's presentation of the experience of the foreign other and his presentation of the experience of the foreign world. The home world can be seen as a kind of primordial sphere at a second level (cf. Held 1991, 308), and Husserl himself writes: "Double sense of the foreign: 1) foreign human beings as other; 2) foreign human beings as human beings of other home fellowships, other cities, other nations. Relativity of 'empathy'; ad 1): empathy through which the unity of a normal community of existing persons is given, and correlatively, a world comprehensible to them all. . . . Ad 2): empathy of a new kind, empathy into a foreign people, appropriating their tradition, their national surrounding world with its historicity" ("Doppelter Sinn von Fremd: 1) fremde Menschen als andere; 2) fremde Menschen als Menschen anderer Heimgenossenschaften, anderer Städte, anderer Völker. Relativität der 'Einfühlung'; ad 1) Einfühlung, durch welche Einheit einer normalen personalen Daseinsgemeinschaft gegeben ist und korrelativ eine allverständliche Welt. . . . Ad 2): Einfühlung neuer Weise, Einfühlung in Volksfremde, Zueignung ihrer Tradition, ihrer völkischen Umwelt mit ihrer Historizität" — Ms. C 16 106a-b).

8. "I understand even others who are genuinely 'incomprehensible' to me precisely as others. And one can say: I do understand anyone who is an other for me in at least the lowest stratum of lived bodily holding sway, lived bodily activity as perceiving, as physical activity having an effect on other physical bodies (pushing, shoving). Even actions that usually proceed in accordance with primal instincts are understood in at least rough typicality" ("Auch den mir eigentlich 'unverständlichen' Anderen verstehe ich eben als Anderen. Und man kann sagen: Jeden, der für mich Anderer ist, verstehe ich mindestens in der untersten Schicht leiblichen Waltens, leiblicher Betätigung als wahrnehmender, als körperlich auf andere Körper wirkende Betätigung (stossend, schiebend). Auch die den Urinstinkten sonst gemäßen Handlungen werden in mindestens roher Typik verstanden"— Ms. C 16 105b).

9. Cf. n. 8 above and Patočka 1990, 95–104.

10. Cf. the following remark by Merleau-Ponty: "Ideal existence is based upon the document. Not, undoubtedly, upon the document as a physical object, or even as the vehicle of one-to-one significations assigned to it by the language it is written in. But ideal existence is based upon the document insofar as (still through an 'intentional transgression') the document solicits and brings together all knowing lives—and as such establishes and re-establishes a 'Logos' of the cultural world" (S 121/96–97).

11. Husserl's analysis has a number of similarities with Heidegger's observations regarding Da-sein's *being lost* in the publicness of the "they"; see also Heidegger's analysis of idle talk in § 35 of *Being and Time*.

12. The precise implications that this has for the ontological status of the past cannot be pursued any further here.

13. As we have already mentioned, it is necessary to emphasize the distinction between "world" and "thing," for the world cannot simply be conceived as a huge collection of things. And it is precisely this distinction that comes into its own in the presentation of the world as a historically developing and historically transmitted nexus of sense and correlate of normality. Cf. Bernet 1994, 317.

14. "Das darf natürlich nicht in verkehrter Weise in Frage gestellt werden: als ob ein Ansichsein der Welt schon absolut feststände, als ob eine absolute Bürgschaft dafür, wer weiß woher, etwa gar durch eine Gottheit und göttliche Erkenntnis geleistet oder zu leisten wäre, und nun bloß die Frage ist, wie weit unsere Erfahrungserkenntnis reicht und wie viel auf ihrem Grunde, durch Methode willkürlichen Experimentes und eines vernünftigen Denkens vom wahren Sein der Welt zu gewinnen wäre" (Ms. B I 12 IV 76a–b).

15. "Die Unbestimmtheit ist nicht eine Unvollkommenheit unserer Erkenntnis in bezug auf eine im voraus in voller Bestimmtheit feststehende und seiende Welt, sondern gehört zum Seinssinn der Welt selbst rein als Welt der Erfahrung" (Ms. B I 12 IV 77a).

16. Cf. Mohanty 1986.

17. Husserl writes: "Leibniz said that the monads have no windows. But I think that every psychic monad has infinitely many windows—namely, every

truly intelligible perception of a foreign lived body is such a window. And each time I say, 'please, dear friend,' and my friend responds to me with understanding, then through our open windows, an I-act of my I is passed over into the I of my friend and vice versa; a reciprocal motivation has established a real unity between us—yes, has actually established a real unity" (13/473; cf. 14/260, 14/295). Here it is unmistakably demonstrated that Husserl has subjected the concept of "monads" to a decisive alteration, and this is also why his account cannot be criticized on account of its supposedly sanctioning a classical theory of substances. For more on the relation between Husserl and Leibniz, see Cristin 1990.

18. There is an interesting parallel between Husserl's conception and Davidson's presentation in "On the Very Idea of a Conceptual Scheme" (Davidson 1984, 183–98).

19. Cf. 15/443, 14/216, and Text Nr. 27 in *Zur Phänomenologie der Intersubjektivität III.* Some brief references to Husserl's relationship to relativism are now possible on the basis of this assertion. We have seen that Husserl speaks not only about absolute truth (valid for everyone) but also about truth that is relative to a homeworld—i.e., about a truth that is valid only for a limited sector of the totality of monads. However, the type of relativism that Husserl criticized in the *Prolegomena* to the *Logical Investigations,* and rejected there as self-contradictory, is a type of relativism that would draw the following consequences from the distinction just mentioned: what is true for one life-community (normality) can be false for another, and indeed, unless there are absolute criteria, no decision between them could be made. To put it another way, this type of relativism accepts the possibility that the same predicatively formed complex of affairs (the same proposition) can simultaneously possess more than one truth value. Now it is true that in emphasizing normal, occasional, and pragmatically conditioned truth (cf. Chapter IV.2) in contrast to absolute scientific truth, Husserl has distanced himself from his absolutist position in the *Prolegomena.* Despite this, however, he never did accept the type of relativism under discussion (cf. Soffer 1991). That is to say, that something is valid only for a limited normality does not imply its non-validity for the remainder, but implies that it is not relevant, or else that it is not immediately accessible! "We do not share the same lifeworld with every human being; we do not have all the objects that make up our lifeworld, and determine our personal working and striving, in common with every human being 'on the planet'—even if they are currently in actual community with us, as they could be at any time (insofar as if they are not present, we could come to them and they could come to us). Objects that are there for us—although, to be sure, they are there for us in a shifting apprehension that is sometimes in agreement, sometimes not—are not there for them. And this means that they have no apprehensions of them as these objects at all, no experiences of them, even when they see them and, as we say, see 'our' objects. . . . If we bring a Bantu into this circle of humans, it is clear with respect to our works of art that he does indeed see a thing, but not the object of our surrounding world, 'work of art,' and that he does not even have any meaning intention, any apprehension,

of it as this object, 'work of art.' . . . We can argue with one another over truth and falsehood, being and non-being, in our own world, but not with the Bantu, for as an individual of his own 'we,' he has another surrounding world" (9/496-97; cf. 15/146, 15/166-67). Thus here it is not a matter of the type of relativism mentioned above, for Husserl is apparently claiming that the diverging apprehension performed by a member of a foreign world is not related to the same thing (or to the same aspect of the object) as our apprehension is at all—and for this reason, cannot be in conflict with it, either. But this is also precisely why we cannot exclude the possibility that the immediately incommensurable apprehensions pertaining to various normalities could eventually turn out to complement one another, insofar as they reveal *various* aspects of the matter. And in this case, Husserl's position would have to be characterized as *perspectivism*.

CHAPTER V

1. Cf. Zahavi 1992a and 1992b.
2. Cf. Tugendhat 1970, 175.
3. Thus when it is a matter of the concept of constitution in the *Logical Investigations,* we agree completely with the following remark by Sokolowski: "If subjectivity 'created' sense and objects when it constitutes them, then their contents should be explained by subjectivity. This is not the case; the contents are simply given as facticity, and not as something essentially deducible from subjectivity and its operations. Therefore, subjectivity does not cause or create senses and objects. It merely allows them to come about. It is their condition, and not their cause; consequently, Husserl's doctrine of constitution should not be interpreted in too idealistic a manner" (Sokolowski 1970, 159).
4. This is even acknowledged by Tugendhat himself: "One has grasped the descriptive sense of Husserl's constitution just as poorly when one can ask to what extent this constitution must not be a 'creatio' of the object as when one answers by saying that what is 'generated' is not the object, but only its 'validity-sense'" (Tugendhat 1970, 175).
5. Further reflections can be found in, e.g., Ms. B IV 5 (1933).
6. Cf. Merleau-Ponty, S 222/176.
7. See our remarks on this passage in Ch. II, n. 37, of the present work.
8. This description of constitution is echoed by Heidegger: "'*Constituting*' does not mean producing in the sense of making and fabricating; it means *letting the entity be seen in its objectivity*" (PZ 97).
9. This interpretation is also denied by Tugendhat and Sokolowski: cf. Tugendhat 1970, 177, 212, 217 and Sokolowski 1970, 138, 159, 197-98, 217 (see also n. 3 above).
10. "Konstitution von Seiendem verschiedener Stufe, von Welten, von Zeiten, hat zwei Urvoraussetzungen, zwei Urquellen, die zeitlich gesprochen (in jeder dieser Zeitlichkeiten) immerfort ihr 'zugrundeliegen': 1) mein urtümliches Ich als fungierendes Ur-Ich in seinen Affektionen und Aktionen, mit allen Wesensgestalten an zugehörigen Modis; 2) mein urtümliches Nicht-

Ich als urtümlicher Strom der Zeitigung und selbst als Urform der Zeitigung, ein Zeitfeld, das der Ur-Sachlichkeit, konstituierend. Aber beide Urgründe sind einig, untrennbar und, so für sich betrachtet abstrakt" (Ms. C 10 15b).

11. Landgrebe has explicitly defended this thesis: "Thus I-consciousness is not a mere consciousness of the spontaneity of thoughts as separate synthetic performances in which the sensuous material given in the sensations is unified into the concept of the object; rather, consciousness can only be aware of itself a priori as a thinking consciousness because it is at the same time the consciousness of the leeway or latitude *(Spielraum)* pertaining to the spontaneity of self-motility. . . . But what is this space of leeway or latitude? It is nothing other than the world of our experience, and to begin with, the immediate surrounding world. Thus if the consciousness of the spontaneity of the 'I move myself' belongs inseparably to the possibility of an I-consciousness as the 'representation of the self-activity of a thinking subject,' and if this consciousness includes within itself a leeway or latitude for movement that is none other than the world, then with this, it turns out that I-consciousness is at the same time world-consciousness, and that as such, it is the ground of possibility for sensuous affection. . . . And this should clarify what it means to understand sensing as a mode of being-in-the-world" (Landgrebe 1963, 120). Cf. our presentation of the relationship between horizon and kinaesthesis, Chapter II.4 above.

12. Cf., e.g., Sartre's reflections in *Being and Nothingness:* "Thus the perceptive field refers to a center objectively defined by that reference and located *in the very field* which is oriented around it. Only we do not *see* this center as the structure of the perceptive field considered; *we are the center.* Thus . . . the structure of the world demands that we can not see without *being visible"* (EN 365/418-19). "Thus my being-in-the-world, by the sole fact that it *realizes* a world, causes itself to be indicated to itself as a being-in-the-midst-of-the-world by the world which it realizes. The case could not be otherwise, for my being has no other way of entering into contact with the world except *to be in the world.* . . . Thus to say that I have entered into the world, 'come to the world,' or that there is a world, or that I have a body is one and the same thing" (EN 366/419). In Merleau-Ponty's *Phenomenology of Perception,* we run across the following claim: "The world is inseparable from the subject, but from a subject which is nothing but a project of the world, and the subject is inseparable from the world, but from a world which the subject itself projects. The subject is a being-in-the-world and the world remains 'subjective' since its texture and articulations are traced out by the subject's movement of transcendence. Hence we discovered, with the world as cradle of meanings, direction of all directions *(sens de tous les sens),* and ground of all thinking, how to leave behind the dilemma of realism and idealism, contingency and absolute reason, nonsense and sense" (PP 491-92/430). Finally, as Heidegger explains in *The Basic Problems of Phenomenology,* "World exists—that is, it is—only if Dasein exists, only if there is Dasein. Only if world is there, if Dasein exists as being-in-the-world, is there understanding of being, and only if this understanding exists are intraworldly beings unveiled as extant and handy. World-understanding

as Dasein-understanding is self-understanding. Self and world belong together in the single entity, the Dasein. Self and world are not two beings, like subject and object, or like I and thou, but self and world are the basic determination of the Dasein itself in the unity of the structure of being-in-the-world" (GP 422).

13. That each I is to a certain extent foreign to itself by virtue of its own self-temporalization does not alter what is stated here.

14. Cf. Zahavi 1992a, 144.

CHAPTER VI

1. Including a discussion of post-Husserlian phenomenologists will also allow us to reexamine their relationship to Husserl, for it will turn out that inceptions of their later reflections are already to be found within Husserl himself. (This fact is not really so astonishing, however, for it must be recalled that after his decades-long endeavor to understand intersubjectivity phenomenologically, Husserl left behind so many manuscripts on this theme that from a purely quantitative point of view, they far exceed the number of pages devoted to the analysis of intersubjectivity by all three later phenomenologists combined.) All the same, it has to be granted that in a number of cases, it is only when we take the later phenomenologists into consideration that we develop an eye for the wealth and variety of Husserl's own analyses. We can therefore agree with the following observation by Bernet (1994, 299–300): "To reread Husserl after having read the phenomenologists who define their own thought in terms of their difference from Husserl does offer some surprises. As justified as their critiques may be, these very critiques also bring out aspects of Husserl's thought that his critics are unaware of."

2. One may perhaps ask why we have decided not to include work on intersubjectivity by two such distinguished phenomenological thinkers as Levinas and Ricoeur. From our point of view, there is greater homogeneity and continuity among Husserl, Heidegger, Sartre, and Merleau-Ponty than between them on the one hand and Levinas or Ricoeur on the other. We are convinced of the radicality of Levinas's account, but we also believe that the consequences that Levinas draws from the transcendence of the other require a fundamental revision of certain phenomenological principles. For this reason, it would have been quite difficult to include an investigation of Levinas's position in the present context. In contrast, Ricoeur's work can be considered as an attempt to mediate between phenomenology and the philosophy of language. Thus including Ricoeur would have obscured the very real difference between phenomenology and the pragmatics of language.

3. The same idea can be found in Scheler; cf. n. 16 below.

4. Binswanger makes a similar remark: "By presenting this ontological connection, Heidegger has banished entire libraries on the problem of empathy, the problem of perceiving the foreign as such, the problem of the 'constitution of the foreign I,' and so on, to the realm of history, for what the latter want to furnish proof of and explain is always already presupposed in the

proof and the explanations; the presupposition itself can neither be explained nor proven, but rather only ontologically-phenomenologically 'disclosed'" (Binswanger 1953, 66).

5. We can therefore agree with Sartre's characterization in *Being and Nothingness:* "The empirical image which may best symbolize Heidegger's intuition is not that of a conflict but rather a *crew.* The original relation of the Other and my consciousness is not the *you* and *me;* it is the *we.* Heidegger's being-with is not the clear and distinct position of an individual confronting another individual; it is not *knowledge.* It is the mute existence in common of one member of the crew with his fellows, that existence which the rhythm of the oars or the regular movements of the coxswain will render sensible to the rowers and which *will be made manifest* to them by the common goal to be attained, the boat or the yacht to be overtaken, and the entire world (spectators, performance, *etc.*) which is profiled on the horizon" (EN 292/332).

6. Cf. Sartre's critique, Chapter VI.3.

7. Note that *das Man* has also been translated as "the Anyone" and "the Everyone."

8. As already mentioned (Chapter IV.2), we can also find the same judgment in Husserl to a certain extent. That is to say, if we allow ourselves to be guided in our experience of ourselves and of the world by the intersubjective apperceptions that are sedimented in linguistic usage, instead of judging for ourselves on the basis of the appropriate experiential evidence, this is a betrayal of the idea of self-responsibility, and if we proceed in such a manner, we will never be able to lay open the transcendental foundations. Whether Husserl has assessed the constitutive implications of the anonymous being-with-one-another that characterizes what has been handed down as "normality" more positively than Heidegger does is something that we will investigate later.

9. We are indebted above all to Lübcke 1977, 463, for this interpretation.

10. Cf. Gould 1977.

11. To be sure, Heidegger later formulates the relationship the other way around (see SuZ 317).

12. Attempts have been made to supplement Heidegger's analyses. Löwith writes: "In the 'they,' Dasein as a 'they-self' relieves itself from the burden of being itself. With this, the genuinely positive possibility of being-with-one-another—being where the I and the Thou, the first and the second person, are with one another—is ignored" (Löwith 1928, 80). Binswanger too has taken up this positive possibility in his attempt to find an entirely different answer to the question of "who" Da-sein is, i.e., another answer besides either the inauthentic they-self or the authentic individual self—namely, the dyadic we-self in the sense of the loving being-with-one-another of "mine" and "thine" (Binswanger 1953, 69). In a similar vein, Buber claims that the Heideggerian "disclosedness" of Da-sein to itself is finally a "foreclosure" that closes off any genuine connection with the other, and that the so-called *"Fürsorge"* ("solicitude," "concern") does not actually express any essential relationship to the other. Hence Heidegger is unaware of the true I-Thou relationship, which breaks through the boundaries of the self. Surprisingly,

Buber rates Husserl's contribution to the problem of intersubjectivity far more positively (Buber 1947, 387, 399–409).

13. Cf. Figal 1988, 134–35.

14. We will not explicitly concern ourselves with Sartre's critique of Husserl, since his brief discussion of Husserl is for the most part incorrect—e.g., when Sarte claims that Husserl was only dealing with mundane intersubjectivity (EN 279/317).

15. As a curiosity (and probably not more than this—cf. Arendt's judgment in Martin 1989, 142), it should be pointed out that in a letter to Sartre of October 28, 1945, Heidegger wrote: "I am in agreement with your critique of 'being-with' and with your insistence on being-for-others, as well as in partial agreement with your critique of my explication of death" (Towarnicki 1993, 84).

16. A fundamental claim of Scheler is that in addition to an apriorism of objective thought and cognition, one can also detect an a priori "order of the heart" or "logic of the heart." Thus the emotional elements of mental or spiritual life (feeling, preferring, loving, hating, willing, etc.) are characterized by an original, a priori content and are subject to original, a priori laws (FE 63). In connection with his analysis of this emotional a priori, Scheler then points out that "all morally relevant acts, experiences and states, in so far as they contain an intentional reference to other moral persons" (acts such as obligation, responsibility, love, promising, etc.) "refer, by the very nature of the acts themselves, to other people," without implying that such others must already have been previously encountered in concrete experience (NS 229). Hence our relation to the other is not some empirical fact; on the contrary, the concrete experience of others presupposes an a priori relatedness to one another and simply represents the unfolding of this possibility (NS 61; FE 535). It is for this reason that Scheler can claim that the nature of the intersubjective relation is not at all primarily theoretical but is already embedded in our essential emotional structure. He now relates this assumption to the question of the original essential relationship between I and community (NS 227) and claims that every finite person is as originally a member of a community as he is an individual. The human being does not live a communal life with other persons "from pure accident"— rather, being a (finite) person as such "is just as originally a mater of being . . . 'together'" as it is a matter of being-for-oneself (EM 373). The lived experience of belonging to a community is just as originally available as is the consciousness of oneself or of the world; according to Scheler, this intention "in the direction of community" (EM 373) exists completely independently of whether or not it finds its fulfillment in a contingent experience of others: "even a hypothetical spiritual-corporeal being who had never been conscious of his fellows via the senses would ascertain his membership of a community, his 'belonging', precisely on account of a positive awareness that a whole class of intentions in his *essential* nature was craving and *not finding fulfilment*"—intentions like loving, compassion, promising, requesting, thanking, obeying, serving, or ruling (EM 374). That is to say, "it is by virtue of their intentional *essence*" (i.e., not first "on the basis of their contingent

objects") that there are acts that can "find their fulfillment only in a possible community" (FE 521). Scheler attempts to illustrate his point by speaking of an epistemological Robinson Crusoe. Such a figure would be aware of his relatedness to an intersubjective community even if he had never had a concrete experience of others, and he would possess such an awareness by virtue of the lived experience of a lack of fulfillment of the series of intentions mentioned above, which can only form an objective unity of sense "in conjunction with the *possibility* of a social response" (NS 235, emphasis altered). Although Husserl did not pursue this path as intensively as later phenomenologists did, the following passage testifies to a similar line of thinking: "Since, however, not just my pre-ethical, but my ethical being—my entire human life of intention, my world-life as such—is related by way of others to what exists in the world; since my ethical being is inseparably interwoven with that of possible others; and since my ethical will, my absolute ethical 'should' or 'ought,' is necessarily a will that other ethical subjects do or will exist and that the ethical world must necessarily become an ethical world in common, then my ethical will can never be actually fulfilled in my own, merely private, responsible living and doing" ("Da aber wie mein vorethisches so mein ethisches Sein, mein ganzes menschliches Leben der Intention, mein Weltleben überhaupt, auf das Sein in der Welt durch die Anderen hindurch bezogen ist, da mein ethisches Sein untrennbar mit dem der möglichen Anderen verflochten ist, da mein ethischer Wille, mein absolutes ethisches Sollen, notwendig Wille ist, daß andere ethische Subjekte seien oder werden und ethische Welt notwendig zu ethischer Gemeinwelt werden muß, so kann mein ethischer Wille sich nie wirklich erfüllen im bloß privat eigenen verantwortlichen Leben und Tun"—Ms. E III 4 31a).

17. Gurwitsch (1979, § 18) has also formulated the same critique.

18. Here we can join the critiques of Hartmann, Theunissen, and Aboulafia. Hartmann (1983, 102) writes that the other-as-subject becomes a hypostasis of what is basically an a priori relation to the other, and that although Sartre claims that his view avoids the apriority of the relation to the other, he does not in truth do so. It is similar with Theunissen, who reproaches Sartre for contradicting the very notion that serves as his own guiding idea, since he now attributes the status of absolute evidence to my being-for-others *in general* or *as such (überhaupt)*, not to my concrete and factual encounter with the other (Theunissen 1986, 241–42). Finally, Aboulafia too is correct when he writes: "The introduction of the mistaken look forces Sartre to posit a permanent presence in absence for the other, which, in turn, relies on *a* look of an other for proof of this presence. As a refutation of solipsism this circularity will not do" (Aboulafia 1986, 51).

19. Theunissen is nevertheless justified in pointing out that the so-called "personalizing alter-ation"—i.e., the "alter-ation" that makes me one other among others—has no place in Sartre's analysis of the immediate encounter with the other. That is to say, such "alter-ation" presupposes solidarity, not conflict (Theunissen 1986, 233–34). It is only when Sartre mentions the "Us-object" in connection with his analysis of the various forms of the experience

of the "Us," characterizing the "Us-object" in terms of a situation where both I and the other are objectified by the look of a third party, that he deals with a situation in which I can experience myself as one among others (EN 469/540–41).

20. By looking at me, the other knows what I am and "holds the secret of my being"—a being that I can neither appropriate nor understand (EN 412/473). But two different paths are open to me. On the one hand, "I can attempt to deny that being which is conferred on me from outside" by turning back upon the other "so as to make an object out of him in turn," since the other's objectness for me destroys my objectness for the other (EN 412/473). Thus although my own transcendence is paralyzed by being objectified by the other, the possibility always remains for me in turn to objectify the other (cf. EN 349/400). The objectification of the other is thereby a means of defense on the part of my own being—a means that is always at my disposal, freeing me from my being-for-others precisely by conferring a "being for-me" upon the other (EN 315/359). On the other hand, Sartre also offers a description (reminiscent of Hegel's analysis of the master-slave dialectic) of a way in which I can attempt to recover the freedom that the other possesses (which is precisely the foundation of my being-in-itself) and seize it for myself *without* robbing the other of this character of freedom (i.e., without objectifying the other), insofar as I, as the for-itself, attempt to become my own foundation (EN 128–29/140). And if I could indeed make this freedom my own, then I would truly be my own ontological foundation (EN 412/473).

21. Laing, incidentally, has provided a description of schizoid patterns of experience and comportment that is clearly similar to Sartre's description of this "normal" intersubjective relation. Cf., e.g., Laing 1990a, 46–49, 113.

22. Merleau-Ponty is very well aware that this critique does not affect Husserl's own concept of constitution (see, e.g., the essay "The Philosopher and His Shadow" in *Signs*). According to Merleau-Ponty, Husserl himself discovered the "identity of 're-entering self' and 'going-outside self'" (S 204/161), and he realized by *Ideas II* at the latest that reflection does not "install" us in a closed, self-contained, and transparent medium (S 205/162). Merleau-Ponty's seemingly arbitrary interpretation of Husserl has often been dismissed too hastily by such Merleau-Ponty scholars as Kwant, Madison, and Dillon. As our own interpretation of Husserl has shown, however, Merleau-Ponty understood Husserl better than they do.

23. One also runs across this anonymity in practical dealings within the cultural world. That is to say, it is here that I encounter the presence of others "beneath a veil of anonymity. *Someone* uses the pipe for smoking, the spoon for eating, the bell for summoning" (PP 400/348).

24. See, e.g., O'Neill 1989, Dillon 1978, and—for the most comprehensive treatment—Meyer-Drawe 1984, 175–92.

25. Thus Scheler does actually write that we can take the fact of "identification" or "sense of unity" (the term here is *Einsfühlung* rather than *Einfühlung*) as an indication of the metaphysical unity of all organic life (NS 73–74). Merleau-Ponty's criticism is nevertheless probably unjustified, for what is at stake here is

only a unity of organic life that "in essence, existence and operation, . . . is quite *distinct* from the Spirit, with its personal structure" (NS 76). Hence the thesis of organic unity does not contradict Scheler's constant emphasis upon the *absolute* difference between individual persons (NS 65, 121; cf. Ch. III, n. 13 above), although one can of course inquire whether Scheler is not ultimately confronted with an unbridgeable dualism between the sphere of individual, personal mind or spirit and a communal vital sphere—a dualism that cannot explain the unity of the human being (cf. Owen 1970, 106).

26. Cf. Madison 1981, 43.

27. Further discussions pertaining to this point can be found in Bernet 1992, 84–85.

28. We cannot pursue Merleau-Ponty's philosophy of language in detail. However, it must be emphasized that for Merleau-Ponty, language does not merely serve as a means of communication: "For the speaking subject, to express is to become aware of; he does not express just for others, but also to know himself what he intends" (S 113/90; cf. S 28/20 and PP 459/400-401). At the same time, however, the significance of language—in particular, its significance for intersubjectivity—should not be overestimated, for as Merleau-Ponty also writes: "The function of language is just one particular case of the general relation between self and others, which is the relation between two consciousnesses, of which each one projects itself *in the other*" (1988, 58-59/1973b, 68, trans, altered).

29. See Van Breda 1992.

CHAPTER VII

1. For Apel, see QG 83, 89, and for Habermas, cf. VTH 69. Apel refers critically to Habermas in TP I 16; Apel 1990a, 48; and Apel 1989a, while Habermas expresses reservations about Apel's project of ultimate grounding in VTH 382 ff. and in MC 44, 95-96.

2. Habermas himself points to his Christian Gauss lectures (now published in *Vorstudien und Ergänzungen zur Theorie des kommunikativen Handelns*), in which he explicitly treats the philosophical motives for the turn from the philosophy of consciousness to linguistic pragmatics, whereas in *The Theory of Communicative Action,* this turn was grounded only within the context of the history of social theory (VTH 7; Honneth and Joas 1986, 214).

3. Thus Apel does of course realize that methodological solipsism in no way denies the existence of other subjects; rather, such a position simply denies that the intersubjective relation is a necessary condition of possibility for world- and self-consciousness (TrP 154).

4. Apel acknowledges (TrP 161) that his understanding of Wittgenstein's reflections—an interpretation that is later taken over by Habermas (cf. LSS 204 n. 41)—is strongly influenced by Winch (1958).

5. Apel praises Heidegger in this context, writing that with his concept of "being-with-one-another," Heidegger has slipped in underneath the solipsistic starting point of traditional epistemology: "While the philosophy that pro-

ceeds from the subject of knowledge believes that the being of the other must be constituted as an object of 'my consciousness,' just like the being of a thing of the external world, Heidegger brings to bear the phenomenological-hermeneutical point of view according to which the 'I,' the 'Thou,' and the 'others' are, as givens that can meaningfully be intended, constituted 'equiprimordially' from out of the 'being-with-one-another' of our being-in-the-world. In addition, he recognizes that in the 'public' way of interpreting the world, the individual's ability to have an opinion is always already anticipated by the traditionally and linguistically conditioned pre-understanding in the mode of the 'they' that 'initially and for the most part' guides even the individual's self-understanding in the behavior characterized as average everydayness" (TP I 264). In an essay written seven years later, however, Apel states that Heidegger is still caught up in an existential-ontological variety of methodological solipsism (TrP 131 n. 55), and it turns out that on the whole, his appraisal of Heidegger has gone down considerably over the years. Apel's usual reproach toward Heidegger is that he has missed the problem of the validity of truth (TP I 35, 41, 43) and ultimately winds up in a "forgottenness of the Logos" (TP I 273). What is in my opinion an appropriate critique of Apel's interpretation of the early Heidegger of *Being and Time* is found in Lorenz and Mittelstraß (1967).

6. Hence Apel does not at all see the transformation of transcendental philosophy mentioned above as weakening the radicality of the transcendental manner of posing the question in favor of, say, quasi-transcendental arguments (DV 113)—and it is precisely here that Apel's path diverges from Habermas's.

7. Thus Apel also claims that the conditions of the possibility and validity of world-constitution can by no means lie in a "pure consciousness," insofar as such a consciousness could hardly "secure any meaning from the world"—not only because I can only have valid intended meanings when there is language (TrP 48) but also because world-constitution is only possible through a living, bodily, "in-person" engagement of the knowing and understanding consciousness: "In order to arrive at a constitution of meaning, consciousness—which is basically 'eccentric'—must become engaged concentrically; that is, embodied in the Here and Now. Any constitution of meaning refers back, for example, to a particular perspective which expresses a standpoint. Once again, this means a living engagement on the part of the knowing consciousness" (TrP 48). Hence Apel even speaks of a *bodily a priori* of knowledge (see TrP 60—where the direct reference to the lived body that is captured in Apel's phrase "'Leibapriori' der Erkenntnis" is obscured by translating it in this case as "'life-a priori' of consciousness"—and see also Apel 1963), as well as of a *cognitive-anthropological* radicalization of the Kantian critique of knowledge (TrP 48–49; UE 240).

8. Later, in connection with our attempt to provide a phenomenological response, we shall come back to a number of further criticisms raised by Habermas; however, see also PT 44 ff. and Habermas 1992a, 18–19, for his own catalogue of objections.

9. Thus Habermas understands his critique of Husserl as a general critique of any phenomenological theory of intersubjectivity (cf. PT 40–42).

10. Habermas wants to make a fundamental distinction between *sense or meaning* and *validity*. Even as early as *Knowledge and Human Interests*, he notes that one has to differentiate the categorial sense of an empirical statement from its implied validity claim, i.e., the claim that it can be discursively cashed in. Whereas the aspect under which we experience something in the world is reflected in the categorial sense, and whereas this sense is contained in the propositional content of a speech act, the validity claim is contained in the performative part of the speech act, since it is this that reflects the claim that what is said there is to be intersubjectively binding. It is against this background that Habermas would now want to introduce a further distinction between *objectivity* and *truth:* namely, although the objectivity of experiences does indeed consist in the fact that they can be intersubjectively shared, this objectivity should not be confused with the truth of a claimed statement (EI 386). Objectivity is what appears in actions whose outcomes are controlled; it implies that everyone can count on whether a specific action will succeed or fail to produce a particular result. But in contrast to truth, objectivity is by no means measured in arguments.

11. Habermas expresses this view with greater precision in later additions to his *Vorstudien und Ergänzungen zur Theorie des kommunikativen Handelns,* for what is said there is that at bottom, talk of "consensus" as a criterion for truth is misleading, and that in the future, it would be better to speak of a *discourse theory of truth.* That is to say, the sense of truth is precisely not the circumstance that a consensus was reached as such; rather, the sense of truth is that whenever we enter into discourse, anywhere and at any time, a consensus can be reached in such a way that this consensus can be demonstrated to be a grounded one. Hence it is not the factual consensus that is decisive, but carrying through the process of discourse, and Habermas stresses that the meaning of the concept of truth must be explained with reference to a *procedure* of cashing in truth claims (VTH 160). Thus Habermas also occasionally characterizes communicative reason as purely procedural (PDM 316; PT 35; MC 7, 36; cf. Alexy 1989, 81, 88).

12. The risk of dissent is inherent in any actual communicative process, and in *Postmetaphysical Thinking,* Habermas attempts to make a catalogue of the most important ways out of it: simply mending the breach; shelving controversial validity claims and leaving them undecided, with the result of shrinking the common basis of shared convictions; making a transition to discourse on a larger scale, although we are not certain what the outcome will be, or what further problems will emerge along the way; breaking off communication altogether, or ultimately replacing it with strategic action (ND 84).

13. In addition, Habermas emphasize that "at each stage of development of personal identity, the identity conditions for persons in general, as well as the basic identity criteria for specific persons, change"; newborns are identified in a different sense than are adults who can identify themselves (TCA II 412 n. 62). Elsewhere he distinguishes between symbiotic, egocentric, sociocentric/objectivistic, and universalistic stages of development (VTH 198).

14. "[Es liegt im Sinne der mundanen Erfahrung, daß] das erfahrene Reale wirklich ist mit dem Seinssinn, den es als Korrelat des Systems einstimmiger möglicher Erfahrung aller mit mir möglicherweise in Konnex tretenden miterfahrenden Subjekte hat, oder den es in der Weise hat, daß das jeweils wirklich Erfahrene horizonthaft verweist auf eine Einstimmigkeit in der fortgehenden und immer wieder herzustellenden Synthesis möglicher Erfahrung, eigener und beliebig in Mitfunktion tretender Erfahrung von Mitmenschen. Eben damit ist impliziert eine zu konstruierende Idee, die des totalen Systems möglicher Erfahrungen aller miteinander und möglicherweise mitfungierenden Subjekte im Horizont der jeweiligen möglichen Modalisierungen und Korrekturen" (Ms. A VII 2 22b).

15. Here two further problematic reproaches coming from Habermas can only be mentioned briefly. 1) On more than one occasion, Habermas has accused the transcendental-philosophically oriented philosophy of consciousness of being confronted with an unbridgeable dichotomy between the extramundane position of the transcendental I and the intramundane status of the empirical I (ND 275-76; PDM 300-301; cf. Wellmer 1977, 487). Either it understands the subject as that which stands over against the world as a whole and masters it, or else it takes the subject as an entity to be found within the world (Habermas 1992a, 38). However, such a transcendental-empirical self-duplication is, according to Habermas, only unavoidable as long as there is no alternative to an objectifying relation to oneself. In Habermas's view, the problem no longer arises the moment that "linguistically generated intersubjectivity gains primacy" (PDM 297). In our opinion, however, phenomenology conceives the relationship between transcendentality and mundaneity in a much more dialectical fashion than Habermas claims it does (cf. Ch. IV above) — and to all appearances, far more dialectically than Habermas does himself. That is to say, his own central distinction between the ideal (transcendental) linguistic community and the real (empirical) linguistic community is a typical example of the dichotomy he is criticizing (cf. Nagl 1988, 354-61). 2) Habermas claims in *Postmetaphysical Thinking* that the modern philosophy of consciousness dissolves the individual thing into "material of sensation" (PT 122), and he often reproaches it — in the context of referring to the concept of constitution, as well as in other places — for being animated by an untenable idealism that is incompatible with the insights of historical materialism, e.g., when it speaks, in his words, of a "mental spontaneity that brings everything forth out of itself" — a notion that he refers to as a "transcendental illusion" (PT 143; see also PDM 321-22). Although Habermas frequently speaks of the weaknesses of the model of constitution (cf., e.g., VTH 27, 30), he himself has never analyzed the concept of constitution in detail; rather, he unproblematically assumes that its significance has already been elucidated. Our analysis in Ch.V.1, however, shows that Husserl's concept of constitution (and the concept of constitution does indeed appear chiefly in Husserl's works) implies neither the animation of the "material of sensation" nor a kind of absolute idealism in the sense just mentioned. At the same time, however, we would not

want to deny that the concept of constitution is in fact incompatible with a materialism (be it analytic or historical materialism—cf. n. 18 below).

16. See also Rasmussen 1991, 111; Nagl 1988, 350; Ebeling 1990, 45; and Frank 1986, 12. The same insight is formulated by Luhmann as well, when he writes that intersubjectivity is not an alternative to subjectivity. To be sure, Luhmann has a polemical project in mind when he does this, for he claims that "intersubjectivity" is the formula for a predicament in which one can no longer sustain or define the subject. Instead of this, he proposes his own systems theory account (Luhmann 1986, 41–42). Although both systems theory and structuralism have also been (justifiably) criticized from the side of phenomenology, their critique of the philosophy of the subject—as formulated, for instance, by Lévi-Strauss—is still much more coherent than the linguistic-pragmatic critique, for systems theory and structuralism are not afraid of drawing the full consequences of their positions.

17. Habermas's reflections were influenced by Mead's symbolic interactionism, and for this reason it is worth turning briefly to Mead in order to understand Habermas's concept of self-consciousness. Like Habermas, Mead speaks of the social character of the self: "The process out of which the self arises is a social process which implies interaction of individuals in the group, implies the pre-existence of the group. . . . Thus, there is a social process out of which selves arise and within which further differentiation, further evolution, further organization, take place" (Mead 1962, 164). Of even more interest is that Mead goes on to emphasize that if one were to identify "self" with sheer consciousness (of something), then it would indeed be possible to speak of an individual self (Mead 1962, 164, 169). However, he wants to make a sharp distinction between consciousness and self-consciousness: "Consciousness, as frequently used, simply has reference to the field of experience, but self-consciousness refers to the ability to call out in ourselves a set of definite responses which belong to the others of the group. Consciousness and self-consciousness are not on the same level. A man alone has, fortunately or unfortunately, access to *his own* toothache, but that is not what we mean by self-consciousness" (Mead 1962, 163, emphasis added). "Self-consciousness . . . is definitively organized about the social individual, and that, as we have seen, is not simply because one is in a social group and affected by others and affects them, but because (and this is a point I have been emphasizing) his own experience as a self is one which he takes over from his action upon others. He becomes a self in so far as he can take the attitude of another and act toward himself as others act. . . . The taking or feeling of the attitude of the other toward yourself is what constitutes self-consciousness, and not mere organic sensations of which the individual is aware and which he experiences" (Mead 1962, 171–72). With a formulation that recalls Sartre (a similarity that is explicitly treated in Aboulafia 1986), Mead concludes that "to be self-conscious is essentially to become an object to one's self in virtue of one's social relations to other individuals" (Mead 1962, 172). Husserl would naturally deny that the I is a product of reflection. As we have expressed it, in a far from elegant formulation, the ontification of the I is preceded by an

ever-present, non-intentional, pre-reflective self-awareness [see also Zahavi, *Self-Awareness and Alterity: A Phenomenological Investigation* (Evanston, IL: Northwestern University Press, 1999) — trans.].

18. A further problem — one that lies at the center of the dispute between Henrich and Habermas — is Habermas's naturalism (cf. Henrich 1986, 507). That is to say, one has to ask how, against the background of this naturalism, it is possible to ascribe a critical, emancipatory potential to the subject (and here we are not even considering the problem of how a discourse theory of truth could be conceptually compatible with naturalism). Habermas does indeed deny that naturalism necessarily "requires the subject to give a naturalistically alienated description of itself" and to "recognize itself in its world" solely in grammatical terms designed to express "things and events," emphasizing instead the difference between his own position and that of a scientistically oriented analytic materialism (PT 20-21). There is undoubtedly a distinction between these positions. The question is merely whether Habermas, having distanced himself from the philosophy of the subject, still has the means at his disposal to ground such a distinction theoretically (see also Düsing 1986, 76-88).

19. With regard to the reproach of being fixated on an orientation toward the object, an equivocation in the concept of an "object" must be pointed out. That something is an object can mean in this context either simply that it is perceived, or that it is apprehended and interpreted as a thing. When I have an experience of others, what I experience is the other. But this experience is not an experience of an "object," is not a "subject-object" relationship in the sense that I apprehend the other as a thing. On the contrary, I as subject experience the other as a subject, i.e., as inaccessible and transcendent — and for this reason it is already a matter of a subject-subject relationship. Of course, the intersubjective character of the relation is intensified the moment we include communication and the process of "alter-ation." But it must still be maintained that there is already a distinction between a thing presenting itself and another subject manifesting itself — a distinction that is already at work in the pure and simple experience of others. It is precisely for this reason that it is problematic to accuse phenomenology of being unable to establish any subject-subject relation on account of its theory of intentionality. On the other hand, one can legitimately object that as long as experience is taken as the point of departure, there will always be an asymmetry between the experiencing subject and the experienced subject. But this asymmetry belongs to intersubjectivity per se, and one can only postulate the abolition of the asymmetry if one describes intersubjectivity from the derived, abstract, external perspective of a third observer.

20. Cf. Zahavi 1992a, Ch. III.2.

21. Habermas's presentations of Husserl's analyses are occasionally marred by elementary mistakes. In *Vorstudien und Ergänzungen zur Theorie des kommunikativen Handelns*, for example, Habermas presents Husserl's notion of sensuous intuition and reproaches Husserl for not having noticed that every perception has a surplus that outruns what is currently actually given, which is why any sen-

suous experience can always be problematized by new experiences (VTH 47–48). But this is precisely what Husserl's investigation of horizon intentionality had brought to light. Another problematic assertion is Habermas's claim that in the paradigm of the philosophy of the subject, the truth of a judgment is traced back to the subject's certainty that his representation corresponds with the object (Habermas 1992a, 17). But "evidence," in the phenomenological sense, is not at all related to the presence of a correspondence between "representation" and "object." Without going into detail about Husserl's theory of truth at the moment, it is still completely clear that Husserl does not understand truth as a relationship of correspondence, but as a relationship of fulfillment. We can speak of truth when the meant object is given originarily, which means: when the signitive intention is intuitively fulfilled. Knowledge can thereby be understood as a kind of identification (or synthesis of coincidence) between what is given in the merely signitive intention and what is given when the signification is fulfilled, i.e., between the given appearing matter or affair and the word whose sense has thereby come to fulfillment (19/538–39[668–69]). "In the unity of fulfilment, the fulfilling content coincides with the intending content, so that, in our experience of this unity of coincidence, the object, at once intended and 'given', stands before us, not as two objects, but as *one* alone" (19/57[291]). Hence the relationship of fulfillment is a relation between act-correlates, not between intra- and extra-mental objects. Moreover, in *Formal and Transcendental Logic*, Husserl distinguishes between two types of evidence, a distinction that is important in this context. On the one hand, there is the evidence of the "truly existing predicatively formed affair-complex in the mode itself-givenness"; on the other hand, evidence means "itself-givenness of the correctness of the judicial meaning, by virtue of its fitting the evidence, in the first sense: that is to say, the categorial objectivity as itself-given" (17/151–52[146]). Thus although Husserl does speak of a type of truth at the pre-predicative level, he insists on understanding knowledge in the genuine sense not merely as the presence of an intuition of the object (as the intuitive givenness of the object) but as a genuine synthesis of identification that takes place in linguistically expressed predicates and in judgments (cf. Rosen 1977, § 19, and Zahavi 1992a, Ch. IV.2–3). Finally, perhaps it should be added that Husserl would also claim that insofar as an argument can bring predicatively formed affair-complexes themselves to direct givenness, it can in fact be regarded as an intuition (i.e., a categorial one). That is to say, he understands intuition as an act that brings objectivity itself to givenness for us (and sometimes what is required for this is precisely an intellectual accomplishment), rather than as an act that is particularly linked with sensuous perception. Thus intuition is not non-discursive per se, but non-signitive (cf. Chapter II.3).

22. It is interesting to notice that this point can also be applied in connection with consensus. Although a consensus can turn out to be erroneous (e.g., the conviction that there are no black swans), this happens on the basis of a new (evident) consensus or a new evidence that claims intersubjective agreement in its turn. Skirbekk has pointed to the possibility that a factual consensus

may be in need of correction, and further points out that we are obliged to accept as valid whatever we have acknowledged under the best possible conditions to date to be true and correct. Simultaneously, however, we are conceding the possibility that what we have accepted in this way as the best argument could be surpassed by a still better argument. And he is right to speak in this connection of a *melioristic fallibility* (Skirbekk 1982, 74–75), which is also taken up by Apel in the following passage: "*Fallibilism* is always already *meliorism*, which means, among other things, that the requirement concerning falsifiability in principle—a requirement postulated by Popper, for example—does not arise from the metaphysical presupposition of the futility of all human cognitive efforts, but rather from the methodological presupposition of the corrigibility of all factually attainable scientific propositions or theories. But what is involved in this methodological presupposition is the quasi-Kantian postulate of the unitary interpretation of the world as a 'regulative principle' of the investigation" (TP II 161).

23. Moreover, in spite of his harsh criticism of the concept of evidence, Habermas occasionally appeals to the intuitive plausibility of his theory (e.g., VTH 438), and he also often refers to the experience of the "peculiarly constraint-free force of the better argument" (TCA I 24; cf., e.g., VTH 144). But a traditional term for this force is precisely "evidence." Cf. Ilting 1976.

24. Cf. Cobb-Stevens 1990b, 53, and Zahavi 1991, 169–70.

25. These remarks are directed against the use Apel and Habermas make of Wittgenstein's arguments; we cannot exclude the possibility that other interpretations could escape our critique.

26. In the meantime, this claim has also emerged outside of the narrow circle of those involved in the pragmatics of language. For example, Ebeling—who defines his own work as an attempt to fashion a theory of the subjectivity of the subject following both Heidegger and Habermas (Ebeling 1990, 11)—writes that it is the linguistic-pragmatic investigations of the *linguistic* subject that have provided for the first time a sufficient documentation of a theoretically legitimized intersubjectivity as such (Ebeling 1990, 81).

27. Because of the aim guiding our analyses, a number of important aspects have indeed been treated only in cursory fashion, and they would definitely have to be taken up were we to work out our account in more detail. What is at stake here is above all a more precise determination of *passivity* (in self-affection and in hyletic affection), since it is indispensable for a thorough understanding of the interconnection between subjectivity, intersubjectivity, and world; of *history*, since it is central for grasping the intersubjectivity of temporality; and last, but by no means least, of *language*.

REFERENCES

1. WORKS OF HUSSERL

A. Unpublished manuscripts

A III 9 (1920–21)
A VI 14A (1930)
A VII 1 (1933 or 1934)
A VII 2 (1934)
A VII 12 (1932)
B I 12 IV (1926–30)
B I 14 XI (1934)
B IV 5 (1933–34)
C 2 I (1931)
C 3 I (1930)
C 3 III (1931–32)
C 8 I (1929)
C 10 (1931)
C 16 I (1931–32)
C 16 IV (1932)
C 16 V (1931)
C 16 VI (1932)
C 16 VII (1933)
C 17 I (1931)
C 17 II (1930–31)
C 17 III (1931)
C 17 IV (1930 and 1932)
C 17 V (1931–32)
D 4 (1921)
D 13 I (1921)
D 13 XIV (1921)
D 14 (1931–33)
E III 4 (1930)
E III 9 (1931 and 1933)
K III 6 (1934–36)
K III 12 (1935)

B. Husserliana

Husserliana 1. Cartesianische Meditationen und Pariser Vorträge. Ed. Stephan
Strasser. Den Haag: Martinus Nijhoff, 1950, rpt. 1973. *The Paris Lectures.*
Trans. Peter Koestenbaum. The Hague: Martinus Nijhoff, 1964 (1/3-39).
Cartesian Meditations: An Introduction to Phenomenology. Trans. Dorion
Cairns. The Hague: Martinus Nijhoff, 1960 (1/43-183).

Husserliana 2. Die Idee der Phänomenologie. Fünf Vorlesungen. Ed. Walter Biemel.
Den Haag: Martinus Nijhoff, 1950, rpt. 1973. *The Idea of Phenomenology.*
Trans. Lee Hardy. Dordrecht: Kluwer Academic Publishers, 1999.

*Husserliana 3, 1-2. Ideen zu einer reinen Phänomenologie und phänomenologischen
Philosophie. Erstes Buch. Allgemeine Einführung in die reine Phänomenologie.* Ed.
Karl Schuhmann. Den Haag: Martinus Nijhoff, 1976. *Ideas Pertaining to a
Pure Phenomenology and to a Phenomenological Philosophy. First Book. General In-
troduction to a Pure Phenomenology.* Trans. Fred Kersten. The Hague: Marti-
nus Nijhoff, 1982.

*Husserliana 4. Ideen zu einer reinen Phänomenologie und phänomenologischen Phi-
losophie. Zweites Buch. Phänomenologische Untersuchungen zur Konstitution.* Ed.
Marly Biemel. Den Haag: Martinus Nijhoff, 1952. *Ideas Pertaining to a Pure
Phenomenology and to a Phenomenological Philosophy. Second Book. Studies in the
Phenomenology of Constitution.* Trans. Richard Rojcewicz and André Schu-
wer. Dordrecht: Kluwer Academic Publishers, 1989.

*Husserliana 5. Ideen zu einer reinen Phänomenologie und phänomenologischen Phi-
losophie. Drittes Buch: Die Phänomenologie und die Fundamente der Wissen-
schaften.* Ed. Marly Biemel. Den Haag: Martinus Nijhoff, 1952, rpt. 1971.
*Ideas Pertaining to a Pure Phenomenology and to a Phenomenological Philosophy.
Third Book. Phenomenology and the Foundations of the Sciences.* Trans. Ted E.
Klein and William E. Pohl. The Hague: Martinus Nijhoff, 1980 (5/1-137).
*Ideas Pertaining to a Pure Phenomenology and to a Phenomenological Philosophy.
Second Book. Studies in the Phenomenology of Constitution.* Trans. Richard
Rojcewicz and André Schuwer. Dordrecht: Kluwer Academic Publishers,
1989, 405-30 (5/138-62).

*Husserliana 6. Die Krisis der europäischen Wissenschaften und die transzendentale
Phänomenologie. Eine Einleitung in die phänomenologische Philosophie.* Ed.
Walter Biemel. Den Haag: Martinus Nijhoff, 1954, rpt. 1962. *The Crisis of
European Sciences and Transcendental Phenomenology: An Introduction to Phe-
nomenological Philosophy.* Trans. David Carr. Evanston, IL: Northwestern
University Press, 1970 (6/1-348, 357-86, 459-62, 473-75, 508-16).

Husserliana 7. Erste Philosophie (1923/24). Erster Teil. Kritische Ideengeschichte. Ed.
Rudolf Boehm. Den Haag: Martinus Nijhoff, 1956.

*Husserliana 8. Erste Philosophie (1923/24). Zweiter Teil. Theorie der phänomenolo-
gischen Reduktion.* Ed. Rudolf Boehm. Den Haag: Martinus Nijhoff, 1959.

Husserliana 9. Phänomenologische Psychologie. Vorlesungen Sommersemester 1925.
Ed. Walter Biemel. Den Haag: Martinus Nijhoff, 1962. *Phenomenological
Psychology: Lectures, Summer Semester, 1925.* Trans. John Scanlon. The
Hague: Martinus Nijhoff, 1977 (9/3-234). *Psychological and Transcendental
Phenomenology and the Confrontation with Heidegger (1927-1931).* Ed. and

trans. Thomas Sheehan and Richard E. Palmer. Dordrecht: Kluwer Academic Publishers, 1997 (9/237-349, 517-26).

Husserliana 10. Zur Phänomenologie des inneren Zeitbewusstseins (1893-1917). Ed. Rudolf Boehm. Den Haag: Martinus Nijhoff, 1966. *On the Phenomenology of the Consciousness of Internal Time (1893-1917).* Trans. John Barnett Brough. Dordrecht: Kluwer Academic Publishers, 1991.

Husserliana 11. Analysen zur passiven Synthesis. Aus Vorlesungs- und Forschungsmanuskripten 1918-1926. Ed. Margot Fleischer. Den Haag: Martinus Nijhoff, 1966.

Husserliana 13. Zur Phänomenologie der Intersubjektivität. Texte aus dem Nachlass. Erster Teil: 1905-1920. Ed. Iso Kern. Den Haag: Martinus Nijhoff, 1973.

Husserliana 14. Zur Phänomenologie der Intersubjektivität. Texte aus dem Nachlass. Zweiter Teil: 1921-1928. Ed. Iso Kern. Den Haag: Martinus Nijhoff, 1973.

Husserliana 15. Zur Phänomenologie der Intersubjektivität. Texte aus dem Nachlass. Dritter Teil: 1929-1935. Ed. Iso Kern. Den Haag: Martinus Nijhoff, 1973.

Husserliana 16. Ding und Raum. Vorlesungen 1907. Ed. Ulrich Claesges. Den Haag: Martinus Nijhoff, 1973. *Thing and Space: Lectures of 1907.* Trans. Richard Rojcewicz. Dordrecht: Kluwer Academic Publishers, 1997.

Husserliana 17. Formale und transzendentale Logik. Versuch einer Kritik der logischen Vernunft. Ed. Paul Janssen. Den Haag: Martinus Nijhoff, 1974. *Formal and Transcendental Logic.* Trans. Dorion Cairns. The Hague: Martinus Nijhoff, 1969 (17/5-335).

Husserliana 18. Logische Untersuchungen. Erster Band. Prolegomena zur reinen Logik. Ed. Elmar Holenstein. Den Haag: Martinus Nijhoff, 1975. *Logical Investigations.* 2 vols. Trans. J. N. Findlay. London: Routledge & Kegan Paul, 1970, 41-247.

Husserliana 19, 1-2. Logische Untersuchungen. Zweiter Band. Untersuchungen zur Phänomenologie und Theorie der Erkenntnis. Ed. Ursula Panzer. Den Haag: Martinus Nijhoff, 1984. *Logical Investigations.* 2 vols. Trans. J. N. Findlay. London: Routledge & Kegan Paul, 1970, 248-869.

Husserliana 22. Aufsätze und Rezensionen (1890-1910). Ed. Bernhard Rang. Den Haag: Martinus Nijhoff, 1979. *Early Writings in the Philosophy of Logic and Mathematics.* Trans. Dallas Willard. Dordrecht: Kluwer Academic Publishers, 1994.

Husserliana 24. Einleitung in die Logik und Erkenntnistheorie. Vorlesungen 1906/07. Ed. Ullrich Melle. Dordrecht: Martinus Nijhoff, 1984.

Husserliana 25. Aufsätze und Vorträge (1911-1921). Ed. Thomas Nenon and Hans Rainer Sepp. Dordrecht: Martinus Nijhoff, 1987.

Husserliana 26. Vorlesungen über Bedeutungslehre. Sommersemester 1908. Ed. Ursula Panzer. Dordrecht: Martinus Nijhoff, 1987.

Husserliana 27. Aufsätze und Vorträge (1922-1937). Ed. Thomas Nenon and Hans Rainer Sepp. Dordrecht: Kluwer Academic Publishers, 1989. "Renewal: Its Problem and Method." Trans. Jeffner Allen. In *Husserl: Shorter Works.* Ed. Peter McCormick and Frederick A. Elliston. Notre Dame, IN: University of Notre Dame Press, 1981, 326-31 (27/3-13).

Husserliana 29. Die Krisis der europäischen Wissenschaften und die transzendentale Phänomenologie. Ergänzungsband. Texte aus dem Nachlass 1934-1937. Ed. Reinhold N. Smid. Dordrecht: Kluwer Academic Publishers, 1993.

C. Other works

Husserl, Edmund. "Entwurf einer 'Vorrede' zu den 'Logischen Untersuchungen' (1913)." Ed. Eugen Fink. *Tijdschrift voor Filosofie* 1 (1939), 106-33, 319-39. *Introduction to the Logical Investigations: A Draft of a Preface to the Logical Investigations (1913)*. Trans. Philip J. Bossert and Curtis H. Peters. The Hague: Martinus Nijhoff, 1975.

———. *Erfahrung und Urteil. Untersuchungen zur Genealogie der Logik* [1939]. Ed. Ludwig Landgrebe. Hamburg: Felix Meiner, 1972, rpt. 1985. *Experience and Judgment: Investigations in a Genealogy of Logic*. Trans. James S. Churchill and Karl Ameriks. Evanston, IL: Northwestern University Press, 1973 (EU).

———. *Briefwechsel.* Ed. Elisabeth Schuhmann and Karl Schuhmann. Vol. 7, *Wissenschaftlerkorrespondenz.* Dordrecht: Kluwer Academic Publishers, 1994.

2. WORKS OF OTHER AUTHORS

Aboulafia, Mitchell. *The Mediating Self: Mead, Sartre, and Self-Determination.* New Haven, CT: Yale University Press, 1986.

Adorno, Theodor W. *Zur Metakritik der Erkenntnistheorie.* Frankfurt am Main: Suhrkamp, 1981.

Aguirre, Antonio. *Genetische Phänomenologie und Reduktion.* Den Haag: Martinus Nijhoff, 1970.

———. *Die Phänomenologie Husserls im Licht ihrer gegenwärtigen Interpretation und Kritik.* Darmstadt: Wissenschaftliche Buchgesellschaft, 1982.

Alexy, R. "Probleme der Diskurstheorie." *Zeitschrift für philosophische Forschung* 43 (1989), 81-93.

Allen, Jeffner. "Husserl's Overcoming of the Problem of Intersubjectivity." *The Modern Schoolman* 55 (1978), 261-71.

Almeida, Guido Antônio de. *Sinn und Inhalt in der genetischen Phänomenologie E. Husserls.* Den Haag: Martinus Nijhoff, 1972.

Ameriks, Karl. "Husserl's Realism." *The Philosophical Review* 86 (1977), 498-519.

Andrew, W. K. "The Givenness of Self and Others in Husserl's Transcendental Phenomenology." *Journal of Phenomenological Psychology* 13 (1982), 85-100.

Apel, Karl-Otto. "Das Leibapriori der Erkenntnis. Eine Betrachtung im Anschluß an Leibnizens Monadenlehre." *Archiv für Philosophie* 12 (1963), 152-72.

———. *Transformation der Philosophie.* Band I, *Sprachanalytik, Semiotik, Hermeneutik;* Band 2, *Das Apriori der Kommunikationsgemeinschaft.* Frankfurt am Main: Suhrkamp, 1973 (TP I, TP II). [Partly trans. in] *Towards a Transformation of Philosophy.* Trans. Glyn Adey and David Frisby. London: Routledge & Kegan Paul, 1980 (TrP).

———. "Zur Idee einer transzendentalen Sprachpragmatik." In *Aspekte und Probleme der Sprachphilosophie.* Ed. J. Simon. Freiburg: Alber, 1974, 283-326.

———. "Das Problem der philosophischen Letztbegründung im Lichte einer transzendentalen Sprachpragmatik." In *Sprache und Erkenntnis.* Ed. Bernulf

Kanitscheider. Innsbruck: Institute für Sprachwissenschaft der Universität Innsbruck, 1976, 55–82; "The Problem of Philosophical Fundamental Grounding in Light of a Transcendental Pragmatic of language." Trans. Karl Richard Pavlovic. *Man and World* 8 (1975), 239–75. Rpt. as "The Question of Grounding: Philosophy and Transcendental Pragmatics of Language." In *Karl-Otto Apel: Selected Essays*. Vol. 2, *Ethics and the Theory of Rationality*. Ed. Eduardo Mendieta. Atlantic Highlands, NJ: Humanities Press, 1996, 68–102 (QG).

———. "Transformation der Transzendentalphilosophie: Versuch einer retrospektiven Zwischenbilanz." In *Philosophes critiques d'eux-mêmes*, Vol. 4. Ed. A. Mercier. Bern: Peter Lang, 1978, 9–43.

———. "Warum transzendentale Sprachpragmatik? Bemerkungen zu H. Krings 'Empirie und Apriori. Zum Verhältnis von Transzendentalphilosophie und Sprachpragmatik.'" In *Freiheit als praktisches Prinzip*. Ed. H. M. Baumgartner. Freiburg: Alber, 1979a, 13–43.

———. *Die Erklären : Verstehen–Kontroverse in transzendental-pragmatischer Sicht*. Frankfurt am Main: Suhrkamp, 1979b. *Understanding and Explanation: A Transcendental-Pragmatic Perspective*. Trans. Georgia Warnke. Cambridge, MA: MIT Press, 1984 (UE).

———. "Intentions, Conventions, and Reference to Things: Dimensions of Understanding Meaning in Hermeneutics and in Analytical Philosophy of Language." In *Meaning and Understanding* Ed. H. Parret and J. Bouveresse. Berlin: De Gruyter, 1981, 79–111. Rpt. as "Intentions, Conventions, and Reference to Things: Meaning in Hermeneutics and the Analytic Philosophy of Language." In *Karl-Otto Apel: Selected Essays*. Vol. 1, *Towards a Transcendental Semiotics*. Ed. Eduardo Mendieta. Atlantic Highlands, NJ: Humanities Press, 1994, 51–82.

———. "Comments on Davidson." *Synthese* 59 (1984), 19–26.

———. "Grenzen der Diskursethik? Versuch einer Zwischenbilanz." *Zeitschrift für philosophische Forschung* 40 (1986), 3–31. "Limits of Discourse Ethics? An Attempt at a Provisional Assessment." Trans. Eduardo Mendieta. In *Karl-Otto Apel: Selected Essays*, Vol. 2, 192–218.

———. "Linguistic Meaning and Intentionality: The Compatibility of the 'Linguistic Turn' and the Pragmatic Turn' of Meaning-Theory within the Framework of a Transcendental Semiotics." In *Critical and Dialectical Phenomenology*. Ed. Hugh Silverman and Donn Welton. Albany, NY: State University of New York Press, 1987, 2–53. Rpt. as "The 'Pragmatic Turn' and Transcendental Semiotics: The Compatibility of the 'Linguistic Turn' and the 'Pragmatic Turn' of Meaning Theory within the Framework of a Transcendental Semiotics." In *Karl-Otto Apel: Selected Essays*, Vol. 1, 132–74.

———. "Normative Begründung der 'Kritischen Theorie' durch Rekurs auf lebensweltliche Sittlichkeit?" In *Zwischenbetrachtungen im Prozeß der Aufklärung*. Ed. Axel Honneth et al. Frankfurt am Main: Suhrkamp, 1989a, 15–65.

———. "Sinnkonstitution und Geltungsrechtfertigung." In *Martin Heidegger. Innen- und Außenansichten*. Ed. Forum für Philosophie Bad Homburg. Frankfurt am Main: Suhrkamp, 1989b, 131–75.

————. "Linguistic Meaning and Intentionality: The Relationship of the A Priori of Language and the A Priori of Consciousness in Light of a Transcendental Semiotic or a Linguistic Pragmatic." In *Phenomenology and Beyond: The Self and its Language*. Ed. H. A. Durfee and D. F. T. Rodier. Dordrecht: Kluwer Academic Publishers, 1989c, 102–18.

————. "Ist Intentionalität fundamentaler als sprachliche Bedeutung? Transzendentalpragmatische Argumente gegen die Rückkehr zum semantischen Intentionalismus der Bewußtseinsphilosophie." In *Intentionalität und Verstehen*. Ed. Forum für Philosophie Bad Homburg. Frankfurt am Main: Suhrkamp, 1990a, 13–54.

————. *Diskurs und Verantwortung*. Frankfurt am Main: Suhrkamp, 1990b (DV).

————, ed. *Sprachpragmatik und Philosophie*. 3rd ed. Frankfurt am Main: Suhrkamp, 1982.

Arp, Kristana. *A Critical Reconstruction of Husserl's Intersubjectivity Theory*. Ann Arbor, MI: UMI, 1987.

————. "Intentionality and the public world: Husserl's treatment of objectivity in the Cartesian Meditations." *Husserl Studies* 7 (1991), 89–101.

Ballard, Edward G. "Husserl's Philosophy of Intersubjectivity in Relation to his Rational Ideal." *Tulane Studies in Philosophy* 11 (1962), 3–38.

Barral, Mary Rose. *Merleau-Ponty: The Role of the Body-Subject in Interpersonal Relations*. Pittsburgh, PA: Duquesne University Press, 1965.

Bartels, M. "Sprache und soziales Handeln. Eine Auseinandersetzung mit Habermas' Sprachbegriff." *Zeitschrift für philosophische Forschung* 36 (1982), 226–34.

Baumgartner, H. M. "Geltung durch Antizipation." In *Kommunikation und Reflexion*. Ed. W. Kuhlmann and D. Böhler. Frankfurt am Main: Suhrkamp, 1982, 46–53.

Becker, Oskar. *Beiträge zur phänomenologischen Begründung der Geometrie und ihrer physikalischen Anwendungen*. Tübingen: Max Niemeyer, 1973.

Berkeley, George. *Philosophical Works*. London: Dent, Everyman's Library, 1985.

Bernet, Rudolf. "Bedeutung und intentionales Bewußtsein. Husserls Begriff des Bedeutungsphänomens." *Phänomenologische Forschungen* 8 (1979a), 31–63.

————. "Perception as a Teleological Process of Cognition." *Analecta Husserliana* 9 (1979b), 119–32.

————. "Die ungegenwärtige Gegenwart. Anwesenheit und Abwesenheit in Husserls Analyse des Zeitbewußtseins." *Phänomenologische Forschungen* 14 (1983), 16–57.

————. "Le monde et le sujet." *Philosophie* 21 (1989), 57–76.

————. "Husserl and Heidegger on Intentionality and Being." *Journal of the British Society for Phenomenology* 21 (1990), 136–52.

————. "The Other in Myself." In *Tradition and Renewal I*. Ed. D. Boileau and J. Dick. Leuven: Leuven University Press, 1992, 77–93.

————. *La vie du sujet*. Paris: Presses Universitaires de France, Épiméthée, 1994.

Bernsen, N. O. "Elementary Knowledge: Transcendental Pragmatics without Consensus Theory and Ideal Community of Communication." *Acta Sociologica* 25 (1982), 235–47.

Biemel, Walter. "Die entscheidenden Phasen der Entfaltung von Husserls Philosophie." *Zeitschrift für philosophische Forschung* 13 (1959), 187–213. "The Decisive Phases in the Development of Husserl's Philosophy." In *The Phenomenology of Husserl: Selected Critical Readings*. Ed. and trans. R. O. Elveton. Chicago, IL: Quadrangle Books, 1970, 148–73; 2nd ed., Seattle,WA: Noesis Press, 2000, 140–63.

Binswanger, Ludwig. *Grundformen und Erkenntnis menschlichen Daseins.* Zurich: Max Niehans, 1953.

Birmingham, Peg E. "*Logos* and the Place of the Other." *Research in Phenomenology* 20 (1990), 34–54.

Boehm, Rudolf. *Vom Gesichtspunkt der Phänomenologie.* Den Haag: Martinus Nijhoff, 1968.

———. "Zur Phänomenologie der Gemeinschaft. Edmund Husserls Grundgedanken. In *Phänomenologie, Rechtsphilosophie, Jurisprudenz.* Ed. Th. Würtenberger. Frankfurt am Main: Vittorio Klostermann, 1969, 1–26.

Böhler, D. "Zur Geltung des emanzipatorischen Interesses." In *Materialien zu Habermas' 'Erkenntnis und Interesse'.* Ed. Winfried Dallmayr. Frankfurt am Main: Suhrkamp, 1974, 349–68.

Bouckaert, L. "Ontology and Ethics: Reflections on Lévinas' Critique of Heidegger." *International Philosophical Quarterly* 10 (1970), 402–19.

Bourgeois, Patrick L., and Sandra B. Rosenthal. "Role Taking, Corporeal Intersubjectivity, and Self: Mead and Merleau-Ponty." *Philosophy Today* 34 (1990), 117–28.

Brand, Gerd. *Welt, Ich, und Zeit. Nach unveröffentlichten Manuskripten Edmund Husserls.* Den Haag: Martinus Nijhoff, 1955.

———. "Edmund Husserl: Analysen zur passiven Synthesis." *Philosophische Rundschau* 17 (1970), 55–77.

———. "Edmund Husserl: Zur Phänomenologie der Intersubjektivität." *Philosophische Rundschau* 25 (1978), 54–79.

———. "Die Normalität des und der Anderen und die Anomalität einer Erfahrungsgemeinschaft bei Edmund Husserl." In *Alfred Schütz und die Idee des Alltags in den Sozialwissenschaften.* Ed. Walter M. Sprondel and Richard Grathoff. Stuttgart: Ferdinand Enke, 1979, 108–24.

Brentano, Franz. *Wahrheit und Evidenz.* Hamburg: Felix Meiner, 1962.

———. *Psychologie vom empirischen Standpunkt I–II.* Hamburg: Felix Meiner, 1971–73.

Brough, John. "The Emergence of an Absolute Consciousness in Husserl's Early Writings on Time-Consciousness." *Man and World* 5 (1972), 298–326.

Bruzina, Ron. "Solitude and community in the work of philosophy: Husserl and Fink." *Man and World* 22 (1989), 287–314.

Buber, Martin. *Dialogisches Leben.* Zurich: Gregor Müller, 1947.

Cairns, Dorion. *Conversations with Husserl and Fink.* Ed. Husserl-Archives, Louvain. The Hague: Martinus Nijhoff, 1976.

Carr, David. "The 'Fifth Meditation' and Husserl's Cartesianism." *Philosophy and Phenomenological Research* 34 (1973), 14–35.

Carrington, Peter J. "Schutz on Transcendental Intersubjectivity in Husserl." *Human Studies* 2 (1979), 95–110.

Claesges, Ulrich. *Edmund Husserls Theorie der Raumkonstitution.* Den Haag: Martinus Nijhoff, 1964.

———. "Zweideutigkeiten in Husserls Lebenswelt-Begriff." In *Perspektiven transzendentalphänomenologischer Forschung.* Ed. Ulrich Claesges and Klaus Held. Den Haag: Martinus Nijhoff, 1972, 85–101.

Cobb-Stevens, Richard. *Husserl and Analytic Philosophy.* Dordrecht: Kluwer Academic Publishers, 1990a.

———. "Being and Categorial Intuition." *Review of Metaphysics* 44 (1990b), 43–66.

Courtine, Jean-François. "Intersubjektivität und Analogie." *Phänomenologische Forschungen* 24/25 (1991), 232–64.

Cristin, Renato. "Phänomenologie und Monadologie. Husserl und Leibniz." *Studia Leibnitiana* 22 (1990), 163–74.

Cunningham, Suzanne. *Language and the Phenomenological Reductions of Edmund Husserl.* The Hague: Martinus Nijhoff, 1976.

———. "Husserl and Private Languages: A Response to Hutcheson." *Philosophy and Phenomenological Research* 44 (1983), 103–11.

Dallmayr, Fred. "Reason and Emancipation: Notes on Habermas." *Man and World* 5 (1972), 79–109.

———. "Heidegger on Intersubjectivity." *Human Studies* 3 (1980), 221–46.

Dallmayr, Winfried. "Sinnerlebnis und Geltungsreflexion: Apels Transformation der Philosophie." *Philosophische Rundschau* 25 (1978), 1–42.

Dauenhauer, Bernard P. "A Comment on Husserl and Solipsism." *The Modern Schoolman* 52 (1975), 189–93.

Davidson, D. *Inquiries into Truth and Interpretation.* Oxford: Clarendon Press, 1984.

De Boer, Theo. *The Development of Husserl's Thought.* The Hague: Martinus Nijhoff, 1978.

Depraz, Natalie. "Les figures de l'intersubjectivité. Étude des Husserliana XIII–XIV–XV." *Archives de Philosophie* 55 (1992), 479–98.

Derrida, Jacques. *Edmund Husserl's "Origin of Geometry": An Introduction.* Trans. John P. Leavey, Jr. Stony Brook, NY: Nicholas Hays, 1978; rpt. Lincoln, NE: University of Nebraska Press, 1989.

Descartes, René. *Discourse on Method and Meditations on First Philosophy.* Trans. Donald A. Cress. Indianapolis, IN: Hackett, 1980.

Diemer, Alwin. *Edmund Husserl. Versuch einer systematischen Darstellung seiner Phänomenologie.* Meisenheim am Glan: Anton Hain, 1965.

Dillon, M. C. "Gestalt Theory and Merleau-Ponty's Concept of Intentionality." *Man and World* 4 (1971), 436–59.

———. "Merleau-Ponty and the Psychogenesis of the Self." *Man and World* 9 (1978), 84–98.

———. "Merleau-Ponty and the Reversibility Thesis." *Man and World* 16 (1983), 365–88.

————. "Merleau-Ponty and the Transcendence of Immanence: Overcoming the Ontology of Consciousness." *Man and World* 19 (1986), 395-412.

Dreyfus, Hubert L. "The Priority of *The* World to *My* World: Heidegger's Answer to Husserl (and Sartre)." *Man and World* 8 (1975), 121-30.

Drummond, John J. "Husserl on the Ways to the Performance of the Reduction." *Man and World* 8 (1975), 47-69.

————. *Husserlian Intentionality and Non-Foundational Realism.* Dordrecht: Kluwer Academic Publishers, 1990.

Düsing, E. *Intersubjektivität und Selbstbewußtsein.* Köln: Dinter, 1986.

Ebeling, H. *Neue Subjektivität. Die Selbstbehauptung der Vernunft.* Würzburg: Königshausen & Neumann, 1990.

Elliston, Frederick A. "Husserl's Phenomenology of Empathy." In *Husserl: Expositions and Appraisals.* Ed. Frederick A. Elliston and Peter McCormick. Notre Dame, IN: University of Notre Dame Press, 1977, 213-31.

————. "Sartre and Husserl on Interpersonal Relationship." In *Jean-Paul Sartre: Contemporary Approaches to His Philosophy.* Ed. Hugh Silverman and Frederick A. Elliston. Pittsburgh, PA: Duquesne University Press, 1980, 157-67.

Emerson, M. "Heidegger's Appropriation of the Concept of Intentionality in *Die Grundprobleme der Phänomenologie.*" *Research in Phenomenology* 14 (1984), 175-94.

Esthimer, S. W. *Max Scheler's Concept of the Person.* Ann Arbor, MI: UMI, 1985.

Evans, J. Claude, "Husserl und Habermas." In *Materialien zu Habermas' 'Erkenntnis und Interesse'.* Ed. Winfried Dallmayr. Frankfurt am Main: Suhrkamp, 1974, 268-94.

Fellmann, F. *Gelebte Philosophie in Deutschland. Denkformen der Lebensweltphänomenologie und der kritischen Theorie.* Freiburg: Karl Alber, 1983.

Fichte, Johann Gottlieb. *Die Wissenschaftslehre (1804).* Hamburg: Felix Meiner, 1986.

Figal, G. *Martin Heidegger—Phänomenologie der Freiheit.* Frankfurt am Main: Athenäum, 1988.

Fink, Eugen. "Die phänomenologische Philosophie Edmund Husserls in die gegenwärtigen Kritik." *Kantstudien* 38 (1933), 319-83. "The Phenomenological Philosophy of Edmund Husserl and Contemporary Criticism." In *The Phenomenology of Husserl: Selected Critical Readings.* Ed. and trans. R. O. Elveton. Chicago, IL: Quadrangle Books, 1970, 74-147; 2nd ed., Seattle, WA: Noesis Press, 2000, 70-139.

————. "Das Problem der Phänomenologie Edmund Husserls." *Revue Internationale de Philosophie* 1 (1939), 226-70. "The Problem of the Phenomenology of Edmund Husserl." Trans. Robert M. Harlan. In *Apriori and World: European Contributions to Husserlian Phenomenology.* Ed. William McKenna, Robert M. Harlan, and Laurence E. Winters. The Hague: Martinus Nijhoff, 1981a, 21-55.

————. "Operative Begriffe in Husserls Phänomenologie." *Zeitschrift für philosophische Forschung* 11 (1957), 321-37. "Operative Concepts in Husserl's Phenomenology." Trans. William McKenna. In *Apriori and World: European Contributions to Husserlian Phenomenology.* Ed. William McKenna, Robert M.

Harlan, and Laurence E. Winters. The Hague: Martinus Nijhoff, 1981b, 56–70.

———. *Studien zur Phänomenologie 1930–1939*. Den Haag: Martinus Nijhoff, 1966.

———. *Nähe und Distanz*. Munich: Karl Alber, 1976.

———. *VI. Cartesianische Meditation*. Teil 1, *Die Idee einer transzendentalen Methodenlehre*. Ed. Hans Ebeling, Jann Holl, and Guy van Kerckhoven. Dordrecht: Kluwer Academic Publishers, 1988a. *Sixth Cartesian Meditation: The Idea of a Transcendental Theory of Method*. Trans. Ron Bruzina. Bloomington, IN: Indiana University Press, 1995.

———. *VI. Cartesianische Meditation*. Teil 2, *Ergänzungsband*. Ed. Guy van Kerckhoven. Dordrecht: Kluwer Academic Publishers, 1988b.

Føllesdal, Dagfinn. "Husserl's Notion of Noema." *Journal of Philosophy* 66 (1969), 680–87.

Frank, M. *Was ist Neostrukturalismus?* Frankfurt am Main: Suhrkamp, 1984.

———. *Die Unhintergehbarkeit von Individualität*. Frankfurt am Main: Suhrkamp, 1986.

Frank, M., G. Raulet, and W. van Reijen, eds. *Die Frage nach dem Subjekt*. Frankfurt am Main: Suhrkamp, 1988.

Friedman, R. M. "Merleau-Ponty's Theory of Subjectivity." *Philosophy Today* 19 (1975), 228–42.

Frings, Manfred S. *Zur Phänomenologie der Lebensgemeinschaft*. Meisenheim am Glan: Anton Hain, 1971.

———. "Husserl and Scheler: Two Views on Intersubjectivity." *Journal of the British Society for Phenomenology* 9 (1978), 143–49.

Gadamer, Hans-Georg. "Die phänomenologische Bewegung." In his *Kleine Schriften III*. Tübingen: J. C. B. Mohr, 1972, 150–89. "The Phenomenological Movement." In his *Philosophical Hermeneutics*. Ed. and trans. David E. Linge. Berkeley, CA: University of California Press, 1976. Rpt. (paper) 1977, 130–81.

Gallagher, Shaun. "Hyletic Experience and the Lived Body." *Husserl Studies* 3 (1986), 131–66.

Gould, C. *Authenticity and Being-with-others: A Critique of Heidegger's Sein und Zeit*. Ann Arbor, MI: UMI, 1977.

Grathoff, Richard, and Bernhard Waldenfels, eds. *Sozialität und Intersubjektivität*. Munich: Wilhelm Fink, 1983.

Grondin, J. "Habermas und das Problem der Individualität." *Philosophische Rundschau* 36 (1989), 187–205.

Gurwitsch, Aron. *Die mitmenschlichen Begegnungen in der Milieuwelt* [1931]. Ed. Alexandre Métraux. Berlin: Walter de Gruyter, 1977. *Human Encounters in the Social World*. Trans. Fred Kersten. Pittsburgh, PA: Duquesne University Press, 1979.

———. *The Field of Consciousness*. Pittsburgh, PA: Duquesne University Press, 1964.

———. *Studies in Phenomenology and Psychology*. Evanston, IL: Northwestern University Press, 1966.

Habermas, Jürgen. *Technik und Wissenschaft als 'Ideologie'*. Frankfurt am Main: Suhrkamp, 1969.

———. *Erkenntnis und Interesse*. Rev. ed. Frankfurt am Main: Suhrkamp, 1973 (EI). Partly trans. in *Knowledge and Human Interests*. Trans. Jeremy J. Shapiro. Boston: Beacon Press, 1972 (KHI).

———. "Moralentwicklung und Ich-Identität." In *Zur Rekonstruktion des historischen Materialismus*. Ed. Jürgen Habermas. Frankfurt am Main: Suhrkamp, 1976, 63–91. "Moral Development and Ego Identity." In Habermas, *Communication and the Evolution of Sociality*. Trans. Thomas McCarthy. Boston, MA: Beacon Press, 1979, 69–94.

———. *Zur Logik der Sozialwissenschaften*. Frankfurt am Main: Suhrkamp, 1985 (LSW). Partly trans. in *On the Logic of the Social Sciences*. Trans. Shierry Weber Nicholsen and Jerry A. Stark. Cambridge, MA: MIT Press, 1988 (LSS).

———. "Entgegnung." In *Kommunikatives Handeln. Beiträge zu Jürgen Habermas' 'Theorie des kommunikativen Handelns'*. Ed. Axel Honneth and Hans Joas. Frankfurt am Main: Suhrkamp, 1986, 327–405.

———. *Theorie des kommunikativen Handelns*. Band 1, *Handlungsrationalität und gesellschaftliche Rationalisierung;* Band 2, *Zur Kritik der funktionalistischen Vernunft*. Frankfurt am Main: Suhrkamp, 1988 [rpt. of 4th, corrected ed., 1987]. *The Theory of Communicative Action*. Vol. 1, *Reason and the Rationalization of Society*. Trans. Thomas McCarthy. Boston, MA: Beacon Press, 1984 [trans. of orig. 1981 ed.], Vol. 2, *Lifeworld and System: A Critique of Functionalist Reason*. Trans. Thomas McCarthy. Boston, MA: Beacon Press, 1987 [trans. of 3rd corrected ed., 1985] (TCA I, TCA II).

———. *Vorstudien und Ergänzungen zur Theorie des kommunikativen Handelns*. Frankfurt am Main: Suhrkamp, 1989a (VTH).

———. *Nachmetaphysisches Denken. Philosophische Aufsätze*. Frankfurt am Main: Suhrkamp, 1989b (ND). Partly trans. in *Postmetaphysical Thinking: Philosophical Essays*. Trans. William Mark Hohengarten. Cambridge, MA: MIT Press, 1992; rpt. (paper) 1993 (PT).

———. *Der philosophische Diskurs der Moderne. Zwölf Vorlesungen*. Frankfurt am Main: Suhrkamp, 1991a. *The Philosophical Discourse of Modernity: Twelve Lectures*. Trans. Frederick G. Lawrence. Cambridge, MA: MIT Press, 1987 [trans. of orig. 1985 ed.] (PDM).

———. "An Intersubjective Concept of Individuality." *Journal of Chinese Philosophy* 18 (1991b), 133–41.

———. *Texte und Kontexte*. Frankfurt am Main: Suhrkamp, 1992a.

———. *Moralbewußtsein und kommunikatives Handelns*. Frankfurt am Main: Suhrkamp, 1992b. *Moral Consciousness and Communicative Action*. Trans. Christian Lenhardt and Shierry Weber Nicholsen. Cambridge, MA: MIT Press, 1990 [trans. of orig. 1983 ed., with an additional essay] (MC).

Hall, Harrison. "Intersubjective Phenomenology and Husserl's Cartesianism." *Man and World* 12 (1979), 13–20.

———. "The Other Minds Problem in Early Heidegger." *Human Studies* 3 (1980), 247–54.

———. "Was Husserl a Realist or an Idealist?" In *Husserl, Intentionality, and Cognitive Science*. Ed. Hubert L. Dreyfus. Cambridge, MA: MIT Press, 1982, 169–90.

Hammacher, K. "Fichtes und Husserls transzendentale Begründung der

Intersubjektivität und die anthropologische Fragestellung." *Archivio di Filosofia* 54 (1986), 669–84.

Haney, Kathleen M. *A Re-Evaluation of Husserl's Theory of Intersubjectivity.* Ann Arbor, MI: UMI, 1992.

Harlan, Robert M. *The I and the Other: A Reformulation of Husserl's 5th Cartesian Meditation.* Ann Arbor, MI: UMI, 1978.

———. "Must the Other be derived from the I? Towards the reformulation of Husserl's 5th Cartesian Meditation." *Husserl Studies* 1 (1984), 79–104.

Harney, Maurita J. *Intentionality, Sense, and the Mind.* The Hague: Martinus Nijhoff, 1984.

Hart, James G. "Constitution and reference in Husserl's phenomenology of phenomenology." *Husserl Studies* 6 (1989), 43–72.

Hartmann, K. *Die Philosophie J.-P. Sartres.* Berlin: De Gruyter, 1983.

Heidegger, Martin. *Prolegomena zur Geschichte des Zeitbegriffs* [1925]. Ed. Petra Jaeger. Frankfurt am Main: Vittorio Klostermann, 1979. *History of the Concept of Time: Prolegomena.* Trans. Theodore Kisiel. Bloomington, IN: Indiana University Press, 1985 (PZ; German page numbers are included in the English translation).

———. *Sein und Zeit* [1927]. 16th ed. Tübingen: Max Niemeyer, 1986. *Being and Time.* Trans. Joan Stambaugh. Albany, NY: State University of New York Press, 1996 (SuZ; German page numbers are included in the English translation).

———. *Die Grundprobleme der Phänomenologie* [1927]. Ed. Friedrich-Wilhelm von Herrmann. Frankfurt am Main: Vittorio Klostermann, 1975. *The Basic Problems of Phenomenology.* Trans. Albert Hofstadter. Bloomington, IN: Indiana University Press, 1982 (GP; German page numbers are included in the English translation).

———. *Wegmarken.* Frankfurt am Main: Vittorio Klostermann, 1978. *Pathmarks.* Ed. William McNeill. Cambridge: Cambridge University Press, 1998.

Held, Klaus. *Lebendige Gegenwart.* Den Haag: Martinus Nijhoff, 1966.

———. "Das Problem der Intersubjektivität und die Idee einer phänomenologischen Transzendentalphilosophie." In *Perspektiven transzendentalphänomenologischer Forschung.* Ed. Ulrich Claesges and Klaus Held. Den Haag: Martinus Nijhoff, 1972, 3–60.

———. "Husserls Rückgang auf das phainomenon und die geschichtliche Stellung der Phänomenologie." *Phänomenologische Forschungen* 10 (1980), 89–145.

———. "Einleitung." In Edmund Husserl, *Die phänomenologische Methode. Ausgewählte Texte I.* Ed. Klaus Held. Stuttgart: Reclam, 1985, 5–51.

———. "Heimwelt, Fremdwelt, die eine Welt." *Phänomenologische Forschungen* 24/25 (1991), 305–37.

Henrich, Dieter. "Selbstbewußtsein, kritische Einleitung in eine Theorie." In *Hermeneutik und Dialektik.* Ed. R. Bubner, K. Cramer, and R. Wiehl. Tübingen: J. C. B. Mohr, 1970, 257–84.

———. "Was ist Metaphysik, was Moderne?" *Merkur* 448 (1986), 495–508.

———. *Konzepte*. Frankfurt am Main: Suhrkamp, 1987.

Hoche, Hans-Ulrich. "Bemerkungen zum Problem der Selbst- und Fremder-fahurng bei Husserl und Sartre." *Zeitschrift für philosophische Forschung* 25 (1971), 172-86.

Höffe, O. "Kritische Überlegungen zur Konsensustheorie der Wahrheit (Habermas)." *Philosophisches Jahrbuch* 83 (1976), 313-32.

———. "Kantische Skepsis gegen die transzendentale Kommunikationsethik." In *Kommunikation und Reflexion*. Ed. W. Kuhlmann and D. Böhler. Frankfurt am Main: Suhrkamp, 1982, 518-39.

———. "Ist die transzendentale Vernunftkritik in der Sprachphilosophie aufgehoben?" *Philosophisches Jahrbuch* 91 (1984), 240-72.

Hoffmann, Gisbert. "Zur Phänomenologie der Intersubjektivität." *Zeitschrift für Philosophische Forschung* 29 (1975), 138-49.

Holenstein, Elmar. "Passive Genesis: Eine begriffsanalytische Studie." *Tijdschrift voor Filosofie* 33 (1971), 112-53.

———. *Phänomenologie der Assoziation. Zu Struktur und Funktion eines Grundprinzips der passiven Genesis bei E. Husserl*. Den Haag: Martinus Nijhoff, 1972.

Holmes, Richard H. "Is Transcendental Phenomenology Committed To Idealism?" *The Monist* 59 (1975a), 98-114.

———. "An Explication of Husserl's Theory of the Noema." *Research in Phenomenology* 5 (1975b), 143-53.

Honneth, Axel, and Hans Joas, eds. *Kommunikatives Handeln. Beiträge zu Jürgen Habermas' 'Theorie des kommunikativen Handelns'*. Frankfurt am Main: Suhrkamp, 1986.

Horster, D. "Der Kantische 'methodische Solipsismus' und die Theorien von Apel und Habermas." *Kantstudien* 73 (1982), 463-70.

Hösle, V. "Die Transzendentalpragmatik als Fichteanismus der Intersubjektivität." *Zeitschrift für philosophische Forschung* 40 (1986), 235-52.

Hougaard, E. "Some Reflections on the Relationship Between Freudian Psycho-Analysis and Husserlian Phenomenology." *Journal of Phenomenological Psychology* 9 (1978), 1-83.

Hoyos, G. "Zum Teleologiebegriff in der Phänomenologie Husserls." In *Perspektiven transzendentalphänomenologischer Forschung*. Ed. Ulrich Claesges and Klaus Held. Den Haag: Martinus Nijhoff, 1972, 61-84.

Huizing, K. *Das Sein und der Andere*. Frankfurt am Main: Athenäum, 1988.

Hutcheson, Peter. "Husserl's Problem of Intersubjectivity." *Journal of the British Society for Phenomenology* 11 (1980), 144-62.

———. "Husserl and Private Languages." *Philosophy and Phenomenological Research* 42 (1981a), 111-18.

———. "Solipsistic and Intersubjective Phenomenology." *Human Studies* 4 (1981b), 165-78.

———. "Husserl's Fifth Meditation." *Man and World* 15 (1982), 265-84.

Hyppolite, Jean. "L'intersubjectivité chez Husserl." In his *Figures de la pensée philosophique. Écrits de Jean Hyppolite (1931-1968)*, Vol. I. Paris: Presses Universitaires de France, 1971, 499-512.

Ilting, K.-H. "Geltung als Konsens." *Neue Hefte für Philosophie* 10 (1976), 20-50.

Joas, Hans. *Praktische Intersubjektivität*. Frankfurt am Main: Suhrkamp, 1980.
Johnson, Galen A., and Michael B. Smith, eds. *Ontology and Alterity in Merleau-Ponty*. Evanston, IL: Northwestern University Press, 1990.
Kaelin, Eugene F. "Merleau-Ponty, Fundamental Ontologist." *Man and World* 3 (1970), 102-19.
Kant, Immanuel. *Kritik der reinen Vernunft*. Hamburg: Felix Meiner, 1976.
Kellner, H. "On the Cognitive Significance of the System of Language in Communication." In *Phenomenology and Sociology*. Ed. Thomas Luckmann. Harmondsworth: Penguin, 1978, 324-42.
Kern, Iso. "Die drei Wege zur transzendentalphänomenologischen Reduktion in der Philosophie Edmund Husserls." *Tijdschrift voor Filosofie* 24 (1962), 303-49. "The Three Ways to the Transcendental Phenomenological Reduction in the Philosophy of Edmund Husserl." Trans. Frederick A. Elliston and Peter McCormick. In *Husserl: Expositions and Appraisals*. Ed. Frederick A. Elliston and Peter McCormick. Notre Dame, IN: University of Notre Dame Press, 1977, 126-49.
———. "Selbstbewußtsein und Ich bei Husserl." In *Husserl-Symposium Mainz 27.6./4.7.1988*. Ed. Gerhard Funke. Mainz: Akademie der Wissenschaften und der Literatur/Stuttgart: Franz Steiner, 1989, 51-63.
Keyes, C. D. "An Evaluation of Levinas' Critique of Heidegger." *Research in Phenomenology* 2 (1972), 121-42.
Klemm, D. E. "Levinas' phenomenology of the Other and language as the Other of phenomenology." *Man and World* 22 (1989), 403-26.
Knoblauch, Hubert. "Zwischen Einsamkeit und Wechselrede: Zur Kommunikation und ihrer Konstitution bei Edmund Husserl." *Husserl Studies* 2 (1985), 33-52.
Kojima, Hiroshi. "The Potential Plurality of the Transcendental Ego of Husserl and its Relevance to the Theory of Space." *Analecta Husserliana* 8 (1978), 55-61.
Kozlowski, R. *Die Aporien der Intersubjektivität*. Würzburg: Königshausen & Neumann, 1991.
Krings, Hermann. *System und Freiheit*. Freiburg: Karl Alber, 1980.
Kripke, Saul. *Naming and Necessity*. Oxford: Blackwell, 1980.
Kuhlmann, W. "Kant und die Transzendentalpragmatik." In *Kants transzendentale Deduktion und die Möglichkeit von Transzendentalphilosophie*. Ed. Forum für Philosophie. Frankfurt am Main: Suhrkamp, 1988, 193-221.
Kuhlmann, W., and D. Böhler, eds. *Kommunikation und Reflexion*. Frankfurt am Main: Suhrkamp, 1982.
Küng, Guido. "The Intentional and the Real Object." *Dialectica* 38 (1984), 143-56.
Kwant, Remy C. *The Phenomenological Philosophy of Merleau-Ponty*. Pittsburgh, PA: Duquesne University Press, 1963.
Laing, R. D. *The Divided Self*. Harmondsworth: Penguin, 1990a.
———. *Self and Others*. Harmondsworth: Penguin, 1990b.
Lakoff, George. *Women, Fire, and Dangerous Things: What Categories Reveal about the Mind*. Chicago, IL: University of Chicago Press, 1987.

Landgrebe, Ludwig. *Der Weg der Phänomenologie. Das Problem der ursprünglichen Erfahrung.* Gütersloh: Gerd Mohn, 1963.

———. *Phänomenologie und Geschichte.* Gütersloh: Gerd Mohn, 1968.

———. "A Meditation on Husserl's Statement: 'History is the grand fact of absolute Being.'" *Southwestern Journal of Philosophy* 5 (1974), 111-25.

———. "The Problem of Passive Constitution." Trans. Donn Welton. *Analecta Husserliana* 7. Dordrecht: D. Reidel, 1978, 23-36.

Langsdorf, Lenore. "The Noema as Intentional Entity: A Critique of Føllesdal." *Review of Metaphysics* 37 (1984), 757-84.

Larrabee, Mary Jeanne. "The noema in Husserl's phenomenology." *Husserl Studies* 3 (1986), 209-30.

———. "Genesis, motivation, and historical connection." *Man and World* 22 (1989), 315-28.

Lee, Nam-In. *Edmund Husserls Phänomenologie der Instinkte.* Dordrecht: Kluwer Academic Publishers, 1993.

Lenkowski, William J. "What is Husserl's Epoche: The Problem of the Beginning of Philosophy in a Husserlian Context." *Man and World* 11 (1978), 299-323.

Levinas, Emmanuel. *Le temps et l'autre* [1947]. Paris: Quadrige PUF, 1989. *Time and the Other.* Trans. Richard Cohen. Pittsburgh, PA: Duquesne University Press, 1987.

———. *Totalité et infini.* The Hague: Martinus Nijhoff, 1961, rpt. 1971. *Totality and Infinity.* Trans. Alphonso Lingis. Pittsburgh, PA: Duquesne University Press, 1969.

———. *Théorie de l'intuition dans la phénoménologie de Husserl.* Paris: J. Vrin, 1963, rpt. 1989. *The Theory of Intuition in Husserl's Phenomenology.* Trans. André Orianne. Evanston, IL: Northwestern University Press, 1973.

———. *Ethique et infini.* Paris: Libraire Arthème Fayard, 1982.

Lingis, Alphonso. "Hyletic Data." *Analecta Husserliana* 2 (1972), 96-101.

———. "The Perception of Others." *Philosophical Forum* 5 (1974), 460-74.

Lippitz, Wilfried. "Der phänomenologische Begriff der 'Lebenswelt' — seine Relevanz für die Sozialwissenschaften." *Zeitschrift für philosophische Forschung* 32 (1978), 416-35.

List, E. "Diesseits und jenseits des Subjekts." *Philosophische Rundschau* 36 (1989), 416-35.

Locke, John. *An Essay Concerning Human Understanding.* Ed. J. W. Yolton. London: Dent, Everyman's Library, 1985.

Lohmar, Dieter. "Hjemverdenens ethos og den overnationale etik." In *Subjektivitet og Livsverden i Husserls Fænomenologi.* Ed. Dan Zahavi. Aarhus: Modtryk, 1994, 123-44.

Lorenz, K., and J. Mittelstraß. "Die Hintergehbarkeit der Sprache." *Kantstudien* 58 (1967), 187-208.

Löwith, K. *Das Individuum in der Rolle des Mitmenschen.* Munich: Drei Masken, 1928.

Lübcke, P. "Forholdet mellem Fēnomenologi og Hermeneutik belyst ud fra den unge Heidegger med hensyntagen til udvalgte dele af Husserls og Gadamers forfatterskab." Copenhagen, unpublished manuscript, 1977.

Luhmann, Niklas. "Intersubjektivität oder Kommunikation: unterschiedliche Ausgangspunkte soziologischer Theorienbildung." *Archivio di Filosofia* 54 (1986), 41-60.

Luther, Arthur R. *Persons in Love: A Study of Max Scheler's Wesen und Formen der Sympathie.* The Hague: Martinus Nijhoff, 1972.

Macann, Christopher. *Presence and Coincidence.* Dordrecht: Kluwer Academic Publishers, 1991.

McCarthy, Thomas. *The Critical Theory of Jürgen Habermas.* Cambridge, MA: MIT Press, 1991.

Madison, Gary B. *The Phenomenology of Merleau-Ponty.* Athens, OH: Ohio University Press, 1981.

Marbach, Eduard. *Das Problem des Ich in der Phänomenologie Husserls.* Den Haag: Martinus Nijhoff, 1974.

Marras, A., ed. *Intentionality, Mind, and Language.* Chicago, IL: University of Illinois Press, 1972.

Martin, B., ed. *Martin Heidegger und das 'Dritte Reich'.* Darmstadt: Wissenschaftliche Buchgesellschaft, 1989.

Matthiesen, Ulf. *Das Dickicht der Lebenswelt und die Theorie des kommunikativen Handelns.* 2nd ed. Munich: Wilhelm Fink, 1985.

Mays, Wolfe. "Genetic Analysis and Experience: Husserl and Piaget." *Journal of the British Society for Phenomenology* 8 (1977), 51-55.

Mead, George Herbert. *Mind, Self, and Society: From the Standpoint of a Social Behaviorist.* Chicago, IL: University of Chicago Press, 1962.

Meist, K. R. "Monadologische Intersubjektivität. Zum Konstitutionsproblem von Welt und Geschichte bei Husserl." *Zeitschrift für philosophische Forschung* 34 (1980), 561-89.

———. "Die Zeit der Geschichte. Probleme in Husserls transzendentaler Begründung einer Theorie der Geschichte." *Phänomenologische Forschungen* 14 (1983), 58-110.

———. "Intersubjektivität zwischen Natur und Geschichte. Einige Anmerkungen über Probleme einer transzendentalen Letztbegründung." *Phänomenologische Forschungen* 24/25 (1991), 265-304.

Melle, Ullrich. *Das Wahrnehmungsproblem und seine Verwandlung in phänomenologischer Einstellung.* Den Haag: Martinus Nijhoff, 1983.

Mensch, James R. *Intersubjectivity and Transcendental Idealism.* Albany, NY: State University of New York Press, 1988.

Merleau-Ponty, Maurice. *Phénoménologie de la perception.* Paris: Gallimard, 1945. *Phenomenology of Perception.* Trans. Colin Smith. London: Routledge & Kegan Paul, 1962; rpt. [with translation revisions by Forrest Williams] Atlantic Highlands, NJ: Humanities Press, 1976 (PP).

———. "Le primat de la perception et ses conséquences philosophiques." *Bulletin de la Société Francaise de Philosophie* 41 (1947), 119-53.

———. *Sens et non-sens* [1948]. 5th ed. Paris: Les Éditions Nagel, 1966; *Sense and Non-Sense.* Trans. Hubert L. Dreyfus and Patricia Allen Dreyfus. Evanston, IL: Northwestern University Press, 1964 (SNS).

———. *Éloge de la philosophie.* Paris: Gallimard, 1953; *In Praise of Philosophy.* Trans. John Wild and James M. Edie. Evanston, IL: Northwestern University Press, 1963.

———. *Signes*. Paris; Gallimard, 1960; *Signs*. Trans. Richard C. McCleary. Evanston, IL: Northwestern University Press, 1964 (S).

———. *Le visible et l'invisible*. Ed. Claude Lefort. Paris: Gallimard, 1964. *The Visible and the Invisible*. Trans. Alphonso Lingis. Evanston, IL: Northwestern University Press, 1968 (VI).

———. *The Primacy of Perception and Other Essays*. Ed. James M. Edie. Evanston, IL: Northwestern University Press, 1964 (PrP).

———. *Résumés de cours. Collège de France 1952–1960*. Paris: Gallimard, 1968. *Themes from the Lectures at the Collège de France 1952–1960*. Trans. John O'Neill. Evanston, IL: Northwestern University Press, 1970 (RC).

———. *La prose du monde*. Ed. Claude Lefort. Paris: Gallimard, 1969. *The Prose of the World*. Trans. John O'Neill. Evanston, IL: Northwestern University Press, 1973a (PM).

———. *Consciousness and the Acquisition of Language*. Trans. Hugh J. Silverman. Evanston, IL: Northwestern University Press, 1973b.

———. *Merleau-Ponty à la Sorbonne. Résumé de cours 1949–1952*. [Grenoble]: Cynara, 1988.

Meyer-Drawe, Käte. *Leiblichkeit und Sozialität*. Munich: Wilhelm Fink, 1984.

Mirvish, Adrian. "Sartre, Hodological Space, and the Existence of Others." *Research in Phenomenology* 14 (1984), 149–74.

Miller, I. "Perceptual Reference." *Synthese* 61 (1984), 35–59.

Mohanty, J. N. "The 'Object' in Husserl's Phenomenology." *Philosophy and Phenomenological Research* 14 (1953–54), 343–53.

———. *Edmund Husserl's Theory of Meaning*. The Hague: Martinus Nijhoff: 1964.

———. "Husserl's Concept of Intentionality." *Analecta Husserliana* 1 (1970), 100–32.

———. *The Concept of Intentionality*. St. Louis: Warren H. Green, 1972.

———. "'Life-World' and 'A Priori' in Husserl's Later Thought." *Analecta Husserliana* 3 (1974), 46–65.

———. "Consciousness and Existence: Remarks on the Relation between Husserl and Heidegger." *Man and World* 11 (1978), 324–35.

———. "Intentionality, Causality, and Holism." *Synthese* 61 (1984), 17–33.

———. "Phänomenologische Rationalität und die Überwindung des Relativismus." *Phänomenologische Forschungen* 19 (1986), 53–74.

Moneta, Giuseppina C. *On Identity: A Study in Genetic Phenomenology*. The Hague: Martinus Nijhoff, 1976.

Morris, Phyllis Sutton. *Sartre's Concept of a Person: An Analytic Approach*. Amherst, MA: University of Massachusetts Press, 1976.

———. "Sartre on the Transcendence of the Ego." *Philosophy and Phenomenological Research* 46 (1985), 179–97.

Moser, P. K. "Beyond the Private Language Argument." *Metaphilosophy* 23 (1992), 77–89.

Munono Muyembe, B. *Le regard et le visage: De l'altérité chez Jean-Paul Sartre et Emmanuel Lévinas*. Bern: Lang, 1991.

Nagl, L. "Zeigt die Habermassche Kommunikationstheorie einen 'Ausweg aus der Subjektphilosophie'? Erwägungen zur Studie *Der philosophische Diskurs der Moderne.*" In *Die Frage nach dem Subjekt*. Ed. M. Frank, M. Raulet, and W. van Reijen. Frankfurt am Main: Suhrkamp, 1988, 346–72.

Natanson, Maurice. *The Social Dynamics of George H. Mead*. The Hague: Martinus Nijhoff, 1973.

———. "The Problem of Others in 'Being and Nothingness.'" In *The Philosophy of Jean-Paul Sartre*. Ed. Paul Schilpp. La Salle, IL: Open Court, 1982, 326–44.

Nitta, Yoshihiro. "Husserl's Manuscript 'A Nocturnal Conversation.'" *Analecta Husserliana* 8 (1978), 21–36.

Nusser, K,-H. "Totalität ohne Subjekt. Zu Habermas' Theorie des kommunikativen Handelns." *Zeitschrift für philosophische Forschung* 39 (1985), 590–600.

Øfsti, A. *Das 'Ich denke' und Kants transzendentale Deduktion im Lichte der sprachphilosophischen (pragmatischen) Wende*. Trondheim: Tapir Forlag, 1988.

O'Neill, John. "Der Spiegelleib. Merleau-Ponty und Lacan zum frühkindlichen Verhältnis von Selbst und Anderen." In *Leibhaftige Vernunft. Spuren von Merleau-Pontys Denken*. Ed. Alexandre Métraux and Bernhard Waldenfels. Munich: Wilhelm Fink, 1986, 236–57. "The Specular Body: Merleau-Ponty and Lacan on Infant, Self, and Other." In his *The Communicative Body: Studies in Communicative Philosophy, Politics, and Sociology*. Evanston, IL: Northwestern University Press, 1989, 58–73, 242–44.

Owen, T. J. *Phenomenology and Intersubjectivity*. The Hague: Martinus Nijhoff, 1970.

Patočka, Jan. *Die natürliche Welt als philosophisches Problem. Phänomenologische Schriften I*. Stuttgart: Klett-Cotta, 1990.

———. *Die Bewegung der menschlichen Existenz. Phänomenologische Schriften II*. Stuttgart: Klett-Cotta, 1991.

Piper, A. "Ethik als Verhältnis von Moralphilosophie und Anthropologie. Kants Entwurf einer Transzendentalpragmatik und ihre Transformation durch Apel." *Kantstudien* 69 (1978), 314–29.

Pietersma, Henry. "Knowledge and Being in Merleau-Ponty." *Man and World* 23 (1990), 205–23.

Poltawski, A. "Constitutive Phenomenology and Intentional Objects." *Analecta Husserliana* 2 (1972), 90–95.

Presseault, J. *L'être-pour-autrui dans la philosophie de Jean-Paul Sartre*. Brussels: Desclée de Brouwer, 1970.

Putnam, Hilary. *Reason, Truth, and History*. Cambridge: Cambridge University Press, 1981.

Rang, Bernhard. *Kausalität und Motivation*. Den Haag: Martinus Nijhoff, 1973.

———. "Repräsentation und Selbstgegebenheit." *Phänomenologische Forschungen* 1 (1975), 105–37.

Rasmussen, David. M. "Exploration of the *Lebenswelt*: Reflection on Schutz and Habermas." *Human Studies* 7 (1984), 127–32.

———. *Reading Habermas*. Oxford: Blackwell, 1991.

Reeder, Harry P. "Language and the Phenomenological Reduction: A Reply to a Wittgensteinian Objection." *Man and World* 12 (1979), 35–46.

———. *Language and Experience: Descriptions of Living Language in Husserl and Wittgenstein*. Lanham, MD: Center for Advanced Research in Phenomenology/University Press of America, 1984.

Reese-Schäfer, W. *Karl-Otto Apel zur Einführung.* Hamburg: Junius, 1990.
———. *Jürgen Habermas.* Frankfurt am Main: Campus Verlag, 1991.
Rescher, N. *Human Knowledge in Idealistic Perspective.* Princeton, NJ: Princeton University Press, 1992.
Ricoeur, Paul. *Husserl: An Analysis of His Phenomenology.* Trans. Edward G. Ballard and Lester E. Embree. Evanston, IL: Northwestern University Press, 1967.
———. "Phenomenology and Hermeneutics." In his *Hermeneutics and the Human Sciences.* Ed. and trans. John B. Thompson. Cambridge: Cambridge University Press, 1981, 101-28.
———. *Soi-même comme un autre.* Paris: Éditions du Seuil, 1990. *Oneself as Another.* Trans. Kathleen Blamey. Chicago, IL: University of Chicago Press, 1992.
Rohr-Dietschi, Ursula. *Zur Genese des Selbstbewußtseins.* Berlin: De Gruyter, 1974.
Römpp, Georg. "Der Andere als Zukunft und Gegenwart: Zur Interpretation der Erfahrung fremder Personalität in temporalen Begriffen bei Levinas und Husserl." *Husserl Studies* 6 (1989a), 129-54.
———. "Truth and Interpersonality: An Inquiry into the Argumentative Structure of Heidegger's Being and Time." *International Philosophical Quarterly* 29 (1989b), 429-47.
———. *Husserls Phänomenologie der Intersubjektivität.* Dordrecht: Kluwer Academic Publishers, 1992.
Rosen, Klaus. *Evidenz in Husserls deskriptiver Transzendentalphilosophie.* Meisenhaim am Glan: Anton Hain, 1977.
Russow, L.-M. "Heidegger and the Problem of Being-with." *Southwestern Journal of Philosophy* 11 (1980), 127-41.
Sallis, John. "On the Limitation of Transcendental Reflection or Is Intersubjectivity Transcendental?" *The Monist* 55 (1971), 312-33.
Sapontzis, S. F. "Community in 'Being and Time'." *Kantstudien* 69 (1978), 330-40.
Sartre, Jean-Paul. *La transcendance de l'ego. Esquisse d'une description phénoménologique* [1936]. Ed. Sylvie Le Bon. Paris: J. Vrin, 1978, rpt. 1988. *The Transcendence of the Ego: An Existentialist Theory of Consciousness.* Trans. Forrest Williams and Robert Kirkpatrick. New York: Farrar, Straus and Giroux, The Noonday Press, 1957 (TE).
———. *L'être et le néant. Essai d'ontologie phénoménologique* [1943]. Paris: Gallimard, Tel, 1976, rpt. 1982. *Being and Nothingness: A Phenomenological Essay on Ontology.* Trans. Hazel E. Barnes. New York: Washington Square Press, 1966 (EN).
Scanlon, John D. "Consciousness, the Streetcar, and the Ego: Pro Husserl, Contra Sartre." *Philosophical Forum* 2 (1971), 332-54.
Scheler, Max. *Wesen und Formen der Sympathie. Der "Phänomenologie und Theorie der Sympathiegefühl"* [1913]. 5th ed. Frankfurt am Main: Verlag G. Schulte-Bulmke, 1948. *The Nature of Sympathy.* Trans. Peter Heath. London: Routledge & Kegan Paul, 1954; rpt. Hamden, CT: The Shoe String Press, 1973 (NS).

———. *Der Formalismus in der Ethik und die materiale Wertethik. Neuer Versuch der Grundlegung eines ethischen Personalismus* [1913/1916]. 5th ed. Ed. Maria Scheler. Bern: Francke Verlag, 1966. *Formalism in Ethics and Non-Formal Ethics of Values: A New Attempt toward the Foundation of an Ethical Personalism.* Trans. Manfred S. Frings and Roger L. Funk. Evanston, IL: Northwestern University Press, 1973 (FE).

———. *Vom Ewigen im Menschen.* Erster Band, *Religiöse Erneuerung.* Leipzig: Der Neue Geist-Verlag, 1921. *On the Eternal in Man.* Trans. Bernard Noble. New York: Harper & Brothers, 1960 (EM).

———. *Schriften aus dem Nachlaß I.* Bern: Francke Verlag, 1957.

Schelling, Friedrich Wilhelm Joseph von. *System des transzendental Idealismus.* Leipzig: Felix Meiner, 1911. *System of Transcendental Idealism (1800).* Trans. Peter Heath. Charlottesville, VA: University Press of Virginia, 1978.

Schmidt, James. *Maurice Merleau-Ponty: Between Phenomenology and Structuralism.* London: Macmillan, 1985.

Schneider, H. J. "Gibt es eine 'Transzendental-' bzw. 'Universalpragmatik'?" *Zeitschrift für philosophische Forschung* 36 (1982), 208–26.

Schroeder, W. R. *Sartre and his Predecessors.* London: Routledge & Kegan Paul, 1984.

Schroyer, T. "Die dialektischen Grundlagen der kritischen Theorie." In *Materialien zu Habermas' 'Erkenntnis und Interesse'.* Ed. Winfried Dallmayr. Frankfurt am Main: Suhrkamp, 1974, 41–70.

Schuhmann, Karl. *Die Fundamentalbetrachtung der Phänomenologie.* Den Haag: Martinus Nijhoff, 1971.

———. *Husserls Staatsphilosophie.* Freiburg: Karl Alber, 1988.

Schütz, Alfred. *Der sinnhafte Aufbau der sozialen Welt. Eine Einleitung in die verstehende Soziologie* [1932]. Frankfurt am Main: Suhrkamp, 1991, Schutz, Alfred. *The Phenomenology of the Social World.* Trans. George Walsh and Frederick Lehnert. Evanston, IL: Northwestern University Press, 1967.

Schutz, Alfred. *Collected Papers I. The Problem of Social Reality.* Ed. Maurice Natanson. The Hague: Martinus Nijhoff, 1962.

———. *Collected Papers II. Studies in Social Theory.* Ed. Arvid Brodersen. The Hague: Martinus Nijhoff, 1964.

———. *Collected Papers III. Studies in Phenomenological Philosophy.* Ed. Ilse Schutz. The Hague: Martinus Nijhoff, 1966.

Schütz, Alfred, and Aron Gurwitsch. *Briefwechsel 1939–1959.* Ed. Richard Grathoff. Munich: Wilhelm Fink, 1985. *Philosophers in Exile: The Correspondence of Alfred Schutz and Aron Gurwitsch, 1939–1959.* Trans. J. Claude Evans. Bloomington, IN: Indiana University Press, 1989.

Searle, John R. *Intentionality.* Cambridge: Cambridge University Press, 1983.

Seebohm, Thomas M. *Die Bedingungen der Möglichkeit der Transzendentalphilosophie.* Bonn: Bouvier, 1962.

———. "The Other in the Field of Consciousness." In *Essays in Memory of Aron Gurwitsch.* Ed. Lester Embree. Lanham, MD: Center for Advanced Research in Phenomenology/University Press of America, 1984, 283–303.

Sinha, Debabrata. "Der Begriff der Person in der Phänomenologie Husserls." *Zeitschrift für philosophische Forschung* 18 (1964), 597–613.

Sinn, Dieter. "Die transzendentale Intersubjektivität bei Edmund Husserl mit ihren Seinshorizont." Unpublished dissertation, Heidelberg, 1958.

Skirbekk, G. "Rationaler Konsens und ideale Sprechsituation als Geltungsgrund? Über Recht und Grenze eines transzendentalpragmatischen Geltungskonzepts." In *Kommunikation und Reflexion*. Ed. W. Kuhlmann and D. Böhler. Frankfurt am Main: Suhrkamp, 1982, 54–82.

Smith, David Woodruff. "Husserl on Demonstrative Reference and Perception." In *Husserl, Intentionality, and Cognitive Science*. Ed. Hubert L. Dreyfus. Cambridge, MA: MIT Press, 1982, 193–213.

———. "Content and Context of Perception." *Synthese* 61 (1984), 61–87.

———. "Husserl and Frege." *Journal of Philosophy* 84 (1987), 528–35.

Smith, David Woodruff, and Ronald McIntyre. "Husserl's Identification of Meaning and Noema." *The Monist* 59 (1975), 115–32.

———. *Husserl and Intentionality*. Dordrecht: D. Reidel, 1982.

Soffer, Gail. *Husserl and the Question of Relativism*. Dordrecht: Kluwer Academic Publishers, 1991.

Sokolowski, Robert. *The Formation of Husserl's Concept of Constitution*. The Hague: Martinus Nijhoff, 1970.

———. *Husserlian Meditations*. Evanston, IL: Northwestern University Press, 1974.

———. "Intentional Analysis and the Noema." *Dialectica* 38 (1984), 113–29.

———. "Husserl and Frege." *Journal of Philosophy* 84 (1987), 521–28.

Solomon, Robert C. "Husserl's Private Language." *Southwestern Journal of Philosophy* 5 (1974), 203–28.

Sommer, Manfred. "Fremderfahrung und Zeitbewußtsein. Zur Phänomenologie der Intersubjektivität." *Zeitschrift für philosophische Forschung* 38 (1984), 3–18.

Spiegelberg, Herbert. "The 'Reality-Phenomenon' and Reality." In *Philosophical Essays in Memory of Edmund Husserl*. Ed. Marvin Farber. Cambridge, MA: Harvard University Press, 1940, 84–105.

———. *The Phenomenological Movement: A Historical Introduction*. 3rd rev. and enl. ed. with Karl Schuhmann. The Hague: Martinus Nijhoff, 1982.

Srubar, Ilja. "Von Milieu zur Autopoiesis. Zum Beitrag der Phänomenologie zur soziologischen Theoriebildung." In *Phänomenologie im Widerstreit*. Ed. Christoph Jamme and Otto Pöggeler. Frankfurt am Main: Suhrkamp, 1989, 307–31.

Stein, Edith. *On the Problem of Empathy*. Trans. Waltraut Stein. The Hague: Martinus Nijhoff, 1964; 3rd rev. ed. Washington: ICS Publications, 1989.

Strasser, Stephan. "Grundgedanken der Sozialontologie Edmund Husserls." *Zeitschrift für philosophische Forschung* 29 (1975), 3–33.

———. "Monadologie und Teleologie in der Philosophie Edmund Husserls." *Phänomenologische Forschungen* 22 (1989), 217–35.

Ströker, Elisabeth. "Husserls Evidenzprinzip. Sinn und Grenzen einer methodischen Norm der Phänomenologie als Wissenschaft." *Zeitschrift für philosophische Forschung* 32 (1978), 3–30 "Husserl's Principle of Evidence: The Significance and Limitations of a Methodological Norm of Phenomenology as a Science." Trans. Robert Pettit. In *Contemporary German Philosophy*, Vol. I.

Ed. Darrel E. Christiansen et al. University Park, PA: The Pennsylvania State University Press, 1982, 111–38.

———. "Phänomenologie und Psychologie. Die Frage ihrer Beziehung bei Husserl." *Zeitschrift für philosophische Forschung* 37 (1983), 3–19. "The Role of Psychology in Husserl's Phenomenology." In *Continental Philosophy in America.* Ed. Hugh J. Silverman, John Sallis, and Thomas M. Seebohm. Pittsburgh, PA: Duquesne University Press, 1983, 3–15.

———. "Intentionalität und Konstitution. Wandlungen des Intentionalitätskonzepts in der Philosophie Husserls." *Dialectica* 38 (1984), 191–208.

Theunissen, Michael. *Der Andere. Studien zur Sozialontologie der Gegenwart.* 2nd ed. Berlin: Walter de Gruyter, 1977. *The Other: Studies in the Social Ontology of Husserl, Heidegger, Sartre, and Buber.* Trans. Christopher Macann. Cambridge, MA: MIT Press, 1984. Rpt. (paper) 1986.

Thompson, J. B. "Universal Pragmatics." In *Habermas: Critical Debates.* Ed. J. B. Thompson and D. Held. Cambridge, MA: MIT Press, 1982, 116–33.

Tito, Johanna Maria. *Logic in the Husserlian Context.* Evanston, IL: Northwestern University Press, 1990.

Toulement, René. *L'essence de la société selon Husserl.* Paris: Presses Universitaires de France, 1962.

Towarnicki, Frédéric de. *À la rencontre de Heidegger: Souvenirs d'un messager de la Forêt-Noire.* Paris: Gallimard, 1993.

Tugendhat, Ernst. *Der Wahrheitsbegriff bei Husserl und Heidegger.* Berlin: Walter de Gruyter, 1970.

Tymieniecka, Anna-Teresa. "Imaginatio Creatrix." *Analecta Husserliana* 3 (1974), 3–41.

Uygur, Nermi. "Die Phänomenologie Husserls und die 'Gemeinschaft'." *Kantstudien* 50 (1958/59), 439–60.

Vaitkus, Steven. *How is Society Possible? Intersubjectivity and the Fiduciary Attitude as Problems of the Social Group in Mead, Gurwitsch, and Schutz.* Dordrecht: Kluwer Academic Publishers, 1991.

Valone, James J. "The Problem of Intersubjectivity in Transcendental and Mundane Phenomenology." *The Annals of Phenomenological Sociology* 2 (1977), 63–86.

Van Breda, Herman Leo. "Maurice Merleau-Ponty et les Archives-Husserl à Louvain." *Revue de métaphysique et de morale* 67 (1962), 410–30. "Merleau-Ponty and the Husserl Archives at Louvain." Trans. Stephen Michelman. In Merleau-Ponty, *Texts and Dialogues.* Ed. Hugh J. Silverman and James Barry, Jr. Atlantic Highlands, NJ: Humanities Press, 1992, 150–61, 178–83.

Van Buren, John. "The Young Heidegger and Phenomenology." *Man and World* 23 (1990), 239–72.

Van Eecke, Wilfried. "The Look, the Body, and the Other." In *Dialogues in Phenomenology.* Ed. Don Ihde and Richard M. Zaner. The Hague: Martinus Nijhoff, 1975, 224–46.

Wagner, B., and H. Zipprian. "Intersubjectivity and Critical Consciousness: Remarks on Habermas's Theory of Communicative Action." *Inquiry* 34 (1991), 49–62.

Wagner, Hans. "Kritische Betrachtungen zu Husserls Nachlass." *Philosophische Rundschau* 1 (1953-54), 1-22, 93-123. "Critical Observation Concerning Husserl's Posthumous Writings." In *The Phenomenology of Husserl: Selected Critical Readings*. Ed. and trans. R. O. Elveton. Chicago, IL: Quadrangle Books, 1970, 204-58; 2nd ed. Seattle, WA: Noesis Press, 2000, 192-242.

Waldenfels, Bernhard. *Das Zwischenreich des Dialogs. Sozialphilosophische Untersuchungen in Anschluss an Edmund Husserl.* Den Haag: Martinus Nijhoff, 1971a.

———. "Weltliche und soziale Einzigkeit bei Husserl." *Zeitschrift für philosophische Forschung* 25 (1971b), 157-71.

———. *Der Spielraum des Verhaltens.* Frankfurt am Main: Suhrkamp, 1980.

———. *In der Netzen der Lebenswelt.* Frankfurt am Main: Suhrkamp, 1985.

———. "Erfahrung des Fremden in Husserls Phänomenologie." *Phänomenologische Forschungen* 22 (1989), 39-62. "Experience of the Alien in Husserl's Phenomenology." Trans. Anthony J. Steinbock. *Research in Phenomenology* 20 (1990), 19-33.

Waldenfels, Bernhard, Jan M. Broekman, and Ante Pažanin, eds. *Phenomenology and Marxism.* Trans. J. Claude Evans, Jr. London: Routledge & Kegan Paul, 1984.

Wallner, Ingrid M. "In defense of Husserl's transcendental idealism: Roman Ingarden's critique re-examined." *Husserl Studies* 4 (1987), 3-43.

Wellmer, Albrecht. "Kommunikation und Emanzipation. Überlegungen zur sprachanalytischen Wende der kritischen Theorie." In *Theorien des historischen Materialismus.* Ed. A. Honneth and U. Jaeggi. Frankfurt am Main: Suhrkamp, 1977, 465-500.

Weymann-Weyhe, W. *Das Problem der Personeinheit in der ersten Periode der Philosophie Max Schelers.* Emsdetten: Heinr. & J. Lechte, 1940.

Whitford, M. *Merleau-Ponty's Critique of Sartre's Philosophy.* Lexington, KY: French Forum, 1982.

Wider, K. "Hell and the private language argument: Sartre and Wittgenstein on self-consciousness, the body, and others." *Journal of the British Society for Phenomenology* 18 (1987), 120-32.

———. "Through the looking glass: Sartre on knowledge and the prereflective *cogito.*" *Man and World* 22 (1989), 329-43.

Winch, P. *The Idea of a Social Science.* London: Routledge & Kegan Paul, 1958.

Wittgenstein, Ludwig. *Philosophische Untersuchungen/Philosophical Investigations* [bilingual edition]. Trans. G. E. M. Anscombe. 3rd ed. New York: Macmillan, 1958.

Yamaguchi, Ichiro. *Passive Synthesis und Intersubjektivität bei Edmund Husserl.* Den Haag: Martinus Nijhoff, 1982.

Zahavi, Dan. "Induktion og Essentialisme hos Aristotles." *Filosofiske Studier* 12 (1991), 157-83.

———. *Intentionalität und Konstitution. Eine Einführung in Husserls Logische Untersuchungen.* Copenhagen: Museum Tusculanum Press, 1992a.

———. "Constitution and ontology: Some remarks on Husserl's ontological position in the *Logical Investigations.*" *Husserl Studies* 9 (1992b), 111-24.

———. "Réduction et constitution dans la phénoménologie du dernier Husserl." *Philosophiques* 20 (1993), 363-81.

———. "Intentionality and the Representative Theory of Perception." *Man and World* 27 (1994a), 37–47.

———. "Husserl's Phenomenology of the Body." *Études Phénoménologiques* 19 (1994b), 63–84.

———. "Beyond Realism and Idealism: Husserl's Late Concept of Constitution." *Danish Yearbook of Philosophy* 29 (1994c), 44–62.

———. "The Self-Pluralisation of the Primal Life: A Problem in Fink's Husserl-Interpretation." *Recherches Husserliennes* 2 (1994d), 3–18.

———, ed. *Subjektivitet og Livsverden i Husserls Fænomenologi*. Aarhus: Modtryk, 1994e.

Zeltner, H. "Das Ich und die Anderen. Husserls Beitrag zur Grundlegung der Sozialphilosophie." *Zeitschrift für philosophische Forschung* 13 (1959), 288–315.

Ziarek, K. "Semantics of Proximity: Language and the Other in the Philosophy of Emmanuel Levinas." *Research in Phenomenology* 19 (1989), 213–47.

INDEX OF NAMES